GREEN VILLAGE HEROES

The Story of

Burscough Football Club

Its History and Its Origins

John Yates

and

Stan Strickland

GREEN VILLAGE HEROES

ABOUT THE AUTHORS

'Green Village Heroes' is effectively two books in one, the contributions of the two authors, John Yates and Stan Strickland, having been written and researched independently, only coming together for the final planning of the book.

Many of the major events in this club's history will, therefore, be visited twice, but from entirely different vantage points. John Yates writes with the panache you would expect of a sports journalist of nearly forty years standing, who has spent a major part of his life following his village football club. He re-creates the excitement of the past fifty years with the knowledge that only first-hand experience of those events can provide. Stan Strickland takes a more in depth look at the development of the club itself, based on painstaking research and enquiry. He uses, and liberally quotes from, archive material and conversations with club officials and players, past and present, to build up a compelling picture of the village football club right back to its roots in the last century.

John Yates was born in Burscough in 1943 and from an early age followed the exploits of his village soccer club.

This was hardly surprising as his late uncle, Johnny Baldwin, was one of the founder members of the club and a man who during his time held a wide range of offices, including chairman, trainer and groundsman.

John attended St. John's Church of England School, Burscough Secondary School, and Southport Technical College before joining the Ormskirk Advertiser in 1959 as a junior reporter, covering both news and sport.

He was lucky enough to report Burscough's first ever excursion into the first round proper of the F.A. Cup against Crewe Alexandra...only five months after the start of his career in journalism.

John left the Ormskirk Advertiser to join the Skelmersdale Reporter in 1969, covering the affairs of Skelmersdale United in their glory years and reported on their 4-1 victory over Dagenham in the F.A. Amateur

Cup Final.

In 1973 he was appointed Editor of the Darwen Advertiser and News and then towards the end of the decade took over the Editorship of the Prescot and Huyton Reporter and the Kirkby Reporter.

In 1982 he was appointed Editor of the Rugby Leaguer, introducing colour to the international magazine for the first time, before taking up his present post as Deputy Editor/Sports Editor of the St. Helens Reporter.

Married to Christine, who is manageress of the Thresher Off Licence in Burscough, the couple have two daughters, Jacqueline and Catherine, and twin granddaughters, Katie and Kirsty.

John is also Secretary of Burscough Cricket Club - a post he has held for more than twenty years.

Stan Strickland was born in Liverpool in 1943. He first gained an interest in non-league football in the 1950s, following the giant-killing exploits of the New Brighton side which reached the fourth round proper of the F.A. Cup, a side which included former Burscough players Stan Hurst and Johnny Vincent. He went on to become a regular visitor at many of the other non-league grounds on Merseyside, including, Earlestown, Guinness Exports, Skelmersdale United, South Liverpool and Burscough.

A fanatical follower of Liverpool from their Second Division days, then through the successful Shankly years, he eventually tired of the time, hassle and cost involved in following a big city club.

Never much of a footballer himself, playing for Old Holts third eleven in the Liverpool Old Boys League was the pinnacle of his career, it has proved no obstacle to him spending a lifetime shouting and yelling 'advice' at others on how to play the game.

Between 1976 and 1979 he managed Ashfield F.C. in the Skelmersdale & District Sunday League, achieving lasting fame after administering neat Dettol to an open knee wound which resulted in the most amazing recovery by an injured player ever seen on Blaguegate playing fields. He then went on to referee in the same league for a further three years.

After 30 years working as a Product Engineer with Delco Electronics in Kirkby, he accepted an early retirement package in 1993 and volunteered for the position of Secretary of Burscough Football Club. After three months in that post he had sat in the director's box at Goodison Park twice and been to two cup finals with Burscough. He was heard to ask.... 'Do we do this every season?'.

Stan Strickland now lives in Ormskirk with his wife, Sally. They have a son, Paul, and two daughters, Kerrie and Jennie.

First published as a Limited Edition
September 1996

© John Yates and Stan Strickland, 1996

All rights reserved
Unauthorised duplication
contravenes existing law

ISBN 0-9528431-0-2

Published
by
Stan Strickland
109 Redgate
Ormskirk
Lancashire L39 3NW
(Tel: 01695 574722)

for
Burscough Association Football Club

Cover design: Stan Strickland/Ipswich Book Company Ltd.
*Front cover: Bobby Langton in action; 1947-48 Lancashire Junior Cup winners;
1995-96 North West Counties League Challenge Cup winners*

Printed in Great Britain by
Ipswich Book Company Ltd., Ipswich, Suffolk

This book is dedicated to
Mr. Frank Parr
*in recognition of a lifetime's devotion
to
Burscough Football Club.*

CONTENTS

	Acknowledgements	8
	Foreword - 1	9
	Foreword - 2	10
Part 1	Burscough AFC (1946-1996) by John Yates	13
Part 2	A Village Football Club by Stan Strickland	51
	Introduction	53
	The 'First' Burscough	55
	Burscough Rangers	67
	Burscough Vics & Lathom Juniors	97
	Burscough Football Club	111
Part 3	A Tribute to Frank Parr	179
Part 4	Reference Section	189
	Match Records - Introduction	190
	Burscough Rangers 1906 - 1935	192
	Burscough F.C. 1946 - 1996	222
	The Goalscorers	304
	Burscough v. Skelmersdale United	305
	Victoria Park	306
	The Present	310
	Club Officials 1946 - 1996	313
	List of Subscribers	316
	Roll of Honour	320

ACKNOWLEDGEMENTS

The Authors wish to thank the following for their contribution to making this book possible, by supplying photographs, press cuttings, missing statistics, etc., but most of all for sharing their memories of Burscough football:

Frank Parr, Stuart Heaps, Mark Parr, Roy Baldwin, Bill Fairclough, Ellen Baybutt, Gordon Cottle, Stan Harvey, Gilly Houghton (ex-Burscough F.C.), Tommy 'Tut' Aspinall (ex-Burscough Vics), Dick Abram (ex-Burscough Vics), John Melling (ex-Burscough F.C.), Jack & Marion Crompton of Ormskirk, Mrs. Rose Smith, the late Bob Langton, Edie Harrison, Nell Disley, Bill Pye (son of Rangers' player Tommy Pye), Kenny Spencer (former Manager Burscough F.C.), R.H.Holcroft (former Secretary Burscough F.C.), the late Fred Parr, Phil Brown of Fleetwood, Tom Walmsley, Mrs. Lee (Ormskirk Library), Tom Galvin (ex-Burscough F.C.), Albert Gore (ex-Rangers, Vics, Lathom Juniors & Burscough F.C.), Mrs. Mary Martland, Keith Martland, Geoff Howard (Ormskirk Advertiser), Jim Bridge (former Vice-Chairman Burscough F.C.), Ronnie Barker (former Secretary Burscough F.C.), David Haworth (Rossendale United F.C. historian), Louis Bimpson, Chris Mahood (former Secretary Burscough F.C.), Bobby Warren (ex-Burscough F.C.), Eric Berry (grandson of John Berry), Michael Braham (Southport F.C. historian), Geoff Wilde (Southport F.C. statistician), Marlene Guy (daughter of Rangers' player Nat Rawlins), Paul Cowburn (North West Counties League statistician), the late Harry Gibbons (ex-Burscough Vics), Tommy Barnes (Bootle F.C. historian), Ian Bagshaw (Chorley F.C.), Colin Hunt & Les Rawlinson (Liverpool Echo photograph library), Tom Sault (New Brighton F.C. historian), Paul Lawler (Formby F.C.), Rod & Josie Prescott of Appley Bridge, J.E.Hinchliffe (Chairman, North West Counties Football League), Malcolm Flanagan (South Liverpool F.C. historian), Joe Vose (ex-Lathom Juniors, Burscough Vics & Burscough F.C.), Terry Kelly (former Treasurer Burscough F.C.), Donald Scott (ex-Ormskirk Wednesday F.C.), Jim Aspinall (ex-Burscough F.C.), Charlie Jones (former Manager Burscough F.C.), Jimmy Sutcliffe, Pete Whittle, Bob Gibbons (ex-Burscough Vics), John Williams (Liverpool Echo), Frank Postlethwaite (ex-Burscough F.C.), Alvin McDonald (former Assistant Manager Burscough F.C.), Larry Carberry (ex-Ipswich Town & Burscough F.C.), John Culshaw, Gary Martindale (Notts County, ex-Burscough F.C.), John Spencer, Graham Glover (ex-Burscough F.C.), Ian Rawstorne, John Vincent (ex-Burscough F.C.), John Coates (ex-Burscough F.C.), Alex Blakeman (ex-Burscough F.C.), Ray Coleman (former Manager Burscough F.C.), Miles Hadfield (Ormskirk Champion), David Chalmers & Keith Forshaw (Southport Visiter), K.Suffell, Mrs. Ann Mentha (née Martland), Ted Green (ex-Burscough F.C.), John Parr (ex-Burscough F.C.), Christine Huyton (daughter of Bob Langton), John Disley (ex-Burscough F.C.), Dave Walbank (ex-Burscough F.C.), Billy Jaycock (ex-Burscough F.C.), Frank Walmsley, Alan Alty (ex-Burscough F.C.), Florrie Wilkes, Jim Spencer, Brian Robinson (ex-Burscough F.C.), & Geoff Clarke (former Secretary Burscough F.C.).

Thanks to Roger Nelson, for proof-reading the book prior to publication, also, Julie Walker and Gill Robinson of the Ipswich Book Company Ltd., for their help and guidance in getting the book into print.

FOREWORD - 1

It is both a pleasure and privilege to be asked to express my thoughts on the first 50 years of Burscough Football Club.

My initial introduction to Burscough Football Club was through Wesley Bridge, one of the club's leading goalscorers in their early days. He had a great love for Burscough, stating it was a wonderful club run by very keen football enthusiasts who were doing an excellent job. His assessment was correct. As a young County Secretary needing help in finding a ground for a cup semi-final, I spoke to Wesley Bridge and he arranged for the use of Burscough F.C. That was the start of a wonderful friendship which has never diminished throughout my years as Secretary of the Lancashire Football Association.

The Association has been privileged over the years to use the ground on many occasions. It can truthfully be said, guests and ourselves have always been received with the friendliness and hospitality that characterises Burscough Football Club. I know our former President, Arthur Horrocks, loved attending games at Burscough. He met so many friends that his half-time interval drink would usually be extended well into the second half.

Any organisation is only as good as the people who are in charge of its affairs. In this respect Burscough Football Club have been especially well served. They have had some outstanding club servants, both administratively and on the football side. They have a record of achievement of which they can justifiably feel very proud.

Fifty years is a long time but one constant factor throughout that period has been the presence of the current Chairman, Frank Parr. He has given a lifetime of outstanding service to 'his' beloved Burscough Football Club. Frank Parr has been rewarded by The Football Association presenting him with their 50 Year Award for service to the game of football. He is a most worthy recipient of the honour.

This book, however, is a celebration for all who have been associated with Burscough F.C. We applaud and congratulate the club on the magnificent achievements of their first 50 years. They have already made their mark at every level of the game. We can be assured Burscough Football Club will go forward to the next milestone of 75 years with even greater confidence in their future.

J. Kenyon
Secretary
Lancashire F.A.

FOREWORD - 2

Burscough Football Club was the first team I covered on a regular basis as a journalist. It was in the early 1970s when I was starting my reporting career with the Southport Visiter and the Linnets were in the Cheshire League.

For a young hack, being involved with the club was an exciting time. The team was packed with skilful players who produced an entertaining brand of football. Home or away, there was rarely a dull moment.

Since those days I have covered sporting occasions across the world, from the Los Angeles Olympics to the World Club Championship in Tokyo. Yet I can truly state that Leo Skeete's blistering goal against Skelmersdale United in the semi-finals of the Liverpool Non-league Senior Cup remains one of the most glittering memories. Burscough, if I recall correctly, had fought back from a couple of goals down to level the scores, and with a large crowd going wild Leo cut in from the left, beat two defenders, and sent a scorching shot into the net.

Following Burscough introduced me to the realities of football at part-time level - like going to Prestwich Heys where the dressing rooms were so small the players had their team talk in the cafeteria. Press facilities, were, well, a challenge. It was my job to phone regular updates from Victoria Park to papers like the Liverpool Echo and Staffordshire Sentinel. The problem was that the telephone was out of sight of the pitch so there was always the risk I would miss some vital action.

My other abiding memory is of the then manager, Kenny Spencer, who would often give me a lift to and from matches from my home in Southport. He didn't take offence if I gave the team stick, and his post-match celebrations/commiserations gave me a taste for Scotch which has stood me in good stead ever since!

Congratulations to the club on its 50th anniversary. Burscough FC has played an important part in my life, and I wish the committee, players, staff and supporters many happy and successful seasons to come.

Charles Lambert
Sports Correspondent
BBC North West

PART 1

BURSCOUGH AFC (1946-1996)

by

John Yates

BURSCOUGH AFC (1946-1996)

IN THE BEGINNING

The storm clouds of war had only just disappeared over the horizon and ration books were still an essential part of daily life when a group of sporting enthusiasts met at the Cambridge Hotel in Liverpool Road North during the early months of 1946 to lay the foundation of the Club.

Jack Sturgess, proprietor of a Liverpool Road North sewing company, was elected as the first president with Johnny Baldwin taking on the role of chairman; Dick Holcroft acting as secretary; and Teddy Dutton, licensee of the Cambridge Hotel, in charge of financial affairs.

Two teams were entered in the Liverpool County Combination - and while the reserves failed to set the world alight - the performance of the senior side gave a strong hint that glorious and glittering days could be around the corner.

But Burscough didn't exactly make an auspicious start to the season, going down 5-2 at Prescot B.I. on Saturday, August 31st.

A report of the match in the Ormskirk Advertiser, dated Thursday September 5, 1946, stated:

'Burscough opened their Liverpool County Combination programme on Saturday when they visited Prescot where they were opposed by a strong BI Social team. The Linnets were prominent early on and might very easily have gone ahead in the first two minutes, Davenport hitting the foot of the post and Vose smashing the rebound over the bar. Subsequently, Prescot settled down to fast and accurate football and in a fierce onslaught Dutton brought Higham down just outside the penalty area, the centre forward scoring from the free kick with a great shot which Meadows almost saved. Jones came near for Burscough following a corner, but then Marsh crossed the ball to Davenport whose final pass was netted by Ray Monks. However, just before half-time Higham restored Prescot's lead.'

The report went on: 'Higham then completed his hat-trick two minutes after the interval, Burscough making vain appeals for offside. The visitors hit back hard and good work by McCrae resulted in Davenport reducing the arrears, but Higham completed a good afternoon's work by scoring a fourth goal and a further goal came before the end.'

The Burscough team on that historic first day was: Meadows; Holdsworth, Dutton; Maher, Lloyd, Jones; Marsh, Monks, Davenport, Vickers, and Vose. The Linnets' goals were scored by Monks and Davenport.

Defeat, however, was quickly avenged as the two clubs met the following week at Victoria Park, where Burscough triumphed by the odd goal in seven.

Slowly but surely they came to terms with the pace and quality of soccer needed to succeed in what was a highly competitive league, eventually finishing third in the first division championship race.

Burscough won 16 of their 28 league games, scoring 74 times and conceding 41 goals, and were only pipped on goal difference for runners-up spot by arch-rivals and neighbours Skelmersdale United.

Liverpool 'A' were champions, losing only once while amassing 48 points, but the Linnets were more than pleased with their first season's work in a league which also included Ellesmere Port Town, Earlestown, Everton 'A', UGB (St. Helens) and Earle.

Cup ties were few and far between. In fact, Burscough were only involved in two competitions, the Liverpool Challenge Cup and the George Mahon Cup.

They reached the third round of the Challenge Cup before bowing out 3-2 at Prescot B.I., but were KO'd in the opening round of the George Mahon Cup, tumbling to a 1-0 home defeat against Liverpool 'A'.

UNIQUE TREBLE

As the 1947-48 season got under way, local lads Harry Sutton, Jimmy Aspinall, Matt Brennan and Frank Postlethwaite had firmly established themselves as first team regulars, and with ace marksman Wesley Bridge firing the ammunition up front, Burscough embarked on what turned out to be the greatest nine months in the club's history.

By the second week in May 1948, three glittering trophies had found their way to Victoria Park - the coveted Lancashire Junior Cup, the George Mahon Cup and the Liverpool Challenge Cup.

In all, Burscough played 15 cup ties that season, 14 of which were won and with a 50-14 goal ratio.

The only tie they lost was an F.A. Cup second round home clash against Rhyl on October 4th. But the Linnets, who had beaten Bangor City 3-1 in the previous round, had some financial consolation as the gate receipts, at a shilling a time, totalled £115 7s 6d......the highest of the season at Victoria Park.

League form was a little patchy up to Christmas but as the excitement of chasing three cups gathered momentum in the new year, fans began dreaming of a unique treble.

In the Junior Cup, recognised as Lancashire's greatest non-league knockout competition, Southport Reserves were beaten 3-1, Atherton Collieries despatched 4-0, Clitheroe hammered 7-0, and Barrow defeated 2-0, paving the way for a final showdown against Fleetwood at Bloomfield Road,

Blackpool, on Saturday 13th March 1948.

The tie, which attracted a crowd of 6,726, burst into life after 20 minutes when left winger Airey slotted Fleetwood ahead but by the half-hour mark underdogs Burscough were level, thanks to a stunning goal from skipper and inside right Joe Kelly.

It was the inspiration needed and five minutes into the second half right winger Alan Woolley forced the ball over the line after superb work by Bridge.

When the final whistle sounded hundreds of an estimated 3,000 Burscough fans swarmed all over the pitch and carried their heroes shoulder high to the front of the stand where the trophy was handed over.

Centre half Postlethwaite still remembers the day vividly. 'It's a moment I will always treasure and when we returned to Burscough, which was only a little village at the time, the reception we received was out of this world,' he said.

'When our coach came over the railway bridge all we could see was a mass of faces....the streets were filled with people, all wanting to get a glimpse of the famous trophy.'

The two teams on that memorable day were - Burscough: Sutton; Aspinall, Langley; London, Postlethwaite, Brennan; Woolley, Kelly, Bridge, Lunt, Saunders.

Fleetwood: Bakewell; Tuson, Dearden; Rawcliffe, Williamson, Hall; Bond, Hough, Strachan, Cutting, Airey. Referee: Mr. J.Robinson (Blackburn).

The players had hardly time to draw breath before facing Ellesmere Port Town in the semi-final of the George Mahon Cup at South Liverpool on 31st March. And at half-time it looked as though their treble dreams were about to go up in smoke.

Burscough were 3-0 down at the interval, but came storming back to win 4-3, thanks to a late goal from Johnny Buckley, which set the stage for their second cup final of the season, this time against Earlestown.

South Liverpool was again the venue but on this occasion the Linnets suffered few scares and goals from Woolley and Buckley completed the second part of the treble bid.

Cup fever, which had been gripping the village for several months, now reached unprecedented heights as Burscough's opponents, and possible party poopers in the final of the Liverpool Challenge Cup, at Haig Avenue, Southport, on May 8 1948, were none other than deadly rivals Skelmersdale United.

But in front of a crowd of 8,046, who paid £624 in gate receipts, Burscough romped to a 4-1 victory.

Centre forward Bridge opened the scoring after only 90 seconds, and although United equalised through Powell just before the interval, they were swept aside in the final 45 minutes.

Woolley restored Burscough's lead after a pile-driver from winger Tom Saunders (later to become Liverpool Youth Development Officer and a man who helped to establish the Anfield dynasty) had rebounded off goalkeeper Roughsedge, and then a double strike from Bridge wrapped up victory.

Bridge's hat-trick took his goals tally for the season to a staggering 70 - still a club record nearly fifty years on.

Cup success, however, hit the Linnets' hopes of clinching the Liverpool County Combination title. They finished fifth with 44 points from 34 games, 18 of which they won.

They scored 104 goals but at the same time conceded no fewer than 77. From 8th

Above: Action in the Burscough goalmouth during the George Mahon Cup Final played on Saturday 10th April 1948. In front of a crowd of 4,280 at South Liverpool's Holly Park ground, Burscough won 2-0 against 'bogey' side Earlestown. Goalscorers were Alan Woolley and Johnny Buckley.

Below: Mrs. Garner, the daughter of George Mahon, presents the Cup to Burscough captain Joe Kelly after a famous victory. The smiles of the onlooking supporters say it all. The Cup had returned to Victoria Park with the Rangers, the Vics, and now, it was Burscough's turn.

November 1947 to 13th March, the following year they played 20 games without defeat, equalling the record of the old Burscough Rangers in the 1914-15 season.

AFTER THE LORD MAYOR'S SHOW....

After the euphoria and success of that never-to-be-forgotten 1947-48 season, it was inevitable that Burscough would lose some of their better players to Lancashire Combination clubs and this proved the case.

Only goalkeeper Harry Sutton, skipper Kelly, wing half Wilf London, top scorer Bridge and Buckley stayed at Victoria Park for the full duration of the 1948-49 campaign.

But the Linnets started the season like an express train, winning their first nine league games, in which they scored a staggering 46 goals.

They hammered Crompton Recs twice (10-0 and 9-0) and crushed UGB (St. Helens) 9-1. Strange as it may seem, the ten goal demolition of Crompton (still the joint highest victory in the club's history) was achieved when they wore numbers on their shirts for the first time.

They could not, however, maintain the momentum and seven defeats from eight successive league and cup ties left them too far adrift in the County Combination title race to make any real impact.

Eventually, they finished the season in eighth place with 41 points from 34 games, 18 of which they won. They scored 101 goals and conceded 69.

The biggest gate, not surprisingly, was recorded for the visit of Skelmersdale United on 25th September when 3,800 fans, paying £128 4s 2d, saw Burscough triumph 3-1.

Hopes of repeating their previous season's cup treble also evaporated before the end of 1948 season with a 2-0 away defeat at Barrow in the Lancashire Junior Cup, followed by a controversial exit from the Liverpool Challenge Cup at the start of the new year.

Burscough won their second round tie 2-0 against Earlestown at Victoria Park but the visitors lodged a protest against full back Seddon, claiming he wasn't eligible to play.

As a result, the County F.A. ordered the tie to be replayed at the same venue and on this occasion Earlestown won 2-1.

The Linnets did, however, reach the semi-final of the George Mahon Cup but went down 2-0 to St. Helens Town at Skelmersdale.

Bridge again topped the scoring charts with 51 goals, Harry Penkeyman hit 15 and skipper Kelly and Harry Bergin both found the net 13 times.

ONE IN THE EYE FOR NELSON

More than 12,000 spectators, paying receipts of £845 14s, flocked through the turnstiles at Ewood Park, the home of Blackburn Rovers, on Thursday 27th April 1950, and witnessed one of the biggest upsets in the non-league soccer calendar.

Little Burscough, already on their way to clinching the Liverpool County Combination first division title, had been given no hope of overcoming mighty Nelson, kings of the Lancashire Combination, in the final of the Lancashire Junior Cup.

But the scribes were left eating their words as the lively Linnets lifted the coveted

The 1949-50 Lancashire Junior Cup winning side, pictured before the kick-off at Ewood Park, Blackburn. Back left to right: Wilf London, Joe Simpkin, Chris Lynn, Harry Sutton, Jimmy Aspinall, Joe Kelly, Ned Gregson (Trainer). Front left to right: Harry Penkeyman, Wesley Bridge, Gilly Houghton, Stan Jones, Bill Morris. Photograph kindly loaned by Gilly Houghton. In 1996, Gilly lived in Whitefield, Manchester.

trophy for the second time in three years on the strength of a 2-1 victory.

'Centurion' in the Northern Daily Telegraph the following night summed up the match perfectly when he said: 'Nelson were put out of their usual smooth stride by a side which played the ball a vital few seconds earlier, snapped into the tackle and covered brilliantly in defence.'

'Perhaps Nelson felt the strain of a recent series of games, or were caught on the rebound after the knowledge that they had won the Lancashire Combination championship.'

'But far too often they were beaten in attack by Burscough's quick-thinking defenders who nipped in to intercept and banged the ball anywhere for safety.'

Wesley Bridge grabbed Burscough's first goal in a thrill-a-minute first half, and although Nelson equalised 10 minutes after the break through Burns, Bridge struck again to restore the underdog's one goal advantage, which they held on to until the final whistle.

For the record the two teams that night were - Burscough: Sutton; Aspinall, Lynn; London, Morris, Houghton; Penkeyman, Simpkin, Bridge, Kelly, Jones.

Nelson: Tattersall; Wigglesworth, Thompson; Coates, Johnson, Coyne; Woodhead, Ward, Webber, Burns, McManus.

The tie was played early evening and, when news filtered through to people in the village that the team would be returning home immediately with the trophy, the streets were soon overflowing.

The Ormskirk Advertiser on the following Thursday reported: 'The team arrived back in Burscough by motor coach shortly before 10.30 pm and the enthusiastic crowd gave them a great reception, waving green and white colours and streamers.'

The sound was so deafening that when the players and officials tried to address the fans from the club stand at Victoria Park they could hardly make themselves heard.

But the main theme of the speeches, apart from commiserating with skipper Harry Bergin, who had to miss the final due to injury, was 'now let's take the championship.'

And that Burscough duly did, pipping Skelmersdale United by one point as a result of a 3-1 victory over Cromptons Recs at Ashton-in-Makerfield on Saturday 8th May 1950.

It was the first time since 1926-27 that the name of Burscough had appeared on the championship trophy and fitting testimony to the most consistent side in the league.

Astonishingly, they never lost a league fixture away from home that season after going down 3-2 at UGB (St. Helens) on 21st August...a run of 13 games.

They won 25 of their 34 league fixtures, scoring 96 goals, conceding 35 and amassing a total of 54 points.

Burscough also won 8 of their 13 cup ties and the number of wins (33) was a new record, beating the 32 achieved during their treble triumph.

The biggest attendance of the season, and a record at that time, was 4,128 (receipts £215 7s 0d) for an F.A. Cup tie against Wigan Athletic on 15th October 1949.

RECORD CROWDS

Success breeds success - but it can also lead to a seemingly never-ending backlog of fixtures.

This proved to be the case in the 1950-51 season when Burscough played a total of 51 games, of which no fewer than 19 were cup ties.

Yet they still rung down the curtain of an energy-sapping campaign in glorious style by defeating St. Helens 3-1 in the final of the Liverpool Challenge Cup at Springfield Park, Wigan, on 14th May 1951 - their 16th game in 29 days.

It was a tremendous show of character, endurance and no small measure of skill as goals from Aspinall, Kelly and Woods enabled the Linnets to lift the trophy for the second time in three years.

The team that day was: Sutton; Stone, Lynn; London, Morris, Brennan; Aspinall, Kelly, Woods, McGrail, Waugh.

Cup soccer had also dominated the early part of the season and at one stage it looked as though the club were on course to reach the first round Proper of the F.A. Cup for the first time in their short history.

After victories over both St. Helens Town and Haydock C & B, a 2-0 triumph at the expense of Bootle and a 3-2 success against Skelmersdale United, only Wigan Athletic, then one of the most powerful non-league sides in the country, stood in their path to glory.

It was a tie which fired the imagination of soccer-lovers throughout the region and was reflected in the attendance at Victoria Park.

No fewer than 4,798 fans flocked through the turnstiles, paying £280 in gate receipts, and it still stands today as the Club's biggest ever attendance.

But, sadly for Burscough, the result went the wrong way, Latics cruising to a 2-0 victory.

October proved to be quite a month for records as 21 days earlier Victoria Park had housed its largest ever league gate - 3,526 fans paying receipts of £168 11s for a derby clash against Skelmersdale United.

The demands of cup soccer, however, dented Burscough's hopes of clinching their second County Combination championship. They eventually finished in sixth spot, collecting 38 points from their 32 league games.

The auld enemy, Skelmersdale United, emerged as champions with 49 points, one more than Everton 'A'.

DEVASTATING IMPACT

Spoiled by almost unprecedented success since the end of the war, Burscough fans were left somewhat deflated during the following two seasons when they failed to win a single piece of silverware!

They finished seventh in the championship race during the 1951-52 campaign (their lowest ever position) and 12 months later were sixth.

But events on the field in the latter half of 1952 were hardly dull with the explosive emergence of centre forward Louis Bimpson from junior football in Rainford.

'Big Louie,' as he was affectionately known by the fans, spent less than six months at Victoria Park before being snapped up by Liverpool for £500 (a massive fee for a non-league player in those days), but not before he had made a devastating impact.

Not only did he score seven goals in an 8-0 thrashing of Southport Trinity in a Liverpool Challenge Cup tie at Victoria Park on November 1st, but finished leading scorer with 24 goals despite joining Liverpool halfway through the season.

Bimpson, who is the only Burscough F.C. player to compete in an F.A. Cup Final at Wembley (he played outside right in the

Louis Bimpson, pictured in his Liverpool playing days. Louis was born in Rainford on the 14th May 1929. He joined Burscough from Rainford North End in 1952, and was transferred to Liverpool in January 1953. During his career, he played a total of 181 Football League matches, scoring 61 goals. Photograph kindly loaned by Louis, who now lives in Burscough.

Blackburn Rovers team which was beaten 3-0 by Wolverhampton Wanderers in 1960), still remembers his seven-goal haul vividly.

'I only had about ten games in the first team before my move to Anfield but the game against Southport Trinity still sticks in my memory. Every time I touched the ball, it seemed to finish up in the net.'

Bimpson's meteoric rise to fame is also recalled with a great deal of self-satisfaction by Burscough's senior vice-president Derek Watkinson.

At the time, Derek was a cub reporter with the Ormskirk Advertiser and reckons that he played a part in 'selling' Louis to Liverpool.

Derek says: 'I've always maintained that John Houghton, who was sports editor at the time, and I sold Louis to Liverpool through our reports.'

'As the weeks went by, we gave him headlines like 'Brilliant Bimpson Bombshell,' 'Louis' Wonder Goals,' and 'Sensational Bimpson,' etc.

'But more importantly, we began to 'invent' league scouts who were 'beginning to converge' on Burscough.'

'At the time, we used to telephone during and after the game summarised reports to the Liverpool and Preston evening football papers and usually managed to slip in the 'scouts in attendance' bit.'

And it eventually paid dividends, Liverpool boss Don Welsh snapping up Bimpson's signature in the now demolished Wheatsheaf Hotel in Burscough Street, Ormskirk, on Wednesday 28th January 1953.

Says Derek: 'I still have my notes of the deal. Burscough received £500, a further £250 if Louis played 10 Central League games and an additional £500 if he played 10 first team games.'

In fact, Louis eventually played 100 games for the Anfielders at first team level, scoring 40 goals. He also had a spell at Blackburn, as mentioned earlier, Bournemouth and Rochdale before coming full circle and rejoining the Linnets for the 1963-64 season - 10 years and 10 months after his initial departure.

'I had a marvellous decade in League football and don't regret a minute of it,' says Bimpson.

And he adds philosophically: 'I am not envious of the money top professionals earn today. When I first went to Liverpool, I received a basic £14 a week with a £2 bonus for a win but enjoying the sport and the life that went with it was more important than the money.'

'I was able to visit different parts of the world and I wouldn't swap my memories for anything.'

DAZZLING START

Strange as it may seem, Burscough's lack of trophy success over the previous two years kick-started the club into seeking a higher standard of football and they were admitted to the Second Division of the Lancashire Combination at the start of the 1953-54 season.

Most of the players who had brought glory to Victoria Park in the early post-war days had now been allowed to seek pastures new, or had retired gracefully from the game, and with Liverpudlian Charlie Jones becoming the first ever manager, his team was not surprisingly jam-packed with Scousers.

He recruited a large number of players from his previous club, Bootle, and they formed the nucleus of a team which over the next few years kept Burscough at the pinnacle of the non-league game.

They made a dynamic impact, lifting the Second Division title at the first time of asking with a team which more often than not read: Stan Hurst; Jimmy Cookson (capt), Arthur Green; Ron Wilson, Joe Brazier, Bobby Warren; Wally Burnett, Joe Hart, Johnny Vincent, Billy Thompson and Johnny Disley.

Burscough won 33 of their 42 league fixtures, scoring a staggering 155 goals (a figure which they are never likely to match again). Including cup ties, they played a total of 55 games and scored no fewer than 180 goals at an average of 3.27...and just for good measure the Reserves won the Liverpool County Combination Second Division title.

Centre forward Vincent led the way with 60 first team goals - the second highest individual return in the club's history - while flying winger Burnett hit the target 21 times.

Third in the scoring stakes with 17 was Disley, arguably the most skilful and gifted player ever to pull on the Linnets' shirt.

Dazzling Disley, as he was dubbed by the fans, wore his shorts down to his knees in Alex James style and possessed almost as many soccer tricks as his more famous Scottish counterpart.

At times Disley seemed to have the ball tied to his boots and his mesmeric ball control bewildered and bemused teams from Burnley to Barnoldswick.

But the big question fans were asking during the close season was: Could Disley and his team-mates continue to dazzle against much tougher opposition in the First Division?

The answer was, to a great degree, a resounding 'yes.' Although they didn't win the championship in the 1954-55 season, they finished in fourth place and that was no mean feat when looking at the quality of the teams above them at the end of the season.

Accrington Stanley Reserves claimed the title with 68 points, 14 more than Rossendale United and 16 ahead of Wigan Athletic, who only pipped Burscough for third spot on superior goal difference.

The seniors had little success on the cup front but the Reserves enhanced their growing reputation by defeating Fleetwood Hesketh 3-2 in the final of the Liverpool Challenge Cup at Haig Avenue - the home of Southport F.C.

GREATEST ACHIEVEMENT

Bobby Warren was a tough tackling wing half who would run through a brick wall in his quest for success every time he pulled on a green shirt.

He never gave less than 100 per cent commitment and epitomised a rock solid defence which was the backbone of Burscough's first ever Lancashire Combination First Division title triumph in the 1955-56 season.

Bobby, now living in Kirkby but still as enthusiastic as ever about the game and the club he served as player and coach for more than a decade, recalls: 'For most of the lads, including myself, winning the Championship was our greatest achievement at Victoria Park.'

Pictured here at a Supporter's Club function held at the British Legion in the early 1950s are, left to right: John Wilkes, Florrie Wilkes, Maggie Spencer, Bob Pate, Tom Spencer, Vera Hollins, Mrs. Pate, Unknown, Unknown, Mrs. Watkinson. Florrie Wilkes, who kindly loaned the photograph, and Maggie Spencer worked for many years in the Victoria Park canteen.

'There were some tremendous teams around at the time, such as Wigan Athletic, Netherfield, Horwich RMI, Lancaster City and New Brighton, but we proved to be the best.'

'I had the cultured Brian Finnigan and Ronnie Wilson alongside me at half back, two exceptional full backs in Jimmy Aspinall and skipper Arthur Green, and Stan Hurst, the finest goalkeeper in the non-league game at that time.'

And the facts back Bobby's assessment of the most miserly defence in the Lancashire Combination. In lifting the title, Burscough conceded a mere 37 goals in 38 championship clashes.

They won 26 games, lost only five and rattled in no fewer than 96 goals while claiming a final points haul of 59 - two more than Horwich and nine better than Accrington Stanley Reserves.

Burscough were also involved in 13 cup ties, winning seven including the final of the Liverpool Senior Non-league Cup when they defeated New Brighton 1-0 at Goodison Park.

Genial Joe Hart topped the goalscoring charts with 32 followed by Johnny Disley (22), John Hendry (18) and Stan Jessop (15). Wee winger Jessop, signed from neighbours Chorley, proved an astute acquisition and his goalscoring prowess from the left flank played a major role in the overall success of the team.

The Reserves, too, had a highly successful season in the Lancashire Combination Second Division, finishing fourth with 47 points from 34 games.

Skelmersdale United were champions with 51 points - one ahead of Droylesden and three in front of Wigan Athletic Reserves.

By now one or two new faces had been introduced, like chunky winger Dennis 'The Menace' Walmsley - a Southport plumber who mesmerised leaky defences, and brilliant ball-playing inside forward Des Steele.

But while looking on paper to have an even stronger team than the one which lifted the title, Burscough failed to retain their crown in the 1956-57 season.

An early indication that it would be tougher second time round came in the second game when Burscough travelled to Morecambe - eventually to finish third in the table - and were hammered 6-1

In fact, in 44 league and cup games the Linnets conceded 75 goals - 25 more than 12 months earlier when they were involved in 51 fixtures. But they were never able to solve a weakness at left back, and with several other players failing to find any kind of consistency, they finished a rather disappointing fifth in the table. Their league record read: P 38 W 19 L 12 D 7 F 86 A 58 PTS 45.

For the second successive season Hart headed the scoring charts with 31 followed by the equally consistent Disley who finished with 20.

But, significantly, no other player reached double figures and left both officials and fans pondering whether the almost unprecedented success which the club had enjoyed since the end of the Second World War was coming to an end.

The next two seasons - 1957-58 and 1958-59 - added weight to the growing theory, soon to be reversed, that the Burscough bubble had burst.

They finished 14th (their worst ever position) and 12th respectively and only managed to win 19 out of 84 league games during this period.

They did, however, enjoy a fair amount of cup success, reaching the semi-final of the Lancashire Junior Cup before losing 1-0 to Horwich RMI and battled their way to the final of the Lancashire Combination Cup where they were beaten 2-0 by New Brighton.

But although they were unaware of it at the time, their fleeting glimpse of glory in sudden-death soccer was the stepping stone to the greatest cup exploit in the Club's history....

F.A. CUP GLORY

Saturday 14th November 1959, is a date indelibly etched in the minds of every Burscough supporter over the age of 40.

A never-to-be-forgotten occasion when cup fever on an unprecedented scale gripped the tiny West Lancashire village.

For the first time in their history, the club had battled through to the first round proper of the F.A. Cup and standing in their path towards further glory was Fourth Division Crewe Alexandra - the first ever Football League club to set foot inside Victoria Park for a competitive match.

'The interest in the tie was phenomenal,' recalls present Chairman Frank Parr.

'Everyone wanted to see the game and the demand for tickets was unbelievable.'

As a result, officials were forced to improvise in order to accommodate everyone who wanted to see a David versus Goliath clash which not only captured the imagination of every football follower in the County, but TV, radio and the national press.

An SOS was issued to the local farming community to provide trailers, which during the days leading up to the tie were stationed the full length of the pitch where the Barons Club now stands.

The additional standing room enabled Burscough to cram in 4,200 fans who paid record gate receipts at the time of £420 9s 0d.

And the fans almost tumbled off their trailers when Burscough snatched a dramatic early lead through winger Jimmy Jones. But their joy was short-lived as Crewe, superbly led by former Everton and Welsh international Bert Llewellyn, cashed in on defensive errors to earn a 3-1 victory.

But the fairy-tale magic which surrounds the F.A. Cup had unfolded before disbelieving eyes in the last qualifying round at Ellesmere Port Town.

Burscough were not given a hope of ousting the Cheshire League club - unbeaten at home for more than two years - and just to make the task even more mountainous they were forced to play a crucial part of the tie with goalkeeper Harry Smelt operating on the left wing.

But Smelt, with his arm in a sling after being injured while making a vital save,

F.A. CHALLENGE CUP COMPETITION

1st ROUND

BURSCOUGH
v.
CREWE ALEXANDRA
KICK-OFF 2-15 p.m.
Saturday, 14th November, 1959

Grand Souvenir Programme

Price 4d.

The Burscough team lines up in front of a packed grandstand, prior to the F.A. Cup Tie with Crewe Alexandra.
Back left to right: Frank Richmond (Trainer), Tony Greenwood, Don Baker, Albert Ashurst, Bobby Warren, Ray Prentice, Charlie Jones (Team Manager)
Front left to right: Dennis Walmsley, Arthur Rowley, Arthur Green, Des Steele, Joe Hart, Jimmy Jones - David Ashcroft (Mascot)

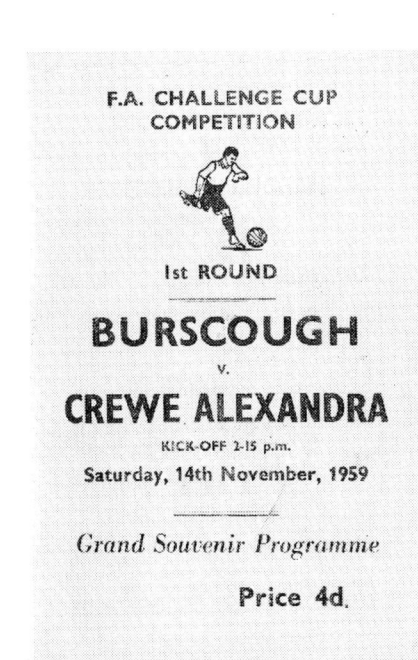

showed courage beyond the call of duty and made a vital contribution as the Linnets achieved an astonishing 2-1 victory.

In all that season, Burscough were involved in a total of 12 cup ties in varying competitions, of which seven were won, but inevitably it left them with a backlog of fixtures, 15 having to be completed in the last two months of the season, and any hopes of regaining the Lancashire Combination title quickly disappeared.

They eventually finished sixth with 48 points from 42 matches - 19 adrift of champions Chorley.

Arthur Rowley - arguably the hardest striker of a dead ball ever to wear a Burscough shirt - topped the goalscoring charts with 42 and a fair share came from cannonball-like free kicks.

His final total should actually have been 43 - but he had one chalked off by a referee many thought needed a pair of glasses! In one league game at Victoria Park, he unleashed a thunderbolt of a shot which struck the stanchion in the back of the net and rebounded back into play before the man in the middle had realised what had happened.

INTO THE SIXTIES

As the countdown to the 1960-61 season got under way optimism was sky-high at Victoria Park. And why not? Their F.A. Cup exploits the previous year and a top six spot in the league table suggested that even better times were on the horizon.

But, although it wasn't immediately apparent, the Sixties signalled the start of a rather traumatic period in the club's history.

Despite finishing joint third with Wigan Athletic in the Lancashire Combination with 64 points from their 32 matches, Burscough won just one of their nine cup games in a variety of competitions and at the same time gates were noticeably on the decline.

Even the arrival on the scene of Harry Lyon - who was regarded as a cult figure by the faithful fans - failed to boost attendances.

Harry, an old fashioned style centre forward in the Nat Lofthouse mould, certainly made his presence felt on the field...scoring 33 of Burscough's final goals tally of 88.

Then, in the 1961-62 campaign, he wrote his name in the club's history books by becoming the first Burscough player to hit a half-century of goals in the First Division of the Lancashire Combination.

Harry found the net 56 times as the rampaging Linnets scored no fewer than 135 goals in their 52 league and cup matches.

Incredibly, only one match was lost at home that season - but what a stunning defeat it turned out to be. Morecambe came to Victoria Park in an F.A. Cup tie and handed out an amazing 8-1 drubbing.

It remains Burscough's biggest defeat in the competition - home or away - and is still remembered by those lucky or unlucky enough to be present.

Several other players came into prominence during the season, including a strong tackling centre half by the name of Bob Jones.

Bob went on to be a magnificent servant of the club and captained them to their 1966-67 Lancashire Junior Cup success...a fitting reward for a player who had green blood running through his veins.

By now Pat Murphy, who had managed, among other clubs, Wigan Athletic and had been involved in top level coaching in Germany, had taken over the management reins from Charlie Jones and his training sessions were legendary...players regularly collapsing with sheer fatigue as he whipped them into shape.

And if he wasn't happy with the team's performance on the pitch, everyone sitting in the stand at half-time would know all about it...his bluer-than-blue dressing room rockets invariably reached their ears!

BIG FREEZE

The big freeze of 1963 turned soccer at all levels into total chaos - and Burscough suffered like the rest.

From Christmas Eve 1962 until March 2nd of the following year the club played only three matches as severe frost and snow left the whole country whiter than white.

As a result the Linnets were forced to play a staggering 18 matches during April in order to complete their fixtures at the end of what was a rather poor season.

This was reflected in average gate receipts of a meagre £10. The Club finished 16th in the 22-strong Lancashire Combination, gaining a paltry 35 points from 22 matches.

On the cup front, their best run came in the Liverpool Non-League Cup when they reached the semi-final stage. But after drawing twice against South Liverpool, they eventually went down 3-2 to the Merseysiders.

Burscough scored a total of 88 goals in 52 competitive matches, Rigby leading the way with 14. Their lack of scoring prowess that season can be gauged by the fact that only two other players, Dennis Walmsley (13) and Albert Finlay (12) reached double figures.

Victoria Park was also an early starting point that season for a youngster who, while never scaling any great heights as a defender, became one of the most successful non-league managers of the 1970s.

Roy Rees went on to lead neighbours Skelmersdale United to triumph in the F.A. Amateur Cup against Dagenham in 1971 and was the man largely responsible for launching the phenomenal Liverpool career of Steve Heighway, bringing him to White Moss Park as a raw university student and helping to develop his talents.

Roy later managed Altrincham and went on to coach in America.

CLUB IN CRISIS

The season of the big freeze also coincided with a period of great uncertainty concerning the club's immediate future.

Burscough finished 16th in the Lancashire Combination and only improved by one rung on the ladder 12 months later, their performance matched by attendances at Victoria Park which slumped to less than 100 spectators.

Even the return of Louis Bimpson after spells at Liverpool, Blackburn Rovers, and Rochdale in November 1963 failed to boost gates.

Matters went from bad to worse and during the 1964-65 season the Linnets spent most of the campaign attempting to avoid a drop into the Second Division, finishing in their worst-ever position of 20th after gaining only 11 wins from 42 games.

As a result Burscough were forced to take drastic action to keep the game alive in the village.

Joe Hull, who was chairman at the time, and president Sam Curtis launched a 'Save Burscough F.C. Fund' with the help of the Ormskirk Advertiser, warning the people of the village that if they didn't get behind the club it would go out of existence.

Fortunately, through their straight talking and a great deal of hard work, the crisis was avoided and by the start of the 1965-66 campaign Burscough were on a much sounder financial footing.

There were also signs of improvement on the playing front, even allowing for the fact that the Club only finished in 16th position with 32 points.

By now Bobby Langton, the former England international winger, had taken over the reins of manager and introduced some precocious young talent, including inside right Micky Worswick, later to move to neighbours Skelmersdale United and play at Wembley in the 1967 F.A. Amateur Cup Final, left winger and practical joker Kenny Worden, and former Skelmersdale United and Wolves outside right Kenny Hodge.

They were cemented alongside the existing playing staff, including Jimmy 'Mr. Perpetual Motion' Hammell, who in the eyes of many fans was the Linnets' outstanding player of the 1960s.

Like all good wingers, Jimmy was king of the right touchline and he was able to destroy defences by his speed off the mark and ability to keep the ball glued to his feet. He also netted his fair share of goals, which was an added bonus.

Burscough were now producing the kind of football which brought the fans flocking back through the turnstiles and with Langton adopting a philosophy of 'I don't care if they score six, as long as we score seven,' Victoria Park was the place to go for goals and entertainment.

Bobby's cavalier approach to the game was eventually rewarded when Burscough lifted the Lancashire Junior Cup for the first time in 17 years, defeating South Liverpool 1-0 at Springfield Park, Wigan, on April 26, 1967....the same week as neighbours Skelmersdale United crashed to a 3-0 defeat against Enfield in an F.A. Amateur Cup Final replay at Maine Road, the home of Manchester City.

It was a feather in the former Bolton, Blackburn and Preston North End winger's cap to lift the county's premier non-league trophy after some tremendous ties on the way to the final.

Both Rossendale United and Wigan Athletic were KO'd after replays but it was even tougher in the semi-final....Burscough taking three games to extinguish the challenge of Chorley.

Not surprisingly, they were not at their best for the final after playing a staggering 12 games in the previous 24 days and it was a tribute to Langton's training methods that they were able to overcome their rivals in what was a rather low key affair.

Defences dominated for long spells at a time and extra-time looked a distinct possibility until South full back Arthur Goldstein, under pressure from Linnets' inside forward Tony Corbett, lobbed the ball over his own goalkeeper's head into the inviting net.

Langton said later: 'This is my proudest moment since taking over as manager. The lads were tremendous tonight and showed great character and resilience. Let's hope this result will be a stepping stone to even greater achievements.'

Burscough didn't exactly set the world alight in the league, finishing in 14th position, but were involved in one of the most bizarre matches in the Club's entire history.

Above: Pictured in the dressing room at Springfield Park, with the Lancashire Junior Cup. Back left to right: John Coates, Dave Parker, Johnny Baldwin. Middle left to right: Bob Langton (Manager), Ronnie Lawson (Committeeman and a lifelong supporter of the club), Roy Johnson, Terry Finlay, Kenny Hodge, Mick Phoenix, Alan Tordoff, Bill Tyrer (Committee), Joe Hull (Chairman). Seated left to right: Tony Fitzgerald, Tony Corbett, Bob Jones, Kenny Worden, Charlie Daniels, Jimmy Hammell.

Below: Action from the Lancashire Junior Cup tie at Morecambe in March 1968, Burscough losing 1-0. Goalkeeper John Coates leaps high to gather the ball watched by Tony Fitzgerald (No.11) and Bob Jones (No.5). Coates went on to play in the Football League with Southport and played in Morecambe's 1973-74 F.A. Trophy winning side at Wembley.

The date in question was April 3, 1967...pencilled in for a visit from arch-rivals and neighbours Skelmersdale United, who were on the way to Wembley in the F.A. Amateur Cup.

Fans packed into Victoria Park expecting to see Skelmersdale's high-fliers in action but United's ebullient chairman at the time, Bill Gregson, didn't want to risk any of his top players on the eve of a crucial cup tie....and signed on the complete Connah's Quay team from North Wales to represent the club.

Larger-than-life Gregson thought it was a masterstroke, particularly as he was breaking no rules in signing players from another league, but Burscough officials were furious and claimed the fans had been conned.

However, the Linnets' blushes were spared to some extent when they took both points from the White Moss Park Welshmen, winning 2-1.

CONTROVERSY

Burscough failed to build on their Junior Cup triumph and, in what was a rather uneventful 1967-68 season, finished 14th in the league.

Their inconsistency was reflected in the match-by-match statistics...they won only four of their first 14 league and cup fixtures; then lost only once in the next 14 games before failing to gain maximum points from eight matches which followed.

Defensively, they were short of quality players and in 53 league and cup outings conceded 86 goals...12 more than they scored.

The Reserves, however, did bring some glory to the club, winning the Liverpool County Combination Second Division title and the Lord Wavertree Cup.

New blood was now high on Langton's agenda and it arrived when Burscough, who had traditionally recruited from Merseyside, moved into other parts of Lancashire and secured the likes of midfield maestros Kenny Dumican and Kenny Miller, creative inside forward Ivor Swarbrick and Rainford-based Graham Glover, who had been playing with Prescot Cables.

But no-one set the fan's adrenalin flowing more than Brian Robinson, a centre forward who achieved cult status at Victoria Park with his prolific goalscoring.

The no. 9 shirt had previously been filled by some of non-league soccer's crack marksmen, such as Wesley Bridge, Johnny Vincent and Harry Lyon, but Robbo's scoring feats were equal to his hot-shot predecessors and when he eventually hung up his boots he had scored close on 150 goals for the club.

In his first season, 1968-69, he hit the half century mark as the Linnets finished fourth in the table, 15 points behind champions Great Harwood.

They won 23 of their 42 matches and rattled in no fewer than 110 goals in a season when all the top five clubs topped the ton.

Burscough also reached the final of the Lancashire Combination Cup, but went down 6-5 in a two-legged thriller to Marine.

The Mariners won the first leg at College Road and held Burscough to a 4-4 draw in a classic second leg which had the fans on tenterhooks from start to finish.

But it was activities off the field which dominated the headlines as the season drew to a close. The Northern Premier League was about to get off the ground and five established members of the Lancashire Combination, including champions Great Harwood and Marine, opted to join the new set up and three others moved into the

Cheshire League.

It left league officials scrambling around to attract the right calibre of club to maintain their highly rated status, and although it wasn't evident at the time, this was the beginning of the end for a non-league competition which in the 1950s and early 1960s was the equal of any from Land's End to John O'Groats.

Burscough had also looked into the possibility of joining the Cheshire League set up but stayed loyal to the Combination for a further season and this proved a wise decision....the following May they were crowned champions for the first time since 1956.

They finished with 64 points from 38 matches, three more than Prestwich Heys and four ahead of Chorley in a title race which went down to the wire.

In an amazing topsy-turvy finale, the Linnets beat their nearest rivals, Prestwich Heys, 1-0 on April 8, 1970, thanks to a goal by Dumican, but then three days later the Mancunians blasted the Championship race wide open again by winning the return by a staggering 7-0.

However, Burscough's nerve held and they sealed the title in their final fixture at Dukinfield Town, goals from Kenny Jarvis (2), Robinson and Chris Booth giving them a 4-0 triumph.

The Linnets also reached the third qualifying round of the F.A. Cup before crashing out in a controversial replay against old rivals Wigan Athletic at Victoria Park.

The destiny of the tie hinged on one decision by the referee when Langton's boys were leading 2-1...and, inevitably, that man Robinson was at the centre of the controversy.

The ace striker, clearly being held back by a Wigan defender, wriggled clear of his marker and smashed the ball into the net.

But to the amazement of almost everyone in a crowd of nearly 2,000 the man in the middle brought play back and awarded Burscough a free kick.

His failure to apply the advantage rule cost Burscough dear....Wigan netting twice in the final six minutes to set up a last qualifying round tie against Skelmersdale.

INTO THE CHESHIRE LEAGUE

Anyone who thought Burscough were going to be out of their depth when they waved goodbye to Lancashire Combination football after 17 years' membership and joined the Cheshire League at the start of the 1970-71 season, were greatly mistaken.

The team, which had lifted the Combination title as their swan-song, quickly showed they had nothing to fear and with the addition of Leo Skeete, a deadly finisher both on the ground and in the air, to play alongside ace markman Robinson, Burscough finished runners-up in the championship race...a tremendous feat.

They collected 60 points from their 42 league matches and scored 106 goals - more than any other club - but conceded 61 which shows in cold calculated facts why they didn't win the title.

The Linnets were great entertainers, with the Skeete-Robinson partnership striking terror into the heart of defences from Oswestry to Oldham.

Liverpudlian Skeete grabbed 39 goals, including four hat-tricks, and Robinson weighed in with 27 - five of which came in one game against New Brighton at Victoria Park.

Their most devastating performance came against Skelmersdale United on April 6, 1971...18 days before the White Moss Park outfit lifted the F.A. Amateur Cup at Wembley by defeating Dagenham 4-1.

Robinson hit a hat-trick and Skeete grabbed a brace as United were humiliated 5-0 in front of their own disbelieving fans.

United's boss Roy Rees blamed his team's 'below-par performance' on their involvement in the F.A. Amateur Cup but the truth of the matter is that on the night Burscough were in a class of their own and would have beaten any non-league club in the country.

The dynamic duo were again among the goals during the following season, 1971-72, but Robbo topped the charts on this occasion with 22 - three more than his co-striker.

Unfortunately, apart from 10 goal Johnny Rogers, later to make a big impact with Wigan Athletic, and midfield maestro Kenny Dumican, who netted 12 times, no other players reached double figures and Burscough's hopes of a first Cheshire League title evaporated.

The disappointment of failing to win the title 12 months after finishing runners-up was partly erased by their success in lifting the Liverpool Non-league Cup with a comprehensive 4-1 victory over Formby at Victoria Park, thanks to goals from Robinson, Skeete, Dumican and Dave Parry.

Burscough had reached the final with a 3-0 home victory over Skelmersdale United in front of their biggest crowd of the season....1,500 fans paying gate receipts of £260.

It was Kenny Spencer's first trophy success since replacing Langton as manager in 1971 and a great boost for the lad who was born and bred in the nearest house to Victoria Park.

And the star of the show that night, as the BBC's sports correspondent Charlie Lambert recalls in his foreword to the book, was the highly talented Skeete who scored a stunning goal.

But Skeete, who was as deadly as a finisher in the air as on the ground, gave the management team at Victoria Park more headaches than they care to remember.

The late Bill Martland was chairman at the time and there were occasions, just hours before the kick off when he had to send his farm hand Tony Dutton and 'chauffeur' Bernard Derbyshire hunting for the 'missing striker.'

'We often had to go into Liverpool and knock him up out of bed and on other occasions we found him sitting on a bench in the village, refusing to turn out unless Billy paid him a few extra quid,' said Bernard.

And Bill invariably had to cough up!

The season was also significant for one other reason...Burscough played their first-ever home match under floodlights. This was against Oswestry Town on March 9, 1972, and the Linnets celebrated the occasion by winning 3-1.

Spencer, a keen and enthusiastic coach who was always willing to learn from others, cast his net far and wide to bring in more young talent to keep Burscough in the forefront of non-league soccer and on the eve of the 1972-73 season also persuaded the vastly experienced Alan Swift to return to the club after a spell at Skelmersdale United, where he won an F.A. Amateur Cup winners' medal.

Burscough had originally spotted Swift playing in Southport junior league football during the late 1960s and he eventually developed into arguably the club's most versatile

Kenny Spencer was first a player, then a successful manager with Burscough, bringing the Cheshire League Cup to Victoria Park in 1974-75 season. Anyone photographed in the fashions of the 1970s deserves some sympathy, but at least Kenny's trousers are not visible! In 1996, he was scouting in the North West for Luton Town.

player in their 50 year history.

He could play in any position from full back to left winger and whatever jersey he was handed never looked out of his depth.

Spencer once said of the Southport-born ace: 'Despite being an amateur player, Alan always adopted a professional attitude. Irrespective of where he played, he almost inevitably emerged as the man of the match.'

Swift was unable to inspire Burscough to lift the title - they finished seventh - but helped them secure a place in the final of the two-legged Cheshire League Cup for the first time in their history.

Confidence was certainly sky-high after Burscough had established what looked an unassailable 3-0 home win in the first leg over Rossendale United, but they were blitzed 5-0 in the return at Dark Lane.

They were three goals down almost within the blinking of an eyelid and at the end of a 90 minute mauling could have conceivably suffered an even more embarrassing defeat.

It was a bitter pill to swallow but Burscough obviously learned from the experience...12 months later they were the bride and not the bridesmaid.

They lifted the trophy with a 2-1 aggregate victory over Marine thanks to an inspirational performance from a new hero to emerge at Victoria Park.

Little Joe Flaherty always played on a short fuse, and his back-chat often landed him in hot water with the referees, but there was no disputing the fact he had an abundance of talent when channelled in the right direction.

His 79th minute goal, which clinched Burscough's victory over Marine in the second leg of the Cheshire League Cup Final, after the teams had drawn 1-1 in the first leg, oozed sheer class.

Highly talented winger Phil Spencer, who had scored Burscough's goal in the first leg, did most of the spadework but Flaherty's finishing was clinical and at the end of the tie he was mobbed by the celebrating fans.

Burscough's cup winning side was: Alty, Stokes, Shannon, Miller, Bannister, Swift, Glover, Flaherty, Dumican, Bennett, Spencer.

The win more than compensated for their defeat two days later in the second leg of the Lancashire Floodlit Cup by Great Harwood.

The first leg at Victoria Park ended goalless, but the North East Lancashire side won the return 5-3...the Linnets' goals coming from Flaherty (2), and a Spencer penalty.

Burscough were also to the fore in the Championship race until the turn of the year but couldn't maintain the momentum and had to be content with seventh position - 15 points behind champions Leek Town.

The season was also significant for the departure of three club officials who had given sterling service to the club over many years. Secretary Chris Mahood, Treasurer Terry Kelly and Vice-chairman Jim Bridge all stepped down from office, expressing the view that it was time to make way for new blood.

TRAUMATIC TIME

Burscough's inability to hold on to their more gifted players, due to a large extent on their lack of finance, went a long way to stifling success in the next couple of seasons.

Body blow number one came with the departure of Joe Flaherty at the start of the 1975-76 season. The will-o'-the-wisp striker, who had hit 30 goals in the previous campaign, joined former Skelmersdale United boss Roy Rees at Bangor City, keen to build on his reputation as one of the most lethal marksmen on the non-league scene.

It left a huge void to fill - and although Phil Spencer, Kenny Dumican and new signing John Foy from Skelmersdale United netted more than 40 goals between them - no other players reached double figures and Burscough finished a bitterly disappointing 12th in the table - their lowest position since joing the Cheshire League.

But any hopes they had of launching a serious championship challenge the following season quickly vanished when they won only four of their first 12 league fixtures before suffering body blow number two....Phil Spencer moving to Runcorn for a three figure fee in November 1976.

Action from the Stafford Rangers v Burscough F.A. Trophy game on Saturday 10th January 1976. Burscough lost 4-0 in front of a crowd of 2,300. Kenny Crisp looks on, as Joey Flaherty appeals to the linesman for support.

The highly talented left winger had been a key figure in the Linnets' set up, able to combine his creative skills with lethal finishing and from this point a season already going downhill accelerated into a mini crisis.

A 5-0 pre-Christmas thrashing by South Liverpool in the F.A. Trophy led to manager Kenny Spencer and his coach, Harry McNally, parting company with the club.

Spencer, who had never been short of ambition, almost immediately joined Southport as Youth Development Officer, while McNally eventually progressed to the more illustrious heights of team manager at Wigan Athletic and Chester, illustrating how success can be achieved from humble beginnings.

Burscough refused to be panicked into naming a long-term successor, and although they had nine applications for the post, they turned to two former players, Bob Jones - a centre half who gave sterling service to the club during the 1960s - and Brian Robinson to hold the fort on a temporary basis.

Both acquitted themselves well to the task, and while results did not improve a great deal, Burscough were able to climb away from the lower reaches of the table.

They eventually finished 14th in the 22-strong competition and even though it represented their worst-ever position since switching leagues, officials were just happy that stability had returned to the club following a traumatic few months.

THE BULL AND THE MATADOR

George Rooney wasn't exactly a tried and tested manager when he took over the reins at Victoria Park in May 1977....his only real coaching experience having been gained as second team coach at Skelmersdale United and during a spell at Bangor City.

Many thought his appointment a huge gamble - and likely to backfire - but he quickly gained the respect and admiration of the fans, particularly with his F.A. Cup adventures.

Like one of his predecessors, fellow Liverpudlian Charlie Jones, George had an uncanny knack of being able to spot raw talent in the Merseyside junior leagues and nuturing it for the benefit of Burscough's soccer-loving public.

He introduced a host of new faces, including John Moran, a full back able to mix his defensive duties with imaginative attacking; rock-solid central defender Al Bowen; and Billy Jaycock, a fearless centre forward who would put his body on the line in a never-ending thirst for goals.

And it was Jaycock's exploits in front of goal which inspired the Linnets to battle their way into the first round proper of the F.A. Cup for the first time in 18 years.

He hit two goals in a 3-0 third qualifying round tie against Chorley and snatched a smash-and-grab winner in a 1-0 fourth qualifying replay win at Morecambe.

But Burscough's dreams of facing a Football League club for only the second time in their history were shattered when they were drawn away to Northern League outfit Blyth Spartans.

Graham Glover, who skippered the club at the time, still vividly recalls his feelings when hearing the draw.

'It was the most disappointing moment of my 11 years at Burscough. I was coming towards the end of my career and dearly wanted a crack at a Football League club before hanging up my boots but it wasn't to be.'

An Ian Mutrie goal gave Blyth a 1-0 win, but Graham still feels that Burscough were worthy of at least a draw against a ruthlessly efficient and hard tackling Northern League side who went on to reach the fifth round before losing to Stoke City at St. James Park, Newcastle.

'It was a tough and bruising encounter and some of the tackling made you shudder but we competed well and could have snatched a replay,' said Graham.

And even Blyth boss Brian Slane acknowledged at the time: 'Burscough are the best side we have played this season.'

The teams that day - November 26, 1977 - Blyth: Clarke, Waterson, Guthrie, Alder, Scott, Dixon, Houghton, Mutrie, Carney (S), Dagless, Carney (R). Sub: Johnson.

Burscough: Lawson, Moran, McGrady, Clarke, Bowen, Glover, Shallcross, Durnin, Jaycock, Madine, Garrity. Sub: Appleyard.

Unfortunately, the Linnets were unable to produce their cup form on the domestic front and finished 14th in the championship stakes - exactly the same position as 12 months earlier.

Re-establishing the club as one of the leading lights in the Cheshire League was still Rooney's top priority and during the close season more newcomers joined the Victoria Park ranks, including wee winger Syl Nolan from Kirkby; the versatile Tony Bannister, brother of Queens Park Rangers' ace Gary Bannister; crafty left winger Tony Duffy; and tough tackling half back Jimmy Lundon from Waterloo Dock.

It gave Burscough greater strength in depth and this was reflected in their early season form when they won six of the first seven fixtures - all played away from home due to re-seeding problems at Victoria Park.

However, they were unable to maintain their momentum and finished the campaign fifth - a massive 19 points adrift of champions Horwich RMI.

The arrivals in the summer of 1979 of former Manchester City and Blackburn Rovers midfield man Tommy Reed; versatile defender Keith Garland; and rangy striker Steve Taylor, who had experience with Bury, were seen as the final pieces in Rooney's title-winning jigsaw and only one defeat in the first 16 league and cup games suggested he was on the right track.

But, in what turned out to be an action replay of the previous season, Burscough again finished fifth, trailing 16 points behind champions Stalybridge Celtic, and also lost the services of their ambitious manager, who moved on to Winsford United.

But not before Rooney had left his mark indelibly on the pages of the club's history book...guiding the Linnets to the first round proper of the F.A. Cup and a never-to-be-forgotten tie against Sheffield United, a sleeping giant of the game.

A thumping 6-1 first qualifying round victory over Chorley gave an early indication that Burscough's sights were firmly fixed on a place in the first round for the second time in three seasons and this was confirmed with further wins over Netherfield (2-0), Rossendale United (4-0) and Horden Colliery Welfare (2-0).

It set the stage for a David versus Goliath clash at Bramall Lane on Saturday

---

Opposite: Alex Blakeman on target at Bramall Lane only to be foiled by Sheffield United 'keeper Steve Conroy, who made a brilliant save. Looking on is Billy Jaycock. Blakeman was the only Burscough player to ever span three decades with the club. He first played for Burscough in 1977-78 season, played through the 1980s - although not continuously, and began 1990-91 season with the club. Alex remembers a period when he went 'over two years without missing a game for Burscough.'

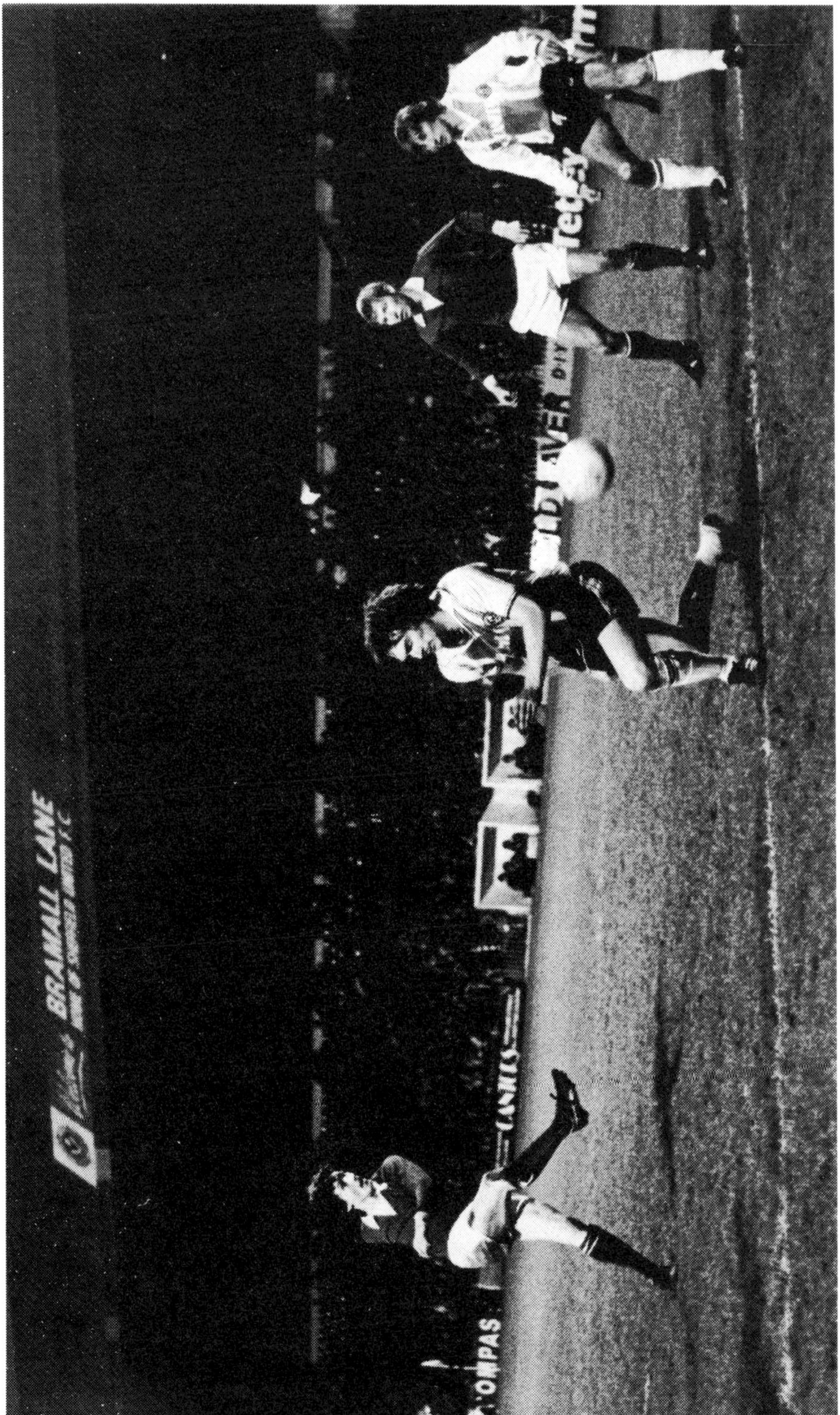
BRAMALL LANE

1979-80 Season. The team that faced Sheffield United. Back left to right: Gordon Hoskin (Vice-Chairman), Geoff Clarke (Secretary), Jimmy Wield (Trainer), Tommy Reed, Billy Jaycock, Kevin O'Brien, Al Bowen, Mike Tickle, Ken Hilton (Treasurer), Jimmy Murray (Committee).
Front left to right: Steve Taylor, Tony Bannister, Syl Nolan, Jimmy Lundon, Frank Parr (Chairman), Keith Garland, Tony Duffy, Alex Blakeman, John Moran.

November 24, 1979, after Burscough, who had originally been pulled out of the hat first, were forced to switch the tie to the other side of the Pennines following talks with the police over ground safety and a 3,000 ceiling on any tie at Victoria Park.

The match, played in front of 14,209 fans who paid gate receipts of £18,000, captured the imagination of the sporting press and on the morning of the showdown the Yorkshire edition of the Daily Express added extra spice to the occasion with a banner back page headline which proclaimed: 'The Bull and the Matador.'

'The Bull' was Burscough's hard-as-nails half back and skipper Jimmy Lundon and the 'Matador' Sheffield United's £160,000 Argentinian international Alex Sabella who were due to come face-to-face in what was considered one of the key duels of the 90 minute battle.

But the newspaper hype meant little once the tie got underway and Rooney's worst pre-match fears turned into reality.

He had warned on the eve of the clash: 'The first 15 minutes are going to be sheer hell for our lads. Sheffield will throw everything at us and we'll feel as if our lungs are at bursting point. The pace will come as a shock to our players but if we can overcome the initial onslaught, then our confidence will grow and the longer we can keep the scoreline blank, the better our chances will be of causing an upset.'

The trouble was, Burscough were only able to keep the Third Division side at bay for a mere 60 seconds!

A free kick, awarded just outside the penalty area, was lofted into the goalmouth and as the Linnets defence stood motionless, John McPhail nipped in and glided the ball beyond the advancing Kevin O'Brien.

To their credit shell-shocked Burscough refused to bow to the inevitable and for an hour produced a gutsy, backs-to-the-wall fight, but two goals in quick succession from Mick Speight and former Arsenal man John Matthews ended any hopes of a giant-killing feat.

The teams that day were - Sheffield United: Conroy, Cutbush, Kenworthy, McPhail, Tibbott, Matthews, Speight, Sabella, Garner, Bourne, Butlin. Sub: Flood.

Burscough: O'Brien, Garland, Moran, Tickle, Blakeman, Reed, Nolan, Lundon, Jaycock, Taylor, Duffy. Sub: Bannister.

Consolation in defeat came with the club's £7,000 pay day, the money being pumped into improving ground facilities as Burscough began looking at the possibility of climbing higher in the non-league ladder.

HELLO.....GOODBYE !

Cliff Roberts will go down in club history with an unenviable record...the shortest serving manager in 50 years.

He took over the helm as the curtain came down on the 1979-80 campaign and lasted only 11 games the following season....nine of which Burscough lost....and was replaced by former Chorley, Morecambe and Leyland Motors player David May.

Fortunately, one of the Linnets' two victories during Roberts' brief stay came at the expense of Prestwich Heys in the F.A. Cup and it was the launching pad for May to rocket the club into the first round proper of the competition for the fourth time.

But, just like 1978, Burscough were left cursing their luck when they failed to land a money-spinning tie against a Football League club...being drawn at home to top non-league outfit Altrincham who, ironically, included in their line-up John Davison, the current boss at Victoria Park.

And it was Davison and his team-mates who emerged 2-1 victors of a dour tie watched by 1,207 fans, former Burscough favourite John Rogers and Jeff Johnson scoring the vital goals.

Dave Perry hit the Linnets' consolation goal in a tie left back Alex Blakeman will never forget. Alex was forced to don the goalkeeper's jersey early in the second half...just like fellow defender Arthur Green had to do 21 years earlier in the same competition at Ellesmere Port....and produced a string of stunning saves to keep the tie alive.

The teams that day were: Burscough: Hamilton, Waugh, Crisp, Blakeman, Stokes, Durnin, McFerran, Gray, Gamble, Jaycock, Perry. Sub: Griffiths.

Altrincham: Connaughton, Allen, Bailey, Owen, Davison, Barrow, Heathcote, King, Rogers, Howard. Sub: Whitbread.

But not for the first time Burscough failed to build on their cup run and a string of poor results led to May being replaced by Bryan Griffiths towards the end of the season....the club's third manager in seven months.

Griffiths, a former Formby and Southport boss, could do little to stem the tide during the final month of the season and Burscough finished 16th, their worst-ever position in the Cheshire League.

FIRST-EVER CHAMPIONS

Griffiths started his team building plans during the summer of 1981 and at the same time stamped his own brand of authorative organisation on the club.

The players quickly responded to his demands as he turned Burscough into a difficult side to beat.

This was illustrated by the fact that, in finishing third in what was the last Cheshire League season before the introduction of the North West Counties League set up, the Linnets' defence achieved 18 'shut outs' and in a further 25 games conceded just one goal per fixture.

The only blip was an astonishing 7-0 thrashing at Winsford United - the worst defeat in Griffiths' reign.

But by the start of the first North West Counties League season, Griffiths believed he had laid the foundations of a side capable of becoming the first winners of the new competition.

His defence boasted ball-winning central defenders 'Pop' Doyle and the vastly experienced Jimmy Horrocks; adventurous full back Mick Fagan, son of Liverpool legend, Joe Fagan; striker John Veacock; and the up and coming winger John Brady.

Ormskirk-born Brady, who was later to ply his skills at a higher level of non-league soccer, had the rare ability of being able to combine creative wing play with goalscoring prowess and his all-round contribution was an influential factor in Burscough lifting their first championship since 1970.

Brady finished top scorer with more than 25 goals to his credit, but the Linnets had players in most positions capable of finding the net.

In fact, in their final Championship-clinching fixture of the season at Prescot,

1982-83 Season. The Management team with the inaugural North West Counties League Championship Trophy, pictured at the Club's Presentation Evening in May 1983. Left to right: Mike McKenzie, Bryan Griffiths, 'Tosh' Malone, John Moran.

Burscough's goals in a 2-0 triumph came from headers by central defenders Doyle and Horrocks.

The title wining line-up was: O'Brien, Fagan, Mulhall, Doyle, Horrocks, Johnston, Redmond, Pennell, Donnelly, Nolan, Brady. Sub: Quinn.

But the celebrations were somewhat deflated when Griffiths announced he was leaving....due to what he described as the club's 'lack of ambition'.

Burscough had decided to snub the chance of automatic promotion to the Northern Premier League, insisting that they had insufficient finances to move into a higher grade of soccer because of the added expenditure involved, and that was the straw which broke the camel's back as far as Griffiths was concerned.

He said at the time: 'I am not leaving under a cloud, but I am very disappointed with the club's lack of ambition. They have spurned, on financial grounds, the chance of playing in a higher grade of football. I can understand the situation regarding finance but personally I would have liked the club to have thought a little more about it before reaching their decision. They could have talked to me or the players about it and I am sure everybody would have had a go for one season. If it didn't work out, we could have returned to the North West Counties League. I cannot deny this has helped me make my decision to leave, but there are other factors.'

Ironically, Burscough's consistency that season also shut the door on a talented 18-year-old defender they had signed from Southport. Shaun Teale only made fleeting appearances before moving on, but as most knowledgeable soccer folk will know he went on to carve out a successful career playing alongside Paul McGrath at the heart of the Aston Villa defence.

TEN BARREN YEARS

Whether Burscough were right or wrong in rejecting the chance of competing in a higher grade of football is a matter of conjecture, but the end of Griffiths' reign coincided with the beginning of the club's least successful spell in their history.

Not one piece of major silverware winged its way to Victoria Park in the next ten years until Russ Perkins' highly talented outfit lifted the North West Counties League Cup, defeating Nantwich Town 2-1 at Gigg Lane - the home of Bury F.C. - on Thursday, April 22, 1993.

But there was little to suggest that the 1980s would produce so little success when Mike McKenzie stepped into Griffiths'shoes and named former Burscough favourite, Billy Jaycock, as his second-in-command.

Both possessed a wide knowledge of the local non-league scene and quickly showed their talent-spotting ability by snapping up a young centre forward who, in true Burscough tradition, had an insatiable appetite for scoring goals.

John Coleman, signed from Kirkby Town, simply loved finding the net, and while at times he could be accused of being selfish in and around the penalty area, he invariably delivered the goods.

In his two explosive seasons at Burscough, Coleman hit more than 50 goals and was a major influence in steering the Linnets into fourth spot at the end of the 1983-84 season - eight points behind champions Stalybridge Celtic - and then played an equally important role as third place was achieved the following season when only six points separated champions Radcliffe Borough and five of their challengers.

Coleman is still scoring goals at the time of writing for Morecambe in the GM Vauxhall Conference and no doubt insisting, as he did during his time at Victoria Park, in taking the penalties. He used to grab the ball before anyone could claim it and quickly place it on the penalty spot!

But his move to Marine during the summer of 1985 and then McKenzie's decision to quit at the beginning of 1986 left Burscough in a spot of bother of their own, reflected in the fact that they parted company with a further six managers, Ray Coleman, Dennis Smith, Mike Ryman, Albie Donnerly, Mike Scott and ex-Ipswich full back Larry Carberry, in five traumatic years.

During this period they only managed to finish in the top half of the table once and then suffered the ultimate indignation...becoming the first-ever Burscough team to be relegated.

And just to add salt to their wounds they toppled into the North West Counties League Second Division after having points deducted for playing an ineligible player, Joey Hunt, from Marine.

Originally, Burscough finished third from bottom, ahead of both Salford and wooden spoonists Chadderton, but the loss of points plunged them into a relegation spot.

It caused the club a great deal of embarrassment and no-one had a redder face than Chairman Frank Parr, a long-serving member of the League management committee.

But he and his fellow committeemen were determined not to allow Burscough to slip into non-league oblivion and turned to Russ Perkins, a former Lancaster City boss, as their potential saviour.

It proved a masterstroke as Perkins, adopting the same philosophy as one of his predecessors, Bobby Langton, allowed his players to express themselves freely on the

Progress in the F.A. Vase was a feature of the 1990s under manager Russ Perkins, the club twice reaching the last 32, and once, the last 16. A large crowd was present at Victoria Park for this fourth round tie against Eastwood Hanley. Played on Saturday 18th January 1992, Burscough's Wembley dreams were shattered as Eastwood won by the only goal of the game. In the thick of the action is Tony Rigby (No. 11), who later joined Bury, with Kevin Still and Jimmy Clark in attendance.

park and during his four-year stay provided some of the most entertaining and attractive football seen at Victoria Park for more than a decade.

In his first season at the helm, Perkins steered the Linnets to fourth spot but due to a complex chain of events involving other leagues and ground facilities it was good enough to earn a promotion spot behind Blackpool Mechanics, Newcastle Town and champions Bamber Bridge.

While promotion had been gained through the back door, Burscough were now re-emerging as a force in the semi-professional game and they emphasised this point by reaching the final of the League Cup where they were unlucky to lose 1-0 to Northern Premier League-bound Ashton United at mud-splattered Gigg Lane....Chris Shaw scoring the match-winner in the opening stages.

'The Heavens Weep for Burscough' screamed the headline in the following week's Ormskirk Advertiser - and it hit the nail on the head.

Torrential rain leading up to the kick off turned the pitch into little more than a quagmire but despite falling behind, Burscough adapted far better to almost unplayable conditions and Ashton, who had already clinched the North West Counties first division title, were extremely fortunate to emerge victors.

Perkins was justifiably proud of his players and their performance. 'We were great but on the night the ball simply would not go into the net,' the manager reflected at the post-match press conference. Perkins and his players, quite clearly, found it difficult to hide their bitter disappointment but 12 months later the heartbreak was all forgotten....Burscough returning to Gigg Lane and earning a 2-1 victory over Nantwich Town in front of a crowd of 500.

Full back Brendan Doyle gave the Linnets an early lead when he collected a short pass from midfield general Tony Quinn and lashed home an unstoppable 18 yard piledriver.

Striker Sean Togher added a second before half time following slick approach play from Martin Lowe and Kevin Still, but Burscough were unable to build on their 2-0 lead and had to endure some anxious moments after Nantwich cut the deficit through Adrian Dunn 15 minutes from time.

Teams - Burscough: Robinson, Doyle (B), Owen, Howard, Doyle (A), Knox, Quinn, Lowe, Togher, Martindale, Still. Substitutes: Trewhitt, Stafford.

Nantwich Town: White, Royall, Wright, Boon, Woodhouse, Diskin, Dunn, Notice, Dawson, Giblin, Scarlett. Substitutes: Jones, Aguis.

But the season was still far from over for a side who, while a little inconsistent in the league, found cup football stimulating and on the eve of their triumph over Nantwich had sensationally KO'd a strong Everton side 2-0 in the semi-final of the Liverpool Senior Cup at Goodison Park.

Not even the inclusion of multi-million pound Scottish international Mo Johnson could put the frighteners on Perkins' outfit and thanks to goals from the Doyle boys, Brendan and Andy, Burscough booked a place in the final against GM Vauxhall Conference neighbours Southport.

The final was also played at Goodison Park and Burscough were hoping that lightning would strike twice.

But despite outplaying the Sandgrounders for long spells at a time, they toppled to a 2-1 defeat.

Steve Haw's 11th minute goal gave Port an early boost but sustained pressure led to

Action from the Liverpool Senior Cup Final against Southport, played at Goodison Park on Tuesday 11th May 1993. Gary Martindale goes up for the ball with Southport 'keeper Paul Moore, Martin Lowe waits to pick up any pieces. Southport won 2-1, with Kevin Still scoring for the Linnets.

Kevin Still equalising, only for the Seasiders to clinch the trophy 11 minutes from time.

The final attracted a crowd of 1,813 and while disappointed at the outcome, Perkins said later that his side's performance 'reflects well on football in the North West Counties League.'

'We got back in the game with a fabulous goal but then gave away a soft one,' declared Perkins.

The Burscough team was: Robinson, Doyle (B), Doyle (A), Owen, Howard, Quinn, Lowe, Knox, Still, Togher, Martindale.

POT OF GOLD

When Russ Perkins was first appointed manager before the start of the 1991-92 season, Burscough were going nowhere, having just been relegated to the second division of the North West Counties League.

But Perkins picked up the club by its bootlaces, assembling a side which played fluent, adventurous and attractive soccer and this was reflected in his achievements....promotion in his first season; two appearances in the final of the League Cup; one appearance in the final of the Liverpool Senior Cup; and a highly respectable third position in the NWCFL first division at the end of 1993-94 season.

He didn't, however, lift the prize Burscough sought more than anything else, the league title, and paid the ultimate penalty when the powers-that-be at Victoria Park decided not to retain his services at the end of the 1994-95 after finishing eighth in the championship race...

It wasn't a decision that had the full backing of the fans, but the club committee felt that Perkins had taken the club as far as he could and a change was needed at the top if they were eventually to gain Unibond League status.

And they turned to former Altrincham defensive king-pin John Davison - one of the most experienced non-league players in the country - to shape their future as the countdown to the 1995-96 campaign got under way.

Davison, who had represented his country at non-league level, knew from day one that he faced a difficult job in shaping a title-winning side and, while Burscough led the championship race at one stage, they could not maintain the momentum and finally finished in fifth position with 77 points from 42 games, 15 adrift of title winners Flixton.

But there was a pot of gold at the end of the rainbow for Davison in his first season of management at Victoria Park...Burscough's second League Cup Final triumph at Gigg Lane, Bury, in the space of four seasons.

And they achieved victory against all the odds, beating red-hot favourites Flixton 1-0 with what can best be described as a patched-up attack.

Top marksman Terry McPhillips had left a bitter taste in the mouths of club officials when he opted to join Ashton United only weeks before the end of the season and with hot-shot Mick McDonough failing a fitness test on the eve of the final, Burscough were almost bereft of attacking options.

The only recognised goalscorer to step out of the Gigg Lane tunnel was little Andy

The winning goal in the North West Counties League Challenge Cup Final at Gigg Lane, Bury, on Thursday 25th April 1996. Andy Howard cuts in from the left and lets fly in the 73rd minute, substitute Phil Farrelly (No.15) got a touch and the ball flew high into the net for the only goal of the game. Photographs courtesy of the Ormskirk Advertiser.

Howard and he was joined up front by full-back-turned-temporary-striker Neil 'Jocky' Hanson.

It seemed to be mission impossible....but Davison had not read the script.

He packed his defence and midfield with ball-winners, taking nothing for granted, and for almost an hour he played a game of containment.

But with Flixton unable to demolish a green wall of defiance, and running out of attacking ideas, Burscough gradually gained the ascendancy before Davison produced his masterstroke of a tactical battle he was now winning hands down.

Phil Farrelly, who had been playing most of the season at Winsford United, emerged from the bench and was credited with the match-winning second-half goal.

Mind you, he knew little about it....Howard's centre-cum-shot hitting him on the shoulder and ricochetting into the back of the net.

But you make your own luck in football and Davison will be hoping it will be a stepping stone to greater things as Burscough celebrates 50 years of village football.

It's ours! Tommy Knox and skipper Ged Nolan celebrate League Challenge Cup Victory at Gigg Lane. Looking no less pleased is Kevin Still. It was the third Challenge Cup medal for both Still and Knox..

PROUDEST MOMENT

There have been many magical moments to savour in the 50 years since Burscough cast aside the storm clouds of war and brought peace-time soccer back to Victoria Park.

Many older fans look no further than the post-war years to recall their fondest memories and, in particular, that never-to-be-forgotten 1947-48 season when the Linnets captured three pieces of silverware...the Lancashire Junior Cup, the George Mahon Cup and the Liverpool Challenge Cup.

It was a momentous achievement for a small village club to complete such a prestigious treble and just how great can be gauged from the fact that Burscough have never won three major trophies in a season since.

Other supporters may feel that lifting the Lancashire Combination premier division title in the 1955-56 season during an era when the standard of non-league football was possibly higher than any other time was the crowning glory, while a good case could be put forward for the club's first excursion into the opening round of the F.A. Cup in 1959.

On that occasion they were drawn at home to Crewe Alexandra who became the first Football League club to visit Victoria Park in one of the world's greatest knockout competitions.

But one man who has experienced all the highs, and quite a few lows, during an unbroken half century of dedicated service to the club is in no doubt about his most treasured memory...and it's nothing remotely concerned with winning trophies.

Chairman Frank Parr declared: 'My proudest moment was the events which unfolded on Thursday, March 24, 1994, when we transferred two of our players to Football League clubs.'

Striker Gary Martindale signed for Bolton Wanderers and midfielder Kevin Formby joined Rochdale, soon to be followed to Spotland by another of the club's talented midfielders, Alex Russell.

Added Frank: 'Clubs like ours are a breeding ground for up and coming talent and it gives you a buzz when they make progress in the game, knowing you have played a part, however large or small, in it.'

'But to have three players moving into the Football League in such a short space of time reflected great credit on our club and our manager at the time, Russ Perkins.'

Since then Martindale has fulfilled every footballer's dream by playing in a Wembley final, leading the Notts County attack against Bradford City in the Second Division play offs.

And Liverpudlian Martindale, who joined the Midland club for £170,000 from Peterborough after being given a free by Bolton Wanderers, is the first to admit that without his 'schooling' at Victoria Park this would never have been possible.

'I owe the club a great deal.'

PART 2

A VILLAGE FOOTBALL CLUB

by

Stan Strickland

INTRODUCTION

There are undoubtedly many people better qualified than myself to write about the fifty year history of Burscough Football Club, people who have been witness to the events of that period. However, in researching local newspaper archives to document the club's playing record over that period, I have encountered so much fascinating detail and gained such an interest in the history and the origins of the club, that I felt there would never be a better opportunity to publish that research in a way that best illustrates this great club of ours and its achievements.

As a comparative newcomer, my contribution is largely about the club and how it has developed, hence, I make no serious attempt to pass opinions on people, players, or games, I didn't know or see.

Since 1946 the Ormskirk Advertiser, or to give it its original grand title, 'The Ormskirk Advertiser, Southport Advertiser, and Agricultural and Mining Intelligencer for West Lancashire,' has consistently covered club affairs and even to this day it is one of the few local newspapers to regularly report in person on the home and away fixtures of a club at regional level. The Advertiser records are the major source of information regarding the development of football in this area, they are an absolute goldmine for any researcher, and I acknowledge their considerable contribution to the documentation of the club's history and offer my thanks for their permission to reproduce the many extracts used.

This story is to celebrate Burscough Football Club reaching its fiftieth year. The fact that a village team, albeit a large village, has managed to not only retain senior status over such a period, but also to win major trophies and gain a position of enormous respect in the football world, is something of which Burscough should be extremely proud.

It also tells the story of the teams that went before, the teams who, like ourselves, have fought so passionately to ensure that the village of Burscough should be represented at the highest possible level in the game of Association Football. So much of our history stems from those days - our ground, our colours, our nickname, and more - that I believe it would be foolish not to recognise their part in the development of this club. After all, if we don't put on record their achievements, who else will? I found that as I researched the past so much of what I discovered was relevant to where Burscough Football Club stands today.

In Ernest Rosbottom's fine book, 'Burscough - The Story of an Agricultural Village,' Burscough is described as 'an ordinary place, a village scarcely known outside the immediate district.' The successful exploits of Burscough Football Club have, on occasion, threatened that anonymity.

This is also a story about one man's incredible dedication to that club.

Stan Strickland
Secretary
Burscough Football Club
April 1996

THE 'FIRST' BURSCOUGH
1880 - 1900

Football came comparatively late to Lancashire. In 1878 it was still considered a game dominated by the gentlemen amateurs from the south of England. Significantly, the 1878-79 F.A. Cup saw the amateur's domination threatened for the first time, when Lancashire side Darwen reached the fourth round and only lost to the eventual winners, Old Etonians, after two replays. It proved a milestone, and the days of those gentleman amateurs were now numbered, as teams from central Lancashire went on to dominate English football in the 1880s. Burscough's position on the main canal and railway network would have ensured regular contact with this football revolution now sweeping the county.

The first Burscough Association Football Club was formed in 1880 and played their opening match against Croston on December 9th of that year. The match was played at Burscough, with Burscough winning 3-0. It was reported:
The game was very fast and the backs and forwards had plenty to do and the Burscough forwards showed some very fair passing, especially during the latter part of the game.
During the 1881-82 season the Liverpool newspapers carried news of 'a big win' by Everton Football Club, which had been formed three years earlier. It was reported they had 'beaten Burscough by eight goals to nil'. Where the game was played was not documented, at that time Everton were playing on the south west corner of Stanley Park, it would be another ten years before they moved to Mere Green Field and renamed it Goodison Park. The future of the two clubs would go on to develop in widely different directions.

Southport Football Club played their first Association Football match on the 12th November 1881 against Bootle Second, after converting from the Rugby Football code. The following week, in Southport's second fixture, they lost by 'one goal and one disputed goal to nil' at Burscough.

The following season Southport were again the visitors to Burscough on the 16th December, the Southport Visiter commented:
The ground was better than expected but still very heavy to play on. The reds kicked off against a strong wind and took the lead after ten minutes when Melross made a brilliant run along the right wing and centred for Briggs to score. Just before half-time Burscough equalised through Thorougood. In the second half Southport had the better of the play when the greasy ball caused the final shots to be very erratic, but Briggs scored a second goal to leave Southport the winners by two goals to one.
The report went on to say that 'Thorougood, Baldwin, Stephens and Peet were the most conspicious for the losers.'

The same day Burscough second eleven lost to their Southport counterparts by three goals to one. The Burscough team lined up: Tyrer; Smith, Peet; Page, Glover;

Marsden, Whalley, Daly, Glover, Holding, Wainwright.

In those early days, Burscough played on the recreation field belonging to Mr. James Walker, in the area that is now known as Fletchers Drive. The field was also used for the annual Lathom & Burscough Show and Sports and was described at the time as being situated 'midway between Burscough Junction and Burscough Bridge Railway Stations.'

Stanley Rovers were the visitors on Saturday 13th October 1883, Burscough winning 2-1 with this line up: D.Postlethwaite, goal; R.W.Bridge and H.Darby (captain), backs; J.Hunter, H.Harrison and J.Bentham, half-backs; W.Stretch and E.Bridge, left wing; J.Peet and R.Hunter, right wing; C.Thorougood, centre. The following Thursday, the Ormskirk Advertiser reported:

For Burscough R.W.Bridge made some grand kicks and Bentham pleased the spectators by his heading and his tackling.

A week later the reserve side lost 2-1 to a Skelmersdale United reserve side in what appears to have been a football match of some significance for the Skelmersdale club. The Advertiser of Thursday 25th October 1883 informed their readers:

This is the opening game of the Skelmersdale club, they entertained the visitors to a substantial tea at the Wesleyan School where a pleasant evening was passed.

Burscough's first reported competitive game was on Saturday 8th November 1884 when they travelled to play 'Tranmere' in a Liverpool and District Amateur Cup tie. This was quite probably the present Tranmere Rovers club, which had been formed in 1883. Burscough won the match, and went on to beat Earlestown by four goals to one in the next round. News of further progress went unreported.

Reports of Burscough fixtures were somewhat infrequent during this period, with the Ormskirk Advertiser understandably featuring the local Ormskirk sides, of which there were many, more prominently. They appeared to rely almost totally on the club secretary, or occasionally a supporter, sending in reports, hence, when they did appear, many of the opposition goals were considered to be of a questionable nature, and the description of play could be extremely biased, as will become apparent later.

In the Ormskirk Advertiser of October 28th 1886 the following report appeared:
SKELMERSDALE UNITED v BURSCOUGH (1st teams)
This match was played at Skelmersdale on Saturday last in very favourable weather. Burscough won the toss and elected to play downhill.
The United had much the best of the game, but only scored three times during the first half.
However, on turning round, the home team began to press their opponents more severely, and were able to add five more goals to their number, thus winning an easy game by eight goals to one.
The home forwards deserve special praise for the grand passing game they played on Saturday.

It was the first reported 'local derby' between the first teams of the two village clubs, beginning an intense rivalry which has continued for the past 110 years. Skelmersdale United Football Club had been founded in 1882 by a group of local miners and by 1891 they had become founder members of the Lancashire Combination. Burscough's progress was to be a little more leisurely.

On Saturday 11th February 1888, Burscough travelled to play Churchtown in a Southport Senior Cup Tie:

The home team won the toss and took choice of ends, the visitors kicking off with a blazing sun in their face. They scored after five minutes play, and after this gave the home backs a lot of trouble, causing them to kick out to save their charge. After some smart passing the visitors got a second point. Then a miss-kick let in the home team, just before half-time, and lying offside, got the ball through, the referee allowing the point. In the second half the play was of a fast character, and the home team soon got the lead, scoring again afterwards, but the referee disallowed on an offside appeal. After some grand rushes by both sides the home team scored a fourth which was followed by another on the part of the visitors, which the referee, to their disappointment, gave offside, and time was called with the score - Churchtown, four; Burscough, two.

Burscough's team that day was: Goal, R.Reynolds; backs, R.Varley and R.Culshaw; half-backs, R.W.Bridge, T.Bickerstaffe, R.Hunter; forwards, J.Pilkington, J.Stringfellow, W.Leaver, J.Spencer and A.Fenny.

The following season the Advertiser of Thursday 6th December 1888 reported on a game at home to Birkdale South End which came to a rather sudden end:

Played at Burscough on Saturday last, this being the return fixture. The home team kicked off shortly after 3 o'clock, and rushed up the field only to be repulsed by the visiting backs, who soon showed they were not to be trifled with. Burscough strove hard to gain a footing, and were soon rewarded with a

Burscough AFC 1880s - This picture has no names and cannot be precisely dated, however, close scrutiny suggests some of the players and officials are also pictured on the 1895-96 team photograph on page 59. Here they look several years younger so it would be reasonable to believe that this was taken in the late 1880s. The trees in the background indicate that they were by now playing on the Vicarage Field.

goal, Meadows completely beating the visitor's goalkeeper. Birkdale fought hard to equalize, but the home backs were playing a very safe game, and repeatedly checked the visitors forwards. Just before the interval, Livesey put the ball through for the visitors, but as he was standing offside the point was disallowed, and the teams crossed over with the score:- Burscough, one goal; South End, none.

The home team did a lot of pressing in the second half, and one of the forwards gave the visitor's custodian a long shot when he picked up the ball and ran with it beyond the limited distance. The referee at once awarded the home team a free kick, but the visitors would not hear of it, and left the field five minutes before time, Burscough claiming the match by one goal to nil. Burscough team: W.Culshaw, goal; Birch and Varley, backs; J.Bentham, Peet and Stringfellow, half-backs; E.Mayson, W.Leaver, Southworth, J.Spencer and R.Meadows, forwards.

A week later Burscough entertained near neighbours Ormskirk Wanderers, it was described as 'a fast and exciting game terminating in a draw - two goals each.'

In 1888, the Football League was formed, and in the succeeding years county and district leagues quickly followed. By 1895-96 season Burscough were to be found playing in the Liverpool and District Amateur Combination, with a reserve side in the Southport and District League. An early league fixture was against Skelmersdale Albion on Saturday 28th September 1895:

This match was played at Burscough last Saturday in exceedingly hot weather. The homesters were short of J.Stringfellow, W.Harrison and W.Jones, three valuable players, their places being filled from the reserves. Burscough kicked off, and some capital passing between H.Stringfellow and David Iddon resulted in a goal, another coming shortly after from the foot of Forrest. Half-time found the home team leading by two goals to none. In the second half the Albion played a more spirited game but the excessive heat began to tell on the players. From a scrimmage in the goal mouth the visitors registered their only point, and Burscough putting on three more goals won a pleasantly contested game, making their goal average 19 goals against 1 in two Combination matches. Result:- Burscough 5 goals, Albion 1 goal. Burscough team:- Mayson, goal; Nelson and T.Iddon, backs; R.Iddon, Thorougood and J.Iddon, half-backs; D.Iddon, H.Stringfellow, Forrest, Meadows and Smith, forwards.

By the time they travelled to Liverpool to play Crosse at Boaler Street in November, 'before a large attendance', their league record was an impressive: Played 7; Won 6; Drew 0; Lost 1; Goals for 48; Goals against 7.

A complaint that the name of the League infringed on the Liverpool and District *Football* Combination led to a meeting at the Mitre Hotel in Liverpool's Dale Street on the 11th of December 1895. At that meeting a decision was taken to rename the League the 'West Lancashire Amateur Football Combination.'

Later in December, Burscough players Nelson, H.Stringfellow and centre forward Arthur Forrest were selected for the Combination representative side on a tour to Scotland, playing Glasgow Perthshire on New Year's Day and Greenock Overton on January 2nd.

Burscough, by now, were playing on the Vicarage Field in Liverpool Road, and the

Burscough AFC 1895-96 season - A fine photograph of the first Burscough Football Club.

Back (left to right): J.Harrison (Sec.), R.Marsden (Linesman), G.Nelson (Captain), J.Mayson, T.Iddon, George Merritt (Treas.).

Middle Row (left to right): Robert Iddon, W.Jones, J.Iddon, Jimmy Pilkington, (half-backs).

Front Row (left to right): Billy Harrison, Harry Stringfellow, Arthur Forrest, J.Garner, J.Smith, (forwards).

Robert Iddon was a basketmaker; he also played cricket for Mawdesley. He died in 1945, aged 74.

At this time Burscough were playing at the Vicarage Field, but the background appears to be a pavilion or verandah with a high brick wall behind, hardly the Vicarage Field. Pete Whittle of Ormskirk recalls a Mr. Iddon showing him a similar photograph many years ago, and it was his belief that it had been photographed at the rear of the Royal Hotel, which was the team's headquarters at that time.

That this picture has survived is a miracle. It was found in the 1970s lying amongst rubble at Preston Station during the dismantling of left luggage lockers. One of the contractors passed the picture on to a friend in Liverpool who in turn passed it on to the offices of the Ormskirk Advertiser. The photographer was Wragg of Ormskirk

return fixture there with Crosse on Saturday 7th March 1896 attracted an estimated 700 spectators, this, at a time when the population of the village only numbered slightly over 2,000. It was reported:

> The start was delayed on account of the players being photographed for Mr. A.Saunders' magic lantern.

They lost the game and, legend has it, thus began a reluctance to be photographed prior to a game which appears to have survived to this day in Burscough football!

Burscough joined the Liverpool and District Amateur League for 1896-97 season. On Saturday 10th October 1896 they entertained Campbell Collin Athletic in a friendly fixture. The Advertiser described the congenial after-match ambience:

> An adjournment was then made to the Royal Hotel, where a smoking concert was held, the members and friends of both teams spending a pleasant evening.

The following season Burscough moved to the Liverpool and District Amateur Football Alliance. With matches now scattered over a larger area, on both sides of the River Mersey, it was hardly surprising that teams or players occasionally failed to arrive. Communications were still primitive, telephones had not yet been introduced, postal services were still in their infancy, and electricity and bus services were still many years away. Teams travelling in and out of Burscough would have used the through steam trains that operated between Liverpool and Preston and relied on making connections in Liverpool. In those early days of organised football Burscough must have appeared a fairly remote location. On Saturday 1st January 1898 Burscough were due to entertain St. Polycarps in a league fixture. Thursday's Advertiser lamented:

> This Liverpool and District Alliance match was down for decision at Burscough on Saturday last, but for some reason or other the visitors failed to turn up or send an explanation.

However, the Reserves' game at New Lane on the same day went ahead and was reported on the same page. It would be reasonable to assume that the report was written by the New Lane club secretary:

> The first match in connection with the Southport and District League between these two rival teams took place on New Year's morning on the ground of the former club. The weather was splendid and there would be from 300 to 400 spectators present. As the official referee failed to turn up, the two captains tossed up as to who should officiate, with the result that Mr. T.Georgeson took charge of the whistle.
>
> Burscough won the toss, and Forrest kicked off for the home team. After a spell of midfield play the home left got away, and the extreme man centred. Bromley secured possession, and passed back again to Ashcroft, that player had no difficulty in beating Mayson, amidst great cheers.
>
> New Lane got away nicely but found Ogilvie a hard nut to crack, as he was playing in good form. However, Forrest and Sephton got through, and the latter gave Mayson a very warm daisycutter to negotiate. The goalkeeper fumbled the ball, so that it went over the line, and the home players appealing for a goal, the referee rightfully decided in their favour, so that New Lane were now two goals ahead of their boastful rivals.
>
> There was now only one team in it, and that team was not Burscough. The home halves were playing a clinking game, Pilkington's tackling and placing being very conspicious. Time was soon afterwards called, and New Lane won a

great game by two goals to nil.

It is only fair to state that throughout the second half Burscough only had ten men, as at the conclusion of the first moiety Rowley accidentally fell on a piece of glass and was incapacitated for the remainder of the game.

The following were the teams: New Lane: Smith, goal: Whalley and Lea, backs; Pilkington, Hope and Peet, half-backs; Sturgess, Bromley, Forrest, Sephton and Ashcroft, forwards.

Burscough Reserve: Mayson, goal; Ogilvie and Disley, backs; Seddon, Iddon and Winrow, half-backs; Harding, Harrison, Rowley, Baybutt and Lewis, forwards.

New Lane played on a field adjacent to the canal bridge. Their outside right that day was Jack Sturgess, who will continue to feature prominently for many years to come, as the Burscough football teams progressed from displaying their skills on that farm field down New Lane to winning trophies in some of the grandest soccer stadiums in the county.

A week later, the Advertiser briefly reported on a league match between Burscough and Tranmere Rovers Reserves:

LIVERPOOL & DISTRICT AMATEUR FOOTBALL ALLIANCE
1897-98 SEASON
(up to & including 19th March 1898)

	P	W	D	L	F	A	Pts
Aintree	15	13	1	1	71	16	27
Linacre Bible Class	18	11	3	4	55	30	25
Bramall's Tuts	15	10	2	3	39	13	22
Rainhill	14	9	2	3	41	20	20
Burscough	**17**	**7**	**6**	**4**	**38**	**23**	**20**
Tranmere Rovers Reserve	14	8	1	5	48	24	17
Kirkdale Reserve	13	3	3	7	15	26	9
St. Polycarps	15	3	3	9	8	42	9
Egremont Recreation	14	3	0	11	15	40	6
Stanley Vics. R.	17	1	4	12	11	72	6
Liverpool Butchers*	12	1	1	10	7	41	3

* Liverpool Butchers have taken up Walton Breck's fixtures

Played at Burscough on Saturday last, the home team winning easily by five goals to nil. Burscough team:- Lewis, goal; T.Iddon and R.Iddon, backs; T.Hargreaves, Winrow and H.Craft, half-backs; Gouge, Eastham, R.Finch, J.Hardman and A.Smith, forwards.

Bad behaviour at football matches, normally considered a modern disease, was already prevalent and many local match reports contained graphic detail of this. There were incidences of teams walking off if a decision was not to their liking, match officials were threatened, and criticism of opponents and officials printed in the correspondence columns of the local newspaper could be quite vitriolic at times. The game was highly physical, with the charging of the goalkeeper fairly relished. Inter-village rivalry was intense and it required very little provocation by players or supporters to ignite already inflamed passions. The Ormskirk Advertiser dated 22nd September 1898 campaigned for improvement and shared this homespun wisdom with local supporters:

Complaints are already being made as to the conduct of certain sections of spectators at some of the football matches. It is stated that the old trick of shouting to the players to 'take' certain men was resorted to, and in one quarter an appeal is made to club executives to sternly discountenance this sort of thing.

A contemporary publishes the following rules as being suitable for posting up on the various grounds so as to assist in maintaining law and order:-

1.- Read well your rules before offering criticism. Having learned them, applaud good play without favour.
2.- Always respect the referee's ruling, and don't make idiots of yourselves by shouting yourself hoarse after his whistle has sounded.
3.- If your team gets beaten don't use swear words to them because it's rude, but help them on to victory another day by encouragement.
4.- Do not yell unkind things at a player because he makes a mistake, or you will only make a bigger one yourself, and possibly upset him.
5.- If it rains, and you have an umbrella, don't let it drip down the man's kneck in front of you, but rather get wet yourself. It saves unpleasantness - to him.
6.- Support your club both away and at home, and let your rivals see your loyalty; and above all pass through the turnstile, and don't jump the fence.

After one season in the Alliance, Burscough rejoined the Liverpool and District Amateur League. On Saturday 12th November 1898 they travelled to Huyton to play a league fixture with Huyton Recreation. Not for the last time they were to field a somewhat depleted team:

Played at Huyton in dull weather and before a fair attendance. Burscough only played eight men but they held their own up to half-time. Ridpath scoring for them. Half-time; Huyton Rec, one goal, Burscough, one goal.
Early on in the second portion the visitors goalkeeper strained his leg and was not so active as in the first half. Nevertheless, the visitors, although three short, played their opponents a rattling good game, but in the end had to acknowledge defeat by four goals to one.

At that time, games between New Lane and Burscough were a major feature of the Christmas holiday period in the area. The matches attracted large crowds, were fiercely contested, and carried the 'local derby' status that would later be accorded fixtures against Ormskirk and Skelmersdale teams. New Lane was one of several communities around Burscough built in the nineteenth century to house boatmen and their families. The Leeds-Liverpool canal was then in its hey-day and Burscough was a thriving centre for the industries that had grown up on and around the canal. No doubt there would be much boasting and betting among the boatmen as to the outcome of these games and many of the most fiercely contested matches over the years to come were between teams representing the communities along the canal. The Advertiser of 29th December 1898 reported:

These local rivals met at Burscough on Monday last, before a very good attendance. G.Ogilve turned out for the first time this season with the homesters. Burscough had the upper hand all through, their combination being superior to their opponents, backed up by a strong defence, Whalley being seldom troubled owing to the fine back play of Ogilve and Disley (1). The result of an exciting game was:- Burscough 6 goals, New Lane none.
Burscough team:- Whalley, goal; J.Disley (1) and G.Ogilve, backs; J.Disley (2), A.Merritt and H.Pilkington, half-backs; Mullen, Turner, Forrest, Baybutt and W.Lewis, forwards.
Referee, Mr. John Spencer.

The same edition also reported a league fixture away to Liscard Y.M.F.S. which resulted in a 5-0 defeat:

When the visitors arrived it was found that six players were missing, owing to the festive season, consequently six substitutes had to be chosen to make up the eleven.

On Saturday 4th March 1899 Burscough played a friendly fixture against another local side, Burscough Town. A match report was submitted for publication in the following Thursday's Advertiser:

This match was played on the ground of the former on Saturday last in a heavy snowstorm. Neither teams were at their full strength. The Town kicked off against the falling snow, but despite this fact they fairly held their own, Baybutt scoring for the homesters. On restarting, the Town pressed, Mayson saving several shots in succession. The homesters then broke away and scored a soft goal, and this was the state of affairs at the interval. In the second half the homesters obtained three goals in the luckiest possible fashion, the Town goalkeeper making no effort to save, and the final whistle blew with the score as above. It was hard lines on the visitors to be beaten by such a large margin as at no time of the game were they overplayed, in fact, if anything, they had three parts of the game. Had the goalkeeper been changed the score would have been vastly different.

The report had obviously been written by a Burscough Town official or supporter who believed his team had suffered a most dreadful injustice. Two weeks later the same correspondent had ingeniously found an even more effective way of improving his team's performance, when he reported on a '3-3 draw' against Burscough Bible Class, however, all was not quite as it appeared:

LIVERPOOL & DISTRICT AMATEUR LEAGUE
1899-1900 SEASON (up to & inc. Sat. 10th Feb. 1900)

	P	W	D	L	F	A	Pts
Formby & Rangers	11	8	2	1	26	10	18
Ormskirk Park Recs	12	7	2	3	26	14	16
Prescot Rovers	8	7	0	1	26	8	14
Huyton Quarry	11	5	2	4	33	17	12
Prescot Juniors	9	5	2	2	19	11	12
Huyton Recreation	9	4	1	4	12	9	9
Skelmersdale Swifts	10	1	4	5	12	22	6
Burscough	9	2	1	6	8	29	5
Whiston Ramblers	7	0	2	5	3	13	2
Ogdens	8	0	0	8	5	36	0

To the Editor of the Ormskirk Advertiser

Sir. In writing the following letter I would like to call your attention to the unsportsmanlike action of some individual or individuals connected with the Burscough Town F.C. in handing in to your office a report of the above match which was entirely void of foundation, portraying the match as a draw of three goals each, this being their only recourse to prevent the insertion of the correct report. The report as rendered by me was perfectly correct, and gave a true account of the game, ending in a win to our team by six goals to one, and was also approved of by Mr A.E.Bridge the referee, against whom the Town team had no objections to make.

Albert E.Ashcroft
Hon. Secretary
Burscough Bible Class F.C.

Burscough continued into 1899-1900 season playing in the Liverpool League, but by now results had deteriorated and there was frequently difficulty in fielding a full eleven. A report of a six goal defeat by Prescot Rovers in the Advertiser of 22nd February 1900 did not paint a very promising picture of the club's future:

These teams met at Burscough on Saturday last before a poor gate.

The home side lacked the services of several of their best players, including the two Vaughans, Cassidy and Ridpath. Reserve players were obtained with difficulty and these were handicapped in having to play in ordinary boots and garb.

The following season they failed to re-appear and it was left to minor league clubs, such as Burscough Swifts, to represent the football interests of the village until someone bigger came along. There would be a five year wait.

BURSCOUGH RANGERS
1905 - 1935

'Born Autumn 1905 following the decease after an inglorious career of the much vaunted Burscough Central AFC whose colours were black and white halves, and who lost every match they played and who died young.'

So wrote Mr. J.W.Berry to describe the formation of the Burscough Rangers Football Club over ninety years ago. John Berry later became Rangers' secretary and over the years he kept a small leather pocket book with precise and meticulous details of the club's results and achievements, which his family have mercifully preserved until the present day.

During their first season Rangers played friendly games only, using the Vicarage Field as their home ground. A Rangers match that season away to Hawkshead Congregational was reported in the Ormskirk Advertiser dated 11th January 1906:

This match was played at Southport on Saturday last on a heavy ground. The visitors won the toss and had the advantage of a strong wind, and led at the interval by two goals to nil. On resuming the visitors kept up the pressure and added another goal. Southport retaliated and scored two questionable goals, but despite their utmost endeavours to score, the Rangers were finally left winners of a pleasant game by three goals to two.

A few weeks later, in March, they beat Ormskirk Y.M.C.A. by three goals to one, with the Rangers lining up: R.Parr; Jim Gore, J.Edwardson; Walter Smith, W.Bentham, J.Baldwin; Jimmy Pye, Jack Radcliffe, R.Stringfellow, T.Lowe and James Ashton.

Rangers' original colours were blue and chocolate squares or halves, however a meeting was called to discuss changing colours. It was suggested by Mr. Berry that a 'Ranger' was a person whose job was among the fields and forests, so the colour should be green, and the colour green was to become synonymous with Burscough teams until the present day. Early team photographs suggest that this happened within a year of their formation, although the change to an 'all green' jersey was recorded in 1909. Burscough Rangers' nickname was 'The Linnets.'

[Ornithology note: Many people have been mystified as to why Burscough teams are called 'the Linnets' when the team play in green, while a linnet is predominantly brown. The nickname undoubtedly derives from the greenfinch which 'Collins Pocket Guide to British Birds' also refers to as a green linnet. It was normal, particularly in this area, to call the bird a green linnet, rather than a greenfinch.]

In 1906, Rangers became members of the Southport and District Amateur League, starting off with a 6-0 win against Birkdale Working Lads. After finishing in third position, they gained a place in the Senior Section the following season, when a reserve side was also entered in the Ormskirk and District Amateur League.

On Wednesday 29th April 1908 Rangers secured their first trophy, when they won

Burscough Rangers 1905-06 Season - Photographed shortly after formation in front of the Stanley Institute, which had been completed in 1902. Back left to right: W.Lewis, Unknown, J.Edmondson, Unknown, John Aspinwall (father of Jimmy Aspinall), Unknown, E.Lamb?. Middle left to right: Unknown, R.Stringfellow, W.Bentham, Walter Smith, Unknown. Front left to right: James Ashton, J.Baldwin, Sam Jowett, Jack Radcliffe, Jimmy Pye. The Rangers had not yet changed to the traditional all green shirts.
Photograph kindly loaned by Mrs. Rose Smith, daughter-in-law of Rangers' player Walter Smith.

the Southport 2nd Senior Charity Cup, beating Churchtown Congregationals 2-1 in the final, at the Central Ground, Southport. The Advertiser described their glorious homecoming:

> On their return home later in the evening, the victorious team, with the Cup in their possession were accorded a healthy reception. They were met at the station by a bugle band of the Boy's Brigade, a procession was formed, and a march made through the village, the utmost enthusiasm prevailing. An adjournment was afterwards made at the Royal Hotel, where complimentary speeches were made and the toasts of the players and officials enthusiastically honoured.

SOUTHPORT & DISTRICT AMATEUR LEAGUE [SENIOR DIVISION] 1908-09 SEASON

	P	W	D	L	F	A	Pts
Southport Emmanuel	16	11	5	0	47	14	27
Blowick	16	11	1	4	43	21	23
Banks St. Stephens	16	9	2	5	45	24	20
Burscough Rangers	16	8	3	5	39	37	19
Birkdale	16	8	2	6	35	30	18
Southport Working Lads	16	6	4	6	34	37	16
Park Villa Reserves	16	4	2	10	36	42	10
Birkdale Working Lads	16	3	1	12	16	54	7
Crossens Institute	16	1	2	13	26	60	4

In 1908, Rangers were to leave the Vicarage Field and make a historic move to Mart Lane. It came about in somewhat unforeseen circumstances.

The area that would later be known as Victoria Park, had been acquired by James Martland Limited in 1887 from the Earl of Derby's Estate, having previously been farmed and occupied by Mr. William Spencer.

The Ormskirk Advertiser of 7th May 1908 reported on a planning application by the Burscough Wesleyans' Cricket Club. Approval was granted, by the Lathom and Burscough Urban District Council, for them 'to build a cricket pavilion in Mart Lane, subject to a bond being entered into to remove the building if so required.' The pavilion was built on the site of what is now the Community Centre. Walter Martland, the son of James Martland, was the president and captain of the cricket club at that time, and it was reported that he laid out and presented a cricket ground to the club 'at large cost.' Burscough Wesleyans played their first cricket match on the new ground on Saturday 16th May 1908.

As the 1908 cricket season drew to a close, so the Advertiser's football correspondent was able to review the local club's prospects for the forthcoming season:

Burscough Rangers promise to have another good season. Though a comparatively young organisation it is none the less an active one and has done a lot to re-awaken the interest in football in Burscough that prevailed some eight or ten years ago. Further interest in the game should be aroused by the formation of another club - Burscough Wesleyans - and in conjunction with the Rangers they have obtained an excellent ground in Mart Lane. Each club will play at home on alternative Saturdays so that supporters of the game can always be assured a match.

Prior to the First World War, cricket was played where the football ground is now

Burscough Rangers 1907-08 season - Winners of the Southport 2nd Senior Charity Cup.
Back row (l to r): Jack Radcliffe (Trainer), W.Bentham, Jack Disley, John Aspinwall (Right-back), R.S.Gibson (Goalkeeper), W.Lewis (Left-back), J.Lyon, H.Bentham, J.Edmondson, E.Lamb, W.Parr
Middle row (l to r): J.Baldwin (Right-half), R.Stringfellow (Centre-half), Walter Smith (Left-half)
Front row (l to r): James Ashton (Outside-right), Jimmy Pye (Inside-right), James Gore (Centre-forward), Sam Jowett (Inside-left), R.Gore (Outside-left). Team pictured on the Vicarage Field.
Photograph kindly loaned by Mrs. Rose Smith.

Mr. Walter Martland, pictured in later years. In 1908, he laid the first cricket pitch at Mart Lane, which eventually became the present Victoria Park football ground.
Photograph kindly loaned by Walter Martland's granddaughter, Mrs. Ann Mentha.

located and, based on the evidence of early photographs, the football pitch was sited parallel to the present pitch, but approximately 30 yards closer to the railway.

Still in the Southport League, Rangers' first game at Mart Lane was scheduled for Saturday 26th September 1908 against Southport Wesleyans, but the game never actually took place. Southport Wesleyans may have scratched as they did not complete their league fixtures, or the game might have been postponed due to dreadful thunderstorms reported in Burscough that week, so bad 'that lightening was stated to have removed one of the shoes from a horse's hoof.'

Two weeks later, on Saturday 10th October 1908, in their first competitive fixture at Mart Lane, Rangers beat Southport Territorials by fourteen goals to nil, a winning margin they would never surpass. Played before 'a good gate' the team that day was: Iddon; J.Aspinwall, W.Lewis; J.Baldwin, R.Stringfellow, W.Smith; J.Ashton, J.Pye, J.Gore, S.Jowett and R.Gore.

The following week Churchtown Congregationals were the visitors. Despite so many of their opponents having church connections, reports suggested that the Christian spirit did not always prevail... 'shady tactics were used by the visitors and Gore and one of the 'Congos' men got to loggerheads, the consequence being marching orders for both players.' Sam Jowett, a prolific goalscorer for Rangers at that time, scored two more in a 4-1 victory and the following January signed an amateur form for Preston North End where he was reported to have 'played for the reserve team in two matches.' Jowett later became a teacher at Aughton Street School in Ormskirk.

As the 1909-10 season commenced, several open dates were advertised by the Rangers secretary for friendly fixtures, with interested parties invited to apply to; 'R.Stringfellow, Lord Street, Burscough.' Already entered in the Southport & District League, the problem regarding a shortage of fixtures was quickly resolved as the first team was also accepted into membership of the Ormskirk & District League. A fixture list was drawn up to avoid any conflict and the team responded by finishing the season as winners of the Southport competition, having remained unbeaten at Mart Lane.

A Southport Shield fixture away to Birkdale St. Johns in January 1910 resulted in a 7-0 defeat, hardly surprising considering Rangers fielded 'a part team only, the others refusing to strip because of the severe cold.'

Later that year, the cancellation of a fixture between Burscough Swifts and Lathom Park gave notice that the Rangers were now emerging as the major football force in the village:

The Lathom Park team journeyed to Burscough with a strong eleven, on arriving at the Swifts ground, however, the home team failed to put in an appearance, preferring to watch a local team - the Rangers - there is no excuse for them and their reputation as sportsmen will doubtless suffer.

Burscough Swifts, who played at the Elm Road ground, were then playing in the Ormskirk and District League, and it came as no surprise when they disbanded shortly afterwards.

The nearby Leeds-Liverpool canal continued to play a prominent role in the everyday life of Burscough at that time, with many local people employed in work on or around the canal. For an away match at Appley Bridge on Saturday 20th January 1912, the Rangers' supporters travelled by barge for this eagerly awaited local derby. The visitors won 4-1, helped by a Tommy Ashton hat-trick:

This important 'local derby' took place at Appley Bridge last Saturday. When the teams lined up, a record crowd of excited spectators were present, quite 400 hailing from Burscough. A unique feature in connection to the match was the presence of 200 boatmen, who had been conveyed per canal in a boat specially arranged for the occasion.

Although classed as a 'friendly', there was much rejoicing as a result of this prestige victory over a local side playing in the higher rated Lancashire Alliance. In 'remarkable' after-match scenes, 'the large crowd of Burscoughites present demonstrated their joy in various ways in truly uproarious fashion.'

The following month a game between Rangers Reserves and Marshside Reserves at Mart Lane was subject 'to several stoppages as a consequence of events during the game.' The Advertiser on 15th February 1912 reported:

Burscough Rangers players, officials and ground have been suspended. The management committee of the Southport & District Amateur League on Thursday last enquired into the disturbances at the Burscough Rangers ground on Saturday February 3rd and as the unseemly proceedings were held to be the fault of the Burscough club, drastic remedies have been applied, the whole of the officials, players and ground of the Rangers being suspended pending the action of the Lancashire Football Association.

A week later Rangers lodged an appeal against the decision. Their appeal proved successful and following an inquiry by the Lancashire F.A. at Preston on 1st March it was announced:

After hearing the evidence, the committee immediately raised the suspension, ordered the appeal fee to be refunded, and vetoed the league's right of further action in the matter, which they the league had reserved. In view of the fact that the Rangers club were somewhat responsible they were ordered to pay the costs of the meeting.

At this time Burscough were undoubtedly the poor relations to Ormskirk in football terms. An Ormskirk team had been formed in 1909, and by 1910 they had become members of the Liverpool County Combination and were well supported. Their derby matches with Skelmersdale United attracted over 2,000 spectators to Ormskirk. Collieries at Skelmersdale started the morning shift one hour earlier so that spectators could get to the game in time, and special trains had to be laid on to carry the hundreds of travelling supporters.

Ormskirk played at the Victoria Athletic and Pleasure Grounds, which was sited between Churchfields and Cottage Lane. It had a grandstand and three pavilions, and was also used for cycling and pony riding. John Berry described it thus:

> Ormskirk had a beautiful ground, it was fenced with a cycling cinder track right round it, but the stand accommodation was paltry, although in addition to the stand there was an open elevated cinder terrace on one side.

[In October 1914, two weeks after losing an F.A. Cup Tie away to Chester, Ormskirk folded and the ground was closed, it was then cultivated during the Great War. Ormskirk football never recovered from the loss of the Victoria Athletic Ground.]

BURSCOUGH RANGERS v. ORMSKIRK

Jan 28 1922	at Burscough	L'pool County Comb	W 3-1
Apr 29 1922	at Ormskirk	L'pool County Comb	W 5-0
Dec 25 1922	at Ormskirk	L'pool County Comb	W 2-1
Jan 1 1923	at Burscough	L'pool County Comb	W 2-1
Jan 1 1924	at Burscough	L'pool County Comb	D 2-2
Jan 26 1924	at Ormskirk	L'pool County Comb	L 2-6
Dec 6 1924	at Burscough	L'pool County Comb	W 3-0
Dec 25 1924	at Ormskirk	L'pool County Comb	L 0-1
Apr 13 1925	at Burscough	Hall Walker Cup	D 1-1
Apr 20 1925	at Ormskirk	Replay	W 4-1
Sep 5 1925	at Ormskirk	L'pool County Comb	W 4-1
Dec 12 1925	at Burscough	L'pool County Comb	W 4-1

RANGERS' RECORD: P.12   W.8   D.2   L.2   F.32   A.16

This balance of power was now about to dramatically change as Rangers made the first move in their bid to broaden their horizons and bring a better class of football to Burscough. The Ormskirk Advertiser of Thursday 12th September 1912 imparted the news:

> Burscough Rangers will commence the season, on Saturday next, as members of the Lancashire Alliance, when Whitley Amateurs of Wigan, will be opposed at Mart Lane. In entering the Alliance the Club is incurring considerably more expense, and they rely on their supporters giving them all possible assistance in their endeavour to provide a better class of football than has been hitherto witnessed in Burscough.
>
> Gate admission will be threepence this year, but season tickets are on sale at the low price of two shillings each. The Club will take part in the Liverpool Junior and Wigan Cup competitions. Two old players in James Gore and James Ashton are captain and sub-captain respectively.
>
> The ground has been completely enclosed, and is in fine condition. All concerned, both players and public, are looking forward to a successful season.

The Rangers' supporters were hardly known for their reticence or false modesty, so would undoubtedly have lost little time in informing their larger Ormskirk neighbours of this latest development. It was an attitude that did not always find favour with the Ormskirk based local newspaper:

> There are no more enthusiastic supporters to be found in any 'port' than in Burscough. Nor is their enthusiasm confined to the masculine sex. The women are just as loyal, ask anyone who has been. But, why this antagonism to Ormskirk, who bear no animosity?

Back in those 'good old days' it was reported that in a local fixture a spectator had attacked one of the match officials. The Advertiser tried to re-assure its readers that behaviour at football matches had not deteriorated but in the process painted a mind-boggling picture:

> A recent case of assault upon a linesman has resulted in the offender being sent to prison for a month. One is apt to forget that this is no modern

development, as some of the old time references will tell you with with grim humour. They can afford to smile now, but it was no laughing matter when, in days when the officials are not protected as they are now, they were chased over adjourning fields by a crowd thirsting for their blood and pelted with stones like some pariah dog.

On Saturday 19th April 1913 Rangers won the Wigan Cup by beating fierce rivals Golborne United 4-2 in the final at Flapper Fold, Atherton:

The English Cup Final wasn't the only final decided on Saturday, as anyone visiting Burscough about 2 o'clock would have thought on seeing the 200 or more green and white bedecked enthusiasts who made the long journey to Atherton to witness their team meet and defeat the redoubtable Golborne United, who had headed both league and cup competitions.

The successful team was: Appleton; Harry Ball, W.Morris; Taylor, Billy Aspinwall, James Gore; James Ashton, Jimmy Pye, Tommy Ashton, Walmsley and Albert Smith. Rangers' full back W.Morris was the first reported professional player in Burscough football.

Albert Smith later recalled, 'I well remember the celebrations we had in the Cambridge on our return, with all the boatmen. We were always turned out immaculately by a lady who laundered the team's kit. Our shorts were starched and made 'whiter than white' using *Bosco*.'

Burscough Rangers 1913-14 Season - Photographed at Mart Lane in front of the pavilion built by the Burscough Wesleyans' Cricket Club.
Back left to right: J.Gore, Unknown, Charlie Welding, Halsall (Goalkeeper), Popplewell, W.Forshaw, Jack Radcliffe, W.Newland, W.Breiser.
Middle left to right: Jack Disley, John Aspinwall, Masheter, Billy Aspinwall, Rimmer, Harry Ball.
Front left to right: George Merritt, Jimmy Pye, Tommy Ashton, John Culshaw, Riding, Tom Gregson (Trainer).

Burscough Rangers 1913-14 season, pictured in front of the Stanley Institute with the Lancashire Alliance Championship Trophy and the Excelsior Cup. Back left to right: Unknown, Unknown, Jack Radcliffe, Unknown, Unknown, Halsall (Goalkeeper), Popplewell, Bill Postlethwaite, Bill Forshaw, Unknown, Tom Gregson (Trainer). Middle left to right: Masheter, Charlie Welding, Billy Aspinwall, H.Rimmer. Front left to right: John Aspinwall, George Merritt, John Culshaw, Tommy Ashton, Unknown, James Ashton, Jack Disley.

On Wednesday 30th April, Rangers played host to Ormskirk in a 'friendly' at Mart Lane. Burscough won 4-1 in front of 'a record crowd.' It was reported that a special train was run from Ormskirk to the 'Port'. The win being warmly acclaimed by the home supporters, 'who appeared to be as pleased with themselves as if they had lifted the English Cup.'

Then, as now, it was the goalscorers who dominated the headlines. In January 1914 the Advertiser's 'Centre Half' was comparing past and present centre forwards:

Tommy Ashton, the Burscough centre forward has scored over 20 goals for the Rangers this season, and a total of over 50 in the past two seasons. He is quite one of the best pivots we have, and is a worthy successor to Forrest, a great Burscough centre forward of by-gone days.

Many a good tussle have I had with Forrest, whom I used to regard as fit for any First League team when he was in form. The present generation must remember that Burscough have had some excellent football teams, when some of the present Ranger team were probably in petticoats.

Rangers won the Lancashire Alliance that season, clinching the Championship at home to Golborne United on Saturday 7th March 1914:

LANCASHIRE ALLIANCE 1913-14 SEASON

	P	W	D	L	F	A	Pts
Burscough Rangers	10	6	3	1	28	11	15
Golborne United	10	6	0	4	26	21	12
Standish	10	4	3	3	20	18	11
Skelmersdale Mission	10	4	2	4	17	24	8
Standish St. Wilfrids	10	2	2	6	22	29	6
Hindley Green Athletic	10	3	0	7	19	29	6

The Rangers played a great game in the first half and were cheered on to success by a good crowd. Merritt got the first 'blood', by which point Burscough led at the interval, after which the homesters went off with a real burst and scored two more through Pye.

The trophy was presented four weeks later by the League Vice-President, Mr. Witter, when Rangers entertained a Rest of the League eleven at Mart Lane. They also won the Excelsior Cup, beating Standish 3-2 in the Final at Ormskirk, with Tommy Ashton bringing his total to 75 goals over two seasons.

In 1914, Burscough Rangers were elected to the Liverpool County Combination. The 7th of November saw their first meeting with Skelmersdale United, then known as 'The Colliers', in a Combination fixture at Sandy Lane, the teams drawing one goal apiece. Skelmersdale United won the League that season, with Rangers finishing in a commendable second place, but the Burscough officials were far from satisfied:

Had the rules been strictly adhered to, we really won the Championship because we beat Skelmersdale 5-1 at Burscough, but the referee failed to appear, and a friendly was played, but the rules say if the clubs agreed on a substitute referee the match shall be considered a league match. In the re-arranged league match Skelmersdale won 2-1.

Rangers gained consolation by winning the Liverpool Challenge Cup, however, by now, football seemed of relatively little consequence as young men were being summoned to expend their energies elsewhere.....fighting for their very lives.

Following the First World War, Rangers found themselves without a ground as Mart Lane had been cultivated to help the war effort, as had many other grounds in the area, and was not available. They rented a field in Higgins Lane from Mr. R.Travis, changing at the Stanley Institute and walking a quarter of a mile to the ground. Short of players, Rangers joined the Ormskirk and District Amateur League for 1919-20 season. An inauspicious start saw them losing to Skelmersdale Rangers by ten goals to one in their first League game. 'Skipper', writing in the Advertiser, was not best pleased:

Some of the Burscough supporters met me going to the match near the end of the game and remarked I was somewhat late. They did not know that I had been present earlier and had left disgusted, returning just to hear the awful final 10-1. Some said it was 11.

Rangers recovered to win their next three games, including a 4-1 win at Ormskirk Comrades on Saturday 25th October 1919. Their supporters came in for some strong criticism, however:

They of course had the usual enthusiastic following, but some of the younger element ought to curb their tongues, their language at times almost singeing the grass. Bad language at a football field ought not to be tolerated, and particularly when you are winning.

Secretary Berry told me the Rangers were in the reconstruction process, but they are building very nicely with three pre-war men, Pye, Ashton ('Gassy') and Aspinall forming a rare foundation. I liked young Eric Caunce at left-back for the Rangers. Ashton, and his partner Watson, forming the right wing, being particularly dangerous.

Miraculously, newspaper reports following the war seemed to confirm that the

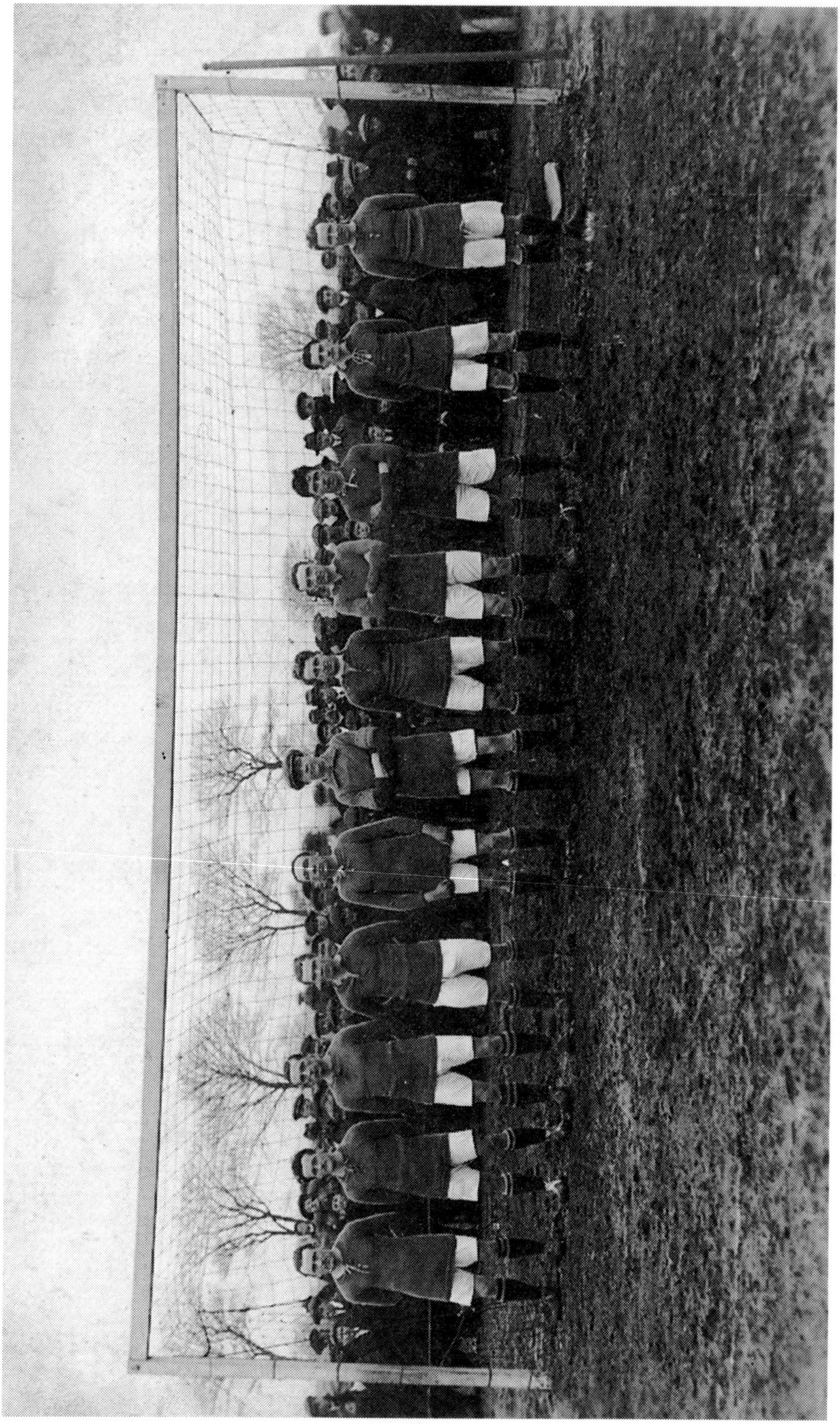

majority of the pre-war Rangers' players survived one of the most murderous conflicts in history, and some of them would continue to play a part in club affairs for many years to come. For a 3-0 win at home to Stormy Albion in November, Rangers were represented by the following eleven: Brookfield; Wareing, Caunce; Foulkes, Aspinwall, Rimmer; J.Ashton, J.Pye, Jenkinson, Blundell, Ireland. Three weeks later there were 'many lusty-lunged supporters from Burscough' present when Rangers went to play on 'the box-like ground of Ormskirk D.S. & S.' After 'Lasher' Gibbons missed an early chance for the home side, Rangers went on to gain an easy 7-2 victory, with Ike Jenkinson scoring four.

ORMSKIRK & DISTRICT AMATEUR LEAGUE 1919-20 SEASON						
	P	W	D	L	F	A	Pts
Skelmersdale Rangers	18	14	1	3	82	25	29
Burscough Rangers	18	13	3	2	63	27	29
Stormy Albion	18	10	4	4	53	28	24
Upholland Moor	18	10	5	4	56	40	23
Skelmersdale Mission	18	9	4	5	52	37	22
Ormskirk D.S. & S	18	7	1	10	54	53	15
Westhead Juniors	18	6	2	10	31	55	14
Rainford Star	18	6	1	11	33	58	12
Ormskirk Comrades	18	2	1	15	30	72	5
Ormskirk Juniors	18	2	1	15	27	86	5

Off the field activities were well supported, when the club held a Whist Drive and Dance on Friday 28th November 1919:

The second event of the tournament series took place on Friday last in the Stanley Institute and was again a pronounced success, all the tickets being sold and the large hall being completely filled. The winners of prizes were:- Ladies; 1. Miss Brewer; 2. Miss Martland; 3. Mrs. Mawdesley. Gents; 1. H.Vickers; 2. H.Disley; 3. H.Martland.

The prizes were kindly presented by Mrs. Hy. Dutton who received the hearty thanks of the company. The arrangements were most efficiently carried out by Mr. & Mrs. Neve and Mr. & Mrs. Johnson, assisted by friends and the club committee.

Despite their poor start in the league that season, Rangers recovered well and tied for first place, before losing a play-off with Skelmersdale Rangers at High Lane by four goals to three.

In 1920-21 season Rangers rejoined the Liverpool County Combination and entered what would prove to be the most successful period in their history. Interest was now at fever pitch, for a match at St. Helens in October against Clock Face Recs it was reported, 'nearly 200 enthusiasts made the journey from Burscough, all the local char-a-bancs being requisitioned.'

On the 30th October 1920, Rangers played host to Skelmersdale United in a league fixture on Travis' Field. There was great pride in both village teams and the game attracted tremendous interest. A special train, packed with supporters from

---

*Opposite: Burscough Rangers line up at Travis' Field on the 13th March 1920 prior to the Liverpool Challenge Cup Semi-final with Skelmersdale United, Skem winning 1-0. There was a crowd of 'over 2,500' paying £55, on what was little more than a pasture field down Higgins Lane. Identified in this picture are Tommy Pye (fifth from right), Jimmy Pye (extreme right), George Merritt (extreme left), Billy Aspinwall (second from left), Rimmer (fifth from left), and goalkeeper Brookfield in centre. The full team that day was: Brookfield; Pinch, Campbell; Rimmer, Aspinwall, Frank Barlow; Merritt, T.Pye, Ike Jenkinson, Pedder, J.Pye.
Photograph kindly loaned by Bill Pye, son of Tommy Pye.*

Skelmersdale, arrived at Burscough Junction station and the visiting supporters marched as a body to the ground led by the famous Skelmersdale Old Prize Band.

The field in Higgins Lane was only surrounded by hedges and was very easy to enter without paying. The entrance charge was 8d, plus 2d extra to sit on a seat by the touchline. When the gate was totalled, it caused a sensation in the district. H.V. (Bert) Berry, was ten years old at the time. He remembered helping his father, who was then secretary of the Rangers, and the treasurer Bill Forshaw, to count the money. 'At first the total came to a few shillings over £100, but then the secretary remembered that he had put in five shillings of his own change to help at the gate. The amount was very sorrowfully deducted and the gate was officially declared at £99 18s 9d.' Not to be denied, however, it became famously known as 'the £100 gate.'

Three months later Rangers lost 4-1 at Sandy Lane in the return league meeting. At that time mock burial announcements in the local newspaper were a popular form of celebration by the victors. Rangers were not to be disappointed:

Mr. Thos. Edwards, President of Skelmersdale United F.C., has received a memorial card, very neatly got up and on which the following lines have been inscribed:-

IN LOVING MEMORY
of Burscough Rangers, who departed this life 22nd January 1921 and were interred on the Sandy Lane enclosure.

Weep not, dear brethren, but be content
Although you were on victory bent
Nobly you fought until the last
But found the collier lads too fast

Two points have gone from the regions of light
Like the vanished hand, they have passed from sight
Like heroes true the best you gave
And the 'Boaties' mourn over the 'Linnets' grave

FROM THEIR LOVING 'SKEM' COUSINS

Rangers were to gain their revenge, however, as Mr. Edwards was also President of the County Football Association, and it would be his official duty over the next few years to preside over a succession of presentations to the Rangers as they went on to win trophy after trophy.

Towards the end of the season Rangers lost a Richardson Cup game at Croston in front of 'a record gate' by three goals to one. Tommy Pye scored all the Croston goals. Croston were well represented at that time and their record against Rangers became second to none. 'Centre Half' wrote after the game:

'Ha's Bursco gone on ?,' asked a burly little five-year-old of me as I was cycling through Burscough Town after the match. 'They've lost,' I ruefully replied, 'it's a bad doo isn't it.' 'Aye-e-e, id is that,' came the answer.

In February, Rangers won the George Mahon Cup for the first time. In the final they overcame Whiston 1-0 at the Sutton Commercial Ground, St. Helens, through a goal by Billy Rigby. In March they played at Anfield in the final of the Liverpool Challenge Cup, losing 4-1 to Skelmersdale United. The gate amounted to £157, with Rangers lining up: Webster; Freeman, Wright; Smith, Horton, H.Rigby; George Merritt, Jack Rowbottom, Jenkinson, Pedder, W.Rigby.

The following season Rangers moved back to the Mart Lane enclosure. Burscough Wesleyans' Cricket Club, without a ground, had disbanded after the war and the football team was now able to make what would prove to be their final move on to the area previously used by the cricket club. The Advertiser dated 25th August 1921 was generous in its praise of their efforts:

The summer has not been an altogether idle time for the various football clubs of the district but perhaps the one that has shown most enterprise is Burscough Rangers who have returned to their old ground in Mart Lane and carried out almost a tranformation scene. They have as far as possible - or as far as funds will allow - paid attention to the comfort of the ground, but it is the dressing room accommodation which has had the most attention. An old stable has been converted into a splendidly equipped pavilion decorated in green and white with excellent bathing facilities. It is no idle boast to say that in this respect the club are better served than any junior club for miles round. There will be a refreshment bar on the ground, and there are separate entrances for the players and spectators.

[The 'converted stable' was used through the 1920s and later converted into a dwelling. It is now occupied by the Baldwin family and known as 'Pavilion Cottage' at 48 Mart Lane. Roy Baldwin recalls that it was actually built as a barn and 'still has the original wide staircase.' Former England international Bob Langton recalled the players changing there, 'one team changed upstairs, and one downstairs.']

Their first match back at Mart Lane was a County Combination fixture with K.L.Allan & Co. (later known as Rainford), the 'Linnets' winning 4-2. There was 'a capital gate on the new (or rather the old) ground in Mart Lane, the receipts totalling over £30 and the turf being in splendid order.' The Advertiser raised one point of concern, however:

LIVERPOOL COUNTY COMBINATION 1921-22 SEASON							
	P	W	D	L	F	A	Pts
Burscough Rangers	24	17	5	2	64	28	39
Frodsham	24	17	1	6	53	27	35
Wigan Boro	24	13	6	5	71	26	32
Ormskirk	24	13	1	10	44	61	27
Whiston Parish	24	11	4	9	43	37	26
Everton 'A'	24	8	9	7	52	44	25
Garston Gas Works	24	10	4	10	43	47	24
Prescot	24	8	7	9	38	45	23
Liverpool 'A'	24	9	3	12	40	51	21
New Brighton Reserves	24	8	1	15	58	62	17
Sutton Commercial	24	6	3	15	47	70	15
St. Helens Junction	24	6	2	16	40	62	14
K.L.Allan & Co.	24	5	3	16	35	74	13

Rangers allowed some 300 on the ground free, on production of the unemployment card. It has since been elicited that the privilege has very largely been abused by people, and very reluctantly the Committee have been compelled to make a charge in future.

At this time facilities for viewing at Mart Lane were fairly basic, with no seats or covered accommodation, however, the demands for spectator comfort, that would be so splendidly fulfilled in later years, were already apparent. It was announced:

The Rangers' Committee have on many occasions been asked by a number of

John Berry, pictured in 1953. For many years the secretary of Burscough Rangers, John Berry kept meticulous records of the Rangers' years in a black leather pocket book. Photograph courtesy of his grandson, Eric Berry.

their patrons to provide a reserved side on their ground, and as many seats as possible for home matches. With a view to meeting this wish to some extent, the Orrell Lane side of the ground will in future be reserved, and an extra charge of 2d each will be made. A certain number of seats will also be provided.

The return to Mart Lane must have suited the Rangers as they finished the season by capturing the coveted Liverpool County Combination Championship for the first time, then, on Thursday May 4th 1922 they travelled to Sandheys Park, New Brighton, to beat Frodsham in the Hall Walker Cup Final.

The Annual General Meeting was held on Wednesday 31st May 1922 at the Stanley Institute where there was 'apparently some misunderstanding about those entitled to attend.' John Parr-Sturgess was voted to the Chair, but later had to vacate the meeting due to 'domestic trouble.'

Hon. Secretary, Mr. J.R.Pardoe reported on improvements to the ground, 'where they had dressing accommodation far superior to junior clubs in their own class, and a welcome new feature had been the provision of a refreshment bar by Mr. E.Wells.'

The club had entered the English Cup and the Lancashire Junior Cup for the first time.

Mr. W.Forshaw, the hon. treasurer, reported a starting balance of £217 5s and a closing balance of £189 7s. Entertainment tax had come to over £150. The loss on the season of £35 13s was the first time in ten years the club had not reported a profit.

Committeeman, Mr. A.Forrest said he considered 'the balance sheet was very satisfactory. They had a very strong team and expense had been incurred on the ground that will not be necessary next season.' Arthur Forrest had been the centre forward of Burscough AFC in 1895.

The committee voted in was: A.Forrest, Geo. Draper, E.Bamber, W.Martland, J.P.Sturgess, R.Gore, James Ashton, Jos. Turner, T.Ashton and A.French.

Further work was carried out on the ground in the summer, which attracted this favourable, yet prophetic, comment from the Advertiser correspondent:

During the summer months, the Rangers committee - who have no superiors and few equals at their jobs - have made several improvements to the ground. The barriers round the playing pitch have been set further back and considerably strengthened and altogether the ground is one of the best appointed in the Combination. I suppose we shall be having a stand someday.

In November 1922, Rangers met Croston, who were members of the West Lancashire League, in the second round of the Lancashire Junior Cup. The Advertiser of Thursday 16th November carried the following report by 'The Scot':

The 'star' match on Saturday was the Lancashire Junior Cup struggle between Croston and Burscough Rangers at the former's ground. The match has attracted considerable local interest, so much so that the L & N.W. Ry. Co. ran a special train, which was packed, while hundreds came by road. I don't think I ever saw a crowd of the type at Westheads on Saturday, for quite 90 per cent were men, youths and lads from the countryside, thus proving what a hold football has on many whose fathers never knew the game at all.

As to the match, I don't think I ever saw a game in which a team was as fortunate as Burscough not to be defeated badly. They were beaten in every department except one, and that was in goal, where Charnley although shaken up and damaged in the first few minutes, played a storming game.

The replay should provide a stiff struggle, for the Rangers are sure to give a better display at Mart Lane than they did on Saturday. If they don't - well the canal is handy.

The game ended in a 1-1 draw. Two weeks later, Victoria Park may well have accommodated in excess of 4,000 spectators for the replay, as a gate described as 'well over £100' was reported. It was to be Croston's finest hour as they won 1-0, and went on to win the Lancashire Junior Cup, defeating Bacup Borough in the final at Deepdale, Preston.

1924-25 season began with high drama, the headline in the Advertiser read; 'Burscough Rangers F.C. prosecuted.' The aptly named Ormskirk Petty Sessional Court was the setting on Friday 5th September 1924, as the club was charged with; 1) failing to collect entertainment tax; 2) using unstamped tickets to place of entertainment; 3) false claim for entertainment tax.

Chairman Arthur Forrest and committeeman George Merritt were summoned to face the charges. It was reported that the offences occurred at a football match at Burscough on Saturday 15th March of that year. The report went on:

There were two entrances to the field at Mart Lane and at one of these the defendants were officiating in a voluntary capacity for the club. There were two prices charged, 9d and 6d, and the tickets should have been stamped indicating the duty.

Mr. Orme, the local excise officer was witnessing the match and afterwards learned that the tickets were unstamped.

At that time a twenty-five per cent entertainment tax was levied on spectators, which the club was responsible for collecting. The Rangers were ordered to pay £1 outstanding tax and slightly over £2 in costs. 'Centre-half' warned other clubs in the area to 'watch out.'

An Ormskirk team had been revived after the war and was to be found competing with Burscough Rangers in the Liverpool County Combination. Initially they played at Burscough Street, on a field next to Hattersleys', but when the Ravenscroft Sports Ground was opened they moved there. This ground had a stand and was situated next to the railway line, between Brook Lane and Bridge Street, on the site of what is now Ravenscroft Avenue.

Burscough Rangers met Ormskirk at Ravenscroft in a Liverpool County Combination fixture on Christmas Day 1924, with the 'Gingerbreadmen' winning 1-0.

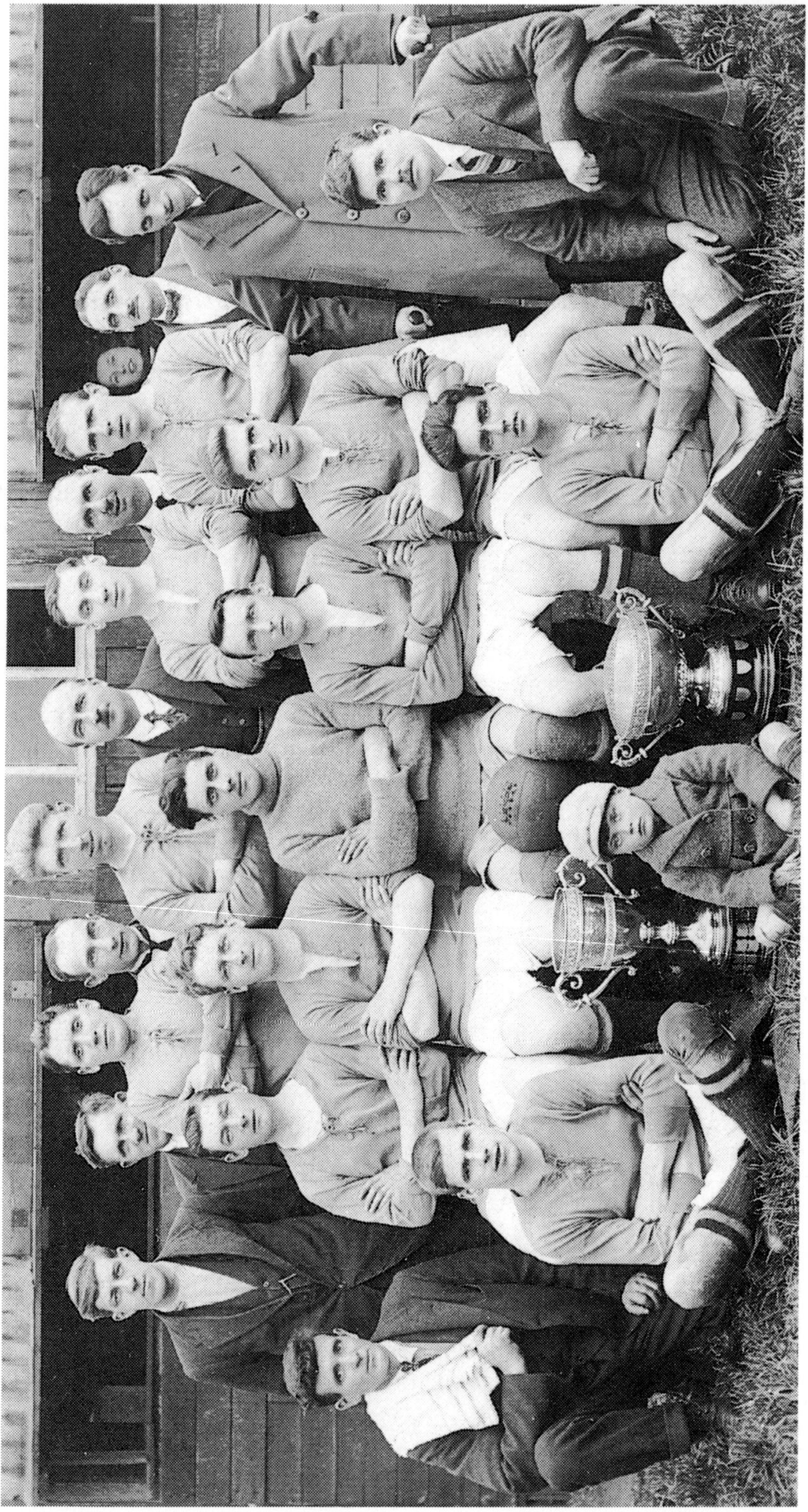

The Rangers lined up that day: Archie Kemp; Bill Ashurst, Billy Green; Billy Aspinwall, Marshall, Frank Barlow; Billy Snape, George Cunningham, Tommy Wyper, Nat Rawlins, Balfour.

Before the end of the decade they too had disappeared from senior football.

Rangers won the George Mahon Cup in 1925-26 season. The semi-final draw had paired them with Skelmersdale United and the Advertiser dated 22nd April 1926 set the big match scene:

Despite the approaching end of season, there was a big attendance at the Sandy Lane enclosure at Skelmersdale last Saturday for the Semi-final of the George Mahon Cup in which United had won the toss for choice of ground against their old and nearest opponents. A special train was run from Burscough, whilst large numbers made the journey on bikes and in motors.

The game finished in a 2-2 draw, with Rangers winning the replay. In the final they beat Harlandic 1-0 at Whiston, Eddie Chatburn scoring from a penalty.

The presentation of trophies by Mr. T.Edwards J.P. of Bickerstaffe, the President of Liverpool County F.A., took place at Messrs. Sandfords' Cafe on Thursday 29th April and afterwards the players were entertained to tea.

On Tuesday 4th May 1926 Rangers beat Skelmersdale United 3-0 to win the Liverpool County Combination Championship:

At the conclusion of the game on Tuesday evening last, Mr. T.Edwards presented the Championship Cup to Burscough Rangers.

He complimented every one of the players, the Committee, and above all their splendid Secretary Mr. Sturgess. Burscough were also fortunate in having a President who was able to 'Bridge' them over their difficulties and if they had not succeeded, well they should have been ashamed of themselves (laughter and applause). The record of the Burscough club was one of which any club might be proud. During the season they had played 22 games, won 19, lost 1, drawn 2, scored 72 goals, against 21, with a total of 40 points (applause).

He then asked Kemp the Burscough captain to accept the very handsome cup. As Kemp came forward he was very heartily applauded. The captain of the Burscough team expressed his delight at receiving the Cup. 'The players had had a very good season, they had played clean and consistent football.'

Opposite: Burscough Rangers 1925-26 season - pictured at Victoria Park with the George Mahon Cup (right) and Liverpool County Combination Championship Trophy.
Back Row (from left): Harry Prescott (Groundsman), Bill Lyon, Bill Ashurst, George Porter, Billy Bennett, Bill Martland, George Cunningham, Bill Johnson (Chairman), Harry Green, Arthur Forrest, Ernie Collins (hon. Treasurer).
Middle Row (from left): Billy Martindale, Tommy Pye, Archie Kemp (captain), Nat Rawlins, Jim Cookson.
Front Row (from left): Tom Gregson (Trainer), Billy Green, Eddie Chatburn, John Parr-Sturgess (hon.sec.)
This picture quite nicely links the past and present clubs. The Secretary of Burscough Rangers, John Parr-Sturgess, became the first President of Burscough Football Club in 1946. Rangers' Committee member Arthur Forrest was, thirty years previously, centre forward of the 1895-96 Burscough A.F.C. team.
H.V.Berry wrote; 'This team, plus Snape (outside-right) and Owen (outside-left) was, in the opinion of many, the best team that Rangers ever had'.
The mascot is 3 year-old Billy Pye, son of Tommy Pye. Bill was living in Richmond Avenue, Burscough in 1996. The woman in the background is a Miss Martland. Bill Fairclough kindly loaned the photograph, which originally belonged to his father.

Mr. J.Berry informed the gathering 'that evening Rangers had completed 1,000 goals in league football'.

The 1,000th league goal was in fact scored by Tommy Pye, who went on to score thirty goals that season. The power of his shot was legendary, a goal in the league fixture at Skelmersdale was described in the match report thus; 'Tommy Pye completed the movement with a terrific shot which must have nearly broke the rigging.'

John Berry gleefully wrote; 'in five meetings, Skelmersdale failed to win once.'

The club's Annual Meeting was held at the Stanley Institute on Tuesday 11th May. Mr W.J.Bridge (President) occupied the chair. It was reported 'there was an excellent attendance, despite the fact that a large political demonstration was being held in the township.' The season had commenced with a balance of £6 18s 9d, and had finished with a balance of £6 1s 2d. Gate receipts from home games were £286 6s 10d and from away games £126 2s 3d. The financial position of the club was considered to be 'very satisfactory indeed.'

Mr Sturgess the secretary felt he could not carry on his duties as 'they were too trying from a health point of view.' Mr. Ernie Collins was appointed treasurer 'amid acclamation.'

Since 1912, Rangers had never finished lower than third in any league. It was time to progress further...

Nothing succeeds like success - and there's really nothing like it. Since Burscough Rangers have got a winning side together the last two or three years, the Club has gone from strength to strength. They have one of the best and most central grounds, Victoria Park, in the Liverpool County Combination and now they are embarking on another important development, via, the erection of a stand. I am told that a start has already been made and that it is going to be completed this summer.

Mr. Sam Hall, the indefatigable hon. secretary of the Club, has been the 'live wire' in the matter. I understand, when he heard three months ago that Everton were making alterations at Goodison, he thought this was the opportunity to equip the Club with a stand at a reasonable cost. The directors of James Martland Ltd, to whom the Club is indebted for the loan of Victoria Park, very kindly granted the necessary permission to erect a stand, and Mr. R.Marsden one of the directors and a staunch supporter promised something more, as did Mr. W.J.Bridge the esteemed President of the Club.

The Supporters' Club also promised co-operation, and last Tuesday week, Mr. Hall and Mr. Dick Orritt journeyed to Goodison Park and purchased a large quantity of good timber at a knock-out price.

The stand will be 60 feet long, with 12 rows of seating and a press box in the centre (thanks very much), and a space reserved for the Committee, with one or two rows of tip-up chairs. There will be a paddock in front of the stand which will be built on brickwork 4 foot 6 inches high. The entrance will be from behind, in the centre.

So the Advertiser reported on 29th April 1926. At the time secretary Sam Hall was the sub-postmaster at Burscough Bridge Post Office. The cost of the stand was estimated to be £200.

Bill Martland was a committeeman of Rangers at this time, and his grandson

Keith Martland remembers, 'he formed a company called Anvil Haulage with his brother Harry. It was their wagons pulled by shire horses that brought the stand from Goodison Park.'

Tom Walmsley, as an 11 year-old, helped with the building of that stand. 'We had sheets of corrugated iron on which to carry materials for the stand. One of the corrugated sheets fell on my leg.' Seventy years later he still carries the scar.

[The stand had originally been erected at the Bullens Road side of Goodison Park in 1895 at a cost of £3,407, but was replaced by the double decker stand in 1926.]

The grandstand was opened on Saturday 28th August 1926, and would continue to give yeoman service, by comfortably housing the football fans of Burscough, for a further sixty years. The Advertiser reported the opening ceremony:

Last Saturday was a red-letter day in the history of Burscough football, for it marked the opening of the new grandstand at Victoria Park, the well appointed headquarters of the Burscough Rangers F.C. The stand which has been erected on the south-west side of the ground is a handsome structure and is splendidly equipped with covered accommodation. It has seating for close on 500 with a directors stand in front and a press box in the middle, while underneath are refreshment rooms, committee rooms and dressing rooms. The structure is the old Bullens Road stand from Goodison Park and the whole has been constructed by voluntary labour, to the lasting credit of those who participated. It would be invidious in this article to enumerate the names of those who took part in the labour and of others who made such generous gifts in the way of material which has enabled the committee to complete the work, but they are entitled to the highest measure of praise, which they are here accorded.

There was a large attendance at the opening ceremony which fittingly enough was presided over by Mr. T.Edwards J.P. of Brookdale, Bickerstaffe, the president of the Liverpool County F.A., supported by Mr. W.J.Bridge, the respected president of Burscough Rangers F.C., and Mrs. Bridge, Mr. E.Bamber (Chairman), Mr. Walter Martland, Mr. W.E.Jones, Mr. J.P.Sturgess, Mr. W.Wells, Mr. S.Hall, Mr. E.R.Collins (hon. sec.), & co., & co.

The two handsome trophies, the Liverpool County Combination Cup and the George Mahon Cup, which the Rangers won last season were proudly exhibited in front of the stand.

Mr. Edwards said it was a great honour for him to have the privilege of presiding over that gathering on such an auspicious occasion.

He thought they could claim that Association Football was the leader of all their English games, for they could get larger crowds than any other form of sport in the country, and its popularity was higher and better maintained than any other sport (hear, hear). They claimed it improved the physique of their young men and those who were connected with it were doing a work of national importance in building up all A1 manhood instead of C3 manhood for the nation.

His recollection of footballers from Burscough went back a long way. During that time he could remember many young fellows from Burscough playing for Skelmersdale United. There was Jimmy Pilkington at outside left, Billy Harrison, Jack Stringfellow and his brother Harry.

Mr. Edwards congratulated the committee of the Burscough Rangers F.C. on their splendid enterprise in providing that stand which was one of the best he had seen for a junior club (applause).

Whilst they claimed a good deal for their sports they must see to it that they did not make them the be all and the end all of their lives. Let them make their religion first, their work or business next, and then their great sport would help them to lead a healthful, contented, and pleasant life (applause).

Mrs. Bridge then opened the stand. She had heard how very hard everyone had worked, for she could not be the wife of the president without him coming home and telling her everything that happened (laughter and applause).

Her husband was very anxious that their club should be a really clean, sporting club.

Mrs. Bridge proceeded, that if they expected ladies to come and see their games, they must come with the full assurance that they were going to enjoy the game without any chance of hearing anything they did not like (loud applause).

She now had much pleasure in declaring the stand open (applause).

Miss Hilda Hesketh and Master Eric Poole, both of the fathers of whom had worked unsparingly on the erection of the stand, then came forward and presented Mrs. Bridge with a handsome bouquet, the little people being rewarded with a sweet kiss from the lady.

The following season began with an English Cup Tie at Hindley Green Athletic. It was reported:

An invitation was extended to the 32 voluntary helpers, tradesmen and others who during the summer evenings built the Grandstand, to participate in a trip to Hindley Green. A party of 24 were able to accept and the start was made by motor coach from the Royal Hotel. The route via Skelmersdale, Upholland and Abbey Lakes was taken, and a glorious view of the countryside was visible before the drop into Upholland village.

Rangers had their best ever run in this famous competition (later called the F.A. Cup). After eliminating Hindley Green, they were drawn away to St. Helens Town in the preliminary round. 'Centre-Half' reported in the Advertiser:

St. Helens were sporting enough to come forward and admit that their ground was not suitable for an English Cup Tie, and so Burscough had another home game.

Great Harwood were the visitors in the qualifying round, Rangers winning 2-0. It was reported 'there was a capital attendance with the ground in splendid condition.' In the second qualifying round Rangers travelled to Chorley. John Berry described it as 'their greatest ever performance,' as goals by Green, Snape and Pye gave them a 3-2 victory.

Some say Tommy Pye won the match, others aver it was Kemp, whilst many say the presence of the Club's lucky mascot had a great deal to do with it.

Some 300 travelled by a special train from Burscough Bridge, others in motors and on bikes, so that in all there would be quite 600 or 700 of the spectators shouting for Burscough.

Rangers' dreams of reaching the competition proper were shattered in the last qualifying round. After Eddie Chatburn had missed an early penalty, the Liverpool County Combination side were soundly beaten 6-1 at Giant Axe by Lancaster Town in front of 4,366 spectators.

The league fixture at home to Everton 'A' caused some excitement locally, as 'the game was filmed for cinema purposes.' The same match was notable for 'the number of ladies present being conclusive evidence that the erection of the stand was justified.'

Games with Skelmersdale United were, as ever, passionate affairs. The New Years Day fixture at Sandy Lane ended in a 3-0 victory for Rangers, 'Skipper' complained:

Only prompt action by police prevented an ugly scene on Saturday. We had the spectacle of players being ordered off. If men cannot play the game without recourse to fighting then they are better out of it.

Later in the season, on a lighter note, 'Skipper' paid tribute to one of the 'unsung heroes' back at Victoria Park:

Mrs. Ackers has throughout the season carried out the catering arrangements. The pleasant smile which accompanies the cup of tea and biscuit has greatly enlarged the pleasure of visits to Burscough.

There was no halting this team, as the Liverpool County Combination Championship Trophy returned to Mart Lane and Bootle Celtic were beaten in the Liverpool Challenge Cup Final at Anfield, Pye scoring the goal in a 1-0 victory. Tommy 'Tut' Aspinall, then a young supporter of Rangers, remembers going to the final with his father. 'There was about 10,000 at Anfield that morning. Tommy Pye scored the goal, he had a terrific shot even though he had lost a couple of toes during the war. After the game we went for some chips, then went to see Dixie Dean playing at Goodison Park in the afternoon against Birmingham City.' Pye scored a total of 47 goals that season, with Nat Rawlins also getting 30.

This was undoubtedly to be the finest team the Rangers ever produced. During eight seasons in the Liverpool County Combination they had achieved three championships, second place twice, and third place on three occasions. The decision was made to apply for membership of the Lancashire Combination. John Berry warned that the village could not support top class football and the Lancashire Combination would prove their downfall.

In 1927-28, their first season of Lancashire Combination football, Rangers made a promising start and by February lay in fifth place, but a 6-3 defeat away to Horwich RMI, after the Rangers had led 3-0 at half-time, signalled a spell of poor results.

BURSCOUGH RANGERS
v. SKELMERSDALE UNITED

Date	Venue	Competition	Result
Nov 7 1914	at Skem	L'pool County Comb	D 1-1
Mar 6 1915	at Burscough	L'pool County Comb	L 1-2
Mar 13 1915	at Ormskirk	L'pool Challenge Cup S/F	D 0-0
Mar 20 1915	at Ormskirk	Replay	W 4-0
Mar 13 1920	at Burscough	Lpool Challenge Cup	L 0-1
Oct 30 1920	at Burscough	L'pool County Comb	L 0-1
Jan 22 1921	at Skem	L'pool County Comb	L 1-4
Mar 28 1921	at Anfield	L'pool Challenge C/Final	L 1-4
Oct 14 1922	at Skem	Lancs Junior Cup	L 1-5
Nov 18 1922	at Burscough	L'pool Challenge Cup	L 1-3
Oct 13 1923	at Burscough	Lancs Junior Cup	W 5-0
Oct 4 1924	at Skem	F.A.Cup	D 0-0
Oct 8 1924	at Burscough	Replay	W 5-0
Nov 15 1924	at Burscough	L'pool Challenge Cup	W 2-1
Jan 3 1925	at Burscough	L'pool County Comb	W 2-0
Feb 14 1925	at Skem	L'pool County Comb	L 2-6
Apr 18 1925	at Skem	Hall Walker Cup	W 2-0
Apr 22 1925	at Ormskirk	George Mahon Cup S/F	D 1-1
Apr 29 1925	at Ormskirk	Replay	L 0-1
Oct 10 1925	at Skem	Lancs Junior Cup	W 2-1
Feb 27 1926	at Skem	L'pool Challenge Cup	W 2-1
Apr 17 1926	at Skem	George Mahon Cup	D 2-2
Apr 21 1926	at Burscough	Replay	W 4-1
Apr 29 1926	at Burscough	L'pool County Comb	W 3-0
Dec 4 1926	at Skem	L'pool Challenge Cup	D 2-2
Dec 11 1926	at Burscough	Replay	W 3-2
Jan 1 1927	at Skem	L'pool County Comb	W 3-0
Jan 15 1927	at Burscough	L'pool County Comb	D 2-2
Sep 17 1927	at Skem	F.A.Cup	W 4-1
Oct 22 1927	at Burscough	Lancs Junior Cup	W 4-0
Oct 11 1930	at Burscough	Lancs Junior Cup	W 1-0
Oct 10 1931	at Skem	Lancs Junior Cup	L 0-1

RANGERS' RECORD: P.32 W.15 D.7 L.11 F.61 A.43

In the F.A. Cup, the joy of a 4-1 victory at Sandy Lane was short lived, as the following week they were expelled from the competition following a protest from the Skelmersdale club that Rangers' player Billy Glover was ineligible.

During 1928, Jack Pears was transferred to Liverpool, although it did not go unnoticed that the Anfield club never paid a fee to Rangers, and later transferred Pears to Rotherham where he gained a place in their Football League side. Fred Rogers, an inside forward, was transferred to Blackburn Rovers for £300. The East Lancashire club were familiar visitors to Mart Lane during the Rangers' years and beyond, and several players trod a well worn path to Ewood Park, no doubt influenced by Rangers' chairman Bill Johnson, a local undertaker, who acted as a scout for Rovers.

LANCASHIRE COMBINATION 1927-28 SEASON

	P	W	D	L	F	A	Pts
Chorley	38	28	3	7	128	49	59
Lancaster Town	38	26	3	9	148	58	55
Horwich RMI	38	23	9	6	111	61	55
Accrington Stanley Res.	38	25	2	11	100	64	52
Rossendale United	38	21	7	10	110	60	49
Dick Kerr's	38	19	4	15	115	93	42
Clitheroe	38	17	8	13	86	81	42
Morecambe	38	17	6	15	92	72	40
Wigan Borough Res.	38	16	8	14	79	72	40
Southport Reserves	38	16	7	15	94	91	39
Burscough Rangers	**38**	**13**	**9**	**16**	**88**	**99**	**35**
Great Harwood	38	12	9	17	97	128	33
Atherton	38	12	6	20	87	114	30
Preston North End 'A'	38	10	10	18	80	108	30
Nelson Reserves	38	12	6	20	80	113	30
Prescot	38	12	6	20	63	128	30
Barnoldswick Town	38	12	3	23	77	114	27
Hindley Green Athletic	38	11	4	23	71	108	26
Darwen	38	10	6	22	68	104	26
Bacup Borough	38	7	6	25	52	109	20

The grandstand was built, but still had to be paid for. To raise funds the Eighth Annual Fancy Dress Dance was held at the Stanley Institute on Friday 20th January 1928. It was reported that 'nearly 300 people attended and the balcony was filled with spectators. The California State Band was in attendance.' The report went on:

> The most original lady's costume was adjudged to be Mrs. Stowe's ingenious presentation of 'Next Year's Cup Winners.' Her dress represented Victoria Park with a football team in play, the figures being done in white applique on a green ground. For head-dress she had a model grandstand complete with spectators.
>
> The gentlemen's prizes were awarded as follows:- Mr. Arthur Seddon as a Sioux Indian Chief with feather head-dress and realistic war-paint; most original, Mr. Thomas Doran as a fearsome skeleton; consolation, Mr. Oswald Crumbleholme, 'Order of the Bath.'
>
> An innovation during the evening was an exhibition of dancing by Miss Muriel Sturgess who was a finalist in the World's dancing championship. Partnered by Mr. James J. Martland, she demonstrated the Yale Blues, Charleston, etc., the exhibition being warmly applauded.
>
> The room was lavishly decorated with gay paper chains, balloons, and fairy-lights by kind permission of Mr. J.R.Horrocks.

Rangers could be well pleased with 1927-28 season, finishing in a respectable 11th place with gates averaging £22 per game. Unfortunately, this would be the highest placing they would ever achieve.

'Centre-half' travelled with the team on New Years Day 1929 to see them win 3-2 against Wigan Borough Reserves:

> Coming home from Wigan I had an entertaining chat with Jim Gore about the early days of Rangers. He is the only foundation member of the committee at

> the present time and he spoke of Will Dutton's help in getting the club going one evening in the chip shop. Burscough have always been blessed with sound administration, and so long as this is continued they will carry on. They are the only village club in the Lancashire Combination and they hold a position of which they have every reason to be proud.

At the end of the season John Berry noted in his pocket book, 'decent season, should have been better, management bad, heavy cash loss.'

Travelling expenses were now greatly increased, but the team still managed to travel in a certain amount of style. Their league fixture at Lancaster City on Saturday 2nd March 1929 was honoured by the presence of the club president, Mr. Wilf Bridge:

> Mr. W.J.Bridge, the Club's President made the journey to Lancaster on Saturday. He was struck with the excellent spirit which prevailed amongst the players. The 'choir' occupy the back seats, and are under the direction of Banner. Ernie Collins has to apply the 'soft pedal' now and again, and is talking of calling the players together midweek for special vocal practice.
>
> There is no doubt that the players travel in comfort. The motor coach is luxuriously equipped, and the driver is a very popular one, he hails from Banks.

Accustomed to success during their County Combination years, Rangers struggled to achieve similar results in the higher league, consequently, support diminished, and there was talk of possible financial problems. There were still good days... on Saturday 18th January 1930 Rangers beat Morecambe 4-0 at Victoria Park with goals from Lonsdale (2), Rogers and Drummond. The Rangers line-up: Hayes; Gorman, Hitchin; Haggar, Clough, Smith; Lonsdale, Banner, Drummond, Rogers and Bamford. The team finished 1929-30 season in 16th place.

In an effort to raise much needed funds for the club, the Burscough Carnival Gala was organised in 1930 by a newly formed committee. The event took place on Saturday 12th August and the procession left Mart Lane at 2 pm. There were various entries from tradesmen in the form of tableaux, etc., and there were jazz bands and morris dancers from all parts of Lancashire and Cheshire. The streets of Burscough were decorated with carnival bunting, especially in Mart Lane, Orrell Lane, Victoria Street, Lord Street, Stanley Street and Red Cat Lane.

Wigan Borough Reserves were the visitors to Victoria Park on the 20th December for a league fixture. The pre-match mood was sombre:

> The teams turned out with black armlets. Two minutes silence was observed in honour of the ill-fated crew of the R101. 'Jesu, Lover of my Soul', was played on a cornet by Mr. E.Draper of Burscough, but the solemnity of the occasion was somewhat spoiled by the yelping of a dog which ought to have been left at home.

In 1931 a decision was taken that would have a major impact on the future of Victoria Park in years to come. With debts of £250 the Club was now in real danger of folding. Rangers approached the, then, Lathom and Burscough Urban District Council, who agreed to purchase the ground as a playing field for the district. It was arranged with the Playing Fields Association who made a grant of over £200 available for organised games. The council bought the ground from the owners, James Martland Ltd., and the grandstand from Rangers for the sum of £150, then rented the ground back to the club.

On Saturday 7th March 1931, Rangers entertained Manchester Central. 'Skipper' wrote:

> *I was disappointed with the support accorded to Rangers. The gate receipts were £8 18s 6d.*
>
> *The weather was not conducive to the comfort of spectators, and I know that many would prefer to sit beside the fire and listen to the Arsenal game. Still, the Club is deserving of better support. Personally, I don't think people realise the amount of trouble and anxiety which a committee has to shoulder to run a football team, and from what I know it will take a big effort to save Burscough from the fate of Ormskirk, who allowed the Town's club to die, and there is now precious little hope of resuscitating it. A football team helps to put a place on the map, and there is no better way of advertising a township than a successful football club.*

The following week Rangers received a cheque for £150 from the council, as payment for the stand, and a further £100 in recognition of the transfer of James Gorman to Blackburn Rovers. Their debt was effectively wiped out and they were still in business.

[Jimmy Gorman was later transferred to Sunderland for £6,000 and became the first former Burscough player to appear at Wembley in the 1937 F.A. Cup Final against Preston North End.]

The council, as the new owners of Victoria Park, now set about making improvements:

> *They had given the pitch a good brush-harrowing and rolling and it looked perfect. The whole field, right up to the railway, has been enclosed in red painted iron railings, while the playing pitch is to be further enclosed with a fence, which will stop gate-crashers.*

A meeting was called on Wednesday 1st April in the Stanley Institute. Four committee members resigned, which left only three remaining. Mr. W.R.Bridge was appointed president for the eighteenth year in succession. Mr. R.Hampson was appointed treasurer and Mr. Sam Hall, secretary. It was clear by now that the somewhat beleaguered Mr. Hall was virtually keeping the club afloat single handedly by his sheer enthusiasm, and to 'loud applause' he announced that the club would be continuing in the Lancashire Combination next season. Sammy Hall would go on to retain an interest in Burscough football for the rest of his life. He later recalled those days in the Lancashire Combination:

> *I took a team to Lancaster in our Lancashire Combination days, Johnny Baldwin (trainer) was outside right. We won 2-1 and the wage bill for eleven players was £8 10s. Lancaster officials were flabbergasted, just as they were disgusted. They had two forwards at £7. Our professionals were Bill Bennett (£1), Nat Rawlins (15/-), Billy Little (25/-), Archie Kemp (10/-), and if they didn't get paid this week it would do again.*

Also attending that meeting as a guest was Alderman E.Clayton Esq., the secretary of Southport Football Club, and when invited to speak, he strongly advocated that Rangers form a supporters club. Within two weeks a supporters club had been formed with Mr. Geo. Draper appointed chairman, Mr. W.Houghton of Burscough Town, hon. secretary and Mr. Rd. Charnock, the Chemist, hon. treasurer.

1931-32 season commenced with the council having completed more work on their newly acquired ground. Comparisons made by 'Skipper' were impressive:

The playing pitch has been levelled, especially at the left hand corner as you go in, and I think the field is almost as level as a billiard table. I wonder what Everton would give for it, if they could transplant it bodily to Goodison Park. The old dressing rooms across the way have been discarded. The players and referee - now 'robe' in rooms underneath the stands where there are baths, the water for which is heated by geysers.

Financial considerations played a major part in the decision to transfer an F.A. Cup Tie away from Victoria Park in October 1931. Darwen were the opponents and it was reported 'the East Lancashire club at the present time are getting excellent support.' The decision was vindicated as Rangers went to Darwen, drew 2-2, and shared a gate of £65. The Rangers team: Rotherham; Sinclair, Taylor; Potter, Pape, Rawlins; R.Rogers, Downey, Williams, Moon, Cartman. Rangers went back to the Anchor Ground for the replay, but with time running out and the scores level, they missed a vital penalty and Darwen went on to win through by five goals to three. Rangers' misfortune was compounded when Darwen continued their progress that season right through to the third round proper where they were drawn away to the mighty Arsenal, losing 11-1.

On the 10th October 1931 Rangers met Skelmersdale United in a Lancashire Junior Cup Tie, with the Sandy Lane side winning 1-0. It was to be the last ever meeting of the two clubs.

By the end of the month, Rangers were lying bottom of the league and the outlook was looking grim, but they kept battling away and just managed to avoid seeking re-election, finishing in 16th place.

1932-33 season was no better, the team was struggling, players were leaving, and 'funds were none too plentiful.' The Advertiser of 11th May 1933 sympathised:

The Committee of the Rangers will not be sorry that the season has closed. It has been a hard fight all through and the support given by the public in general has not been what it ought to have been. They certainly made a good start but when their players went to other clubs the committee were unable to find capable substitutes. Consequently the Rangers began to lose matches, and as is generally known, the public will not follow a losing team.

The Advertiser sought other possible explanations for the falling support. After a match at home to Southport Reserves in January 1933 they concluded:

The attendance was not very encouraging, but I suppose the attractions of the ice were too great for some of the supporters - and with the canal so handy some could scarce be blamed.

Winters were undoubtedly colder then, but a report of 'a stiff wind coming in from Crabtree' during one match at Victoria Park in April 1933, was an expression that would gain instant recognition amongst present day supporters. The Rangers line-up against Southport was: Wally Holt; Smith, Taylor; Billy Birch, McCaughey, Johnny Porter; Pilkington, Gastall, Kay, Dover, Taberon. That month another Rangers player, Frank Ridings, signed professional for Oldham Athletic.

After a match later in the season which attracted a poor attendance, the Advertiser reporter was now considering that the counter-attractions might lie elsewhere:

The wireless is threatening to kill local football. As long as people are content to sit by their fireside and have the privilege of hearing a first class match they are hardly likely to want to go out and watch their local team.

On Saturday 6th May 1933, Burscough Rangers travelled to play Bacup Borough, losing 3-1. Although they did not yet know it, it was to be their last recorded match in the Lancashire Combination.

The following week a benefit match was held at Victoria Park for Nat Rawlins, who had 'sustained a fractured leg the last season but one.'

The benefit match was between a Rangers past and present team: *Mr. Bobbie Hall of Banks has promised to bring with him Johnny Ball, the clever Sheffield Wednesday centre forward, who will be on the line, and probably 'Dixie' Dean will be on the other.*

Whether the great 'Dixie' ever did tread the Victoria Park turf proved impossible to confirm.

John Berry's pocket book recorded his feelings at the end of that season, words which, even today, powerfully capture the end of a dream:
Very poor season. Poor team, spiritless committee. Public entirely apathetic. A season of miserable records. Looks like the end of a long and distinguished career.

Bert Berry later added:
Season 1932-33 was the last for Burscough Rangers. A great team in their day, Lancs Comb football was too big for them and the once proud club finished in disgrace, heavily in debt.

It seemed the book had been closed on the Rangers, but it was all just a little premature. The fight for survival was set to continue for almost two further years before defeat would finally be conceded. The Annual Meeting was held on the 25th May 1933 and attracted appeals for support in the local paper:

Sir - Permit me through the columns of the Ormskirk Advertiser to advise all members and supporters of Burscough Rangers Football Club to attend the very important Annual Meeting to be held this evening in Sandfords' Cafe at 8.00pm. The Club's future is at stake, and the policy of the Club for next season will be decided. It is not too much to say that tonight's meeting is the most vital

Nat Rawlins, who joined Rangers in 1922 and played for them for 10 years before breaking his leg at Chorley in April 1932. Although it caused him to retire from football, Nat went on to become a well known bowler in the Southport area. Two months before he died at the age of 83 he was up a ladder painting the apex of the house ! Photograph kindly loaned by Nat's daughter, Marlene Guy.

in the history of the Club. If you desire to see football in Burscough next season it is most essential you attend this meeting.

'Ranger'

The meeting decided to continue in the Lancashire Combination as dropping back to the Liverpool County Combination 'would not reduce the wage bill.'

A letter to the Advertiser dated 20th July 1933 summed up the club's desperation in its efforts to survive:

Sir - May I through the columns of your valuable paper, in an attempt to draw attention of your Ormskirk readers to the fact that we of the Bursco' Rangers A.F.C. are attempting to make our club not representative of Burscough Bridge alone, but representative of the whole Ormskirk area.

We realise that Burscough Bridge on its own cannot run a club capable of justifying itself to Lancashire Combination status. Proof of this can be found in the past policy of isolation having been so disastrous financially, as there are debts amounting to £200.

The Club's name has undergone a change from that of Burscough Rangers to the more representative one of 'Bursco' Rangers A.F.C., Ormskirk.' Strange colours will adorn the Victoria Park eleven, black and white striped jerseys with black knickers to match will displace the green and white of past seasons.

Francis Walsh
Sec. & Manager

The change of name was never taken seriously, as newspaper reports continued to refer to the club by its traditional name.

Burscough Rangers began 1933-34 season as members of the Lancashire Combination but after they had played four games, all lost, it became clear they could not carry on. The Advertiser of 21st September 1933 reported:

At a special meeting of the Committee of Burscough Rangers Football Club held on Monday night, it was decided owing to financial stress to resign from the Lancashire Combination of which the Club have been members for the past 6 seasons.

It was considered with a liability by the Club of £200 and no prospects of improvement it was impossible to carry on.

Their final game as members of the Lancashire Combination was a League Cup Tie. Albert Gore, who played in that game, recalled 'we travelled to Fleetwood and played on the old North Euston Ground next to the promenade.' Fleetwood, who were then top of the league, won 1-0. The Advertiser described it as 'Burscough's Glorious Exit.' The team that day: Tyrer; Harry Sinclair, Ted Taylor; Ray Monk, Naylor, Nat Taylor; Keegan, Albert Gore, Jack Ingram, Fred Rogers, Wilf Monk.

On 28th September the Rangers met with representatives of the Liverpool County Combination with a view to entering that competition, but were refused immediate membership. A meeting with the West Lancashire League proved more successful, and they were elected as members. Their first league game was on Saturday 21st October 1933 at Victoria Park against Nelson Reserves, Rangers losing 2-1. Despite the reduced standard at which Rangers were now forced to operate, the game found 'Skipper' of the Advertiser in good spirits:

It is amusing to report the circumstances of the small crowd by the pay box. Excitement must have been high because the fence suddenly gave way, carrying with it some of the Rangers' loyal support.

December found 'Skipper' endeavouring to retain his good humour as he reported on a 2-2 draw at home to Fleetwood Reserves:

It is pleasing to note that there is some enthusiasm, in some particular supporters, who are anxious for the success of the club. It was my misfortune to have to vacate my seat in the press box owing to the fading light and I immediately took my seat in the 'Director's Box' in front of a well known lady supporter, who was frequently telling the players to 'shoot themselves.' The climax was reached when Burscough got an equalising goal, for suddenly I felt my hat leave my head as if a whirlwind had struck. I turned round to see the same lady supporter waving it in the air with the utmost delight. Burscough had equalised and it mattered little that the price of eggs showed a slight decline.

WEST LANCASHIRE LEAGUE
1934-35 SEASON
(up to & inc. Sat. 2nd February 1935)

	P	W	D	L	F	A	Pts
Whittingham	17	12	1	4	74	25	25
Bolton Wanderers 'A'	21	10	5	6	54	33	25
Blackburn Rovers 'A'	18	12	0	6	75	32	24
Chorley Reserves	21	11	0	10	48	23	22
County Mental Hospital	16	10	0	6	70	42	20
Calderstones	12	8	0	4	40	35	16
Lancaster Town Reserves	14	7	2	5	34	35	16
Fleetwood Reserves	16	6	3	7	30	22	15
Burnley 'A'	19	6	3	10	33	53	15
Barnoldswick Town	17	7	0	10	36	55	14
Nelson Reserves	17	6	1	10	35	61	13
Burscough Rangers	**16**	**5**	**1**	**10**	**19**	**44**	**11**
Wigan Athletic Reserves	17	5	0	12	26	59	10
Darwen Reserves	17	3	2	12	31	35	8

Following their late start in the West Lancashire League, Rangers were called upon to play two fixtures on New Years Day of 1934. After travelling to Westhoughton in the morning and winning 3-2, they returned to Victoria Park for an afternoon kick-off against Lancaster Town Reserves. Rangers completed an unique double by winning the second game 2-0 with 'only four team changes' reported.

They continued into 1934-35 season playing mainly as amateurs in the West Lancashire League, but they were now hanging on by a thread. On Saturday 12th January 1935 they travelled to Whittingham to play a West Lancashire League fixture, they lost 9-1, it was reported:

Goalkeeper Wally Holt collapsed in the second half, owing to the intense cold.

The end, when it came, was something of an anti-climax, and rather undignified, after all that had gone before. Tucked away beneath an article on 'Profitable Pig-keeping,' the Advertiser of 21st March 1935 informed their readers:

The inevitable has happened and Burscough Rangers have resigned from the West Lancashire League owing to financial difficulties. This step has been anticipated for a long time and it comes as no surprise. The Committee has been struggling for a long time under a great financial burden, and the real blow came when the Ormskirk Urban District Council took possession of Victoria Park and would not grant a further lease following the Liverpool Challenge Cup game with Northern Nomads.

'The Ormskirk Council charged us £20 per season but they have let the ground to the Lancashire Electric Power Company at the low rate of five shillings per match, which I think is grossly unfair,' said Mr.J.Baldwin, the Secretary of the Club.

For the record, the last game that Burscough Rangers ever played was on Saturday 16th February 1935 at Victoria Park, against Northern Nomads in a fourth round replay of the Liverpool Challenge Cup. Nomads won 3-2 and Rangers final goals were both scored by Jack Crowell of Parbold. To rub salt into the wounds, the following season, the same club, the 'club without a home' who had no real roots in the area, Northern Nomads, were granted the use of Victoria Park as their home ground by the local council!

Burscough Rangers had existed for thirty years, before conceding defeat. Mr. John Berry in 1927 had said that 'the village of Burscough could not support top class football.' Mr. Francis Walsh in 1933 had said 'Burscough Bridge on its own cannot run a club capable of justifying itself to Lancashire Combination status.'

Their pessimism at that time was understandable. They were not to know that within eleven years of the Rangers folding, the aftermath of war would create the climate for a new club to emerge in the village, a club that would go on to attract support and achieve the kind of success that would then have seemed an impossible pipe dream.

BURSCOUGH VICS & LATHOM JUNIORS
1935 - 1941

Following the demise of Burscough Rangers in 1935, attention focused on Burscough Vics and Lathom Juniors, now the two most senior clubs in the area. The derby games between the two were always very competitive affairs which attracted enthusiastic crowds to the Vicarage Field. One such game was a Southport League Senior Division fixture reported in the Advertiser on 3rd December 1936 and played in front of 'a large attendance':

It was a derby game last Saturday when Lathom Juniors defeated Burscough Vics in a Southport League game. There was some robust football and fouls were frequent. The Juniors played the ball with more accuracy than the Vics and the team spirit of the Juniors was a great factor in the success of their side.

Burscough Vics were members of the Southport & District Amateur League from 1931-32 season. In 1933 they won the South Division, beating Halsall 5-2 after a play-off at Haig Avenue, Southport. The Southport League Championship was secured by beating North Division winners, Crossens, in a further play-off. Vics wore maroon shirts with a prominent sky blue 'V' displayed on the front.

The centre forward of that team was Dick Abram. Speaking in 1995, Dick recalled; 'we played on the Vicarage Field which had a cricket pitch as well as a football pitch, there were also tennis courts and there were benches around the ground.' During the Second World War the Fleet Air Arm camp was built on part of the field, and now the houses of Peters Avenue and Christines Crescent occupy the site. Dick still proudly possesses his League winners medal from that season.

SOUTHPORT & DISTRICT AMATEUR LEAGUE (SOUTH DIVISION) 1932-33 SEASON							
	P	W	D	L	F	A	Pts
Burscough Vics	21	14	3	4	85	45	31*
Halsall	21	14	1	6	81	42	29*
Brighton Road	20	12	4	4	46	22	28
Ainsdale	20	10	3	6	67	37	25
Burscough P.C.	20	10	1	9	77	63	21
St. Paul's S.	20	8	4	8	45	52	20
Formby Rangers	20	8	2	10	55	49	18
Birkdale S.E.	20	8	1	11	59	77	17
St. Teresa's	20	6	3	11	44	67	15
Farm School	20	3	5	12	32	72	11
Baptist Tabernacle	20	3	0	17	30	72	6

* Inc. play-off match:

Vics once won two trophies in one day. It happened in 1937 when they kicked off at three o'clock in the afternoon against the Skelmersdale Shoe Company and won the Skem medals and trophy with a 3-1 victory. They'd barely time to get changed before shooting off to Haig Avenue for an early evening kick-off against Banks Rangers in the final of the Southport Victoria Cup. Vics won again, this time by two goals to nil, to make it a day to remember. The Vics line-up that day was: Bob Fisher, Joe Hull,

Burscough Vics 1932-33 Season - Southport & District Amateur League Champions.
Back Row (l to r): Jack Spencer (reserve), Dick Aspinwall, Tom Riley, Fred Davis, Issy Banks, Billy Glover, Harry Leyland, Dick Gaskell (reserve).
Front Row (l to r): Billy Orritt, Peter Gregson, Dick Abram, Jimmy Pye, Joe Aspinwall.
Pictured in front of the Cricket Pavilion on Vicarage Field. Spectators at foreground in pavilion (from left): Jimmy Knowles (Loppy), Bill Baldwin, Joe Hull, Albert Gore, Norman Knowles, Jack Gaskell. Jimmy Langton.
This photograph was kindly loaned by Dick Abram, the Vics centre forward at that time. In 1995, Dick, then aged 84, lived in Mill Lane, Burscough.
Loppy looked a character and apparently he was. His party piece was to jump off the Canal Bridge every Sunday. Dick Holcroft remembers when Loppy was going to join the army. Dick suggested he join the cavalry,
Loppy shook his head, 'if they sound the 'Retreat' there's no way I'm waiting around for any damned horse.'

Johnny Porter, Fred Hankin, Jackie Lawson, Bill Gregson, Doug Eastwood, Les Lyon, Harry Culshaw, Bob Langton and Tiggy Baldwin.

Bill Gregson later recalled: 'We went back to the Junction Hotel to celebrate but it was lemonade only, none of us drank in those days. We trained three nights a week and we were football daft.' Bill Gregson went on to achieve fame as chairman of the 1971 F.A. Amateur Cup winning Skelmersdale United side.

One of Vics' most loyal supporters throughout this period was Jimmy Knowles, known to everyone as 'Loppy.' The mere mention of his name, even sixty years later, invariably brings a knowing smile to the face of all those that knew him. Bob Langton recalled being in the Army and playing for his regiment in some remote part of India.

Opposite: Lathom Juniors circa 1936.
Back Row (left to right): Frank Postlethwaite, Tom Riley, Peter Cheetham, Joe Hankin, Ray Lewis, Tommy Tyrer. Front Row (left to right): Nobby Hall, Harry Vickers, Albert Gore, Jimmy Kirby, Dick Gaskell.
Picture taken at the Skelmersdale Shoe Company Ground. The teams then changed in the Engine Public House. Photograph kindly loaned by Albert Gore, who was living in Walnut Street, Southport in 1996. Albert was a centre-forward, who played with his socks down, and could 'head a ball further than many players could kick it.'

Above: Burscough Vics Reserves circa 1935. Pictured on Vicarage Field.
Back Row (l to r): Tom Gregson, Harry Stazicker, Sammy Bourne, Harry Melling, Harry Sharpe, Dick Gaskell, Dick Baldwin, Edgar Peters, Jimmy Disley, James Vickers. Middle Row (l to r): Roy Peters, Tommy 'Tut' Aspinall, Staniforth, John Harrison, Jack Marsden. Front Row (l to r): Harry Gibbons, Unknown.
Photograph kindly loaned by John Melling, nephew of Harry Melling. John, who lives in New Lane, played for Burscough in the 1960s.

Burscough Vics 1936-37 Season. The team that won two cups in one day. Back left to right: Bill Vart, Billy Walsh, Unknown. Middle left to right: Johnny Baldwin (Trainer), John Porter, Len Bamber (Secretary), Fred Hankin, Joe Hull, Bob Fisher ?, Jackie Lawson, Unknown, Dick Baldwin. Front left to right: Jimmy Knowles, Douggie Eastwood, Unknown, Harry Culshaw, Bill Gregson, Bob Langton, Tom Atherton, Tiggy Baldwin. Photograph kindly loaned by Jimmy Sutcliffe.

During the game he heard someone shouting over to him from the touchline. It was only Loppy!

Lathom Juniors had been founded just prior to the First World War and had played down Wheat Lane in the 1920s. They joined the Southport and District League in 1936-37 season, going on to reach the Victory Cup Final. Nobby Hall scored their only goal as they drew 1-1 with Banks Rangers at Haig Avenue on Wednesday 28th April. The following night Juniors travelled to Russell Road for the replay, but went down to a 3-1 defeat.

Juniors played in black and white striped shirts for many years, but changed their colours to 'royal and scarlet' in 1937.

Victoria Park had been used by Northern Nomads since the Rangers had folded in 1935, however, in 1937 the ground once again became the rightful home to local football when Vics and Juniors moved there from the Vicarage Field. Mart Lane saw an early confrontation between the two local rivals on Monday 31st August 1937 in the first round of the Southport Charity Cup. Lathom Juniors won 2-1, with the teams lining up:

Juniors: Blackledge; Riley, Lewis; Postlethwaite, Rothwell, Kirby; R.Gibbons, W.Gibbons, Crompton, Kavanagh, Lee.

Vics: Cheetham; Hull, Drury; Hankin, Lawson, Gregson; Merritt, Forshaw, Gore, Langton, Jimmy Baldwin.

Burscough Vics 1937-38 Season - Winners of the Liverpool Junior Cup, Victory Cup & Colonel White Cup. Pictured in front of the stand at Victoria Park. At this time there was still a paddock area at the front. Back Row (l to r): Johnny Baldwin (Trainer), Bill Vart (Treasurer), Joe Hull, Tommy Cheetham, Bill Gregson, Billy Drury, Tommy Croft. Middle Row (l to r): Len Bamber (Secretary), Jackie Lawson, Fred Hankin, Albert Gore, Tiggy Baldwin, Bill Forshaw, James Vickers (Committee). Front Row (l to r): Nobby Hall, Jack Gaskell, Joe Travis, Tom Atherton. This photograph was kindly loaned by the Forshaw family.

'Skipper' in the Ormskirk Advertiser, who obviously knew a thing or two about football, wrote after the game in words that were to prove one of the biggest understatements of all time:

The best player on the field, in my opinion, was young Bob Langton, the Vics inside left. He was both clever and determined, and with more experience should develop into a good player.

Albert Gore had left the Juniors to join the Vics. Albert remembers it caused 'a bit of a fuss' at the time as there was so much rivalry between the two teams.

On Saturday 16th October, Vics travelled to Southport to play a cup tie against Holy Family, it was reported 'Burscough Vics were in rampant mood' as they won 15-0, with Langton scoring eight times. Albert Gore scored four, with Billy Forshaw getting two and Bill Gregson the other.

The Ormskirk Advertiser of 11th November 1937 broke the news:

Bobby Langton has joined the professional staff of Blackburn Rovers, and we send him our best wishes and good luck.

Dick Abram recalled the day Bob joined the First Division club. 'He was only 17 at the time and he signed for Blackburn in the boiler house at Ainscough's Mill, I remember being called on to witness his signature.' Blackburn paid Vics a fee of £50. Bob's daughter, Christine, still has her father's first contract with Rovers. Bob was paid '£2 10s per week, plus £1 extra when playing in the Central League team.'

Despite having his playing career interrupted by the Second World War, Bob Langton went on to play 11 times for England, as well as making nearly 400 Football League appearances for Rovers, Preston North End and Bolton Wanderers.

Many of the players with the Vics and Juniors at that time would go on to be involved in the running of the new Burscough club after the Second World War, including Albert Gore, Tom Riley, Joe Hull, George Crabb, Harry Vickers and, of course, Johnny Baldwin.

Vics won the Liverpool Junior Cup in 1937-38 season. On Saturday May 14th they travelled to Bootle to meet Simpson's United in the final:

It seemed like old times last Saturday to see Mart Lane with a crowd and the seven coaches which were making the journey to Bootle to cheer the Vics on to victory

Goals by Jack Gaskell, Albert Gore and Tom Atherton saw them gain a comfortable 3-0 win. The same season they went on to win the Colonel White Cup and the Victory Cup, overcoming Banks Rangers in both finals.

The presentation evening took place at the Stanley Institute on Friday 3rd June 1938 where 'a large crowd of dancers assembled.' The report of proceedings went on:

The cups and medals were presented by 'Wally' Halsall, the former Burscough Rangers footballer, and Jack Westby of the Blackburn Rovers F.C.

The Club's little mascot, Bobby Derbyshire, delighted the large gathering with his singing of the Club's signature tune and also the popular song 'The Little Drummer Boy.' He was given an enthusiastic reception.

Refreshments were daintily served by the Ladies Committee, including Mrs. Lamb, Mrs. Vart, Mrs. Gregson, Mrs. Vickers, Miss Peet, Miss Bridge and Mrs. Prescott.

[Wally Halsall had been a young half-back with Rangers in the early 1930s, before joining Marine for whom he played in the 1932 F.A. Amateur Cup Final (a game for which Wally received two shillings and sixpence expenses less eightpence because he had two drinks on the return journey). He signed professional for Blackburn Rovers in 1935, going on to make more than 50 League appearances for them. Aged 83, Wally was still living in Bootle in 1996.]

Bob Derbyshire, the Vics' mascot at that time, can remember the passion that games between the Juniors and Vics generated. 'On one occasion, Johnny Baldwin and George Crabb even came to blows in front of the grandstand at Victoria Park.'

Lathom Juniors met Vics in a Southport League game on Saturday 9th April 1938. The Vics ran out 3-1 winners, Forshaw, Gaskell and Atherton were their scorers, with Bimpson replying for Juniors. The same week a young centre forward called Wesley Bridge was scoring a late equaliser for Ormskirk Wednesday at Goodison Park in the Liverpool Mid-week Cup Final, but that's another story!

Still in the Southport & District League Senior Division, the two clubs met again at Victoria Park on Saturday 14th January 1939 in front of 'a nice gathering of spectators.' Juniors won 2-1 with goals by Joe Vose and Frank Postlethwaite. In February, Tiggy Banks scored six as Juniors slaughtered Parbold United by fifteen goals to nil.

Meanwhile, Vics met Fleetwood Hesketh in a Colonel White Cup semi-final in April, at Windy Harbour Lane, Birkdale. The antics of the Vics supporters at the game attracted a note of censure from the local reporter covering the game:

The Vics supporters while giving encouragement to their team, overdid it, and could have seen the game just as well from the side of the pitch, instead of crowding on to the pitch around the goals. The game was held up ten minutes, and might easily have been abandoned.

Vics completed a successful season by beating Crossens 3-2 in the Watson-Mosscrop Cup Final at Haig Avenue, with goals by Baldwin, Gaskell, and Gregson, giving them a 3-2 victory. Then, the following week, they again met Crossens at the same venue in the Senior Charity Cup Final, this time honours were shared as the teams drew one goal apiece. Vics 'won the toss for the honour of holding the cup for the first six months.'

Juniors' season was only marginally less successful, finishing as losing finalists in the Victory Cup and winning the Skem Medals competition, beating Rainford North End in the Final.

The Advertiser dated 25th May 1939 reported:

An enjoyable evening was held at the Cambridge Hotel, Burscough last Saturday when the Lathom Juniors held their annual supper and social gathering.

Those present included Counc. E.Pickles, the President of the club, Counc. E.Trigg, a great supporter, Ted Langton, Treasurer, and Joseph Langton, Secretary. Unfortunately the club Chairman Jim Welding was absent due to business reasons.

Afterwards the party indulged in community singing, and interspersed were songs by Mr. Peter Cheetham, and selections and social items by Mr. Ted Stack, who was described as the 'Hoscar Harmonica Wizard.'

This was yet another period remarkable for the absence of any major football representation from the Ormskirk area. Apart from the midweek exploits of Ormskirk Wednesday, the Advertiser's sports pages continued to be dominated by coverage of football in the Skelmersdale and Burscough districts.

In 1939-40 season Burscough Vics took a giant leap forward by joining the Liverpool County Combination and become the latest village club to do battle with the old enemy....Skelmersdale United. Despite the outbreak of war in Europe the County Combination would continue to operate for a further two seasons under increasingly more difficult conditions. 'Junius,' writing in the Advertiser, previewed the forthcoming season:

> Burscough Vics F.C. who will make their debut in the Liverpool County Combination this year, are anticipating a successful season and they have already made one or two important signings with this end in view.
>
> Seddon, whom 'Dixie' Dean, the former Everton star and England centre-forward, took with him to Sligo last season, has been signed.
>
> Tim Briscoe, Harry Welding, and W.Evans, all of Skelmersdale, are among the captures, which

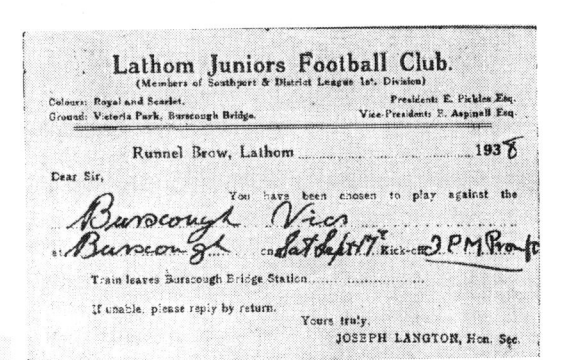

Lathom Juniors pictured at Victoria Park in 1938-39 season. In the background are the two covered entrances from Mart Lane which had been erected by the Burscough Rangers.
Back Row (l to r): Bill (Cocker) Martland, Billy Scanlon, Ted Langton, Bill Gibbons, Tom Riley, George Crabb, Ray Lewis, Unknown, Bob Gibbons, Jack Hurst.
Front Row (l to r): Harry Core, Tiggy Banks, Bill Abram, Jimmy Kirby, Joe Vose.
Photograph and selection card kindly loaned by Joe Vose, who lives at Diglake Farm, Scarisbrick.

also include Jack Rotherham, the former Burscough Rangers goalkeeper, who last season played with Northwich; Sellick, a forward with Marine, and Houghton and Brennan, two players from Dee Joy.

Other players signed include the following: Cheetham (goalkeeper), W.Gregson, H.Armitage (Miranda), and Joe Hull (full backs); Edwards (Orrell), W.Forshaw (Crossens), Tate (Horwich), F.Hankin and Jos. Birch (half-backs); and Atherton, J.Gaskell and Travis (forwards). One or two more important signings are to be made within the next few days.

For Saturday's game at Wargrave, we understand there are still a few vacant seats in the motor coach which leaves the Royal Hotel at 2 p.m.

Mr. T.Bamber is the President of the Club, with Councillor Wm. Martland, Chairman. Mr. Len Bamber is secretary, and Mr. Wm. Vart, treasurer. Mr. Johnny Baldwin is the popular trainer assisted by Ned Gregson, and the Committee is as follows: J.Baldwin, J.Disley, H.Stazicker, T.Gregson, A.Kelly, J.Vickers, H.Prescott, and R.Walmsley.

During the early part of the season Vics played Skelmersdale United twice. On Saturday 30th September 1939 the clubs met at Victoria Park, Skem winning 2-1 in front of a crowd of 'about 1,000.' The following Saturday the two teams met again, drawing three apiece at Sandy Lane.

On Saturday 20th April 1940, Vics entertained Skem in the semi-final of the George Mahon Cup. 'Skipper' was there:

There was quite a 'derby day' atmosphere about Victoria Park on Saturday when Skelmersdale were opposed to Burscough Vics in the semi-final of the George Mahon Cup.

The attendance was quite good but not in keeping with the cup-ties of former days, when the meeting of Skelmersdale and Burscough teams could be relied on to produce receipts of over £40.

The game ended in a 3-3 draw, with Vics captain Billy Forshaw missing a penalty. The Vics team: Rotherham; Briscoe, Holdsworth; Edwards, Gregson, Forshaw; McArdle, Lymer, Hullett, Houghton, Vose. The following week Skem won the replay 4-1 in front of 'nearly 2,000' at Sandy Lane. Skem went on to win the County Combination, with Vics finishing a creditable third.

The war was obviously having its effect and many players had already joined up. A letter to 'Junius' was received from Albert Gore who was stationed at Lille in France 'I have nicely got settled down to the rough conditions here and I am quite happy.' Vics continued to field a team however, and carried on playing in the County Combination the following season.

On Saturday 5th October 1940 Skelmersdale United were again the visitors to Victoria Park. The Advertiser's report of the game by 'Centre Half' made clear that the local population's priorities were now focused elsewhere:

Everything considered both the Burscough Vics and the Skelmersdale United fielded fairly good sides for the first 'Derby' meeting at Victoria Park on Saturday. The Vics turned out as selected but the United were compelled to make a change or two. The ground was, as usual, in excellent condition with a gentle breeze blowing from the Martin Mere goal.

The attendance, particularly at the start, was very thin, but the number increased as the game as the game proceeded.

> But the bulk of the cheering came from the youngsters. Spectators, I suppose are getting beyond being moved by football exchanges.

The game ended in a 2-2 draw, with Seddon and Forshaw scoring for Vics. The home side lined up: Hankin; Banks, Rimmer; Edwards, Gregson, Forshaw; Vickers, Seddon, Cansfield, Travis, Vose. 'Centre Half' went on:

> Welsby the United 15 year-old goalkeeper - a bonny lad - had also a fault. He is too fond of using his feet, when he might with greater advantage make use of his hands. It's a good fault being young, you generally grow out of it.

The difficulty of staging football matches was becoming all too apparent. 'The calls of military service are affecting team selection' was a common observation. For a game at Marine it was reported 'Harry Welding was playing while on leave.' On Saturday 26th October 1940 Vics lost 8-5 to Everton 'A' at Burscough. The Referee failed to appear, so 'Mr. Vart of Burscough undertook the onerous task of refereeing the match.' Marine and St. Teresa's (Norris Green) failed to arrive at Victoria Park for league fixtures due to 'traffic arrangements.' The inevitable began to happen.

The Advertiser of 31st October reported:

> But football is dead now, and though sad to relate it is not surprising to learn that Skelmersdale United have disbanded for the time being.

Sadly, Bob Langton died in 1996 before this book was published. Known more commonly as Bobby Langton during his playing days, he was Burscough's most famous footballing son, winning 11 England caps during a glittering career in League football. Like many of his contemporaries, the Second World War interrupted his career and prevented him winning many more international caps.

This photograph, taken during his time at Bolton Wanderers, epitomises the direct style of wing play for which Bob was renowned. He was always happiest returning to his roots in Burscough and international fame never changed him.

Albert Gore played for Burscough Cricket Club with Bob. He recalls the day Bob learned he had won his first cap against Northern Ireland. He returned from Blackburn by train and went straight to Victoria Park where the cricket was still in progress. 'He never said a word', said Albert. 'We only found out on the wireless that night, but that was typical of him, he never wanted to make a fuss'. Jimmy Aspinall also remembers playing cricket with Bob. 'The Reverend Gadd was playing in our team and Bob came out with a right mouthful in front of him. Bob looked to the sky for forgiveness, but the Vicar never turned a hair.'

An Agreement

made the *Fourth* day of *November* 19*37* between *S. V. Taylor* of *Blackburn* in the County of *Lancashire* the Secretary of and acting pursuant to Resolution, and Authority for and on behalf of the *Blackburn Rovers* FOOTBALL CLUB, of *Blackburn* (hereinafter referred to as the Club) of the one part and *Robert Langton* of *19 Mill Lane, Lathom* in the County of *Lancashire* Professional Football Player (hereinafter referred to as the Player) of the other part **Whereby** it is agreed as follows :—

1. The Player hereby agrees to play in an efficient manner and to the best of his ability for the Club.

2. The Player shall attend the Club's ground or any other place decided upon by the Club for the purposes of or in connection with his training as a Player pursuant to the instructions of the Secretary, Manager, or Trainer of the Club, or of such other person, or persons, as the Club may appoint. [This provision shall not apply if the Player is engaged by the Club at a weekly wage of less than One Pound, or at a wage per match.]

3. The Player shall do everything necessary to get and keep himself in the best possible condition so as to render the most efficient service to the Club, and will carry out all the training and other instructions of the Club through its representative officials.

4. The Player shall observe and be subject to all the Rules, Regulations, and Bye-Laws of The Football Association, and any other Association, League, or Combination of which the Club shall be a member. And this Agreement shall be subject to any action which shall be taken by The Football Association under their Rules for the suspension or termination of the Football Season, and if any such suspension or termination shall be decided upon the payment of wages shall likewise be suspended or terminated, as the case may be.

5. The Player shall not engage in any business or live in any place which the Directors (or Committee) of the Club may deem unsuitable.

Bob Langton's first contract with Blackburn Rovers, dated 4th November 1937, following his signing from Burscough Vics.

> *There is little interest at the present time, and I think the Burscough Vics Committee are to be congratulated on attempting to continue their fixtures in the face of difficult odds.*

When Skem packed up, Joe Vose remembers that 'quite a few of their players came and joined the Vics, including the Pilling brothers.'

On Saturday 15th February 1941 Vics drew 1-1 with Liverpool 'A' at Victoria Park. It was reported 'Fairclough failed to appear, probably due to the 'alert' which sounded a short time before the kick-off'.

Against the odds, Vics battled on, and gained their reward later in the season. On Saturday 29th March Vics played Everton 'A' at Victoria Park. 'Centre Half' was there, and the visit stirred up a few memories for the former player:

> *There were the usual 'old contemptibles' there, it was quite a pleasure to see them again. They have lost none of their old enthusiasm - nor of their professing 'knowledge' of the game! George Merritt sat close by me. He is 75, but he doesn't look it, and I'll gamble he could stick it much longer than many old players twenty years younger. It is many moons since I played against him and longer since I played with Jack Sturgess at New Lane against Burscough one Boxing Day! George had also many years at refereeing. He's a son and grandson who are chips off the old block.*

Vics won the game 5-2 to win the George Mahon Cup, which that season was played on a league basis.

The Liverpool County Combination Championship was to be decided by a play-off between Vics and Liverpool 'A'. The Advertiser of 17th April 1941 previewed the match:

> *A good game is promised for next Saturday on the Skelmersdale United ground when Burscough Vics and Liverpool 'A' play off for the championship of the Liverpool County Combination. Already Vics are the winners of the George Mahon Cup and they are very keen on securing the 'double.'*
>
> *Liverpool's senior team has no match on Saturday so that it is possible a few First Division players may be on view, but in any case the 'A' team invariably have League players in their side.*

Vics clinched the Championship with a 4-0 victory. The trophy was presented to Vics captain Bill Forshaw by the President of Skelmersdale United, Mr. Rd. Forshaw. The Advertiser mischievously went on:

> *Many of the Skelmersdale people present were pleased, but not exultingly pleased, at the result.*

It was a fine way to finish, as Burscough Vics never played again. The games remaining were now comparatively meaningless:

> *Burscough Vics have closed down for the season. Last Saturday they should have played Rootes Athletic away, but owing to transport and other difficulties this was impossible. There were three other games to play, but all three have been cancelled.*

BURSCOUGH FOOTBALL CLUB
1946 - 1996

Burscough Association Football Club was officially formed in 1946, however, the roots of the present club can be traced back just a little further. Bill Vart and Billy Disley entered a team called 'Burscough F.C.' in the Southport & District Amateur League Senior Division in 1944-45 season. They were based at the Stanley Institute and their colours were registered as 'amber and black.' Bill Vart was appointed secretary, with Syd Abram running the team. They opened their fixtures at Victoria Park on Saturday 9th September 1944 against the Civil Service. The following month it was reported that they had beaten Southport Holy Trinity by seven goals to three. The team continued in the Southport League the following season, with a team also being entered in the Junior Section.

Frank Parr recalls the forming of the Burscough Junior side. In 1944-45, he played at Crossens in an under 16 team called Bankfield Minors with, amongst others, Derrick Bradley. As the players became too old for that team so they asked Burscough to form an under 18 team for the older players in the village and also those returning on leave from the forces. A team was entered in the Junior Section of the Southport League for 1945-46 season. John Parr, who later played for Burscough, was then a young supporter of the Juniors. He still recalls that Juniors' side; it was usually picked from: Paddy Moorcroft, Trevor Bridge, John Bromley, Frank Parr, John Rose, Norman Lea, Edwin Castle, Alfie Pemberton, Tommy Bowen, Harry Aindow, Jimmy Harrison, and Stan Gaskell.

Within weeks of starting up, tragedy affected the newly formed team. Burscough Juniors and Ainsdale St. Johns were drawing 4-4 at Victoria Park, the game being described as 'fast, clean football', when the outside right of the Ainsdale club 'fell to the ground, with no-one near him.' A doctor was called and arrived within five minutes, but the young player was declared dead and the game was abandoned.

Late in 1945 an historic meeting was held in the cellar of the Stanley Institute at which the present football club was founded. Dick Holcroft, who became the first secretary, can recall being literally 'dragged off the street' by Johnny Baldwin to attend that meeting. Among those present were; Ronnie Barker, Dick Holcroft, Bill Vart, Johnny Baldwin, Frank Parr, Jack Phillips, Tom Riley and Harry Vickers. Many of those attending had previously been associated with Lathom Juniors and Burscough Vics before the war. It was proposed and agreed that all surviving assets be pooled to form the new club. Jack Phillips voiced his dissent and left the meeting.

Ronnie Barker, at a time when commodities were scarce, proved invaluable by purchasing surplus playing kit for the new team from HMS Ringtail, the Fleet Air Arm camp at Burscough. Ronnie recalls that there was never any question that the team would play in any other colour but green - 'the Burscough colours.'

Frank Parr, then only seventeen years old, was present at that meeting, a member of that founding committee, and now, fifty years later, is Chairman of Burscough Football Club.

Efforts to raise money commenced immediately. Under the heading 'Burscough Football Club,' the Ormskirk Advertiser dated 15th November 1945 carried an advertisement in the front page 'Notices' section:

A dance will be held in the British Restaurant, Friday November 30th 1945, 7.30pm to 12pm. Tickets 2/6 each. Phil Newport (Southport) and his Mayfair Trio.

Early in 1946 the new club went on to hold its first Annual General Meeting at the Cambridge Hotel in Liverpool Road North.

On Thursday 20th June 1946 the Ormskirk Advertiser carried news that Burscough's Derby Cinema was showing Roy Rogers in 'San Fernando Valley,' to be followed by George Formby in 'Turned Out Nice Again.' Deeper into the same edition came news of further efforts to provide much needed entertainment for the war-weary local population:

The Committee of the new Burscough Football Club with the aid of an enthusiastic Supporter's Club, are making great preparations for the coming season. The Club has made application for membership of the Liverpool County Combination and if accepted intend to enter two teams. It is expected that a number of important signings will be made in the next few days. The Supporter's Club has already a membership of over 200 subscribers. Such enthusiasm augurs well for a revival of football in Burscough during the coming season.

Dick Holcroft recalls that, at that time, establishing security of tenure over Victoria Park, which was still owned by the local council, was high on the list of priorities so that much needed work could be carried out on the ground.

Harry Spencer brought his 'horses and harrows' on to Victoria Park to level the ground ready for seeding. Harry's son, Kenny, and Frank Parr can still recall, 'the horses were called Duke and Jipp, they were two Clydesdales belonging to local farmer Tommy Watkinson.'

Burscough Football Club was to have one of the finest playing surfaces in the North West of England over the next fifty years, it would appear that some of the credit may be due to those two long departed shire horses....Duke and Jipp!

Eventually, all was ready, Burscough's application for membership of both a first and second team into the Liverpool County Combination had been accepted, and the Advertiser of 15th August 1946 went on to assess the new club's prospects:

Burscough open their Liverpool County Combination League programme at Victoria Park on Saturday, when the Reserve team entertain Prescot B.I. reserves in a Second Division match on Saturday 31st August. The first team are away in their first game to Prescot B.I.

The following three Saturdays in September will see the first team at home, thus, the public of Burscough will have an early opportunity of according full support to their local club and it is to be hoped they will respond whole-heartedly. Mr. J.P.Sturgess, a great supporter of local football for many years, is the President, Mr. J.Baldwin, who rendered yeoman service to the old Burscough Rangers as trainer, is Chairman, Mr. Dick Holcroft the Secretary, and Mr.

E.Dutton (Cambridge Hotel) Treasurer.

A strong Supporters Club, under the chairmanship of Mr. Jim Vickers, is in being with a membership of over 200, Mr. T.Webster being the Secretary.

The team prospects would appear to be good. The professionals signed include Jack Holdsworth, a full-back of note who played with Fleetwood in the Lancashire Combination, and also played with the old Burscough Rangers. J.Dutton, a prominent Southport player has also been secured for the centre-half position.

Numerous local players have also signed amateur forms, and these include W.Meadow (goalkeeper), J.Rimmer, Mawdesely (right-back), A.Harrison, Burscough (left-back), H.Melling (Burscough), T.Hankin (New Lane), T.Owen (Burscough), Edgar & Roy Peters (Martin Lane), Tiggy Banks (Halsall), all half-backs.

A tall right-half from Liverpool, Geo. Davenport, who has played as a guest player with Cardiff City and Watford, has also been signed together with D.Jones a left-half from Southport and W.McGrae, a Fairfield half-back.

Great things are expected of Jos. Vose, an amateur outside-left from Ormskirk. Arthur Vickers, who gained distinction in services football in India, should be a prominent outside-right. He hails from Burscough. J.Gilbody, a tall Burscough inside-forward has also joined the Club. Wesley Bridge from Maghull will figure at centre-forward, he has dash and skill.

Other forwards to join the Club include H.Gore (Halsall), J.Lowe (Skelmersdale), R.Riding (Burscough), W.Draper (Mawdesley), Jos. Travis (Ormskirk), A.Gore (Burscough) and J.E.Marsh (Lathom).

Burscough Football Club played their first game, a Liverpool County Combination fixture, at Prescot B.I. Social on August 31st 1946. The Advertiser of 29th August previewed the game:

The football loving people of Burscough have a fine opportunity of displaying their interest in the football revival next Saturday when the newly-formed Burscough Football Club open their season in the Liverpool County Combination.

For their first game with B.I. Social at Prescot, on Saturday, Burscough have selected the following team: Meadow; Holdsworth, Dutton; McCrae, Lloyd, Jones; Marsh, Monk, Davenport, Vickers and Vose.

Lloyd played for Shrewsbury Town before the War and gave a good display in the trial game. Marsh played for Skelmersdale last season. Davenport hails from Liverpool and the left wing, Vickers and Vose, are local captures.

The Reserve team are at Victoria Park on Saturday when they entertain B.I. Social Reserves in a Second Division match. A good game is expected and local talent is being given a chance. The team will be: Erickson; Rimmer, Kennedy; Aspinall, Hankin, Greenwood; Bridge, Banks, Tyrer, Draper, Gilbody.

It was hardly the perfect start as Burscough lost the match 5-2, the first goal for the new club being scored by Ray Monk, a former Rangers player. The following week Prescot B.I. were due at Victoria Park for the return fixture:

Burscough supporters are in for a real treat next Saturday, when they will be all out to avenge last week's defeat. Prescot B.I. Social are on view at Victoria

Park and several changes have been made in the Burscough side which is as follows: Meadow; Lloyd, Holdsworth; McCrae, Dutton, Monk; Marsh, Draper, Bridge, Vickers and Vose. Wesley Bridge hails from Maghull and great things are expected of him. The kick-off is 3 p.m.and it is expected a large crowd will be present to greet Burscough's first home game.

Burscough gained their revenge with their first victory by four goals to three. The words about Wesley Bridge were to prove uncannily accurate, as great things were achieved, and he went on to set goalscoring records that still stand to the present day.

The new club's first 'derby' meeting with Skelmersdale United was a Liverpool County Combination Division One fixture on Saturday, November 9th 1946. The game ended in a scoreless draw in front of a crowd of over 2,000 at Victoria Park. Admission was 'less than 1/-,' with gate receipts totalling £85.

Four weeks later in the return fixture another 2,000 spectators were present to see Burscough win 3-1 at Sandy Lane, with three goals by Tommy Saunders (later to become a director of Liverpool Football Club), who had just signed from New Brighton.

The new club attracted tremendous support and interest right from the start. Everyone had an opinion. A letter to the Advertiser, from a supporter using the nom-de-plume 'Green Jersey,' was published in January 1946:

I and many other supporters would like to know why more transport cannot be arranged for away matches. Talk is going around that the seats in the 'bus are for a certain class of people, namely the Committee's relatives, whereas there is no room for the ordinary supporters. If other local clubs can arrange buses for supporters I am sure Burscough can; otherwise they don't deserve support at home or any other place. It's the same old story when you try for a seat 'we are full up.'

BURSCOUGH ASSOCIATION FOOTBALL CLUB
BALANCE SHEET 1946/47

RECEIPTS

	£	s.	d.	£	s.	d.
Balance fwd Season 1945/46				47	3	10
Supporters Club Grant				80	0	0
Season Tickets & Donation				39	1	0
Christmas Draw	17	7	0			
Other Draws	24	15	8			
				42	2	8
Coach Receipts				48	7	0
First Team Gates	357	3	8			
Second Team Gates	93	10	1			
Cup Ties	31	3	11			
Cricket & Football Club (Collection)	3	14	6			
				486	12	2
Refund Southport F.A.				3	0	0
Mr. A.Charnock (Trainers Kit)				1	6	2
				747	12	10

R.H.Holcroft, Hon. Secretary.
E.Dutton, Hon. Treasurer.

PAYMENTS

	£	s.	d.
By Team & Match Exps.	397	1	10
" Referees	19	7	6
" Entertainment Tax	18	15	4
" Trainers Kit & Exps.	27	8	0
" Coaches (Enterprise)	146	10	0
" Playing Outfits	25	3	2
" Ground Exps (Material)	30	4	0
" L'pool County Com. Forms League & Cup Fees	13	7	0
" L'pool County F.A.		15	0
" English F.A. Pro Forms		15	0
" " " Cup 1947/8		10	0
" Lancs Junior Cup	1	2	0
" Lancs County F.A. Fee		2	6
" Printing, Postage, Posters	41	17	0
" Honorariums Secretary	-	-	-
" " Treasurer	-	-	-
" Secretary's Exps.	-	-	-
" Ground Rent	10	0	0
" Treatment for Injured Players	11	9	0
" Cash in Hand	3	5	6
	747	12	10

Audited and found correct
(Signed) R.NICHOLAS
May 8/47

(Signed) GEORGE DRAPER

Green Jersey

The reply from club official Jack Bowen was prompt, forthright, and fairly uncompromising:

> Sir - As a member of the Burscough Football Club committee, I treat with disgust the article written by 'Green Jersey' in last week's Advertiser. The reason more transport has not been arranged for away matches is mainly because transport is difficult to obtain. When transport is available it is worked on a system of 'first come, first served' for a seat.
>
> For instance the other week we managed to obtain two transports to carry 61 supporters to Prescot. Seats were obtainable until 8pm Friday night. Now if 'Green Jersey' and the many other supporters could not find time to reserve a seat from Monday 'til Friday, all I can say that it was sheer neglect on their part. The Committee's relatives are only treated as ordinary supporters and definitely do not receive any special consideration.
>
> J.Bowen

In those early days, many people in Burscough, understandably, saw the club as a re-incarnation of the old Burscough Rangers. One of the stalwarts of Rangers had been Sammy Hall, and, despite then living in Bury, he was a prolific letter writer to the Advertiser on all things connected with Burscough Rangers and the newly formed Burscough Football Club. Writing to the Burscough Football Club committee through the Advertiser, he said:

> Your President was one of the sheet anchors of Burscough Rangers, a name to which they should, and one day will, return.

He referred in his letter to the first president of Burscough Football Club, Mr. John Parr-Sturgess, who had previously been an official of Burscough Rangers. His prediction regarding a change of name has so far proved incorrect, however, Burscough were to have many similarities with the Rangers. They played at Victoria Park, played in green, progressed from the Liverpool County Combination to the Lancashire Combination, and last, but not least, went on to also be called the Linnets.

The grandstand at Victoria Park had been erected by the Rangers in 1926. Sammy Hall reminded the 'new club' just how much they were indebted to the Rangers:

> Has it ever occurred to you to count your blessings? The splendid field on which you play was obtained through the generosity of the directors of James Martland Ltd., coupled with the influence of Mr. John Berry. The rent was £15 a year, and the directors did not expel us when we missed paying it for one season.
>
> You rejoice in a stand that many Third Division clubs would be proud of. The timber came from Everton part of the Bullens Road stand before the double decker was built. County Alderman W.J.Bridge, our President, paid for all of it. We got all of the timber to Victoria Park with an effort. Harry Prescott and I commenced to dig the foundations. Mr. Bridge gave us all the bricks and he also persuaded Ben Turner to lay the bricks. Bricks kept on coming and Ben kept on laying! Later he had the help of two of his joiners Tom Hesketh and Harry Postles. They came willingly along with George Lee, Jim Gore and others. The ladies kept us going in tea - Mrs Chadwick and many whose names I knew not. That stand was built with a cup of tea and a smile - no intoxicants ! The

late John Spencer never failed to give a hand plus his friendly advice, and that stand is a standing monument to voluntary labour.

Johnny Baldwin, your Chairman last year, painted all the metal that adorns the roof, inside and out. Burscough football never had a servant more worthy of the chairmanship. I remember him as a trainer, buying his own commodities, and playing if I was short. Bill Lyons and his friends after 'coaling' ships in the middle of the night used to come in the early morning mixing concrete. The late Jim Harrison finished the job off by painting the name on the front. Billy Martland once found sufficient fencing to go all round the ground. All these men did it because they loved their Burscough football.

In 1947-48 season Burscough made history by winning the Lancashire Junior Cup, the Liverpool Challenge Cup and the George Mahon Cup.

Burscough started off the season, in their first F.A. Cup campaign, with a fine 3-1 win at home to Bangor City. In the next round, Rhyl were the visitors to Victoria Park, but the Welshmen proved too strong, winning 3-0. Goalkeeper Bill Meadow, who at the time of writing lives in Burscough's Mill Lane, recalled the disadvantages of being a local player, particularly a goalkeeper, playing in front of such large crowds. There were over 2,000 spectators present at the Rhyl cup tie and he still remembers, 'the sun got in my eyes and a shot went over my head and into the net for one of their goals. It was weeks before I could show my face in the village again.' Two weeks later he was replaced for a league fixture at Ellesmere Port by Harry Sutton. Bill kept a straight face as he recalled that Burscough lost that game 8-2! Bill Meadow was an amateur, but admitted to occasionally finding 'five shillings in my boot.' Meanwhile, Harry Sutton recovered from that disastrous start to go on and become a regular member of the most successful team in Burscough history.

In the Lancashire Junior Cup Final Burscough met Fleetwood at Broomfield Road, Blackpool. The Advertiser of 11th March 1948 previewed the game:

Burscough, who meet Fleetwood in the final of the Lancashire Junior Cup at Blackpool on Saturday next have very rightly been described as 'the Pride of Burscough' and their record is indeed a noteworthy one.

It is interesting to note that the last time Burscough had such a successful run was in 1914-15 when the old Rangers went 20 games without defeat. They will be out to equal that record next Saturday against Fleetwood. There will be a fleet of motor coaches and special trains conveying over 1,000 supporters to Blackpool, so they will not be without support.

The following week the Advertiser reported on Burscough's triumph by two goals to one:

Enthusiastic scenes were witnessed at Blackpool on Saturday last when Burscough and Fleetwood met in the final of the Lancashire Junior Cup. The club colours - green and red respectively - were much in evidence and there were rattles, bells, and whistles and the like, truly a typical cup final scene. The glorious weather attracted a large crowd, Burscough having at least 2,000 supporters from their own village and locality.

Fleetwood, led by their little mascot were first to take to the field amidst a round of cheers and applause, but this was nothing to the enthusiasm which greeted the Burscough team as they came out led by their popular captain, Joe

Two action shots from the Lancashire Junior Cup Semi-final at Victoria Park on Saturday 14th February 1948. Burscough beat Barrow Reserves 2-0, with goals by Alan Woolley and Frank Postlethwaite, on the way to winning Lancashire's premier non-league competition. Photographs kindly loaned by Jimmy Aspinall.

Above: Against the backdrop of a packed Mart Lane end, Jimmy Aspinall at full stretch in a tussle with a Barrow forward.

Below: Goalkeeper Harry Sutton in action following a Barrow corner kick.

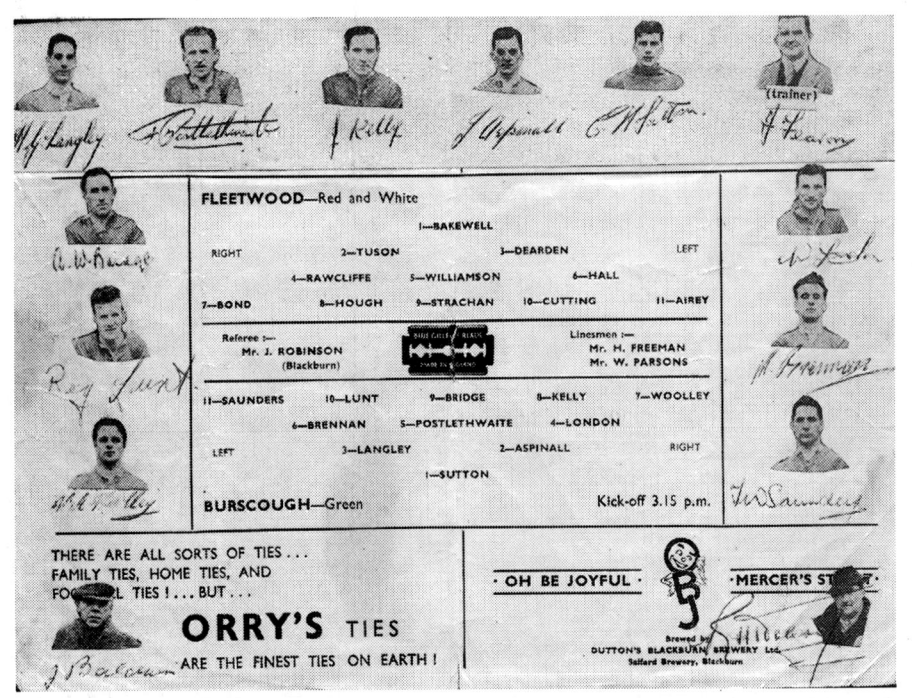

```
FLEETWOOD—Red and White
                    1—BAKEWELL
RIGHT    2—TUSON        3—DEARDEN        LEFT
      4—RAWCLIFFE   5—WILLIAMSON   6—HALL
7—BOND      8—HOUGH   9—STRACHAN   10—CUTTING   11—AIREY

Referee :—                         Linesmen :—
Mr. J. ROBINSON                    Mr. H. FREEMAN
  (Blackburn)                      Mr. W. PARSONS

11—SAUNDERS   10—LUNT   9—BRIDGE   8—KELLY   7—WOOLLEY
        6—BRENNAN   5—POSTLETHWAITE   4—LONDON
LEFT    3—LANGLEY        2—ASPINALL        RIGHT
                    1—SUTTON
BURSCOUGH—Green                     Kick-off 3.15 p.m.
```

THERE ARE ALL SORTS OF TIES...
FAMILY TIES, HOME TIES, AND
FOOTBALL TIES!... BUT...
ORRY'S TIES
ARE THE FINEST TIES ON EARTH!

· OH BE JOYFUL ·   · MERCER'S ST... ·

Brewed by
DUTTON'S BLACKBURN BREWERY Ltd.
Salford Brewery, Blackburn

The Official Programme line-ups for the Lancashire Junior Cup Final at Bloomfield Road, Blackpool on the 11th March 1948. The programme has been autographed by the most successful team in the history of Burscough football.

Kelly. Burscough's team: Sutton; Aspinall, Langley; London, Postlethwaite, Brennan; Woolley, Kelly, Bridge, Lunt and Saunders.
After 21 minutes Fleetwood took the lead. Rawcliffe gained possession and swung over a lovely centre which Airey hit first time into the net giving Sutton no chance. There were jubilant scenes when Burscough got the equaliser in the 34th minute. Brennan worked the ball well and transferred to Joe Kelly, who put in a great shot from about twenty yards into the top of the net.
Half-time: Burscough 1, Fleetwood 1
The Burscough goal had a lucky escape in the first minute on resuming, Postlethwaite almost putting through his own goal. Burscough went ahead after 50 minutes, Bridge took a header from Lunt and his hard shot was diverted and deceived Bakewell, and to make sure Woolley ran up to help the ball in the net. A typical Hampden Park roar greeted the Burscough success. As the final whistle blew swarms of Burscough supporters swept the players off their feet and carried them shoulder high to the Director's box where Councillor S. Pilkington presented the Cup.
Result: Burscough 2, Fleetwood 1
Attendance: 6,726
Gate receipts: £563
Frank Parr recalls 'there was a special train ran to Blackpool with 15 coaches, all full. When we returned with the Cup I can remember Emma Vickers standing outside

the Methodist Church playing her concertina and everyone was singing.' The local paper further described the after match celebrations and the scenes in the village on the team's return:

> *When shall the glory fade! Hats off this week to proud Burscough, who last Saturday brought glory and honour to the Liverpool County Combination and South West Lancashire by winning the Lancashire Junior Cup for the first time in their history.*
>
> *And never was there so much enthusiasm displayed by a Burscough sporting public. Last Saturday the special train took no fewer than 500 to Blackpool and there were well over twenty motor coaches from Burscough alone.*
>
> *After the match milling crowds made their way back to Burscough, there to gather in ever increasing numbers in the centre of the village between the two bridges, and as the motor coach approached tumultuous cheering and wild scenes of enthusiasm were witnessed. Players and officials rode on top of the motor coach through the thronged village, holding the Cup aloft and later returned to their headquarters at the Cambridge, where men have been known to meet!*

The team had now gone 20 games without defeat, equalling a record set by

The treble-winning side of 1947-48, pictured with, from left to right: Liverpool Challenge Cup - Lancashire Junior Cup - George Mahon Cup
Back left to right: Harry Vickers, Jimmy Aspinall, Harry Sutton, George Langley, Frank Parr
Middle left to right: Jimmy Langton, George Crabb, Tom Riley, Albert Gore, Wilf London, Frank Postlethwaite, Matt Brennan, Jack Bowen, Teddy Dutton (Treasurer), Edwin Eastwood, Evan Rimmer
Front left to right: Jack Fearon (Trainer), Dick Holcroft (Secretary), Alan Woolley, Grant, Wesley Bridge, Terry Bowen (mascot), Joe Kelly, Johnny Buckley, Johnny Baldwin (Chairman).
Photograph was kindly loaned by Mr. R.H. (Dick) Holcroft, the first Secretary of Burscough Football Club in 1946. At the time of writing, Dick lives in Briars Brook, Lathom.

Burscough Rangers in 1913-14 season. Frank Parr remembers 'they were due to face South Liverpool Reserves the week after they won the cup, but the Liverpool side got held up at Aintree races and failed to arrive.' Burscough lost their next game and the record remained intact.

A month later it was off to South Liverpool's Holly Park ground for the final of the George Mahon Cup, but only after coming back from a three goal half-time deficit in the semi-final at Ellesmere Port Town. On Saturday 10th April 1948, in front of 4,280 spectators, 'The Greens' beat Earlestown 2-0, with goals by Woolley and Buckley:

The Trophy was presented at the close of the match to Joe Kelly, the Burscough skipper, by Mrs. Garner, daughter of the late George Mahon. Afterwards the Burscough team and officials adjourned to the Grafton Rooms, Liverpool for their well deserved victory dinner. On return to Burscough they were again accorded a warm reception by enthusiastic supporters. The team toured the village in a motor coach and returned to Victoria Park which, in the meantime, had been floodlit for dancing, arrangements being made by Mrs. Vickers, with the loudspeaker arrangements kindly supplied by Mr. Roberts.

8,046 spectators were present at Haig Avenue, Southport on Saturday 8th May 1948 when Burscough won their third trophy of the season by beating Skelmersdale United 4-1 in the final of the Liverpool Challenge Cup. Wesley Bridge scored a hat-trick and again the people of Burscough turned out in force to greet this all conquering team:

It was pleasing to note the enthusiasm which greeted the special coach containing the Burscough team, and their wives and sweethearts, when they returned to the village just before 10 o'clock, following their latest cup victory. Large crowds assemble in the village an hour before the team and officials,

Burscough 7 Ellesmere Port Town 0 - Saturday 6th March 1948. Action from the Liverpool County Combination fixture at Victoria Park. Watched by some young supporters in the foreground, Harry Sutton safely gathers the ball as Matt Brennan looks on. Wesley Bridge scored four of the goals.

This priceless photograph, kindly loaned by John Parr, shows a formidable group of Burscough supporters in Mart Lane ready to travel by Blakemore's Coaches to a cup tie, almost certainly in 1947-48 season. The youngsters at the front are left to right: Roy Halsall (with rattle), Kenny Spencer, Eddie Lawson, Ellis Bracegirdle. Stood behind are, from the left: Unknown, Unknown (with child), Unknown, Marlene Dawson, Gladys Spencer, Mrs. Suffell, Harry Prescott (with cap), Mrs. Fairhurst, Mrs. Aspinall (with famous bell), Nellie Halsall, Nellie Bracegirdle, Alice Walmsley (white shoes), Elsie Forshaw, Bob Forshaw, Mrs. Bracegirdle, Harry Walmsley, Hughie Glover (hidden), Alice Parr, Tommy Dutton, Jim Parr, Bertha Prescott, Bill Martindale. Mildred Disley may be one of the young ladies at the back. The youngsters look like they have been hurriedly tidied up especially for the photo - look at their knees! Kenny Spencer went on to play for, and manage, Burscough. Eddie Lawson became a committee member.

and cheers upon cheers greeted them as they rode slowly through the main thoroughfare to the Club's headquarters at the Cambridge Hotel.

Mr. Dick Holcroft, the Club's popular Secretary, paid tribute to the fine team spirit which had carried the club through one of its stiffest challenges to win the Liverpool Challenge Cup for the third time in the history of Burscough football.

Looking in on this scene of triumph and jubilation was one to who the Club owes much - Mr. Jack Fearon the trainer, who has been largely responsible for moulding together a team which will go down in the history of Burscough football.

Later the team went down to Victoria Park which had been floodlit for dancing to a radiogram, and here large crowds assembled. Speaking through the microphone, Joe Kelly, the popular skipper, thanked the players for their fine spirit, thanked the officials and supporters, and concluded with the words 'the enthusiasm of Burscough wants some beating.'

Wes Bridge also spoke and paid tribute to his colleagues, whose great work had enabled him to score 70 goals during the season. Tommy Saunders added his tribute and spoke of the debt owed to the women-folk who had sacrificed so much for the welfare of Burscough football.

A beautifully iced cake bearing an exact replica of Victoria Park, complete with stands, goalposts and markings, and with the names of all the players, was on view courtesy of Mr. Harry Dickinson.

Wesley Bridge later recalled this as his greatest ever game having scored 'three beauties' to take his total to a record breaking 70.

Burscough's senior citizens still recall the names of those players with pride and affection, they can usually recite the team as quickly and easily as their ten times table.

The club's Annual Meeting was held at the Village Hall in Lord Street on Friday 4th June 1948. Not surprisingly, after such a momentous season, 'over 200 members and supporters attended.'

The club president Mr. J.P.Sturgess presided, supported by Mr. J.Baldwin (chairman), Mr. R.H.Holcroft (hon. secretary) and Mr. E.Dutton (hon. treasurer). Mr. Holcroft reported to the meeting 'Wesley Bridge scored 43 league goals and 14 cup goals with the first team, he also scored 13 goals with the Reserve team.' He paid tribute to the club's trainers Mr. Jack Fearon and Mr. Gregson. He expressed appreciation of Mrs. Morris for her fine work in connection with the club's laundry, the Supporters Club for the grants they had made to the club, and a special word of thanks to Mr. Joe Halsall and his helpers.

Mr. E.Dutton submitted the balance sheet which showed the club started the year with a balance of £3 5s 5d and finished with a total balance in hand of £594 3s 4d. League gate receipts amounted to £742 16s 9d compared with £357 3s 8d the previous year.

1948-49 season started off in much the same fashion with an incredible 35 goals being scored in the first five league matches, including a 10-0 win over Cromptons Recs. The 3-1 league victory over Skelmersdale United in September attracted an estimated 3,800 spectators to Victoria Park, but October saw a dramatic reversal in fortunes, as the team conceded nine goals at Earlestown, then eight goals at Formby.

Bangor City gained revenge in the F.A. Cup with a 4-2 victory, it was reported that 'over 20 coaches' travelled to North Wales. One game during this spell was a 2-1 defeat at Hoghton Road against St. Helens Town. Jim Barrett, in later years the St. Helens chairman, remembers the match well; 'there were 3,018 spectators at that game, in goal for us was a former German prisoner-of-war called Bert Trautmann.'

As results deteriorated so there were rumours of unrest at the club. 'Junius,' in his Advertiser column of 11th November 1948, reported on the 'first stirrings of discontent':

Team spirit is sadly lacking, and I only hope something has been done this week to bring matters to a head. The principle of allowing players to dictate who will play and who will not is not one to be encouraged. There are all kinds of silly rumours going round the village, and I personally would welcome a statement to the effect that many of these are untrue. I would venture to suggest in a true spirit of helpfulness that a Committee of 12 or 14 is far too big to select a team, three, or five at the most are sufficient.

Matters did come to a head. Following comments on team selection, players Postlethwaite and Brennan were expelled from the Club, action that was described as 'far too drastic' in the local press. Frank Postlethwaite admits to several disagreements with club officials. 'It was always more difficult for us local lads to get selected for the first team.' Although local, Frank insists he wasn't a 'villager' - 'I was from Burscough Town!'

1949-50 season brought the first meeting with the mighty Wigan Athletic, then the giants of North West non-league soccer. The occasion was the first qualifying round of the F.A. Cup at Springfield Park. The Burscough programme from the previous week's game with Bootle Reserves detailed the arrangements:

In the next round of the F.A. Cup we meet Wigan Athletic, at Wigan, and the railway authorities have arranged a special train to leave Burscough Bridge at 1.50 p.m. (return ticket, 2/1).

The Club have been allocated 75 stand tickets at 3/- each, and these will be on sale from the Club Secretary or Treasurer after to-day's match.

Burscough were eliminated after a replay at Victoria Park, played in front of 4,128 spectators. Admission to the ground was one shilling with an extra sixpence charged for a seat in the grandstand, the gate receipts totalling £215 7s. Burscough's share of the gate was £93 12s 6d, with Wigan receiving £96 2s 6d. The two ties had been watched by over 11,000 people.

The team were not downhearted, however, as they went on to secure two more trophies that season, when they won the Liverpool County Combination Division One Championship and the Lancashire Junior Cup for the second time, by beating Nelson 2-1 at Ewood Park, Blackburn.

Bob Derbyshire particularly remembers the crowds that travelled to Blackburn. 'At five o'clock that evening you couldn't get through the village, there were so many coaches about.'

Burscough's captain Gilly Houghton was presented with the Cup and forty five years later he recalled that day:

I didn't think we could win this game - until we entered the dressing rooms at Ewood. There we found the Nelson team sitting round a stove, eating meat pies. I thought 'if we can hold them for an hour, those meat pies may lie heavy, and we'll nick a goal in the last quarter.'

Some rare footage of the great Wesley Bridge in action. A crowd of 2,500 was at Victoria Park on Saturday 14th January 1950 to see Burscough beat Stubshaw Cross Rovers 5-0 in the third round of the Lancashire Junior Cup on the way to winning the trophy for the second time. The goalscorers were Bridge, Penkeyman, Jones, Bergin and London.
Above: Bridge challenges for a high ball, with Joe Kelly following in.
Below: Wesley beats a defender to the ball and that magic left boot gets in a shot on target.

Above: A packed Victoria Park watches as Bridge gets in a header on goal, with Harry Bergin to the right of the picture. Below: Bridge again involved in a goalmouth tussle. Also pictured (from left), Bergin, Kelly and Harry Penkeyman. Frank Postlethwaite remembers, 'Wesley came off the field after every game black and blue, but he never complained. He used to score goals from the most incredible angles.' These four photographs were kindly loaned by Frank Walmsley, who can still picture Harry Penkeyman always playing with a handkerchief in his hand - Jim Aspinall reckons he picked up coins from the ground and wrapped them in it!

More action from the same match. Jimmy Aspinall appears to have made an effective tackle on a Rovers forward, with (from left) Chris Lynn, Gilly Houghton, Harry Sutton, Bill Morris, Harry Bergin and Wilf London, also pictured.

The background belies the semi-rural setting of Victoria Park. The goods trains in the railway sidings at Burscough Bridge Station can be seen, with the skyline dominated by the cake factory of I.H.Lavery & Co.

The same view is now equally dominated by the massive new premises of Westbrook Packaging.

Photograph courtesy of Jim Aspinall.

In the event the team played really well and went in at half-time leading 1-0, courtesy of Wesley Bridge's left boot. Unfortunately Wesley was carried off concussed, and at half-time he was still out to the wide on the dressing room table.

There were 15,000 at Ewood that night, and when Nelson equalised their supporters let off a frightening din, but Joe Simpkin picked me off the ground and shouted 'remember those meat pies!' A roar from the Burscough end greeted the emergence of Wesley Bridge from the tunnel. He was still only half-right, but we pointed him towards the Nelson goal - his half-dazed condition seemed to distract Johnston, the Nelson centre half. Wesley rounded him and slotted in the winner. Looking towards the Burscough side of the ground I saw a red-headed Dervish called Lawson doing a war dance in the paddock, to the sound of a bell being rung by Jimmy Aspinall's mother!

Ever since that night I've always had a soft spot for Holland's meat pies!!

12,077 spectators paying £845 were actually reported present as the Burscough captain accepted the trophy:

Gilly Houghton, with justifiable pride, stepped forward to receive the handsome trophy. In a sporting speech he thanked the Burscough supporters and also their 'enemies' in Liverpool County Combination championship circles, but friends in cup tie football for their support.

On their return to the dressing room, the players were besieged with jubilant and admiring Committee men and supporters. The Cup was filled and the players drank 'toasts' of happiness and success.

The team arrived back in Burscough by motor coach shortly after half past ten and an enthusiastic crowd gave them a great reception, waving green and white colours and streamers and sounding victory bells and rattles.

They proceeded to Victoria Park which was floodlit and the admiring throng gathered by the stand to cheer the players

Burscough's team at Ewood Park: Harry Sutton; Jimmy Aspinall, Chris Lynn; Wilf London, Bill Morris, Gilly Houghton; Harry Penkeyman, Joe Simpkin, Wesley Bridge, Joe Kelly, Stan Jones.

After a distinguished 'career' as a player and as a football administrator, Wesley Bridge recalled in later years 'I went to Burscough in 1946 and won the Lancashire Junior Cup twice in three years. I am specially proud of those two cup winning medals, I don't think many amateurs have got two Junior Cup medals to their credit.'

Gilly Houghton later paid this tribute to his former team-mate:

Wesley was a centre forward of the old fashioned style. Most of his goals were scored with his left foot - his right one was strictly for standing on. Legend had it that his right foot had been severely damaged by frost bite during the War. He was quite happy to let that story circulate until someone suggested it was the 1914-18 war!

In what turned out to be his last game of football, he scored a hat-trick in the first half and broke his leg in the second - he never played again.

This was undoubtedly the golden era of Burscough Football Club, attendances of one to two thousand were common, the whole village followed the club's fortunes, the team was successful, and they had a ground that, even then, attracted much favourable comment. Away support was incredible, a week after winning the Lancashire Junior

Cup, a vital league game at South Liverpool attracted 'at least 15 coaches from Burscough, also coaches from Ormskirk and possibly from Skelmersdale.'

At the start of the 1950-51 season the club announced:

Mr. Jack Berry, of Orrell Lane, who has done such good work on the ground, has been appointed an honourary Life Vice-President of the Club in appreciation of his services and also as a tribute to his long connection with football in Burscough in years gone by.

On Saturday 14th October 1950, Burscough entertained Skelmersdale United in the second qualifying round of the F.A. Cup. A crowd of 3,526 paid £168 to watch the game. The match programme asked for supporter's co-operation, as work on developing Victoria Park to cope with crowds of this magnitude gathered pace:

As the Committee are anxious that the work on the covered erection behind the Crabtree end goal should be commenced on Monday a portion of the ground has been roped off. Spectators are asked to keep on the right side of the ropes and refrain from encroaching on the ground which has been reserved behind the goal.

Burscough won 3-2 and were rewarded in the next round, two weeks later, with a home tie against Wigan Athletic. The Liverpool Daily Post of Saturday 28th October 1950 was in expectant mood:

Burscough F.C. have a score to wipe off today, when they oppose Wigan Athletic in the third qualifying round of the F.A. Cup at Victoria Park, Burscough.

The teams met last October in the first qualifying round and Wigan won 5-1 at Burscough, after 2 goals had been shared at Springfield Park the previous week. The total gate receipts for the two games amounted to £559 18s, and a crowd of about 11,000 witnessed them.

The 4,128 spectators who saw the replay was a record for Victoria Park, the gate receipts of £215 7s also being a record. Since then substantial improvements have been effected. Covered accommodation has been increased and it is estimated that a capacity crowd of at least 6,500 people will be present today. Though their County Combination record so far this season is not very convincing, they have lost four of their six games - they have a reputation for being cup fighters. Their team will include 10 of the 11 players which last season equalled a club record of 20 games without defeat.

Their team today will be: Sutton; Aspinall, Lynn; London, Morris, Houghton; Woolley, Bergin, Bridge, Kelly, Jones.

Burscough lost the game 2-0, but a record 4,798 spectators paying £280 were present at Victoria Park that day, still, and likely to remain, the ground record. Jim Bridge, then a young supporter, remembers 'there were so many there, I couldn't see a thing.' Frank Parr is convinced there was more like 6,000 on the ground that day, as they just couldn't cope with the numbers. 'All the club officials were walking round with their pockets stuffed full of money, there was nowhere else to put it!'

It is difficult to comprehend nearly fifty years later, but over four consecutive Saturdays that month, in excess of 13,000 spectators paid to pass through the Mart Lane turnstiles! Ronnie Barker, by now secretary of the club, claimed he was able to tell by looking around the ground what the gate was 'to within five or ten pounds.'

Christmas of 1950 brought one or two minor irritations. Before the Lancashire Junior Cup tie with Cromptons Recs at Victoria Park could be played local farmers had to be called in to remove snow from the playing surface - one advantage of a rural location! The league game away to Formby had to be contested without captain Wilf London who would not play on Christmas Day.

In February 1951, Victoria Park, which had been bought by the local council in 1931 was offered to the club for a sum of £400. The club negotiated and agreed to buy the ground, with the grandstand included, for this sum. It was, without doubt, the shrewdest day's business in the history of Burscough football. A special fund was set up and on Monday April 30th 1951 Liverpool sent a team to Victoria Park to help raise funds for the purchase of the ground. A gate of £45 was taken as Liverpool easily won the game 5-1.

Not every ground visited measured up to the standard of Victoria Park. Every visit, every season, to Haydock led to the travelling Advertiser reporter describing the ground as 'like a slag heap.' In fact the ground was on a slag heap, it had quite a slope and when they tried to level it they ran into serious drainage problems, but as one proud 'Yicker' from Haydock said 'I've seen Pongo Waring playing on there so it can't be that bad.'

On Wednesday 28th February 1951, Huddersfield Town came and signed Arthur Green. 'I was straight on the phone to their chairman,' recalls Ronnie Barker. A £50 donation from Huddersfield quickly followed! However, Arthur Green would later return to Victoria Park and give many more years service to Burscough.

The season ended with yet another trophy, the Liverpool Challenge Cup. 'Sportsman,' in the Advertiser, reported:

Burscough rang down the curtain on football season 1950-51 on Whit Monday morning when before a crowd of 3,000, who paid £170, they defeated St. Helens Town in the Final of the Liverpool Challenge Cup at Springfield Park, Wigan. The 3-1 victory over St. Helens was well deserved, indeed but for a masterly display by Booth, the St. Helens goalkeeper, the margin would have been much bigger.

Wilf London the Burscough skipper said he was glad they had won 'they were the better side without a doubt.' After having lunch at Parbold the players were given a warm reception when they arrived at Victoria Park.

Burscough: Sutton; Stone, Lynn; London, Morris, Brennan; Aspinall, Kelly, Woods, McGrail and Waugh.

Burscough's goals were scored by Aspinall, Kelly and Woods.

For a Liverpool County Combination fixture at home to Liverpool Police on 29th March 1952, Burscough started with only nine men due to the non-arrival of players. After ten minutes a local goalkeeper, Edwin Cliffe from the Ormskirk League, who was attending the game as a spectator, was brought on to play on the wing. Burscough won the game 6-3 and Cliffe scored two of the goals. He never played for Burscough again.

At the club's A.G.M. in June 1952 it was reported that donations of £165 from the Supporters Club, £165 from whist drives, and £50 from Huddersfield Town, had been received. Ground expenses were £185 5s 8d, and £40 had been paid towards the new Crabtree stand. The starting balance had been £118 5s 5d and the closing balance £12 6s 7d. The financial situation was thought 'quite satisfactory considering that the stand had been bought for £400.' £360 had been received towards the Ground Appeal Fund from whist drives, dances and donations. Club officials included Jimmy Johnson, chairman; George Crabb, treasurer; and Ronnie Barker, secretary.

Jimmy Johnson was following in the footsteps of his father, Bill Johnson, who had been chairman of Burscough Rangers in the 1920s.

Ronnie Barker remembers that his devotion to the club often landed him in hot water at home. 'I nearly got chucked out a couple of times, as I was always in Liverpool with Jimmy Johnson, looking at players. By the time I got home my Sunday dinner was often ruined.'

'I remember a game at Skem, where one of our supporters had a swipe at the referee after the game. We were brought up in front of the County F.A., who were determined to find out who the guilty party was. I told Ike Robinson I hadn't seen a thing. I can still remember him looking me straight in the eye and saying, 'Come on Barker, you little bugger, you know who did it', but I stuck to my story.'

Attendances were still impressive, even for the Reserves. Burscough Reserves played Skelmersdale United Reserves at Sandy Lane in September 1952, with 'slightly under 600' spectators present. It was reported that 'it was a pity that rain had marred the attendance.'

On Wednesday 15th October 1952 Burscough played their first game under floodlights when they lost 3-0 to Bootle at Seaforth Stadium.

In November of that year a young centre forward was promoted from the reserves to make his first team debut. Burscough won 8-0 against Southport Trinity in the first round of the Liverpool Challenge Cup. The debutant, Louis Bimpson, scored seven of the goals. The Ormskirk Advertiser was there to record another slice of club history:

Burscough opened the scoring after about 6 mins. Pilson weaving his way down the right and cut in and kicked at goal. Todd half charged the shot down but Bimpson racing in put a pile-driver into the roof of the net.

Goal number two came after 20 mins., and it was a beauty. Bimpson intercepted and dashed past bewildered defenders, beating them with effective body swerves to crash the ball into the net.

Burscough went further ahead 14 mins. from the interval. Bimpson gathered a pass from the right, raced goalwards, and completed his hat-trick, with a shot which gave Todd no chance.

Stan Jones scored the fourth after about 12 mins. This was a goal that came as a result of some unselfish passing. Stan shot well with his left foot from an oblique angle.

Goal number five came from another burst of speed by Bimpson who beat Todd from ten yards.

Bimpson netted again with a smashing right-footer.

After Pilson had done good work, Bimpson completed his second hat-trick.

Not long before time Bimpson scored his seventh goal and Burscough's eighth.

Another Bimpson goal came at the Bootle Stadium on the 17th January. Burscough had travelled to play Bootle Reserves in a County Combination fixture, they won 3-2, aided by a goal that few who witnessed it will ever forget. Jack Hillier, the home 'keeper, drove a goal kick hard and low direct at Louis who managed to get his head in the way of the ball, which cannoned straight back into the net with Hillier stranded.

By the time Burscough played Crossens in the third round of the same competition on Saturday 24th January 1953, Bimpson had scored 22 goals in 13 games. Another two came that day in the presence of scouts from Blackpool, Bolton and Blackburn, as well as Liverpool.

The Advertiser of 29th January 1953 reported:

An important meeting was due to take place in Ormskirk last night, when it was arranged that Louis Bimpson, the 21-years-old Rainford-born Burscough centre forward should sign full-time professional forms for Liverpool.

A motor mechanic, Bimpson was discovered by Burscough when he played in the Skem medals competition last year for Rainford North End for whom he played in the Ormskirk and District League.

As a result of his signing, Burscough will receive a gift of £500 from Liverpool Football Club. They will also receive a further £250 if he plays ten Central League games, with a further £500 if he plays in ten first team games.

[Louis Bimpson went on to play 94 Football League games for Liverpool, scoring 39 goals. In 1959 he joined Blackburn Rovers and appeared for them in the 1959-60 F.A. Cup Final at Wembley. His career also included spells with Bournemouth and Rochdale. During his career he played a total of 181 Football League matches, scoring 61 goals].

Before the season had finished, Liverpool had paid a further £250 for captain and right-half Bill Parker. In March, Billy Pilson joined Stoke City for £300, and in April Billy McLean became a professional with Blackburn Rovers for £300.

On Monday 16th March 1953 the decision was made to apply for membership of the Lancashire Combination:

Burscough Football Club decided at a meeting on Monday night to make immediate application for entry next season in the Lancashire Combination. The Committee felt that there was a need for an improved standard of opposition bringing with it more enthusiastic support from individual clubs. At the moment only Skelmersdale United and Formby would appear to provide that.

At the club's A.G.M. on Thursday 25th June 1953 it was revealed that the club had finished the season with a balance of £1,057, compared to a starting balance of £12 6s 7d. The chief source of income, not surprisingly, was from donations received for players, which totalled £1,600. In addition there was a donation of £270 5s 4d from the Supporters Section - 'a really fine effort.' Gate receipts amounted to £720 1s 3d from all first and second team league and cup games.

Mr. Johnson, the chairman, revealed that 'the club had engaged Mr. Jones, assistant manager of the Bootle Football Club, who has had playing experience with Liverpool, as the team manager.'

Proposing the re-election of Councillor J.P.Sturgess as president for the coming year, Mr. Johnson said that Counc. Sturgess had been president since the Club was formed in 1946, and he has been connected with football in Burscough probably longer than most of them can remember. In reply, Counc. Sturgess said he did not think there was a club of Burscough's standing for miles around with a better ground. In view of the progress made during the past seasons he thought the management should be given a pat on the back for all they had done.

The club's application for membership of the Lancashire Combination was considered at the League's Annual Meeting on Friday 19th June 1953:

Burscough were accepted as members of the Lancashire Combination at the

Annual Meeting at Preston, on Friday night, and next season they will be competing in the Second Division.

This is good news for the sporting public of Burscough and district, and with this in mind the Committee have made a number of useful signings with players like Hurst (formerly of Bootle), Jimmy Aspinall, Green (formerly Huddersfield Town), Cookson (formerly of Bootle), Steve Jones, W.Thompson, Birchall (a noted outside-right), Wilson, Vincent (formerly of Bootle), Dom McGrail and others.

Twenty six years previously Burscough Rangers had been accepted into membership of the Lancashire Combination. They had survived six years, would Burscough fare better?

The answer was to be an unqualified yes, as in the Second Division of the Lancashire Combination, Burscough carried all before them, scoring 155 league goals in the process. The honour of scoring the first goal in the higher league fell to Tom Galvin, as he opened the scoring with a headed goal after just ten minutes, against Lomax at Victoria Park on Wednesday 19th August 1953.

[Tom Galvin, a Liverpudlian, went on to settle in the Burscough area and play a distinguished role in the organisation of local junior football with Dynamo Burscough F.C. In 1996, his contribution to junior football in the area was officially recognised when he was invited to perform the opening ceremony at the new Abbey Lane Playing Fields.]

The team travelled to Padiham on Monday 26th April 1954 and clinched the Championship with a 4-0 win. The Advertiser reported:

For their game at Padiham on Monday night Burscough again had Jackson in goal with reserve left back Higgins deputising for Arthur Green.

Burscough team: Jackson; Cookson, Higgins; Wilson, Brazier, Warren; Burnett, Hart, Vincent, Thompson, Disley.

Burscough soon showed their authority and they played some reasonably good football on a ground which did anything but lend itself to good football. VINCENT scored for Burscough when he converted a pass from Disley to give the goalkeeper no chance. Padiham made spasmodic attacks without becoming really dangerous and no further scoring took place in the first half.

After the interval, HART added a second for the visitors from a cross from the right, and the third goal scored by VINCENT appeared to be offside, but the referee allowed the point.

VINCENT completed the scoring when he went through on his own to score a typical Vincent goal.

After the match there were general rejoicings and congratulations from friend and foe alike. On the return journey the team coach stopped to sample the delights of Whalley and players and officials joined wholeheartedly and enthusiastically in the success toasts.

The same edition reported:

Once again Burscough Football Club have brought honours and distinction to the Village by winning the Championship of Div. 2 of the Lancashire Combination by means of their convincing 4-0 victory over Padiham on the latter's ground on Monday night. Centre forward Johnny Vincent scored three

Two key members of the record setting 1953-54 side were centre forward Johnny Vincent and goalkeeper Stan Hurst.

Above: Johnny Vincent in typical goalscoring action. Here he is pictured playing for New Brighton at the Tower Ground against the magnificent backcloth of the Tower Ballroom (both ground and ballroom are now gone). Vincent only had one full season with Burscough but his 60 first team goals that season gave him a place in the record books that will surely never be beaten. At the time of writing John Vincent lives in Foxhouse Lane, Maghull.

Right: Stan Hurst. Like Vincent, he went on to play for New Brighton, but gave many years service to Burscough. He started off playing his football in the Bootle JOC before joining Charlie Jones at the Bootle club. In many people's eyes he was the Club's finest ever 'keeper. Stan lives in Mart Lane, Burscough, less than 50 yards from Victoria Park.

133

The 1953-54 record breaking side with the Lancashire Combination Division Two Championship Trophy. Back left to right: Jimmy Johnson (Chairman), Johnny Baldwin (Vice-Chairman), Wally Burnett, Jimmy Lowe (Kit-man), Bobby Warren, Stan Hurst, Joe Brazier, Johnny Disley, Arthur Green, Charlie Jones (Manager). Front left to right: Joe Hart, Ronnie Wilson, Jimmy Cookson, Billy Thompson, Johnny Vincent. Photograph kindly loaned by Charlie Jones. In 1996, Charlie was living in Rufford Avenue, Maghull.

of the goals. Burscough's success is an honour of which the players, team manager, trainer and officials can feel justly proud. The Reserve team also achieved League honours by winning the Championship of Div.2 of the Liverpool County Combination only losing two games.

'We are very glad to have such a worthy club like Burscough coming into Div. 1 of the Lancashire Combination,' said Councillor E.W.Raynor, a member of the League Management Committee on Friday evening, when he presented the handsome Combination (Div. 2) Championship trophy to Jimmy Cookson, the Burscough skipper. The presentation took place prior to Burscough's home game with Burnley 'A' and a large crowd witnessed the ceremony. Mr. J.Johnson, Chairman of Burscough Football Club presided and introduced Councillor Raynor who said that since the Club was re-formed in 1946, that was the seventh trophy they had won. Burscough he said owned their own ground and their facilities and amenities were second to none among the Lancashire Combination clubs. After receiving the Trophy Jimmy Cookson thanked the team for their wholehearted efforts, and Mr. Charlie Jones (Team Manager) said the team had trained hard and played hard. The Cup decorated in club colours of green and white together with the Liverpool County Combination (Div. 2) trophy similarly adorned, occupied a place of honour in the 'Directors Box' for the game which followed.

180 goals in total were scored that season, with centre forward Johnny Vincent scoring 60 of them, to beat Wesley Bridge's previous record of 57 first team goals. Vincent signed professional for Wigan Athletic at the end of the season, but he still

remembers clearly his year at Burscough; 'They were a good club, we could play on a Saturday and get caked in mud, but you could be certain that even if we played again on the Monday, all the kit would be spotless and the boots blackened.' Vincent went on, with goalkeeper Stan Hurst, to achieve national recognition as part of the giant killing New Brighton team of 1956-57, which reached the fourth round proper of the F.A. Cup. Both Vincent and Hurst, along with Jim Cookson and Bobby Warren, had been signed from the ailing Bootle club. Tommy Barnes, a renowned historian of Bootle football, wrote in later years, 'Bootle, unable to pay wages (often giving I.O.U.s to their professionals), were unable to compete with Burscough to attract players. The Victoria Park club were in the middle of great times and could bring in the top part-time professionals by offering them lucrative contracts.' Team manager Charlie Jones, formerly at Bootle, remembers bringing those players to Burscough. 'They all got £2, plus £2 win bonus, including myself,' he recalls, 'I didn't believe in some players getting more than others.'

At the club's Annual Presentation Evening held in the Legion Hall on 22nd May 1954, Liverpool manager Don Welsh handed out the well earned medals to the players, including the Reserves, who had won the Liverpool County Combination Division Two Championship under manager Frank Parr. The occasion was 'attended by about 200 people' and dancing was to Wilf Burton and his band.

Although no honours were forthcoming in 1954-55 season the club established itself as a force in Division One of the Lancashire Combination, finishing in a creditable 4th place. The Reserves were successful once more, however, winning the Liverpool Challenge Cup at Haig Avenue, Southport, by beating Fleetwood Hesketh 3-2 after extra time, with goals by Wilkinson (2) and Wright.

The level of support was still extraordinary with the Advertiser reporting that over 800 supporters travelled to Lancaster for a second qualifying round F.A. Cup tie.

The following season the gloomy predictions of the Rangers' years that the village would never produce a successful Lancashire Combination side were consigned to oblivion as Burscough went on to win the First Division Championship. It was arguably the club's finest ever achievement, as the club won a competition that still contained all of the giants of North West non-league soccer, including Wigan Athletic, Chorley, New Brighton, and the then formidable Nelson. What had long been a distant dream to the people involved in Burscough football had finally become reality.

The season started off quietly, but with the attention to detail that has always been characteristic of the club. Chairman Jimmy Johnson informed the Advertiser:

We have had our ground sprayed against the dandelion menace and we are proud of its condition.

The team had played 16 league games without defeat when they faced Marine at Victoria Park on Saturday 10th December 1955. The match programme was wondering 'can we equal Wigan's record - 19 games without defeat. It's asking a lot, but with even luck our boys are capable of it.' There was also 'congratulations to all concerned on both teams holding the top positions in the leagues. Surely for a village this must be a record.' With the help of a Joe Hart hat-trick Burscough won the game 5-0, but lost their next game at home to New Brighton.

The same programme reported that the club's Christmas Whist Drive was on Tuesday 20th December. Tickets were 2/6 each and there were 'the usual prizes - Turkeys,

Opposite: Burscough skipper Arthur Green receives the Lancashire Combination Championship Trophy at Victoria Park on Saturday 5th May 1956 from Alderman E.W.Raynor, a member of the League Management Committee. Among the supporters identified in the grandstand are: Behind the trophy - Herbert Spencer (left) and Tommy Truscott. Seated in the front row are, from the left - Mrs. Marsden, Margaret Melling and Richard Melling. Just behind them are Jack Culshaw (in the trilby) and Alf Rees (with the moustache). Immediately to the left of the trophy is Jimmy Aspinall's wife, Gladys. Towards the back (all wearing spectacles) are, from the left, a young Eric Berry, Mrs. Forshaw, Jim Vickers, and Jack Vickers.

Chickens, Ducks, etc.'

Joe Hart scored a total of 32 goals as the team went on its unstoppable way to the Combination Championship, a team orchestrated by the incomparable Johnny Disley, even now referred to by many supporters as 'the most skilful player to ever pull on a green shirt.'

Frank Parr can still picture the lonely figure of committeeman Bill Tyrer standing on the unprotected 'cricket pitch side' through all kinds of weather, so that he could gain a close-up view of Disley's skills. 'Bill worshipped Disley as a player,' remembers Frank.

Charlie Jones remembers his joy at hearing on the radio that John Disley had been selected for the England Amateur International side but, unfortunately, domestic circumstances at the time made it impossible for Disley to become the first and only Burscough player to represent his country.

Disley and Hart had both played at Formby. 'They knew each others game to a T,' said Charlie. Joe Hart went on to spend almost ten years at Victoria Park, scoring a total of 119 goals - one of only four players to exceed 100 goals for the club.

Lancashire Combination First Division Champions, 1955-56 Season.
Back left to right: Johnny Baldwin (Vice-Chairman), Bobby Warren, Brian Finnigan, Stan Hurst, George Higgins, John McKinley, Bob Millington, Charlie Jones (Manager).
Front left to right: Tommy Scroggins, John Disley, Ronnie Wilson, Arthur Green, Joe Hart.

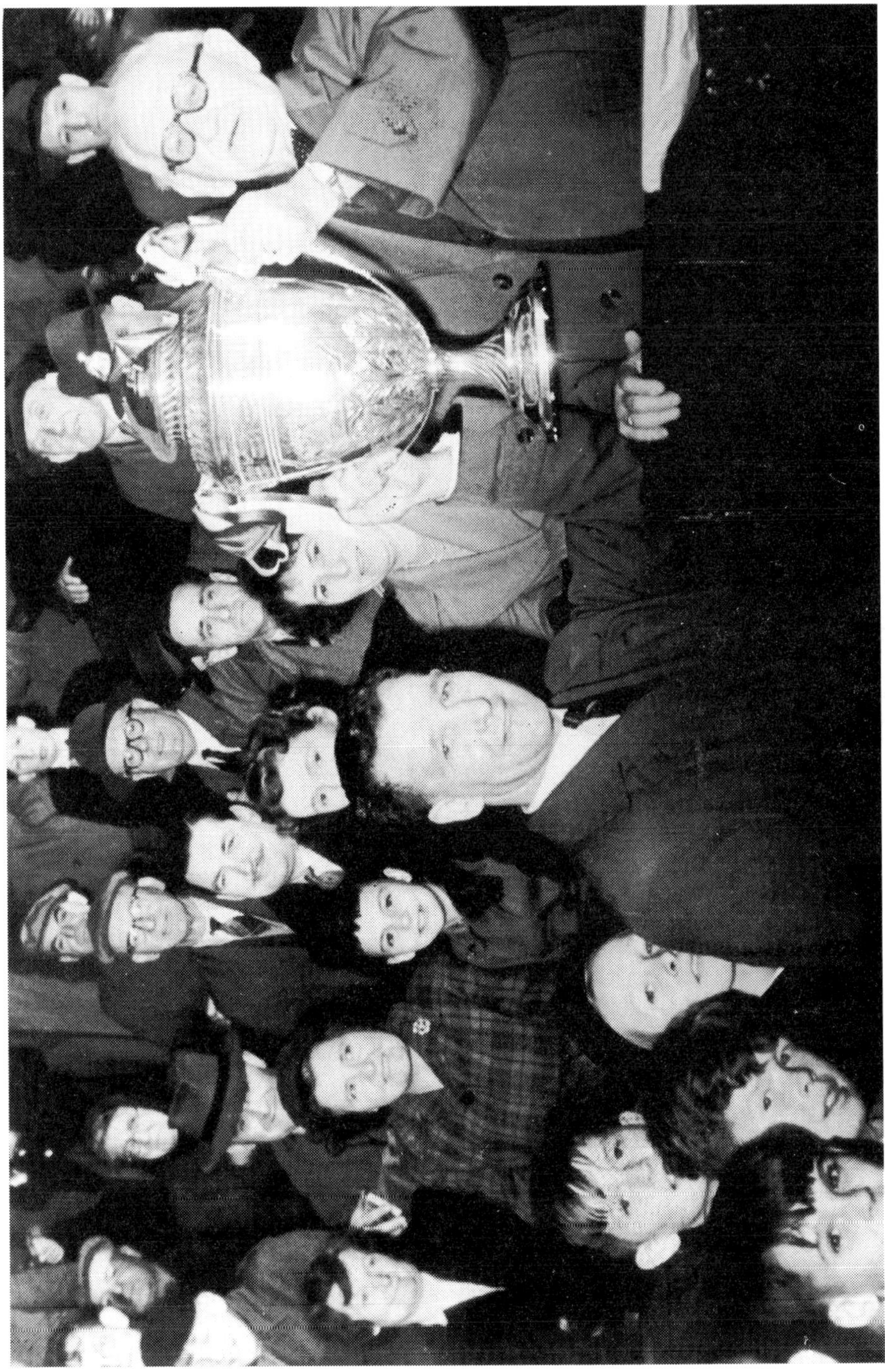

John Disley still remembers his time at Burscough as 'the best days of my life, they were a really homely crowd.'

The Advertiser of 10th May 1956 reported on that season's triumph:

Sharing the points in the last two games of the season - at Fleetwood on Wednesday and Nelson on Friday - Burscough become undisputed Champions of the Lancashire Combination (Div. 1) for the first time in the history of local football. It was a remarkable achievement by a team which has played consistently well all season and has built up a high reputation for some of the best quality football in non-league circles.

The players were given an enthusiastic reception at Victoria Park on Saturday night when they received the Trophy at the hands of Ald. E.W.Raynor of Southport, a member of the Management Committee of the Lancashire Combination. He was received by Mr R.W.Charnock (President of the Club) and Mr. R.Barker (Secretary). Mr. Jim Johnson, the Club Chairman, who has played such a big part in the Club's success in recent years was prevented from attending because of illness.

To see Arthur Green, the popular skipper and left back, receive the Trophy would have been one of the proudest moments of his life; it was indeed the crowning glory for a side which has won admiration on most junior grounds in the County.

A super action shot of Jimmy Aspinall, one of Burscough's finest servants.

A telegram was received 'Hail Champions. Unto you the glory. With you in spirit. - Sammy Hall.'

For good measure, a week later, the club also won the Liverpool Senior Non-league Cup, by beating New Brighton 1-0 at Goodison Park. The lone goal was a 60th minute penalty by the evergreen Jimmy Aspinall, now in his tenth season at Victoria Park. Ronnie Barker later paid tribute to a player who 'never played a bad game, every game was a good game,' although Jim himself recalls, 'my father soon let me know if I had a bad game.' His mother was also one of the club's most enthusiastic supporters, complete with bell! He could have been a professional. After playing for Burscough in the Lancashire Junior Cup Final at Blackpool in 1948, the local League club had offered him terms. Jim recalls, 'I turned them down, I preferred to play with the lads at Burscough.' Born 'over the border' in Lathom, Jimmy Aspinall followed in a family tradition, his father, John, and uncle, Billy, had both played for the Burscough Rangers. His father and uncle were called Aspinwall, but an error on Jim's birth certificate led to him losing a 'W'!

A 'Victory Dance' was held at the British Legion Hall on Friday 1st June 1956

Above: The grandstand that Burscough Rangers brought from Goodison Park in 1926 watches over this local derby with Skelmersdale United on Saturday October 20th 1956. Burscough won 3-1 with goals by Bobby Warren, Johnny Disley and Stan Jessop.

Below: Part of the Victoria Park crowd at the same match, pictured in front of the old canteen, which was replaced by the present canteen in 1960.

when there was 'a crowded attendance.' Present were Mr. R.W.Charnock (President), Mr. Jim Johnson (Chairman), Mr. R.Forshaw and Mrs. Forshaw, Mr. F.Middleton, Mr. and Mrs. J.Hull, Mr.J.Baldwin (Vice-chairman), Mr. R.Ashcroft (Hon. treas.) and Mrs. Ashcroft, Mr. Charlie Jones (Team manager) and Mrs. Jones, Mr. F.Parr and others. Mr. Jim Johnson congratulated the players on the success they had achieved. To win two trophies in one season was a fine performance of which the players could feel justly proud. Mr. Charlie Jones replied on behalf of the players. It was announced that 'Burscough have retained all five professionals - Stan Hurst, George Higgins, Arthur Green, Brian Finnigan and Stan Jessop.'

The following season Chorley were the first visitors to Victoria Park for a league fixture. New signing Ray Williams scored the only goal in a one-all draw. The match programme thanked 'Mr. Charnock (President) and all who helped and donated towards our new playing kit.' The Supporters Section were running football 'Doubles' at 1/- each, giving prizes of £20 weekly.

On Wednesday 29th August 1956, Jim Johnson died suddenly at the age of 53. The next match at Victoria Park was against Darwen and the match programme carried this heartfelt tribute to a great club servant, a man Charlie Jones remembers 'lived for the club':

We cannot find enough words to express our sorrow in losing our greatest friend, nor can we find enough words to express the great work he has done for our Club. His work for our Club will be immortal, and will be remembered for ever.

I am sure we all agree that Burscough has lost a great man, especially in the football world. For in this sphere of life he had a reputation of which anyone could be really proud. Let us hope that we can maintain his standard of sportsmanship, and carry on the work which he had so much energy for, and which he so nobly carried out.

At his funeral there was a floral tribute of 11 white flowers, from manager Charlie Jones and the players, bearing the words 'In memory of a fine gentleman and a great leader.'

Burscough Football Club were barely ten years old yet had already won an incredible 11 major trophies, a standard that would prove impossible to sustain.

In September 1956 the club were unceremoniously dumped out of the F.A. Cup by North Lancashire 'minnows' Milnthorpe Corinthians. In December, Burscough player Stan Jessop travelled with the team to Chorley, signed for Chorley prior to the kick-off, then played against his old team!

The front page of the Ormskirk Advertiser on the 7th February 1957 carried this warning:

The times are not good for local football clubs. Falling gates and rising prices have made non-league football cost more with less income to pay for it. To meet this challenge Burscough Football Club is calling a special meeting of supporters to take place in the British Legion Hall on Friday night.

It was reported the following week that the meeting was 'well attended.' The Supporter's Club's Mr. Bob Forshaw reported that they had already 'paid £633 to the Football Club, and their £1200 target would be met by the end of the season.' Mr. J.Turner (Treasurer) revealed that the club had a total deficit of £479 10s 7d.

Action from the Lancashire Combination Cup Tie between Burscough and Skelmersdale United played at Victoria Park on Saturday 13th September 1958. Skem centre forward, Watkinson, is seen challenging home goalkeeper Albert Ashurst, with Gerry Joyce in the background. Skem won 3-1, with Jeff Aughton scoring the Burscough goal.

Finances couldn't have been that bad, however. Former Burscough player John Parr remembers the club paid for a trip to the Isle of Man during Whitsuntide of 1957, with the team playing and winning two games during their short stay.

Plans were announced to make alterations to the stand in order to build a clubroom, complete with licensed bar. No time was wasted during the summer months, and the following September the Social Club was officially opened:

The new Social Club which has been built below the stand at Victoria Park was opened on Saturday prior to the match with Horwich.

It has been splendidly equipped with the help of Higson's Brewers and there are facilities for refreshments, including tea, and a room for the lady supporters of the Club.

County Ald. W.J.Bridge, who has been connected with Burscough football for over fifty years, and was a former president of Burscough Rangers, accompanied Mrs. Bridge who officially opened the Club. Mrs. Bridge was presented with a bouquet of chrysanthemums by Susan Hull, daughter of Mr. J.Hull, a member of the Committee.

In 1959 the attraction of the nation's foremost football competition was to drive the crowds back to Victoria Park as the club reached the fourth qualifying round of the F.A. Cup, with only one game separating them from entry into the competition proper. The tie at Ellesmere Port Town attracted an attendance of 3,807. The Advertiser's John Yates reported on 5th November 1959:

Burscough made cup history on Saturday when they defeated Cheshire League

Above: Manager Charlie Jones discusses tactics with his team prior to the big match with Crewe Alexandra. Pictured with Charlie from the left: Jimmy Jones, Joe Hart, Des Steele, Bobby Warren, Ray Prentice, Don Baker, Albert Ashurst, Arthur Rowley (hidden) and Dennis Walmsley.

Below: The calm before the storm. This atmospheric picture shows Arthur Rowley practicing his shooting against goalkeeper Albert Ashurst under the glare of the training lights at Victoria Park.

142

Champions Ellesmere Port Town by 2-1. This is the first time in the Club's history that they have made the First Round Proper of the F.A. Cup.

The drama was intense as with the scores level, Burscough goalkeeper Harry Smelt was taken off injured, with full back Arthur Green taking over in goal. Smelt came back with his arm in a sling and played on the wing. With time running out and a replay looking certain, Dennis Walmsley scored the winning goal:

And what a roar went up from the Burscough supporters. They nearly went mad with joy.

Crewe Alexandra were to be the visitors in the first round proper. The draw generated tremendous excitement in the village for the first ever visit of a Football League side:

There is joy in the hearts of all Burscough people in the success of their favourites - the Burscough Football Club - and admiration from all parts of West Lancashire. The achievement at Ellesmere Port on Saturday was splendid and the team, trainer and committee has been the recipient of congratulations. What lies ahead? A tough struggle with Crewe Alexandra on Saturday, November 14th at Victoria Park, Burscough.

There is a note of optimism and secretary Dick Ashcroft has set the victory note with the statement; 'We can win and we hope for a big crowd.'

There is no question of Burscough switching the match to Crewe. The Burscough Committee have the arrangements well in hand and met on Monday evening to decide important matters.

It is not to be an all-ticket match. Admission prices will be 2s in the ground and 5s stand tickets will soon be available. The Committee feel that over 6,000 spectators can be got into the ground. The stand holds about 500 and the Committee are considering putting up a platform on the cricket side. Many years ago bales of hay on carts were used to get the crowd in so they could see. This was in a struggle with the great Wigan Athletic of those days.

The draw on Monday provided intense excitement at Burscough. The townsfolk round about noon were glued to their radio sets. According to Raymond Glendenning, who gave the commentary, eight of the balls in the bag fell to the floor and that incident could have changed the draw. However, Burscough came out second in the draw and for the first time in the history of the Club they entertain a fourth division side.

Not unnaturally, the tie attracted the attention of the national dailies, and it would be easy to imagine them, at the time, scratching their heads and wondering 'where the hell's Burscough.' The Daily Herald managed to locate it, and assigned famous Fleet Street journalist Sam Leitch to pay a visit to the village. The usual well-meaning, but somewhat patronising style of journalism, that non-league sides periodically have to suffer shone through as Sam telexed through his report two days before the big game:

I crossed England yesterday from the big time of the Sunderland international to find Burscough, for the Burscoughs of Soccer are its bread and butter - loyal little clubs with wonderful, down-to-earth characters, who run them for the Lancashire passion which is football.

On the near perfect playing pitch I pumped the strong right hand of Burscough chairman Alf Marsden, a 47 year-old produce merchant, on this flat strip of land which could pass for East Anglia.

Alf, in flat 'at and new gumboots, said; 'We'll win through, there's no doubt about that. Although we play in green shirts, we're certainly not green in Burscough.'

The manager is 39 year-old Charlie Jones, a former Liverpool player. The captain is right-back Arthur Green, 31 year-old transport department worker. Star is 20 goal Arthur Rowley, 26 year-old produce merchant, who has kicked it around pretty slickly for Liverpool, Tranmere and Crewe.

I walked across this wonderful pitch with Alf Marsden, secretary Dick Ashcroft and supporters' club secretary Chris Mahood. Two schoolboys chanted: 'Crewe have no chance, mister.'

After the excitement of an early goal for Burscough, the full time professionals predictably won through by three goals to one, but the home side drew tremendous praise, particularly for their second half display:

By 1 O'Clock Victoria Park was very full and to add to the excitement a Crewe supporter planted a red and white doll on the centre spot. Their triumph was shortlived for several Burscough fans ran on and took the doll and replaced it with green and white rosettes.

After only 7 minutes play Jones put Burscough in the lead with a terrific drive and the cheering was intense.

Crewe were awarded a corner in the 18th minute. Coleman took the kick which went right up into the centre. Out of the blue came the head of Llewellyn and the ball was travelling into the back of the net when Green fisted it over the bar. Referee Hawcroft had no hesitation in awarding Crewe a penalty which Keery converted easily.

In the 22nd minute Crewe took the lead, the ball came across from the left wing, and Ashurst came too far out of the sticks. The ball dropped on the head of Chris Riley, who headed into the empty net.

Three minutes later a slip by Ashurst gave Crewe a commanding lead. Coleman burst through the middle and hit the ball towards goal, Ashurst failed to hold the shot, which bounced out to Llewellyn who tapped the ball into the back of the net.

In the second half Burscough had practically all the play, but for the last minute tackling of the Crewe defence, Burscough might have had a couple of goals.

Up to the final whistle Burscough never gave up fighting and when the whistle sounded schoolboys ran on to the field to congratulate their favourites on their performances.

Attendance: 4,200

Gate Receipts: £412 9s 0d

Burscough's line-up: Albert Ashurst; Arthur Green (capt), Ray Prentice; Tony Greenwood, Don Baker, Bobby Warren; Dennis Walmsley, Des Steele, Joe Hart, Arthur Rowley, Jimmy Jones.

Chris Mahood remembers Arthur Rowley well. 'Arthur had joined Burscough from Tranmere Rovers at the start of that season, in his first match he was scoring from 40 yard free-kicks, I couldn't believe it.'

Left-half Bobby Warren was then a professional with the Club and still has a copy of his Agreement. Bobby earned '£2 per week, with a further £2 per week when playing in First or Reserve Teams.' A bonus of 10 shillings was paid for a win and 5 shillings for a draw, and 'income tax in full to be paid by player.'

Outside-right Dennis Walmsley's lasting memory of the game was the size of the crowd, 'farm carts had been positioned all along the cricket pitch side with about fifty spectators standing on each.' Dennis spent a total of twelve years at Victoria Park, with an enforced two year break for National Service, to become one of the club's longest serving players.

Jimmy Jones remains the only Burscough player to ever score a goal against Football League opposition, however, his story is one of the most tragic to emerge while researching this book. Jimmy had been on Liverpool's books as a junior and had joined Burscough at the start of the 1959-60 season. His sister Sadie recalls: 'He was only about twenty-one, and I think still with Burscough, when he was playing football with his mates, he got his foot caught in a hole in the ground and, not only broke his ankle, but severed his achilles tendon, it was the end of his football career.' By the time Jimmy was twenty-five he had been diagnosed as having Hodgkin's Disease, and although he fought on for several more years, it finally took his life at the age of only thirty-one.

It was not uncommon in those days for players from Liverpool to return home with their 'wages' partly paid in market gardening produce from the fertile lands of South West Lancashire. Many of the local businessmen involved in running the club over the years were produce merchants or market gardeners who made their living off the land. Fred Price, the club president, sold vegetables and imported fruit. Chris Mahood recalls how players finishing work in Liverpool would often be met at the factory gates by one of his lorries waiting to transport them up to Burscough for a match.

At the end of the season team manager Charlie Jones left the club to join New Brighton. Pat Murphy was appointed manager in his place, arriving at Victoria Park from Wigan Athletic, and quickly became notorious for the level of fitness he demanded. Frank Parr can still picture the distress; 'the players were sick after every training session.'

The Advertiser of Thursday 18th August 1960 reported on further improvements for the comfort of spectators at Victoria Park:

The newly erected canteen is still being painted but should be ready for Saturday.
The old canteen is to be used as an office for visitors and the Committee.

The 1960s were hardly underway before concern was being expressed about gates dwindling. The boom times were over, there were now too many alternative forms of entertainment, not least television, and improved transport made it easier for the football follower to support the big city clubs.

A letter from H.V.Berry to the Ormskirk Advertiser on 30th March 1961 made this appeal to the local population:

Football fans may one day have to face up to the unpleasant situation of not only losing their football team, but losing their ground also.
During the last two seasons, the attendances at Burscough home games have dwindled in alarming fashion. At least four hundred one-time supporters no longer come along to Victoria Park.
It is an astonishing fact that forty years ago Burscough Rangers played Skelmersdale United before almost 4,000 spectators on a pasture field, and in

> those days Burscough and Skelmersdale were only small villages.
> If the Burscough team were a bad one there would perhaps be some excuse, but the teams league record is excellent.
> I am not a member of the Committee but I am in close enough contact to know that never in the long history of Burscough football has there been a harder working body of enthusiasts than the present officials and that includes the Supporters Club and their lady helpers.
> There can be only one answer to this sort of support and the public of Burscough must face up to the fact that unless they come along and give their support the days of Burscough F.C. are numbered.

Victoria Park was put to good use on Easter Monday 1961, when the club held its first Carnival Day. Almost 400 people attended:

> Organised by Mr. W.Tyrer and the Committee of Burscough Football Club the event raised approximately £50 for the Old Age Pensioner's Building Fund.
> Star attraction was the grand challenge match between the Burscough's 'over forties' (including guest star, Ron Lawson) and Hollingwood Working Men's Bible Mission A.F.C. from Oldham.

At the club's A.G.M. in July of 1961 it was revealed that the Supporter's Club had donated a massive £3,202 to the club. Gates had averaged £15. Congratulations were offered to Mr. Frank Parr who had recently been appointed to the management committee of the Liverpool County Combination. It was announced that Mr. Fred Price was retiring as president.

On the 7th October 1961, Burscough suffered their heaviest ever defeat at Victoria Park, losing 8-1 to Morecambe in the third qualifying round of the F.A. Cup. Long time supporter Bill Fairclough's abiding memory of that game, however, was Burscough's lone goal scored by Arthur Rowley, 'it went like an absolute rocket, the goalkeeper never moved.' Two weeks later the Advertiser reported that Harry Lyon had scored 'after only six seconds' in a 2-2 home draw with Padiham. Lyon went on to sign for Wigan Athletic at the end of the season after scoring a total of 56 goals. Terry Kelly, who was then a committeeman, remembers seeing the Wigan manager talking to Lyon after a match between the two clubs. He raised 'a big fuss' by accusing Wigan's boss of trying to 'poach' Lyon. The manager denied it, however, and put the blame on his own centre-half for 'tapping Lyon up during the game.' Whatever the truth was, Lyon is remembered as a Springfield Park legend, scoring 264 goals for Wigan in only 380 appearances.

Additional ways of raising finance were sought by the club, now faced with the reality that they would never again be able to survive on gate money alone. Under a heading 'Future Plans' the Advertiser of 20th December 1962 gave details of the club's intentions:

> An ambitious £6,500 scheme comprising licensed club facilities and a hall with a seating capacity of 180 people was outlined by the President of Burscough Football Club, Mr. Sam Curtis J.P. at the Club's Annual Dinner at the Royal Hotel last night.
> Mr. Curtis told members and guests that the Club was receiving very poor support at the home matches and although they had cut down their expenses by £25 per week, it was vital that they had a good social centre in order to pay their way. If it had not been for the fine work of the Supporters' Club they

would be in a sorry state.

The Social Club was opened on Saturday 15th June 1963 by Councillor S.C.Jones, the Chairman of Ormskirk Council. Mr. Curtis recalled the words of former chairman Jimmy Johnson 'I wish we could have decent club premises.' He made special mention of three members of the Supporters' Section who had contributed so much; Mr. W.Church (Chairman), Mr. Robert Watkinson (Secretary) and Mr. Jimmy Bimpson (Treasurer).

Louis Bimpson returned to Victoria Park in December 1963, following a successful career in League football. Local journalist Geoff Howard can still recall his amazement at the sight of the hundreds of fans that had congregated in Mart Lane just to see Louis board the coach for his first game, an away fixture at Bacup.

A headline in the Advertiser 'Dim Future for Burscough' was prominent in July 1964. It was revealed that the club was 'over £500 in the red.' Mr. Ward, the club's secretary, summed up the club's position when he said 'it has been exceptionally difficult maintaining a semi-professional team during the past season on our low gates, and if things do not drastically improve soon, one team will have to be withdrawn next season, probably the Lancashire Combination team.' Mr. Charlie Jones, who had now returned as manager, added that he had recruited 21 amateurs from Merseyside. He stressed that this season they would have to be three-quarter amateur because of the financial position.

It was inevitable in such circumstances the team would struggle. In February an incredible Lancashire Junior Cup Tie ended in a 7-5 defeat at Ashton United on a pitch where the Advertiser's reporter struggled in vain to find 'even one blade of grass.' The travelling Burscough supporters' wit was, as always, to the fore...Bill Suffell wanted to know if Ashton got dirt money for playing there and Bill Martland queried whether they'd let him plant cabbages!

There was no such problems back at Victoria Park. The Lancashire Junior Cup Tie at home to Blackpool Mechanics went ahead despite some atrocious weather. The local newspaper reported:

Victoria Park, the pitch which soaks up water like a sponge. Despite the torrential rain last week there was not puddle or any sign of mud when the teams trotted out.

The team finished 1964-65 season in 20th position, just avoiding relegation.

In January 1965 front page headlines in the Advertiser warned that 'Burscough Football Club is facing Crisis':

The end of Burscough Football Club could be near, unless the people of the village rally round and support the Club in a better manner than they have these past few seasons.

Mr. Joe Hull, the club chairman, was quoted:

The present management committee felt that it was a waste of time trying to carry on continually in the red season after season and scraping the bottom of the pot. People did not realise the position the Club was in and this had to be brought to their notice.

A meeting was held on 22nd February where it was decided to carry on. The following game saw a 'fifty per cent increase in attendance'.

Ideas for raising finance to secure the future of the club were not lacking originality.

A front page feature of the Advertiser dated 1st April 1965 announced:
Greyhound racing is definitely coming to Burscough, the meetings will be held at Victoria Park, home of Burscough F.C.
The Club will receive a substantial rental for the use of their ground, car park fees and the money taken at the bar and from refreshments.
Mr. Joe Hull, the Club Chairman, said yesterday that they had agreed to allow greyhound racing on Monday and Thursday evenings, but stressed that it would be only during the close season.

In April, manager Charlie Jones left the club for the last time to 'take over training and coaching at Skelmersdale United.' He had enjoyed a 'yo-yo' relationship between Burscough and New Brighton during his three spells as manager. Journalist John Yates later wrote; 'he was a shrewd operator, with an excellent eye for spotting raw talent. His knowledge of the non-league soccer scene on Merseyside was second to none, and the players he brought to Burscough proved this.'

Charlie's infectious enthusiasm for the club and the players he brought to Burscough remains undiminished with the passage of time. He has many fond memories of his years at Victoria Park, although events did not always go quite to plan. He remembers signing a centre forward from Wigan Athletic one weekend. During the following week a work-mate pointed out an article in the local newspaper about a footballer that had been killed down the mine. It was the player Charlie had signed.

He also recalls trying to sign a player called Reg Pearce at the end of one season in the 1950s, but he didn't know where he lived. 'I went through the Liverpool telephone directory with Jimmy Johnson and made a list of everyone called 'Pearce'. Then we went around the City knocking on doors until we found him living in Norris Green. He signed a form for Burscough, then went off to a holiday camp, but Winsford United found him and offered him a professional contract. He was later transferred to Luton Town and became an England 'B' International.'

In September 1965 Burscough travelled to Aughton for the first time, to play a 'local derby' with Guinness Exports, losing 4-3.

The previous year Guinness Exports had moved from their home at Bootle Stadium to Middlewood Road, Aughton, the site of the company's social club. The ground was known as Gigfy Park. John Moorcroft, now one of Burscough's most loyal fans, was then a committee member of the Exports Club, and he remembers the ground had superb facilities including 'an indoor heated grandstand and a sunken bath in the dressing rooms.' The club waged a continuous battle to gain

BURSCOUGH'S RECORD
v. GUINNESS EXPORTS

Date	Venue	Competition	Result
Sep 11 1965	at Aughton	Lancs Comb	L 3-4
Feb 26 1966	at Burscough	Lancs Comb	W 3-0
Aug 29 1966	at Burscough	Lancs Comb Cup	D 1-1
Sep 1 1966	at Aughton	Replay	W 1-0
Mar 24 1967	at Aughton	Lancs Comb	W 1-0
Mar 27 1967	at Burscough	Lancs Comb	W 3-0
Aug 24 1967	at Aughton	L'pool Senior N/L Cup	L 0-3
Feb 3 1968	at Burscough	Lancs Comb	L 0-3
Mar 26 1968	at Aughton	Lancs Comb	L 0-1
Mar 25 1970	at Aughton	L'pool Senior N/L Cup	L 1-2

v. ORMSKIRK

Date	Venue	Competition	Result
Apr 9 1971	at Aughton	Cheshire League	W 4-0
Apr 12 1971	at Burscough	Cheshire League	D 1-1
Aug 30 1971	at Burscough	Cheshire League Cup	W 5-2
Mar 31 1972	at Aughton	Cheshire League	W 2-1
Apr 3 1972	at Burscough	Cheshire League	D 1-1
Apr 20 1973	at Aughton	Cheshire League	W 2-1
Apr 23 1973	at Burscough	Cheshire League	W 2-0
Oct 10 1973	at Aughton	Cheshire League	W 1-0
Oct 31 1973	at Burscough	Cheshire League Cup	W 3-0
Mar 16 1974	at Aughton	Cheshire League	W 2-0

BURSCOUGH'S RECORD: P.20 W.12 D.3 L.5 F.36 A.20

local acceptance and support, but met increasing hostility from local residents. Secretary Paul Orr said at the time: 'We are situated in the centre of Aughton surrounded by what are largely upper class types of people - the wrong kind for filling empty terraces at Gigfy Park.'

[After three years in the Lancashire Combination, Guinness joined the Cheshire League in 1968. Despite some fine efforts in the F.A. Amateur Cup, the club still failed to capture the local population's interest, so in one final attempt to improve support, they changed their name to Ormskirk in 1971 and played on in the Cheshire League for three seasons under the town's name. Despite the local apathy, in 1971 they became the first team carrying the Ormskirk name to ever win a senior football trophy, when they won the Liverpool Senior Non-league Cup. In 1974 they failed to gain re-election to the Cheshire League and disbanded...Ormskirk football once more lay dormant.]

A Burscough football legend was appointed as manager in 1965, Mr. Bob Langton. Against all odds 1966-67 season saw them complete a hat-trick of Lancashire Junior Cup successes. Wigan Athletic were the visitors in the second round, the game ending in a one all draw. No-one gave Burscough a chance in the replay, even chairman Joe Hull was heard to say, 'the best chance we've got is to stay at home.' The Springfield Park side believed the replay to be even more of a formality, their match programme notes read:

Our surprise draw at Burscough was nowhere near as bad as the defeat of Glasgow Rangers at Berwick only a fortnight ago. Long live the uncertainty of cup competition. However, we hope there will be no uncertainty about our win against Burscough today!

Does anybody fancy Burscough's chances today on the larger pitch at Springfield Park? Whether they can do as well at Wigan remains to be seen, quite frankly, I can't see them holding 'Latics a second time.

Burscough beat their illustrious opponents 2-1 with goals by Kenny Hodge and Tony Corbett. Appropriately, the final was back at Wigan, with Burscough beating South Liverpool by one goal to nil. The winning goal was a personal tragedy for one player, but another triumphant moment for the village side that had once more captured the county's premier non-league trophy. The Advertiser of 4th May 1967 described the moment perfectly:

The destiny of the Lancashire Junior Cup was decided in one mad, agonising moment four minutes from time...and took the coveted trophy to Burscough for the first time since 1950.

With bated breath the large contingent of Burscough supporters bedecked in green and white, watched as their muscle-aching warriors summoned every ounce of energy in a death or glory bid to snatch victory.

Inside right Tony Corbett, splattered from head to foot in mud, fastened on to the ball midway inside the South Liverpool half of the field, and glided it into the penalty area for his eager colleagues to chase.

The chance seemed lost as right back Arthur Goldstein, watching the flight of the ball like a hawk, looked in complete control of the situation.

But the full back had not noticed Bill Jones race from his line, and as he turned the ball to where he thought his goalkeeper was positioned, he realised in that

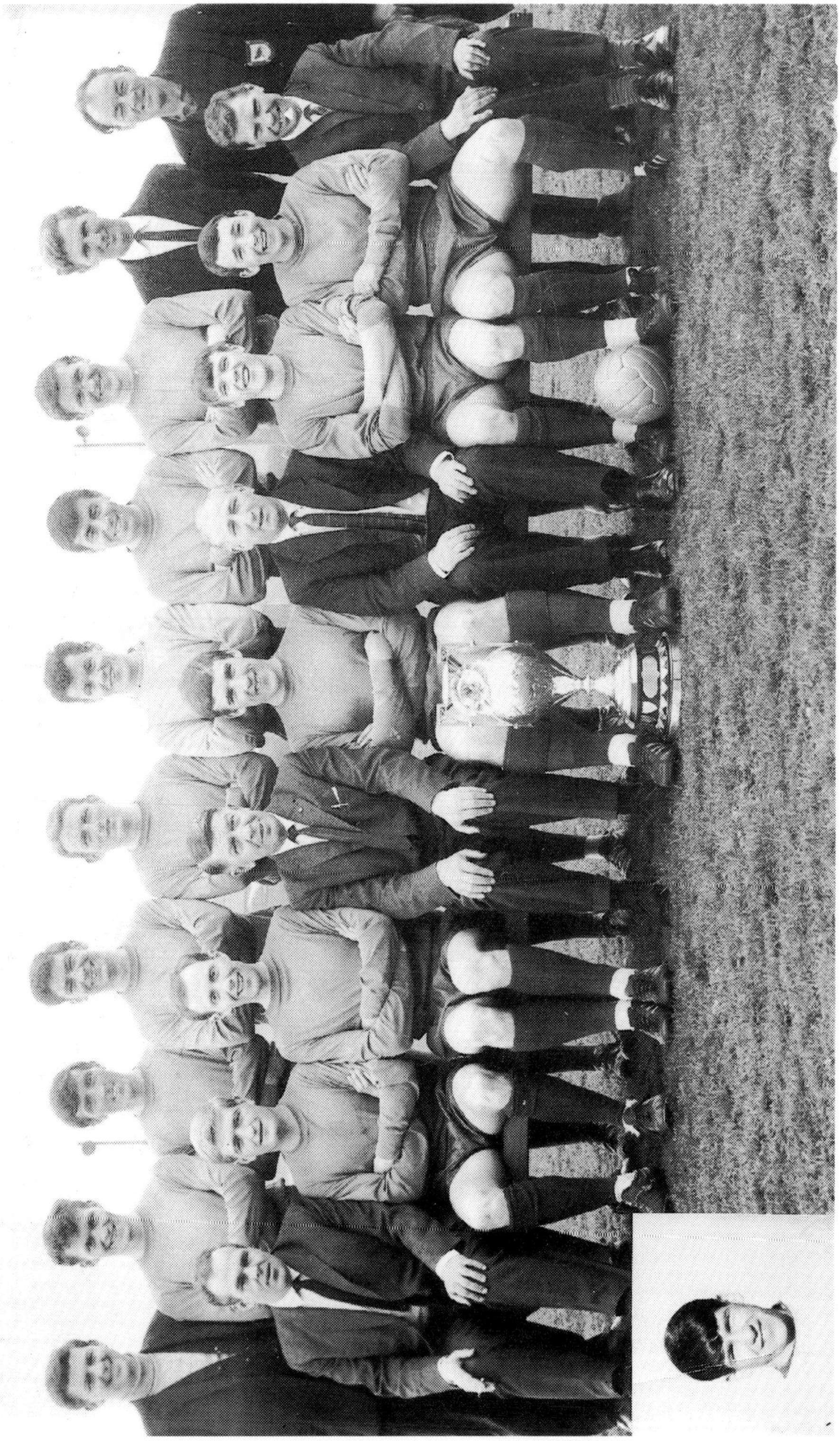

split second that he had 'sold' the cup.

The ball beat a bewildered Jones and rolled slowly but surely into the back of the net. Goldstein, his face twisted in anguish, crumpled to the ground like a deflated balloon, as hordes of delighted Burscough fans leapt over the ramparts and performed a jig in the penalty area.

It was a tragic way for the trophy to be decided but this was cancelled out by the fact that Tony Corbett missed a last minute spot kick after inside left Jimmy Hammell had been pole-axed by Goldstein.

No-one, however, could begrudge Burscough their magnificent win, one of which their players, officials and supporters would never have dreamed possible when they started on the long road to the final at Rossendale way back on January 14th.

Amid great scenes of jubilation, Mr. Arthur Horrocks, a Wigan Athletic director and member of Lancs F.A. presented Bob Jones with the coveted trophy and the players with replicas.

Burscough: Coates; Johnson, Finlay; Tordoff, Jones, Daniels; Hodge, Corbett, Fitzgerald, Hammell, Worden; Sub; Phoenix.

Earlier that season there had been a local derby with a difference. Bill Gregson had by now taken over as chairman at Skelmersdale United, the club had claimed amateur status and their priority was very much winning the F.A. Amateur Cup. The league game at Victoria Park on Monday 3rd April 1967 was being played in the same week as an important Amateur Cup tie. Bill Gregson, true to his showbusiness background, decided on a theatrical gesture by signing on the complete Connahs Quay Nomads side from North Wales to play the game. Burscough beat the 'Welshmen' 2-1 through goals by Fitzgerald and Phoenix.

Away matches still sprung one or two surprises. A game at Netherfield in December 1967 was called off due to an outbreak of foot and mouth disease in the Kendal area. On another occasion, the Advertiser described the Nelson ground at Seedhill as being 'part mud, part artificial turf, part scattered grass,' a challenge for anyone's imagination.

Records galore were in danger at the start of 1968-69 season. The team went fourteen games without defeat, including eleven straight victories. Nelson came to Victoria Park for a Lancashire Combination fixture on Tuesday 3rd September, Burscough winning 10-0, to equal the club's biggest ever victory. During that month the club won all seven fixtures with a truly impressive twenty-nine goals scored and only one conceded. Present vice-chairman Stuart Heaps still recalls vividly the arrival of 'a prolific goalscorer' by the name of Brian Robinson. Robinson scored sixteen of September's twenty-nine goals and went on to score a total of fifty-one over the season, as the team finished in fourth position.

After 17 years in the Lancashire Combination it was time for the club to move on,

---

Opposite: The successful 1966-67 team and officials, pictured with the Lancashire Junior Cup.
Back left to right: Eddie Lawson (Committee), Roy Johnson, Terry Finlay, Tony Fitzgerald, Mick Phoenix, Dave Parker, Charlie Daniels, Alan Tordoff, Jim Bridge (Committee), Harry Gaskell (Trainer).
Front left to right: Terry Kelly (Treasurer), Kenny Hodge, Tony Corbett, Joe Hull (Chairman), Bob Jones, Bob Langton (Manager), Jimmy Hammell, Kenny Worden, Norman Adams (Committee).
Inset: John Coates. Tony Fitzgerald went on to become Chief Scout at Newport County during their Football League days. He now scouts for Notts Forest.

as they applied for membership of the Cheshire County League, and what a way to depart. The Advertiser of Thursday 7th May 1970 reported:

> Burscough are all set to fill their Lancashire Combination Trophy with champagne and toast a tremendous season which will probably hit its peak tonight when Bob Langton's boys travel to Dukinfield looking for one point to clinch the Title.
>
> At time Burscough have played devastating football this season.....a brand of soccer which has set local officials and supporters longing to see them matched with Skelmersdale United.

A 4-0 victory at Dukinfield gave the club its second Lancashire Combination Championship. The Advertiser's Geoff Howard wrote the following week:

> For Burscough Football Club the close season cannot pass quickly enough as they prepare for the first season in the Cheshire League...and the return of the derby battles with the 'old enemy' Skelmersdale United.
>
> For weeks Burscough officials have been ultra-confident that their Lancashire Combination days were numbered...it was officially confirmed this week at the Cheshire League Annual Meeting that the Linnets were voted in with a maximum 23 votes.
>
> It is as though a breath of fresh air has swept through Victoria Park...suddenly the 1970s look distinctly healthy for Bob Langton's boys.
>
> But already Burscough have realised that to really make things surge ahead, Victoria Park will have to have floodlights...a floodlight fund may be set up in the near future.
>
> Middle of the week matches under lights really set the turnstiles clicking. Burscough go into the Cheshire League knowing that they have the finest playing surface in that league.
>
> Burscough will be presented with the Lancashire Combination Championship Trophy next Thursday night when the Player of the Year award will also be presented. The presentation will take place in a huge marquee erected alongside the Social Club.

It was a tremendous achievement on a very tight financial budget. They won thirty of their thirty-eight league games including a run of twelve consecutive league victories, surely a club record.

The decision to leave the Lancashire Combination had not been taken lightly. Burscough had remained loyal to the old established county league and to its administrators, which included Wesley Bridge, longer than many, but it was clear by now that the standard of the competition was gradually being eroded as more and more clubs left to join the now dominant Cheshire County League.

Johnny Baldwin was now groundsman at Victoria Park. His lifetime in Burscough football had included spells as trainer and secretary of Rangers, trainer of Vics, chairman, trainer and now groundsman of Burscough. He used to jokingly tell friends 'when I die, bury me under the centre spot at Victoria Park, so I can hear the kick-off every Saturday.' Charlie Jones can still picture a contented Johnny Baldwin, 'smoking a Woodbine and preparing the boots for Saturday's match.' Ronnie Barker described him as 'a real stalwart of Burscough football, he would do anything for the club.'

The club's A.G.M. in the summer was reported in the Advertiser under the headline 'Tempers flare at Linnets' AGM.' Joe Hull, unerringly described by everyone who knew him as 'a real gentleman,' had been chairman of the club for ten years, but there was now gathering strong support for change. The report went on:

Burscough Football Club's preparations for the new season got off to a rowdy start on Tuesday when more than 100 supporters turned up for the annual meeting.

It was the biggest turnout for an A.G.M. for many seasons and at times discussions became heated with personal attacks on members.

Mr. W.Martland was elected chairman after a ballot which he won by 16 votes.

Chris Mahood, the secretary, reported to the meeting 'the first team clinched the league championship after a thrilling end of season battle for points with Prestwich Heys and Chorley, it was pleasing to leave the Lancashire Combination in a blaze of glory.'

The treasurer, Mr. Terry Kelly, reported a loss for the year of £270. Match receipts amounted to just over £900. Donations from the Sports and Social Club totalled £641, while the '200 Club' brought in £1,561. Match expenses amounted to over £2,000 and ground improvements cost £1,018.

In line with other Cheshire League clubs, admission was being increased to four shillings, with a season ticket to cost three guineas.

Chris Mahood had already been involved with the club for thirteen years. Kenny Spencer, a player during the early 1960s and later to become manager, remembers him 'as the most efficient secretary any club could have.' The job of secretary wasn't without its perils, Chris recalled travelling into Liverpool in 1970 with Billy Martland to sign Leo Skeete, who had been spotted playing in local Sunday football. The area where Leo lived was near Upper Parliament Street in Toxteth and looked somewhat threatening after the rural tranquility of Burscough. He remembers stopping outside an apartment block and a voice alongside him saying, 'You go in Chris, I'll wait in the car.' Chris went on to give another five years service to Burscough, including assuming responsibility for the Social Club, before leaving to become Secretary of the Cheshire League and to 'spend a little time with the family.'

Terry Kelly had been treasurer since 1964. He still recalls the ups and downs of trying to keep the club financially solvent at that time. 'I was the only one with a smile on their face when we lost, as I didn't have to pay out a win bonus. I can still remember Jim Bridge and myself writing so many begging letters that we filled the post box in Red Cat Lane and had to take the rest into the village.' Terry had succeeded Jim Turner as treasurer and paid him this tribute; 'Jim Turner was a tremendous worker for Burscough Football Club over the years, it was Jim that started the first club lottery.'

Skelmersdale United were the visitors to Victoria Park in September 1970. The game was being played against their wishes as a couple of their players were abroad on amateur international duty. Not to be deterred, Skem chairman Bill Gregson met the players at the airport on their arrival home and triumphantly drove them straight to Burscough in time for the kick-off. Meanwhile Leo Skeete, who faced a somewhat shorter journey from Liverpool, did not arrive until after the game had started, being named as substitute. Skem were quickly four goals ahead when Burscough decided to make a substitution. Chairman Bill Martland was so sure that the introduction of Leo would swing the game that he walked on to the pitch with his arm around his star player and 'delivered' him to the referee. Geoff Howard can still picture the look of pure disbelief on the match official's face. Skem still won 4-0.

Over the years Victoria Park had been put to many different uses in order to generate much needed income for the football club. As well as greyhound racing, open air wrestling was staged on the ground, and the early 1970s were notable for the organisation of a summer carnival, attractions included morris dancing, pony and donkey rides, five-a-side competitions and various produce and game stalls.

The club, still under Bob Langton, finished their first season in the Cheshire County League as runners-up to Rossendale United. Jim Bridge, by now a committee member, later paid tribute to the man he considered Burscough's finest manager; 'Bob didn't care if we conceded five, as long as we scored six. If we lost, he didn't say anything immediately, but waited until training on Tuesday when everyone had cooled down.' Terry Kelly also remembers Bob; 'He brought some fine players to the club but often got their names wrong - Jimmy Hammell always got called Jimmy Hamilton.'

Geoff Howard, Sports Editor of the Ormskirk Advertiser, has covered Burscough's games for his newspaper from the early 1960s until the present day. He especially recalls two players from that team....Bob Jones and Kenny Dumican. 'Dumican was a tremendously skilful player and Jones was one of the most consistent defenders I ever saw.' Kenny Spencer also remembers Dumican: 'Knowing what I know now, I realise he had everything, he was the finest player I ever had as a manager.'

At the 1971 Annual General Meeting, Jim Bridge was elected vice-Chairman, with the club's management committee being made up of: J.Draper, F.Parr, E.Lawson, R.Lawson, W.Ward, M.Wilce, E.Stokes and H.Melling.

The promise of floodlights at Victoria Park came true in 1972. In March, the Ormskirk Advertiser broke the news:

To keep pace with other non-league clubs up and down the Country, Burscough Football Club have taken the important and expensive step of installing floodlights at its Victoria Park ground.

The Management Committee is optimistic that the floodlight games will bring a new and valuable source of revenue to Victoria Park and no longer will gate money be lost through early kick-offs.

On Thursday 9th March 1972 the lights came on. The official opening of the new floodlights was by Mr. Ike Robinson, Life Vice-President of the Football Association. The occasion was a Cheshire League fixture with Oswestry Town and the players decided on 'a new floodlit strip of canary yellow shirts and green shorts.' At the time the team had been playing in an all green strip, but the following season were reportedly returning to the traditional green and white at the request of 'many supporters.' The following Thursday there was a big crowd at Victoria Park for the visit of Skelmersdale United in the semi-final of the Liverpool Senior Non-league Cup, a major attraction being the visit of comedian Ken Dodd to help the club celebrate the opening of the new floodlights. Burscough continued the celebrations with a 3-1 victory.

Jim Bridge recalls that 'chairman Bill Martland played a major role in the installation of floodlights at Victoria Park and for a time the novelty value of evening football saw a noticable increase in attendances.'

The floodlights also opened up all kinds of imaginative possiblities for the dedicated staff at Victoria Park. Kenny Spencer, by now the manager, can remember a local resident calling the police at three o'clock in the morning because the floodlights were

Comedian Ken Dodd came to Victoria Park in March 1972, to help celebrate the opening of the new floodlights. Above: 'Doddy' pictured in the stand, complete with rattle and tickling stick, surrounded by local youngsters. Below: More of the large crowd watch from the pitch. This photograph was kindly loaned by John Spencer, who can be seen towards the centre of the picture with his son Brian (in a striped bob-hat) on his shoulder.

The Burscough team that won the Liverpool Non-league Senior Cup at Victoria Park on Wednesday 19th April 1972. Back left to right: Roy Hart, Peter Wassall, Leo Skeete, Brian Robinson, Brian Bannister, Kenny Dumican, Graham Glover, Graham Egerton, Rodney Webb. Front left to right: Dave Parry, Tommy Taylor, Kenny Miller.

on. When the police arrived they found groundsman Norman Forshaw cutting the grass. He was having trouble sleeping, so had decided 'to do something useful!'

In May, Burscough beat Formby to win the Liverpool Senior Non-league Cup, the winning margin was 4-1 with the goals coming from Robinson, Skeete, Parry and Dumican:

> *A two goal blast during an explosive minute near the end of the first half sealed the destination of the Liverpool Senior Non-league Cup for the next 12 months in the Final at Victoria Park. Burscough: Peter Wassall, Rodney Webb, Roy Hart, Kenny Miller, Brian Bannister, Tommy Taylor, Graham Glover, Brian Robinson, Leo Skeete, Kenny Dumican, Ken Parry. Sub: Graham Egerton.*

Kenny Spencer had won a trophy in his first season as manager. Kenny still prides himself on his attention to detail regarding the playing side of the club. When he took over the first thing he did was make sure 'every player had his own football at training, and they were all fitted out with individual tracksuit tops.'

Graham Glover would go on to spend over ten years with Burscough. Graham, now a keen bowler, lives in Rainford and still looks fit enough to get a place in the team. Justifiably, he has tremendous pride in his playing career at Victoria Park and still has the many press reports from that period. Kenny Spencer remembers him as 'an admirable professional.'

1973-74 looked highly promising, as the club reached two finals, but ended in unexpected disappointment. On Thursday 25th April 1974, Burscough lost 2-1 to Skelmersdale United at Victoria Park in the Liverpool Senior Non-league Cup Final. There was controversy after the game following the presentation by a County official. Geoff Howard wrote:

Instead of handing out the medals individually as is customary, Burscough skipper Ian Ledgard and Skem's Keith Barlow found that they had a box containing the lot thrust in their hands and that they had to dish them out themselves in the changing rooms afterwards.

Burscough manager Spencer added 'our spectators were very annoyed about it.'

In the Cheshire League Cup Burscough had faced a mighty two-legged semi-final battle with Leek Town. After a 1-1 draw at Victoria Park, they faced a 1,000 strong crowd in the second leg in Staffordshire. Goalkeeper Alan Alty views it as their finest display during his three years with the club, as goals by Dumican and Spencer saw them through. 'We all played a blinder, it was a tremendous performance under pressure.'

The final, again over two legs, was against Rossendale United:

Burscough coasted to an easy 3-0 lead over Rossendale United on Tuesday night in this first leg of the Cheshire League Cup Final.

Burscough never looked troubled on the Victoria Park pitch and now must be confident of lifting the trophy.

The goals were scored by Joe Flaherty, Alan Swift and Kenny Dumican. A week later Burscough travelled to the Rossendale Valley for the 'formality' of the second leg, but returned home later that evening completely devastated, following an incredible 5-0 defeat.

At the Annual General Meeting held at the Linnets Club on Thursday 15th August 1974 there were 'a total of twenty-nine including officers, committee and members.' The hon. treasurer pointed out that there was a deficit on the year of £838.35 'which showed that the budgeting had not been as accurate as it might have been.' One minutes silence was observed in memory of the late Mr. Johnny Baldwin, 'who had served the club in every capacity since its inception in 1946.'

Later that month Frank Parr was appointed chairman in succession to Bill Martland, a fitting reward after nearly 30 years service with the club. His first words, reported in the Advertiser were:

Obviously the success on the field must be tied in with the success of the social club but I do not want to say anything further until after our first committee meeting.

Words that were to provide a tremendous challenge to many a local journalist over the years to come!

In 1975 Burscough made up for that disastrous defeat at Rossendale United by winning the Cheshire League Cup at the second attempt. After beating Formby, Rhyl, New Brighton and New Mills they came up against Marine in another two-legged final. A 1-1 draw at Victoria Park left the Linnets with it all to do at College Road, but a late Joe Flaherty goal ensured the Trophy finally came to Victoria Park:

It was a proud Kenny Miller who collected the Linnets' first cup in two years from Trevor Hitchin, Chairman of the Cheshire League Management Committee.

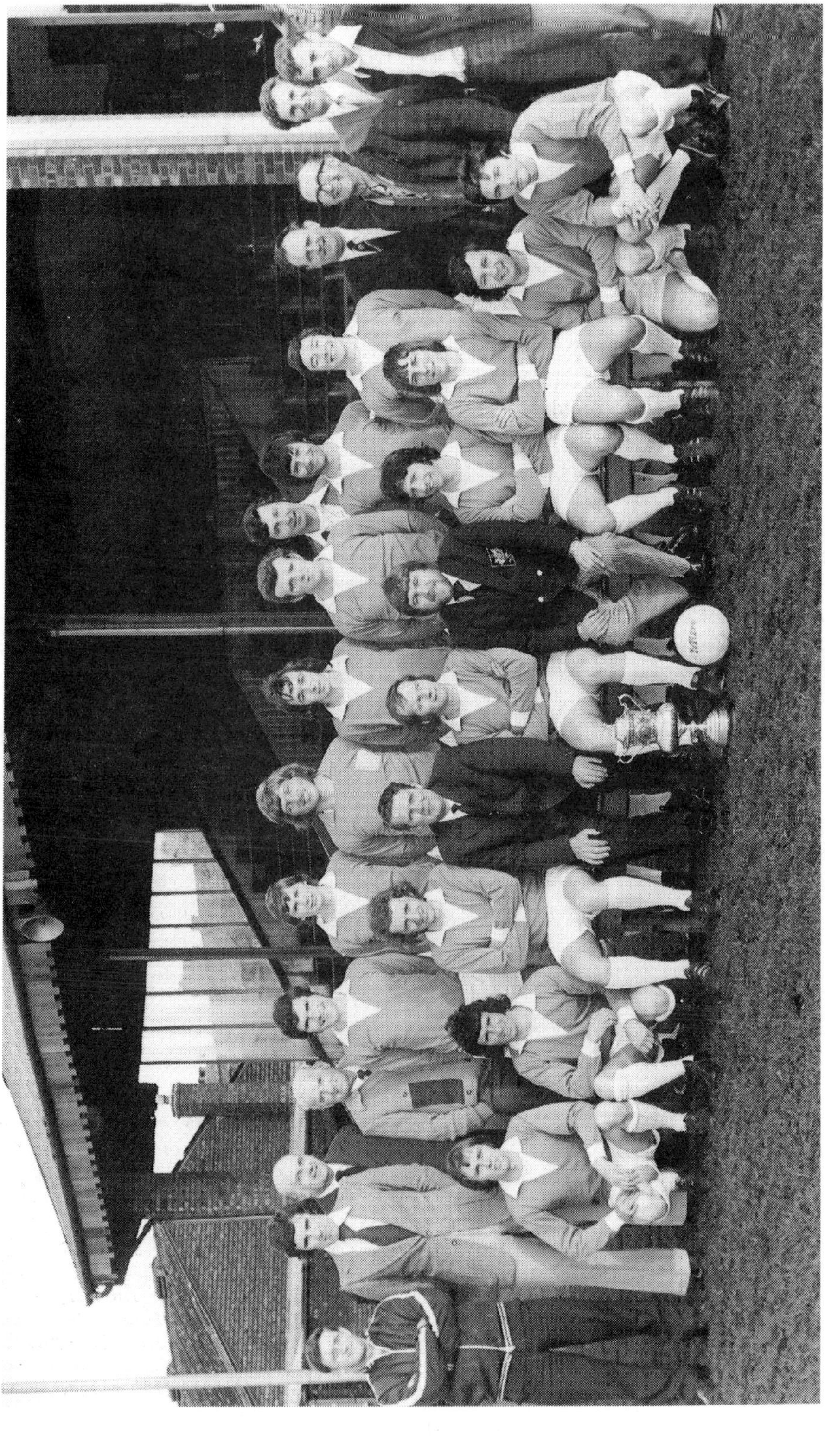

After the match a delighted Kenny Spencer said simply 'It's been a long time waiting for. This was Burscough's fourth cup final in two years and the Cup has come just at the right time.'

He confessed that he never watched the last ten minutes. 'I'm not really worried about the League now, as long as we have something to show for the season.'

Burscough's winning team: Alan Alty; Brian Stokes, Dave Shannon; Kenny Miller, Brian Bannister, Alan Swift; Joey Flaherty, Graham Glover, Kenny Dumican, Gerry Bennett, Phil Spencer. Sub: Tommy Cheetham.

At the A.G.M., Honorary Life Memberships of the club were offered to Mr. Jack Boyes, Miss Ellen Baybutt and Mr. Jimmy Lowe 'for all the work they had done for the Club over many years.'

Chris Mahood, Terry Kelly and Jim Bridge tendered their resignations. It was a major blow, Frank Parr recollects that at that time 'they were virtually running the club. I wondered if we could carry on.'

Carry on they did. Kenny Spencer quit as Manager in December 1976, his parting words were; 'there have been some good times and not too many bad ones.'

At the end of 1976-77 season George Rooney was appointed manager, an appointment that would signal the commencement of a further period of cup success. He replaced Bob Jones, who had been acting as caretaker manager, and was now taking up a business appointment away from the area after fourteen years with the club. It was announced:

A Testimonial for Bob Jones is being held on Tuesday 4th May when a Burscough XI will play an All Stars XI of veteran League players.

In George Rooney's first season Burscough reached the fourth qualifying round of the F.A. Cup to revive hopes of entry into the competition proper for the second time. Morecambe were the opponents, but after a goalless draw at Mart Lane, prospects didn't look too good. Burscough travelled to North Lancashire for the replay on Tuesday 8th November 1977. Geoff Howard was present to report on their triumph:

The victory means a visit to the North East on November 26th when they will face renowned cup fighters Blyth Spartans. Not the draw Burscough would have opted for, but nevertheless one which gives them more than a realistic chance of making the Second Round Proper...and writing a new chapter in Victoria Park history.

The one goal which separated Burscough and Morecambe after 180 minutes of vintage cup football was a lucky one. Nevertheless it was fully deserved. George Rooney's men were the better team on the night.

The goal came at the supreme psychological moment, just one minute before the interval as John Moran crashed in a hard low shot from outside the area and Billy Jaycock raced in to add the finishing touch as Morecambe's keeper

---

Opposite: 1974-75 Season - Cheshire League Cup Winners. Back left to right: Derrick Bradley (Trainer), Bob Jones (Ass. Manager), Gordon Hoskin, Bill Tyrer, Brian Bannister, Dave Shannon, Alan Alty, Unknown, Mick Clarke, Maurice Wilce, Alan Swift, Joe Flaherty, John Robinson, Harry Spencer, Jim Bridge (Vice-Chairman), Don Prentice. Front left to right: Kenny Dumican, Graham Glover, Phil Spencer, Frank Parr (Chairman), Kenny Miller, Kenny Spencer (Manager), Tony Williams, Brian Stokes, Les Gaskell, Gerry Bennett. Dumican scored over 120 goals during his eight years at Burscough. Frank Parr describes Spencer, Flaherty and Dumican as 'the smallest forward line we've probably had, but, by God, they could score goals.'

Byram allowed it to slip from his grasp.

The trip to Blyth ended in 1-0 defeat, but the team were not disgraced, as the North Easterners went on to make history by reaching the last sixteen of the Competition:

'No complaints,' that was the verdict of Burscough chairman Frank Parr after his team's great showing at Blyth.

'The lads fought tremendously hard and I think it would be true to say Blyth were a little better than us on the day.'

The Burscough team that travelled to Northumberland: Mike Lawson; John Moran, Vinny McGrady; Amby Clarke, Al Bowen, Graham Glover; Tony Shallcross, John Durnin, Billy Jaycock, Ronnie Madine, Larry Garrity. Sub: Ian Appleyard.

Billy Jaycock recalls that game as the high point of his time at Burscough. 'Blyth were a good side, with players like Shoulder and Mutrie on their books, who went on to play as professionals. Blyth had a small compact stadium and there was a tremendous atmosphere with about 5,000 inside. Under George Rooney we played it very tight, we had a good midfield and defence and I played very much as a lone striker.'

Burscough may have been disappointed in drawing Blyth, but they were to be compensated in 1979-80 season, a season which would see the club make its biggest F.A. Cup headlines yet.

The draw for the first qualifying round in September paired Burscough with Chorley at Victoria Park. On the Friday evening prior to the game the Lancashire Evening Post carried a comment from Chorley manager Brian Pilkington; 'We are a much better side than Burscough and if we can get an early goal, no-one is going to catch us.'

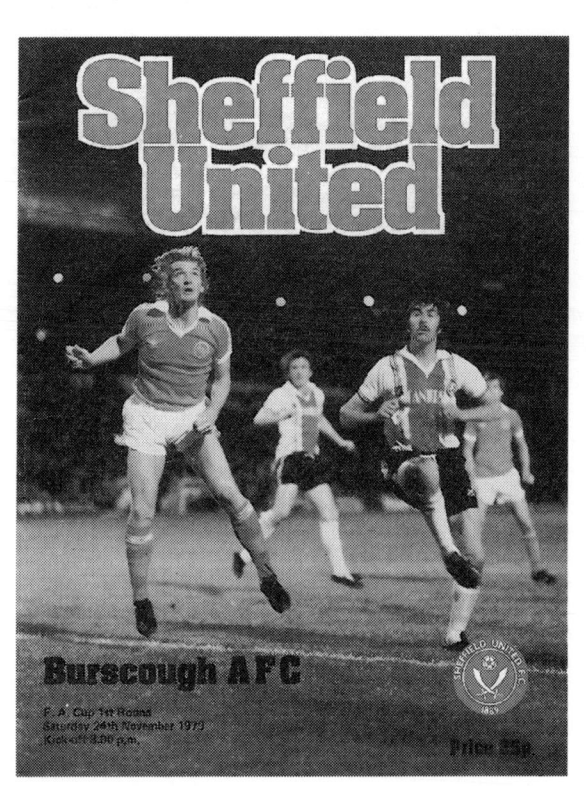

George Rooney said; 'You just don't say things like that about the opposition on the eve of a cup-tie. All I had to do was pin the article on the dressing room wall. They nearly broke down the door to get at 'em.'

Burscough won the match 6-1.

A win at Horden Colliery Welfare in the final qualifying round saw the Linnets in the first round proper. The front page headline of the Advertiser dated 8th November 1979 read 'Cup Jackpot for Local Club.' Geoff Howard went on:

Burscough Football Club have landed the biggest jackpot in the Club's history. The draw for the country's major cup competition has matched them against Sheffield

160

Above: November 1979 v. Sheffield United. Captain Jimmy Lundon leads the team out at Bramall Lane and gets encouragement from one of the 600 Burscough fans who made the journey.

Left: Some of the local youngsters who travelled to Yorkshire.

United.

This David versus Goliath match is the showpiece of the First Round Proper of the F.A. Cup.

Monday's cup draw gave Burscough ground advantage, but within hours the decision had been made to switch the tie to Sheffield United's Bramall Lane ground.

An attendance limit of 3,000, car parking problems, cost of policing and ground improvements meant the staging of the match at Victoria Park was out of the question.

Burscough Chairman Frank Parr's immediate reaction to the draw was 'This is the greatest thing which has happened in my 30 years at the Club.'

Secretary Geoff Clarke remembers; 'It was the draw everyone wanted, at that time Sheffield United were regularly attracting crowds of near 20,000. I phoned the F.A. in London on the Monday, I couldn't believe it when they told me who we had drawn.'

The tie was due to take place on Saturday 24th November 1979:

For the big day out Burscough expect to take about 500 supporters to Sheffield. But the great thing is that the unsung workers who do so much for the Club week after week have received their just reward. People like Bett O'Reilly who does the laundry and Ellen Baybutt, who month after month, year after year runs the most efficient canteen imagineable with the best cuppa to be found in non-league football.

[Ellen Baybutt was still running the canteen until she 'retired' at 80, after which, in the 1990s, she continued to look after the boardroom. Her delicious sponge cake will become part of club folklore. Bett O'Reilly also sold raffle tickets on matchdays, her dedication was legendary. Frank Parr's son, Mark, remembers Chadderton arriving late for a fixture in the 1980s, the players had changed into their playing strip on the coach and came through the turnstile ready to run straight on the pitch where the referee was waiting, but Bett would not let them pass until they had bought a raffle ticket!]

Before the match at Sheffield, chairman Frank Parr paid tribute to his manager; 'I want to take this opportunity of giving George Rooney the credit for what he has achieved since he joined us, particularly in reaching the first round proper twice in three years.'

Not surprisingly, Burscough lost the game 3-0, but a dreadful start could easily have led to humiliation. To their great credit the team kept their heads, battled tremendously hard, and gained the respect of the Yorkshire crowd with a courageous display against the Third Division side:

The last thing on earth Burscough wanted was to fall behind to an early goal. To concede a goal after just 2 minutes 40 seconds was a disaster.

But to those in the crowd who thought that Burscough....first non-league opponents seen at Bramall Lane since Corinthians in 1931...were going to be hit for double figures were disappointed.

In fact for the next hour George Rooney's lads tried their damndest and on a couple of occasions might have levelled the scores.

George Rooney said after the game; 'everything about today has been great.' The Burscough team: Kevin O'Brien, Keith Garland, John Moran, Mike Tickle, Alex Blakeman, Tommy Reed, Syl Nolan, Jimmy Lundon, Tony Duffy, Billy Jaycock, Steve

Taylor. Sub: Tony Bannister.

Ken Hilton was then Burscough's treasurer. He especially remembers the trip to Sheffield:

They treated us like royalty, when we stepped off the coach at Bramall Lane there was a commissionaire to meet us, 'Miss Sheffield United' was waiting to hand us a programme, and our officials were escorted to meet the Sheffield Chairman. I recall Harry Haslam, United's manager, walking in after the game and saying, 'where's Burscough's treasurer - he's the only winner today.'

The club's Annual General Meeting recognised that George Rooney 'did a tremendous job as Manager of Burscough Football Club on a low budget.'

The F.A. Cup continued to dominate in 1980-81 season even though George Rooney had by now moved on to Winsford United. Coincidentally, Morecambe were again the victims in the last qualifying round, Burscough winning 2-0 with goals by Frank Gamble (later to join Derby County) and Billy Jaycock. This time the opponents were to be Alliance League club Altrincham. The Advertiser of 30th October 1980 reported:

The game will kick-off at 2.15 pm as Altrincham were not satisfied that Burscough's floodlights are up to the standard that they are accustomed to playing under.

In front of 1,207 spectators Altrincham won 2-1, with Dave Perry scoring for Burscough:

Manager David May's lads can hold their heads high after being so close to overcoming the ultimate test of character...two goals in arrears capped by the sight of their own goalkeeper Brian Hamilton being stretchered off the field of play.

So close, because not only did they hit back almost immediately by breaking Altrincham's defence, but they could well have forced a replay on the strength of the guts and determination they showed in the second half.

Burscough: Hamilton, Waugh, Crisp, Blakeman, Stokes, Durnin, McFerran, Gray, Gamble, Jaycock, Perry. Sub: Griffiths.

It was a brave performance by the Victoria Park side after losing their goalkeeper. Two rounds later Altrincham were drawn against Liverpool at Anfield. Burscough are left to dream of how events might have developed differently had they won that game.

In April 1981 Bryan Griffiths replaced David May as manager.

The Cheshire County League and the Lancashire Combination were amalgamated in 1982 to form the North West Counties Football League, with Burscough being elected founder members. The new season began ominously with news of another financial crisis, the front page of the Advertiser carrying the appeal; 'Save our Soccer.' Secretary Gordon Hoskin was quoted:

With ever increasing overheads, coupled with a diminishing income and lack of active support both financial and physical locally, it is extremely doubtful if top level non-league soccer can be maintained here at Burscough. It is not our intention to follow so many other clubs into total bankruptcy.

An eighteen year-old defender called Shaun Teale joined the club at the start of the season and although he only played a handful of games for Burscough he went on to achieve fame and fortune later in his career with Aston Villa.

*The team that won the North West Counties League Division One Championship in 1982-83 season.
Back left to right: Mike McKenzie (Asst. Manager), John Veacock, Mike Fagan, John Donnerly, Kevin O'Brien, Dave Elder, Dave Pennell, Peter Doyle, Mick Quinn, John Moran (Trainer).
Front left to right: Bob Johnson, Syl Nolan, John Brady, Bryan Griffiths (Manager), Robbie Griffiths, Ronnie Mulhall, Paul Conchie.*

Despite the gloomy pre-season forecasts, Bryan Griffiths led Burscough on to become the inaugural Champions of the League. They clinched the First Division Title, to pip main rivals Rhyl, with a win at Prescot Cables on Thursday 12th May 1983:

> Burscough duly clinched the League Title in their last match of the season with a victory at Prescot Cables. That tension filled win meant that nearest challengers Rhyl were unable to overhaul Burscough's final total of 59 points.
>
> The first goal when it arrived in the 24th minute was simple enough. A short corner was touched to Brady who swung over a cross right into the path of Peter Doyle who had little option but to accept the chance and gratefully head home.
>
> The second half opened in lively fashion as Brady flashed a shot narrowly wide and then whipped a ball teasingly across the goalmouth.
>
> Whatever Manager Griffiths said at half-time certainly made the players a little more responsive and after 63 minutes they made sure that Burscough would be hailed as Champions when Horrocks headed in from another corner. A minute later a third was almost added when the hard working Donnelly and Nolan combined to open up the Prescot defence and set up Brady whose effort was fired straight at the 'keeper.
>
> Donnelly and Brady again dovetailed superbly in another move before the latter struck the foot of the post with a raking shot from the edge of the box. In their last dangerous move forward Burscough breached the offside trap as Fagan surged forward but unfortunately booted the ball over as the goalkeeper dashed out.
>
> Although the Victoria Park side were crowned the first ever Champions of the

newly inaugurated North West Counties League they are now without the services of Bryan Griffiths - one of the astutest managers on the local scene. His replacement is Coach Mike McKenzie.

Burscough: Kevin O'Brien, Mike Fagan, Ronnie Mulhall, Peter Doyle, Jimmy Horrocks, Johnson, Redmond, Dave Pennell, Alan Donnelly, Syl Nolan, John Brady: Sub. Mick Quinn

Bryan Griffiths had announced his decision to quit before the game. Barry Turnbull, writing in the Advertiser, commented:

Mr. Griffiths insists he is not leaving under a cloud but it is true to say he is disappointed with the Club's lack of ambition, for they have spurned on financial grounds the chance of stepping up a grade by refusing to join the Northern Premier League.

Bryan Griffiths, obviously disappointed, had the final words:

I can understand the situation regarding finances but personally I would have liked the club to have thought a little more about it before coming up with their decision.

They could have talked to me or the players about it and I am sure everybody would have had a go at least for a season. If it didn't work out we could always drop back down again.

The League Championship Trophy was presented to Burscough captain Syl Nolan by League Vice-President Mr. John Williams at a special presentation evening in the Social Club. Leading goalscorer John Brady won the Player of the Year award.

Following this success, Mike McKenzie took over the manager's reigns, and under his guidance the club continued to retain a healthy position in the North West Counties First Division.

An incredible Lancashire Challenge Trophy game at Victoria Park in December 1983 ended in a 7-6 win for Burscough. Two of the home side's goals were scored by Steve Skeete, brother of Leo. In a short but spectacular spell with the club, he scored 11 goals in 7 games before departing to Prescot Cables.

In 1984-85 season they made a strong challenge for the League title, finally finishing in third place. John Coleman scored a total of 39 goals, including scoring from twenty-one consecutive penalties. Although he was occasionally called upon to defend his team against 'the liberal use of the offside trap,' McKenzie was able to reflect on a satisfying season:

It has not been a bad season at all, we finished third in the league, got through to the last qualifying round of the F.A. Cup, and the quarter-finals of the Lancashire Junior Cup and the League Cup.

Burscough had travelled to Newcastle-on-Tyne in the fourth qualifying round of the F.A. Cup to meet Blue Star. The game ended goalless and the winners of the replay the following Wednesday at Mart Lane were to travel to York City. Mike Woods had just joined the club and recalled; 'Blue Star's ground was situated close to the runway at Newcastle Airport and they weren't allowed to erect floodlights, so they wouldn't replay under our lights as they believed it would give Burscough an unfair advantage. Despite playing on a Wednesday afternoon, we still got 400 there.' Unfortunately, the North Easterners went through with a 4-0 victory.

Following McKenzie's departure in 1986, a succession of managers came and went,

Part of the 1,700 crowd that were attracted to Victoria Park by the visit of a strong Liverpool side for the official opening of the Grandstand in August 1988.

Four of the most famous names ever associated with Burscough football were invited guests at the game. From the left: Louis Bimpson, Tom Saunders, Bob Langton and Larry Carberry.

with the club, not surprisingly, enjoying very little success. The final humiliation coming in 1989-90 season when, for the first time in the history of Burscough football, the village football club was relegated, the team scoring only five goals in their final eleven league matches. To make matters worse, the team only finished in a relegation position due to three points being deducted as punishment for fielding an unregistered player.

In 1983 the 'Linnets' Club had been sold, providing the means of clearing the debt which had been stifling progress. The euphoria that had understandably been prevalent when the social club was opened had long since died. Very little of the anticipated revenue that the football club so desperately needed had in fact materialised, despite the tremendous hard work and commitment of so many people during the twenty years of club ownership. It had been a period of sometimes bitter strife, acrimony, and even litigation, and is best dealt with briefly. Jim Turner had warned when the club opened, 'it will cause nothing but trouble,' and he may have been right.

With a potential source of revenue from a social club now gone, the club's focus would now be concentrated more than ever on other means of generating finance. A weekly lottery and sponsorship were now to play the most crucial role as the club set about building the kind of foundations that would ensure that any further opportunities to progress would not be spurned.

No time was lost. In 1986, rather sadly, the grandstand that Burscough Rangers had built over 60 years before was demolished, as the mainly wooden structure no longer complied with new ground safety requirements. A new grandstand, incorporating changing rooms, office accommodation and boardroom, was built with seating for 250 spectators. It was officially opened in Monday 22nd August 1988 by Mr. Syd Rudd, former Secretary of the Liverpool County F.A. and Life Vice-president of the Football Association. Liverpool sent a strong team, including Steve Staunton, Jim Beglin and Mike Marsh, for a celebration match, winning 4-0 in front of a crowd of 1,700. The building of the new stand was a tremendous team effort. Chairman Frank Parr said:

Gerald Thompson and his Company, who erected the new stand, have given help above and beyond what any contract called for. Jimmy Murray and his Manhire Construction Company have not only donated most of the materials for the ceilings, etc. but have also provided free, much of the labour to complete the work. The plumbing and electrical contractors were Holgate Maintenance E.M.H., I.F.S. and Mike Forest. John Moorcroft has given countless hours of free time to us, away from his own joinery business. Walter Gibbons turned his hand to all manner of jobs for us. My Vice-Chairman, Stuart Heaps, has been a jack of all trades throughout the work and has given virtually all his spare time to the project.

Attending the opening ceremony were many of the famous footballing names who had associations with the club, including Bob Langton, Louis Bimpson, Larry Carberry and Tom Saunders. Other guests included Mrs Margaret Edwards, Chairman of West Lancashire District Council and Mr. Ken Hind, the local Member of Parliament. The match programme for the Liverpool visit reported:

The summer break has seen many changes to the ground, firstly the new grandstand and facilities have been completed, yes, including the seats! Perhaps more surprising to most people you will notice that completely new floodlights have been erected. This move follows the storm damage which the old ones suffered earlier in the year. The decision to renew the floodlights was made, they have given 17 years service, and it would not have been cost effective to repair them. The cost of the new lights is £11,000, this was financed by a loan from the District Council, which the club have to pay back over the next five years. Another thing that will be apparent is that a hard standing has been laid all the way around the pitch.

Russ Perkins took over as Manager in 1991 and set about the task of reviving the club's fortunes. In this he was to prove successful, quickly establishing a team that became renowned for the quality of its football.

In his first season the team reached the League Cup Final and were unfortunate in losing 1-0 to Ashton United at a rain-sodden Gigg Lane, however, they would soon return.

1992-93 was to bring tremendous success in cup competitions. The season started in August with a trip to Bramley for an F.A. Cup preliminary round tie. Their opponents, Bradford Park Avenue, were using the local Rugby League stadium as their home ground, but when the team arrived they found the grass six inches high. Club secretary Mike Woods was quoted; 'The team has made a 160 mile round trip for nothing. The grass was ankle-high and totally unsuitable for playing football on.'

The game was called off and ordered by the F.A. to be replayed at Burscough the following week, but the Yorkshire side eventually triumphed after a replay.

Dreams of Wembley glory in the F.A. Vase were high when Cammell Laird came to Victoria Park in January for a fourth round tie, but on the day the Linnets proved second best and their chance of a place in the last sixteen disappeared with a 1-0 defeat.

There was some light 'relief' during the season. A game at Burscough was subject to a lengthy stoppage because of an injury to an opposing player. Supporter Philip Carver will never forget the sight of Burscough goalkeeper Alan Robinson 'getting booked for going off for a pee without the ref's permission.' Robinson, a real character, had hopped over the perimeter fence at the Mart Lane end during the stoppage in play and disappeared into the 'Gents' behind the goal. He reappeared a couple of moments later and took up his position back in goal. As the referee was about to restart the game, his attention was attracted by a the waving flag of a vigilant linesman who had witnessed the evil deed, and Robinson was cautioned for leaving the field of play without permission.

After reaching the semi-final of the Liverpool Senior Cup, Burscough were drawn away to Everton. It was confidently expected that the tie would be switched to Victoria Park, but Everton manager Howard Kendall had other ideas and insisted that Everton retain home advantage. So on Monday 29th March 1993 the Linnets travelled to Goodison Park, and despite facing a Blues team including

Above: Sean Togher shoots the winning goal in the North West Counties League Challenge Cup Final at Gigg Lane, Bury, on Thursday 22nd April 1993.

Below: Some of 'Russ Perkins' Green Army' who travelled to support the team. Among them is a young Graham Jarman who particularly recalls two players from that team - Gary Martindale and Kevin Still. 'They were both good footballers and did the club proud', said Graham.

Above: The victorious 1992-93 team and officials pictured with the League Challenge Cup.
Back left to right: Roy Baldwin, Gordon Cottle, Bill Fairclough (Committee), Brendan Doyle, Tommy Knox, Ian Owen, Sean Togher, Alan Robinson, Steven Perkins, Gary Martindale, Brian Fairclough, Stuart Heaps (Vice-Chairman), Stan Strickland (Secretary).
Front left to right: Andy Doyle, Martin Lowe, Tony Quinn, Russ Perkins (Manager), Sponsor, Frank Parr (Chairman), Bobby Howard (Asst. Manager), Colin Stafford, Kevin Still.

Left: Skipper Tony Quinn lifts the Cup, the other wide smiles belong to Alan Robinson, Gary Martindale, Tommy Knox and Bobby Howard.

David Unsworth and Scottish International Maurice Johnston, emerged victors by two goals to nil. The next morning the Liverpool Daily Post enthused:

> Brilliant Burscough dumped their more illustrious opponents out of the Liverpool Senior Cup thanks to first half goals from full backs Brendan and Andy Doyle.
>
> Despite almost total second half domination, Everton rarely looked like scoring. So much so that Scottish star Mo Johnston was restricted to a few half chances by the impressive Ian Owen.
>
> At the end the tannoy played 'Unforgettable' and for the large travelling Burscough support last night certainly was.

Even better was to come as the team once again reached the League Challenge Cup Final at Gigg Lane, Bury on Thursday 22nd April 1993. Manager Russ Perkins was on holiday in America, but news crossed the Atlantic later that evening of Burscough's 2-1 victory over Nantwich Town. The Advertiser reported that 'it was a triumphant return' after being beaten on the same ground in the previous season's final:

> Burscough made a triumphant return to Gigg Lane to lift their first trophy in a decade. They made a sensational start to last Thursday's match with a goal worthy of any big game. It came after only three minutes when Brendan Doyle cut inside the Nantwich right back and from 20 yards struck a shot straight from Roy of the Rovers.

Sean Togher scored a second, and despite a second half fightback by the Cheshire side, Burscough held on to win the League Challenge Cup. Captain Tony Quinn was presented with the magnificent trophy and celebrations on the pitch were joined by an understandably emotional chairman, Frank Parr, who later said:

> I thought it was a tremendous performance, very professional, and all credit to the lads. And I thought the support we got on the night was absolutely terrific.

The Burscough team on that memorable evening at Gigg Lane was: Alan Robinson, Brendan Doyle, Andy Doyle, Ian Owen, Bobby Howard, Tommy Knox, Tony Quinn, Martin Lowe, Gary Martindale, Sean Togher, Kevin Still, Subs: Gary Trewhitt, Colin Stafford.

This famous old trophy was brought back to Burscough for the first time. Over one hundred years old and hand crafted in solid silver, it had previously been known as the Lancashire Combination Cup.

Two thousand spectators were at Goodison Park on Tuesday 11th May 1993 to witness the final of the Liverpool Senior Cup against Southport, who had just won promotion to the Vauxhall Conference. Burscough lost 2-1, in what was their 68th game of the season. They played some fine football and monopolised possession for long periods, but the more incisive finishing of their opponents proved too much. Matt 'the Hat' Horn in the Advertiser wrote:

> Disappointment and pride were the mixed emotions felt by all those connected with Burscough after defeat in the final of the Liverpool Senior Cup.
>
> The heroic efforts of all 11 players were just not enough to give them victory against Southport. Despite dominating long periods of the game by playing their typical brand of flowing football they went down to a soft goal 11 minutes from time. The winner came just minutes after Kevin Still struck a superb equaliser to give the Linnets hope of a shock victory and their second trophy of the season.

In 1993-94 Burscough made a strong challenge for the League Championship, finishing third and scoring 105 league goals. Victoria Park regulars witnessed a team playing football that will live in the memory forever, but defensive lapses cost too many points and the challenge faded.

Gary Martindale had been signed in January 1993 from Liverpool County Combination side St. Dominics. After having scored 34 goals in 1993-94 season he was already attracting League scouts to Victoria Park. An article in the Football Echo of 12th March 1994 was to trigger off a quite breathtaking chain of events:

Gary Martindale (left) in action for Burscough.

The man who discovered John Aldridge believes he's found an even better prospect - and he has predicted 'goalden' times for his latest prodigy.
Burscough boss Russ Perkins was manager of South Liverpool in 1979 when he sold Aldridge to Newport County, setting him on the road that ended up at Tranmere via Liverpool and Real Sociedad. And Perkins says he has a player who is as good as the young Aldridge...and who could go just as far in the game.
His name is Gary Martindale, he's a 22 year-old striker who is the talk of the North West Counties League scene.

This story alerted Bruce Rioch, manager of Bolton Wanderers, who took Gary for a trial game and came back to sign him on transfer deadline day, Thursday 24th March. In one of the most dramatic days in the club's history, Rochdale then came in with an offer for fellow striker Kevin Formby, whose registration was faxed through to Lancaster Gate from Mart Lane with only minutes remaining to the 5 pm deadline. The Ormskirk Champion, the following week, reported:

Burscough Football Club received the biggest financial boost in their history when leading marksman Gary Martindale and his co-striking partner, Kevin Formby both joined Football League clubs before Thursday's transfer deadline. Although Burscough are at this stage reluctant to discuss the financial arrangements involved, it is believed they will benefit by in excess of £15,000.

At the end of that season Rochdale returned for midfield player Alex Russell to complete one of the most eventful seasons in Burscough's history.

Formby and Russell, who had both stepped down from the Northern Premier League to join Burscough, quickly adjusted to playing at Football League level, with Formby going on to play against Liverpool in an F.A. Cup Tie at Anfield. Martindale later moved on from Bolton to Peterborough United, then, in March 1996, was transferred to Notts County for a fee of £175,000. To cap it all Gary Martindale scored the winning goal for Notts County two months later to take them to the Second Division play-off final at Wembley Stadium.

Gary said at the time of leaving Burscough; 'I've always wanted to be a professional footballer, it shows your dreams will come true if you work hard enough.'

The club never officially confirmed the fees that were received for Martindale and Formby, but it can safely be assumed that they were a club record. However, how do you measure a monetary record? In 1953, Louis Bimpson's accumulative transfer fee to Liverpool finally totalled £1,250, which, at present day values, must equate to more than £30,000. Louis' place in Burscough's history would also appear assured.

At the start of the 1994-95 season Russ Perkins promised; 'Burscough will win the League,' words which were to haunt the club all season as a serious challenge for the championship failed to materialise. Excitement was reserved for the F.A. competitions. A four game marathon with Congleton Town in the F.A. Cup was attracting the attention of the national press, but poor defending when the second qualifying round tie looked won, led to defeat.

Record breaking progress to the last sixteen of the F.A. Vase, which included fine victories against Brigg Town, Arnold Town and Brandon United, left the club only three matches from the dream of a final at Wembley Stadium, when they came up against the inevitable stumbling block - Cammell Laird. In front of an estimated 700 spectators at Rock Ferry, many following Burscough for the first time, the Linnets 'froze' and experienced a 4-2 defeat, a defeat which attracted widespread criticism as to why a team who paid to play could show more commitment and passion. At the end of the season the club decided not to retain Russ Perkins as Manager.

Russ had played a key role in re-establishing the club as a major force in the non-league game, he had built teams that played good football, won a major trophy, took the team to three cup finals, enjoyed F.A. Vase success and generally brought much excitement to the club. Over the four seasons he was at Burscough, the team scored a quite staggering 493 goals, but conceded 350. A man of strong football principles, Russ was convinced that Burscough could win promotion with the kind of exciting, attacking football in which he believed. Unfortunately, all too often defensive naivety would mean that this view was not always universally shared.

Following his departure, Russ had the final word. 'In a way, I have been a victim of my own success. When I came here they were languishing in the Second Division. Now they expect to win the league. I am very disappointed and quite amazed that they have done it.'

At the club's 49th Annual General Meeting, held on the 17th August 1995 in the Community Centre, Mart Lane, it was unanimously agreed to invite Bob Langton to become an Honorary Life Member of the club. Sadly, this was to be one of the last honours to be bestowed on this famous footballer, as he died suddenly at the age of 77 on Saturday 13th January 1996. Born in the village on the 8th September 1918, Bob had travelled the world as an international footballer, but never gave up his Burscough roots. His funeral at the Methodist Church was attended by Burscough Football Club officials and players, past and present, and also by former England footballers Tom

Finney, Nat Lofthouse, Bryan Douglas and Ronnie Clayton. Bob's autographed photograph will continue to take centre stage in the boardroom at Victoria Park and remind visitors for many years to come of Burscough's most famous footballing son.

In May John Davison had been appointed the club's nineteenth manager. A local resident, he arrived with a pedigree of 24 appearances for the England semi-professional side during 14 years as a player with Altrincham. Expectations were, justifiably, set high.

He began the season confidently by offering terms to virtually all of the previous season's playing squad, most of whom elected to remain with the club. Experienced players with Northern Premier League experience were added to the squad and by November the team proudly headed Division One.

An eighteen year-old striker called Lee Trundle had been spotted playing in the F.A. County Youth Cup Final at Victoria Park in April 1995 (attended by Football Association Chief Executive, Graham Kelly). He went on trial to Liverpool but was released early the next season. While other clubs hesitated, Burscough moved in and signed him from St. Dominics. A player of precocious talent, hopes were high that he would follow in the footsteps of Gary Martindale, signed three years earlier from the same Huyton club. In his second game he scored four goals of the highest quality and left the field to a memorable standing ovation. Again, the speed of events was breathtaking, as before the end of the week the club had signed him as a contract professional and within a further five weeks he had signed for Chorley at a reported fee of £7,000. The club had experienced eighteen months of transfer activity not matched since 1953.

Lee Trundle was transferred from Burscough to Chorley on Friday 3rd November 1995, little more than six weeks after signing from Liverpool side, St. Dominics. Here, he is pictured at Victory Park being welcomed by Chorley manager Dave Sutton.

The optimism borne of John Davison's appointment would not be misplaced as the team continued to make a strong challenge for the League Championship only to lose the services of its two main strikers during the critical final stages of the season. Terry McPhillips, while captain of the team, left the club for the second time that season to join Ashton United, while Mick McDonough missed vital games through recurring injury problems. They were major blows and left the manager with the impossible task of finding replacements as the transfer deadline loomed.

The championship challenge eventually died, but the best was yet to come. This was a book looking for the perfect ending...and it got it!

After beating Stantondale, Prescot Cables, Darwen and Holker Old Boys, Burscough had reached the League Challenge Cup Final for the third time in five seasons. Again

The Burscough 'bench' pictured as the final whistle sounds at Gigg Lane for the Linnets second League Challenge Cup victory in four years. Physio Rod Cottam, Gary Trewhitt and Peter King show their delight in the foreground, while manager John Davison appears to be restrained by an over-zealous official in the background. Photographs by courtesy of the Ormskirk Advertiser.

League Chairman Eric Hinchliffe lets Burscough captain Ged Nolan take centre stage as the Cup is held high to the roars of the Burscough supporters. Paul Blasbery, Peter King and Gary Trewhitt are no less ecstatic as they wait to collect their winners medals.

Above: Some of Burscough's magnificent support at Bury, complete with green and white balloons. Among those identified in this shot are Barbara & Andrew Moorcroft, Sue, Chris & Sian Davison, Julie & Kimberley Wright, Graham Jarman, Jean & David Bain, Joe McCall, Ken Taylor & Peter Knowles.

Below: Celebrations on the pitch. Back left to right: Richie Langshaw, Billy Knowles, Darren Saint, Dave Roberts, Tommy Knox, Neil Hanson, Phil Farrelly, Peter King, Paul Blasbery, Danny McVey, Paul Gwyther, Stuart Heaps, Rod Cottam, Roy Baldwin. Front left to right: Chris Stanton, Kerrie King (mascot), Gary Trewhitt, Ged Nolan, Andy Howard, Paul Dawson, Kevin Still, Stevie Horrocks, Mick McDonough.

the final was to be played at Bury F.C.'s Gigg Lane ground, where they would face Champions-elect, Flixton. The Manchester side were reported to be paying big money and entered the match as strong favourites after convincingly beating Burscough two nights earlier in a league fixture.

When Burscough's team coach pulled up at Gigg Lane on Thursday 25th April 1996, manager Davison stood before the still seated team; 'When you get off this coach, I don't want to see you speaking to any of their players before the game. You're here to do a job,' were the printable words he used. This was a game you felt Burscough were not going to lose!

The support was again tremendous. Some of the younger supporters from previous finals were now young adults and no longer Victoria Park regulars, but they had re-united for another big football occasion in order to shout and sing for their local team and help them recapture the glory of 1993. They were not to be disappointed, as they saw a Burscough side battle and contain in the first half, and then with a tremendous second half display, take control of the game and deservedly overcome powerful opponents, the only goal coming from substitute Phil Farrelly after 73 minutes.

The Flixton supporters were left asking after the game; 'who's your No. 8, we didn't know about him?' Andy Howard had been kept under wraps two nights earlier and held back for the final. It was a major phsychological victory for John Davison as Howard's ball skills viciously exposed the limitations of the big Flixton defenders. Geoff Howard, reporting for the Advertiser, described it as 'a tactical battle of wits Davison won hands down with his opposite number in the Flixton camp.' However, it goes down as a team triumph of the highest calibre, made even more meritorious by the loss of so much forward power in the latter stages of the season.

Burscough's victorious team that evening was: Paul Blasbery, Neil Hanson, Chris Stanton, Tommy Knox, Ged Nolan, Peter King, Darren Saint, Andy Howard, Kevin Still, Dave Roberts, Paul Dawson. Subs: Billy Knowles, Gary Trewhitt, Phil Farrelly.

In the club's fiftieth year, the Burscough team marched up the steps into Bury's Main Stand where skipper Ged Nolan was presented with the North West Counties League Challenge Cup by League Chairman Mr. J.E.Hinchliffe.

Ged Nolan lifted the cup high to the supporters' cheers. With a little imagination, and viewed through slightly misty eyes, stood there in the famous green shirt, Ged could easily have been any one of the Burscough skippers who have adopted a similar pose over the past half century....Joe Kelly in 1948, Gilly Houghton in 1950, Jimmy Cookson in 1954, Arthur Green in 1956, Bob Jones in 1967 and 1970, Kenny Miller in 1975, Syl Nolan in 1983, or Tony Quinn in 1993.

Some things have never changed.

PART 3

A TRIBUTE TO FRANK PARR

FRANK PARR

There have been many, many people who have dedicated a major part of their life to Burscough Football Club and the value of their contribution can never be overstated and, hopefully, through the publication of this book, will never be forgotten. However, in this the club's fiftieth year, it is only right and proper that we should pay tribute to the massive contribution made by one man in particular to this club reaching such a proud milestone.

Frank Parr was born on the 28th November 1928 in Burscough. His father was John Parr and his mother was Ellen (née Howard). Frank had two half-brothers by his mother's first marriage, Bob and Tom Walmsley. He also had two brothers, Harry, who was killed in the Second World War, and Fred, a supporter of the club and ex-committeeman, who sadly died in 1995. Frank married Joan Booth in 1959 and they had two children, Kevin and Mark. In 1995, Frank and Joan became grandparents, when a little girl, Elizabeth, was born to Kevin and his wife Joanne.

Frank's mother and father were both bargees on the Leeds-Liverpool Canal. His father operated one of the first steam-driven barges, *Pioneer*, between Ainscough's Mill and Wigan.

The family home was in Victoria Street, overlooking the canal. Tom Walmsley recalls, 'John Parr was friendly with some of the Burscough Rangers' players and it was common in the 1920s for them to call at the Parr home after the game, where there was always a stewpot of cowheel and shinbeef on the go.' Frank's brother, Fred, remembered 'regular visitors included the Wigan based players Billy Ashurst and Billy Green.'

Frank's first job after leaving school was as a butcher's lad for Joe Martland. He used to take the pig's heads home to his mother who would boil them in the washhouse. Frank's job would then be to put them through the mincer to make brawn.

He then served his time as a blacksmith with Ted Davis in Victoria Street, where they shoed many of the farm horses in the area. When he was 18 years old Frank registered for call-up to the forces. The local Farmer's Union official heard about it, and although Frank never discovered precisely why, he didn't get called up, presumably after pressure from local farmers. He worked as a blacksmith until he was 26, when he was advised to give it up because he had suffered a hernia.

Meanwhile, after playing football for the under 16 team of Bankfield Minors in 1944-45 season, Frank turned out at right half for Burscough Juniors, who played at Victoria Park, during 1945-46 season, where he also got his first experience of football administration.

In 1946, he became a founding committee member of Burscough Football Club. Ronnie Barker recalls; 'Frank, along with Johnny Baldwin, did a lot of work on the ground when the club first started.'

In his early years with Burscough he ran the Reserve team. During his period as manager they won the Liverpool County Combination Division Two Championship in 1953-54 and the Liverpool Challenge Cup in 1954-55. Fred Parr recalled in 1995, 'Burscough's chairman Jimmy Johnson was his mentor, Frank thought the world of him.' Charlie Jones can still clearly recall the words of Jimmy Johnson that 'Frank would be a future chairman of the club.'

Frank Parr continued as second team manager into the 1960s and was appointed to the Management Committee of the Liverpool County Combination in 1961.

Chris Mahood recalls 'Frank ran the Reserve side for years, often with no-one helping him. I worked with Frank for 18 years and I can't remember us having a single row.' Not everyone can say that!

Frank took a back seat in club affairs when his children were young, but after a period as vice-chairman, he once more came to the fore in August 1974 when he was appointed chairman of the club, in succession to Bill Martland. He has been chairman ever since.

He was a Vice-President of the Cheshire County League and is still a Vice-President of the North West Counties Football League. He was awarded the Order of Merit by the Lancashire Football Association in 1984 and is currently a Council Member of the same body.

Frank worked for Universal Bulk Handling in Orrell Lane for many years, where he became Works Manager. His last job, prior to his retirement in early 1995, was at Rylands Ltd. in Warrington.

Burscough Football Club reaches its fiftieth year in good health, continues to win trophies and compete with the very best at senior non-league level. The Victoria Park ground, which has been home to the village football club for the best part of one hundred years, has never looked better, is a credit to the club and to Burscough village, and is a fitting monument to the standards Frank Parr has sought to achieve and maintain at Burscough. The club, in particular, and North West football, in general, owes a tremendous debt of gratitude to Frank Parr.

This debt was recognised in June 1996 when he was presented with The Football Association 50 Year Long Service Award for service to the game of football.

Speaking in 1995, former club secretary Ronnie Barker paid this meaningful tribute to Frank; 'It's hard work running a football club and Frank has been involved for 50 years. He deserves an O.B.E.'

1947-48 *A member of the club's Management Committee.*
Left to right:: Teddy Dutton (Treasurer), Jack Bowen, Terry Bowen (mascot), Jimmy Langton, Harry Vickers, Tom Riley, Dick Holcroft (Secretary), George Crabb, Edwin Eastwood, Frank Parr, Johnny Baldwin (Chairman), Evan Rimmer.

c1952 *Included in this photograph taken at one of the club's Hot Pot Suppers in the British Legion are: Frank Parr, Harry Waugh, Steve Jones, Jimmy Wright and Johnny Wishart.*

1953-54 *Manager of Burscough Reserves, Liverpool County Combination Division Two Champions.*
Back left to right: Frank Parr, Jimmy Aspinall, Brian Finnigan, Jackson, Jimmy Wright, George Higgins, Gerry Ashton, Tommy Gaskell (Trainer)
Front left to right: Jim Martland, 'Digger' Stanley, Matt Brennan, Tom Galvin, Len Wilkinson, Billy Birchall.

1955-56 *Manager, Burscough Reserves. Back Left to right:: Frank Richmond (Trainer), Bob McAdam, Jim Martland, Alan Buttons, Joe Brazier, Frank Walsh, Jimmy Wright, Frank Parr. Front left to right: Billy Birchall, Joe Brine, Jimmy Aspinall, Ronnie Wright, Gerry Ashton. Pictured at Sandy Lane, Skelmersdale.*

1959 *The Crewe F.A. Cup Tie attracted much attention from the local and national press. This pre-match photocall includes, from the left at the front: Alf Marsden (Chairman) and Bill Lyon. At the back between the photographers are: Frank Parr, Secretary Dick Ashcroft (partially hidden), Harry Wareing, Freddie Monk, Unknown, Bill Harrison. Lit up in the background is the 'sentry box' where you paid to enter the stand.*

1961-62 *Burscough Reserves. Back left to right: Frank Parr (Manager), Slade, Gaskin, Clarke, Gerry Joyce, Unknown, John Melling, T.Conley.*
Front left to right: Roberts, Taylor, Tony Rimmer, Hume, Keith Reeder.

1974   Frank Parr pictured at Victoria Park in August 1974 following his appointment as Chairman of Burscough Football Club.

1976   A Celebrity Dinner held at the Social Club in December 1976. Back left to right: Dave Raybould (Secretary), Derek Watkinson (now Senior Vice-president of the Club), Frank Dobson (President), Brian Lowe (Treasurer), Gordon Hoskin (Vice-Chairman), Larry Carberry, Wesley Bridge, Bill Bothwell.
Front left to right: Bob Langton, Frank Parr, Joe Mercer, Johnny Wheeler.

1988 Frank Parr welcomes three former players back to Victoria Park in January 1988. From left to right: Jim Cookson, John Disley, Frank, Billy Thompson.

1993 Chairman Frank Parr joins the players on the pitch to celebrate the League Challenge Cup victory over Nantwich Town.

1996 *Fifty years on, Chairman of Burscough Football Club, and still winning trophies. Pictured at Gigg Lane, Bury, following another Burscough triumph. The Trophy is 107 years old, Frank somewhat younger, but they both still look in fine condition after a lifetime in the game.*

PART 4

REFERENCE SECTION

Edited & Researched by Stan Strickland

MATCH RECORDS

This section of the book lists the match by match record of all the games played by Burscough Rangers and Burscough from 1906 to 1996. It records, where known, the date of the game, the opponent, the competition, the venue, the result, and the goalscorers. Additional information is occasionally given regarding the attendance or the 'gate' taken.

J.W. (John) Berry was involved with Burscough Rangers for virtually the whole of their thirty year existence. During this period he kept meticulous details of all the matches they played. The records between 1906, the first season Rangers played competitive football, and 1933, were recorded by him and finely scripted in a small leather pocket book. They are now published in full for the first time and I dedicate this section of the book to his memory.

Strangely, and for a reason I have not been able to establish, John Berry recorded the end of Burscough Rangers upon completion of 1932-33 season, and no further records were kept. Rangers continued for almost two further years, predominantly playing in the West Lancashire League, and the results over that period have been researched by myself. It may have been too painful for him to accept the Rangers' failure to retain their Lancashire Combination status, or he may have believed that the club were no longer representative of the Rangers he knew, and undoubtedly loved. Whatever the reason, there can be no dispute that the Rangers did continue until 1935, before folding.

Upon the formation of Burscough Football Club in 1946, John Berry's son, H.V. (Bert) Berry, continued the family tradition and documented Burscough's match records until 1974-75.

All of the above records, including John Berry's pocket book, have been retained by his grandson J.E. (Eric) Berry until the present day, so we are indeed indebted to the Berry family that a comprehensive record of Burscough football throughout this century has, firstly, been kept, and, more importantly, survived.

Since my appointment as club secretary at the end of 1992, I have kept similar records, but that still left a void of almost twenty years to bridge, from 1975 to 1992.

This period has proved the most difficult to document. Results and league tables have been obtained from old match record books retained by my predecessor Mike Woods, the archives of the *Ormskirk Advertiser* and *Southport Visiter*, old programmes, and from various club historians scattered around the North West, most notably Tom Sault (New Brighton), David

Haworth (Rossendale United), and Malcolm Flanagan (South Liverpool). Paul Cowburn has maintained records of the North West Counties League since its inception in 1982, and he has proved an invaluable source of information covering that period. Finally, missing Cheshire League results were supplied by the Chairman of the North West Counties Football League, Eric Hinchliffe.

The accumulative season by season records of the Burscough Rangers and Burscough are also recorded. During the Burscough Rangers' years, friendly games are included in the accumulative record for each season and in the club's total record. John Berry, in his records, included them, and I saw no reason to change anything. Friendly matches were often viewed at that time as prestige affairs to be treated by the clubs concerned, and the local press, with the utmost gravity.

To prove the point, a widely quoted statistic over the years, has been the 20 match unbeaten run recorded by Burscough Rangers in 1914-15 season. In 1949-50 season, Burscough equalled that record, playing twenty competitive fixtures before losing. However, what is not so widely appreciated, was that Rangers' record included four 'friendly' fixtures. This is not to devalue the achievement, but to emphasise that equal importance was attached to these additional prestige fixtures, which is, perhaps, not so apparent today. Burscough's accumulative record, therefore, only takes into account competitive league and cup games.

BURSCOUGH RANGERS

1906 - 1935

1906/07 Season
Southport & District Amateur League (Second Division)

Date	Opponent	H/A	Competition	Result	Scorers
Sat Sep 1	L & Y Recs	H	Lge	W 2-0	James Gore, James Ashton
Sat Sep 8	Birkdale Working Lads	H	Lge	W 6-0	J.Gore, O.G., Ashton, Sam Jowett
Sat Sep 15	St. Lukes	H	Lge	W 7-1	R.Gore, Jowett, J.Gore, Ashton
Sat Sep 22	St. Pauls	A	Lge	D 1-1	R.Gore
Sat Oct 13	Hawkshead Cong. Inst.	A	Lge	W 6-1	W.Stringfellow, Ashton (2), Jowett (3)
Sat Oct 20	Southbank Wesleyans	H	Lge	W 3-1	J.Gore (2), Jowett
Sat Oct 27	Tarleton Institute	A	2nd Senior Charity Cup	W 2-1	R.Gore, J.Gore
Sat Nov 3	L & Y Recs	A	Lge	L 3-5	Jowett (2), R.Gore
Sat Nov 10	Southport Working Lads	H	Lge	W 3-0	Ashton, J.Gore (2)
Sat Nov 17	Blowick Wesleyans	A	Lge	L 1-7	
Sat Nov 24	Banks St. Stephens Res.	H	Charity Cup	D 1-1	
	Banks St. Stephens Res.	A	Charity Cup replay	D 2-2	
Sat Dec 1	Hawkshead Cong. Inst.	H	Lge	W 1-0	Jowett
Sat Mar 9	Banks St. Stephens Res.	H	Charity Cup 2nd replay	L 1-2	
Sat Mar 16	Blowick Wesleyans	H	Lge	W 3-0	Ashton, J.Gore
	Crossens	H	Lge	L 1-2	
	Crossens	A	Lge	D 2-2	
	Birkdale Working Lads	A	Lge	L 0-3	
	Southport Working Lads	A	Lge	W 3-2	
	Southbank Wesleyans	A	Lge	W 4-0	
	St. Lukes	A	Lge	W 4-1	
	St. Pauls	H	Lge	W 4-1	
Mon Apr 1	Ormskirk Rovers		Medals Comp. 1st Rd	L 0-2	
	at Victoria Athletic Grounds, Ormskirk				

1907/08 Season
Southport & District Amateur League (Senior Division)

Date	Opponent	H/A	Competition	Result	Scorers
Sat Sep 7	All Saints	H	Lge	W 11-1	
Sat Sep 14	Birkdale Working Lads	A	Lge	D 0-0	
Sat Sep 21	Southbank Wesleyans	H	Lge	W 2-0	Jowett (2)
Sat Sep 28	Blowick Wesleyans	A	Lge	L 1-2	
Sat Oct 5	Southport Working Lads	H	Lge	W 5-2	
Sat Oct 12	All Saints	A	Lge	W 3-2	J.Gore (2), J.Baldwin
Sat Oct 19	Birkdale Reserves	H	Lge	W 4-3	Ashton, Jowett (3)
Sat Oct 26	Crossens Institute	H	Lge	W 3-2	Ashton, W.Stringfellow, Jowett
Sat Nov 2	Park Villa Reserves	A	Lge	L 1-2	Jowett
Sat Nov 9	Birkdale Working Lads	H	Lge	W 4-2	J.Gore, Jowett (2), O.G.
Sat Nov 16	Churchtown Cong.	H	Lge	D 3-3	Jimmy Pye, Ashton, O.G.
Sat Nov 23	Burscough Ordnance	A	Lge	W 5-2	Jowett (4), J.Gore
Sat Dec 7	Hesketh Bank	H	Lge	W 4-0	Jowett, Pye, J.Gore (2)
Sat Dec 14	Aughton Casuals	H	Friendly	W 9-6	
Sat Dec 21	Park Villa Reserves	H	Lge	L 1-3	
Wed Dec 25	Aughton Casuals	H	Friendly	W 9-1	
Thu Dec 26	Birkdale Reserves	A	Lge	L 1-2	
Sat Dec 28	Banks St. Stephens A	H	Lge	W 3-1	
Wed Jan 1	Crossens Institute	A	Lge	W 4-3	W.Bentham, Pye (2), Jack Radcliffe
Sat Jan 4	Southport Working Lads	A	Lge	W 2-1	Ashton, Pye
Sat Jan 11	Birkdale Reserves	H	Southport 2nd Senior Charity Cup	W 3-2	Pye (2), Ashton
Sat Jan 18	Southbank Wesleyans	A	Lge	W 3-0	Pye, R.Gore, Bentham
Sat Jan 25	Burscough Ordnance	H	Lge	W 2-0	W.Lewis, J.Gore
Sat Feb 1	Emmanuel	A	Lge	L 1-3	R.Gore
Sat Feb 8	Blowick Wesleyans	H	Charity Cup	W 2-1	Jowett (2)
Sat Feb 22	Hesketh Bank	A	Lge	D 0-0	
Sat Feb 29	Churchtown Cong.	A	Lge	L 1-3	
Sat Mar 14	Emmanuel	H	Lge	L 1-2	
Sat Mar 28	Banks St. Stephens A	A	Lge	L 2-5	
Sat Apr 4	Burscough Ordnance	H	Friendly	D 4-4	
Sat Apr 11	Southport Working Lads *at Park Villa ground*		Charity Cup Semi-final	D 1-1	
Fri Apr 17	Southport Working Lads *at Park Villa ground*		Charity Cup replay	W 2-0	
Mon Apr 20	Aintree Loco's	A	Ormskirk Medals	L 1-2	
Sat Apr 25	Blowick Wesleyans	H	Lge	L 1-2	
Wed Apr 29	Churchtown Cong. *at Central Ground, Southport*		Southport 2nd Senior Charity Cup Final	W 2-1	

1908/09 Season
Southport & District Amateur League (Senior Division)

Sat Sep 5	Burscough Ordnance	A	Friendly	W 5-4	
Sat Sep 12	Southport Working Lads	A	Lge	L 2-4	
Sat Sep 19	Crossens Institute	A	Lge	W 4-2	Pye, Jowett (3)
Sat Sep 26	Stanley Institute	H	Friendly	W 3-0	
Sat Oct 3	Birkdale	A	Lge	W 3-2	Jowett, J.Gore, R.Gore
Sat Oct 10	Southport Territorials	H	Lge	W 14-0	
Sat Oct 17	Churchtown Cong.	H	Lge	W 4-1	Ashton, Jowett (2), R.Gore
Sat Oct 24	Park Villa Reserves	A	Lge	D 2-2	
Sat Oct 31	Blowick Wesleyans	A	Lge	L 2-3	
Sat Nov 7	Emmanuel	H	Lge	D 3-3	Baldwin, Ashton, Jowett
Sat Nov 21	Southport Territorials	A	Lge	W 3-1	Jowett (3)
Sat Nov 28	Banks St. Stephens A	A	Lge	L 0-4	
Sat Dec 5	Skelmersdale Mission Res	H	Friendly	W 9-1	
Sat Dec 12	Crossens Institute	H	Lge	W 5-3	
Sat Dec 19	Park Villa Reserves	H	Lge	W 2-1	
Fri Dec 25	Ormskirk Central	H	Friendly	L 1-2	
Sat Jan 2	Banks St. Stephens A	H	Lge	L 0-4	
Sat Jan 9	Banks St. Stephens A	H	Cup	W 3-1	J.Gore, W.Stringfellow, H.Smith
Sat Jan 16	Birkdale Working Lads	A	Lge		
	abandoned, Rangers winning 2-0				
Sat Jan 23	Churchtown	H	Cup	W 2-1	J.Gore, H.Smith
Sat Jan 30	Birkdale Working Lads	A	Lge	W 4-3	
Sat Feb 20	Blowick Wesleyans	H	Lge	L 1-2	
Sat Feb 27	Birkdale Working Lads	H	Lge	W 1-0	
Sat Mar 20	Birkdale	H	Lge	W 4-0	
Sat Mar 27	Crossens		Cup Semi-final	L 2-3	
	at Marshside ground				
Fri Apr 9	Burscough Wesleyans	H	Friendly	L 3-5	
Fri Apr 16	Emmanuel	A	Lge	D 2-2	
Sat Apr 17	Birkdale	A	Medal Competition	W 2-1	
Sat Apr 24	Southport Working Lads	H	Lge	W 5-2	
Thu Apr 29	Southport Working Lads	A	Medals Final	D 0-0	
Fri Apr 30	Southport Working Lads	H	Medals Final replay	W 3-1	Geo. Hunter (2), 1 unknown

1909/10 Season
Southport & District Amateur League (Senior Division)
also members of the Ormskirk & District Amateur League

Date	Opponent	H/A	Competition	Result	Scorers
Sat Sep 4	Bickerstaffe Mission	H	Ormskirk Lge	W 9-1	Gibbons (4), H.Smith (2), Jowett, Ashton, J.Gore
Sat Sep 11	Banks St. Stephens A	A	Southport Lge	W 2-1	R.Gore, Gibbons
Sat Sep 25	Crossens Institute	H	Southport Lge	W 3-2	
Sat Oct 2	Skelmersdale Mission	H	Ormskirk Lge	D 2-2	
Sat Oct 9	North Meols Working Lads	A	Southport Lge	L 0-2	
Sat Oct 16	Blowick Institute	H	Southport Lge	W 7-2	Gould (3), H.Smith, Ashton, Jowett, J.Gore
Sat Oct 30	Crossens Institute	A	Southport Lge	D 2-2	
Sat Nov 6	Park Villa Reserves	A	Southport Lge	W 3-1	Ashton, Gould, Pye
Sat Nov 13	North Meols Working Lads	H	Southport Lge	D 1-1	Jowett
Sat Nov 20	Skelmersdale Mission	A	Ormskirk Lge	L 1-4	
Sat Nov 27	Banks St. Stephens A	H	Southport Lge	W 3-0	Field, Gould, Ashton
Sat Dec 11	Park Villa Reserves	H	Southport Lge	W 4-0	
Sat Dec 18	Bickerstaffe Mission	A	Ormskirk Lge	L 2-4	
Sat Dec 25	Ormskirk 9th Kings	A	Ormskirk Lge	W 6-1	
Mon Dec 27	Burscough Swifts	H	Ormskirk Lge	W 6-0	
Sat Jan 1	Ormskirk 9th Kings	A	Ormskirk Lge	W 5-0	
Sat Jan 8	Emmanuel	A	Southport Lge	D 0-0	
Sat Jan 15	Ormskirk 9th Kings	H	Stanley Shield	W 3-1	
Sat Jan 22	Birkdale St. Johns	A	Southport Shield	L 0-7	
Sat Feb 12	Mawdesley	A	Ormskirk Lge	L 0-1	
Sat Feb 19	Churchtown Cong.	H	Southport Lge	W 4-0	
Sat Feb 26	Westhead Juniors at Dray & Horses ground		Stanley Shield Semi-final	L 0-2	
Sat Mar 5	Skelmersdale West End	A	Ormskirk Lge	D 1-1	
Sat Mar 12	Westhead Juniors	H	Ormskirk Lge	L 0-4	
Sat Mar 19	Mawdesley	H	Ormskirk Lge	W 7-1	
Fri Mar 25	Emmanuel *morning kick-off*	H	Southport Lge	W 2-1	
Fri Mar 25	Burscough Wesleyans *afternoon kick-off*	H	Friendly	W 1-0	Lewis
Sat Mar 26	Skelmersdale West End	H	Ormskirk Lge	W 2-0	Ashton, W.Stringfellow
Mon Mar 28	Churchtown Cong.	A	Southport Lge	W 1-0	
Sat Apr 2	Rainford Colliery Juniors	A	Ormskirk Lge	D 2-2	
Wed Apr 13	Ormskirk Reserves	A	Ormskirk Lge	L 0-1	
Mon Apr 18	Ormskirk Reserves	H	Ormskirk Lge	L 1-3	
Sat Apr 23	Rainford Colliery Juniors	H	Ormskirk Lge	W 3-0	
Wed Apr 27	Westhead Juniors	A	Ormskirk Lge	L 0-1	
Sat Apr 30	Selected Southport Lge X1	H	Friendly	W 3-1	

1910/11 Season
Southport & District Amateur League (Senior Division)

Date	Opponent	H/A	Comp	Result	Scorers
Sat Sep 3	L & Y Locos	H	Lge	D 3-3	R.Stringfellow, Billy Aspinwall, R.Gore
Sat Sep 10	Burscough Ordnance	A	Friendly	W 5-3	
Sat Sep 17	Birkdale South End	H	Lge	W 8-1	James Ashton, Jowett (2), 5 unknown
Sat Sep 24	Birkdale South End	A	Southport Shield	L 3-5	
Sat Oct 1	Churchtown	A	Lge	L 1-3	
Sat Oct 8	Southport Central A	H	Lge	W 2-0	
Sat Oct 15	North Meols	A	Lge	D 0-0	
Sat Oct 22	Marshside	H	Lge	W 4-1	O.G., Pye (2), McLoughlin
Sat Oct 29	Tarleton	A	Lge	D 3-3	
Sat Nov 5	St. Pauls	A	Lge	W 2-1	
Sat Nov 19	Crossens	A	Lge	L 1-2	
Sat Nov 26	Southport Central A	A	Lge	W 1-0	Pye
Sat Dec 3	Churchtown	H	Lge	W 3-0	Tommy Ashton, J.Ashton, 1 unknown
Sat Dec 10	Appley Bridge	H	Friendly	W 6-1	McLoughlin (2), Baldwin, T.Ashton (3)
Sat Dec 17	Tarleton	H	Lge	W 7-0	T.Ashton (3), McLoughlin (2), Pye, J.Ashton
Sat Dec 24	Crossens	H	Lge	W 3-2	Jowett, T.Ashton, McLoughlin
Mon Dec 26	Elton (Liverpool)	H	Friendly	W 2-1	J.Ashton, T.Ashton
Tue Dec 27	Ormskirk	A	Friendly	W 2-0	
Sat Jan 7	Park Villa Reserves	A	Lge	D 3-3	
Sat Jan 14	Park Villa Reserves	H	Lge	W 10-3	
Sat Jan 21	L & Y Locos	A	Lge	D 2-2	
Sat Feb 4	North Meols	H	Lge	W 3-1	Jowett, George Merritt, 1 unknown
Sat Feb 11	Marshside	A	Lge	D 1-1	
Sat Feb 25	St. Pauls	H	Lge	W 2-1	
Sat Mar 11	Portland St.	H	Lge	W 3-0	
Sat Mar 18	Birkdale South End	A	Lge	D 2-2	
Sat Apr 8	Portland St.	A	Lge	W 3-2	Pye (2), Jowett
Fri Apr 14	Banks A	H	Lge	W 2-1	
Mon Apr 17	Banks A	A	Lge	L 0-1	

1911/12 Season
Southport & District Amateur League (Senior Division)

Date	Opponent	H/A	Comp	Result	Scorers
Sat Sep 9	Marshside	H	Lge	D 3-3	
Sat Sep 16	L & Y Locos	H	Lge	W 4-3	
Sat Sep 23	North Meols Working Lads	A	Lge	L 0-1	
Sat Sep 30	Tarleton	H	Lge	D 3-3	
Sat Oct 7	Marshside	A	Lge	L 0-3	
Sat Oct 14	Banks United	H	Lge	W 2-1	
Sat Oct 28	Norwood Crescent	A	Lge	L 0-1	
Sat Nov 11	Ormskirk Swifts	H	Friendly	W 5-1	
Sat Nov 18	Park Villa Reserves	H	Lge	D 1-1	
Sat Dec 2	Churchtown	H	Lge	W 4-2	
	an appeal caused the game to be replayed				
Sat Dec 9	Crossens Institute	H	Lge	W 4-1	
Sat Dec 16	Norwood Crescent	H	Lge	W 2-1	
Mon Dec 25	Churchtown	H	Lge	W 1-0	
Tue Dec 26	Elton (Liverpool)	H	Friendly	D 2-2	
Sat Jan 6	Churchtown	A	Lge	W 3-1	T.Ashton (2), Pye
Sat Jan 13	Tarleton	H	Major White Cup	W 3-0	J.Ashton, Jowett, J.Gore
Sat Jan 20	Appley Bridge	A	Friendly	W 4-1	Pye, T.Ashton (3)
Sat Jan 27	Crossens Institute	H	Lge	W 6-1	J.Ashton (3), T.Ashton (2), Royston
Sat Mar 2	Crawford Village	H	Friendly	L 2-3	
Sat Mar 9	Crossens Institute	H	Major White Cup	W 7-0	
Sat Mar 16	Banks United	A	Major White Cup	D 1-1	J.Ashton
Sat Mar 23	Banks United	H	Replay	D 2-2	
Sat Mar 30	Banks United		2nd Replay	L 0-1	
	at Park Villa ground				
Fri Apr 5	Melling	H	Friendly	D 1-1	
Sat Apr 6	Appley Bridge	H	Friendly	L 0-1	
Sat Apr 20	North Meols Working Lads	H	Lge	W 4-2	
Tue Apr 23	Park Villa Reserves	A	Lge	L 0-3	
Thu Apr 25	Tarleton	A	Lge	L 0-5	
Sat Apr 27	Banks United	A	Lge	L 0-2	

1912/13 Season
Lancashire Alliance

Tue Sep 3	Skelmersdale Mission	H	Friendly	L 1-2	
Sat Sep 14	Whitley Amateurs	H	Lge	W 6-2	Culshaw, T.Ashton (3), O.G., Bradley
Sat Sep 21	Walkden Central Reserves	A	Lge	D 1-1	John Culshaw
Sat Sep 28	Newsprings	H	Lge	W 4-2	T.Ashton, Taylor (2), J.Gore
Sat Oct 5	Golborne United	A	Lge	L 3-7	
Sat Oct 12	Appley Bridge	H	Lge	W 4-2	Makinson (2), Culshaw, T.Ashton
Sat Oct 19	Ashton YMCA	A	Lge	W 2-0	T.Ashton, Culshaw
Sat Nov 2	Brynn	A	Lge	L 0-6	
Sat Nov 9	Brynn	H	Lge	L 0-2	
Sat Nov 16	Ashton YMCA	A	Wigan Cup	W 3-0	T.Ashton (2), Culshaw
Sat Nov 23	L. & N.W. Permanent Way	H	Liverpool Junior Cup	W 6-2	Culshaw (4), T.Ashton, Bolton
Sat Nov 30	Ashton YMCA	H	Lge	W 2-1	Makinson, T.Ashton
Sat Dec 7	Newsprings	A	Lge	W 2-1	T.Ashton, Makinson
Sat Dec 14	Brynn	H	Wigan Cup	W 2-0	Culshaw, Makinson
Sat Dec 21	Sandhurst	H	Liverpool Junior Cup	W 6-1	Culshaw (4), Makinson (2)
Wed Dec 25	Billinge Albion	H	Friendly	L 1-2	
Thu Dec 26	Elton (Liverpool)	H	Friendly	W 8-0	
Sat Dec 28	Standish	A	Lge	D 2-2	
Wed Jan 1	Walkden Central Reserves	H	Lge	W 5-0	
Sat Jan 4	Ormskirk 9th Kings	H	Friendly	W 3-2	
Sat Jan 18	Alexandra Vics	H	Friendly	D 2-2	
Sat Jan 25	Alexandra Vics	H	Liverpool Junior Cup	L 0-2	
Sat Feb 1	Appley Bridge	A	Lge	D 2-2	Jowett, Taylor
Sat Feb 8	Hindley Green Athletic	H	Wigan Cup	W 6-1	Jowett, T.Ashton (3), Culshaw, J.Ashton
Sat Feb 15	Golborne United	H	Lge	W 3-0	Culshaw (2), T.Ashton
Sat Feb 22	Walkden Central Reserves	H	Wigan Cup	W 6-1	
Sat Mar 1	Standish	H	Wigan Cup	W 7-0	J.Ashton (2), 5 unknown
Sat Mar 8	Golborne United	A	Friendly	L 0-2	
Sat Mar 21	Diamond Match Works	H	Friendly	W 9-0	
Tue Mar 24	Appley Bridge	A	Wigan Cup Semi-final	W 4-0	Pye, Walter Smith, J.Ashton (2)
	Attend: 700		1st leg		
Sat Mar 28	Melling	H	Friendly	W 6-0	
Sat Apr 5	Standish	H	Lge	W 4-1	
Sat Apr 12	Appley Bridge	H	Wigan Cup Semi-final	W 3-2	Pye (2), J.Ashton
			2nd leg		
Sat Apr 19	Golborne United		Wigan Cup Final	W 4-2	Pye, W.Smith, T.Ashton (2)
	at Flapper Fold, Atherton				
Wed Apr 23	Ormskirk	A	Friendly	L 0-1	
Sat Apr 26	Aughton Wanderers	H	Friendly	W 7-2	T.Ashton (2), 5 unknown
Wed Apr 30	Ormskirk	H	Friendly	W 4-1	

1913/14 Season
Lancashire Alliance

Date	Opponent	H/A	Competition	Result	Scorers
Sat Sep 13	Standish	H	Lge	W 4-1	T.Ashton, Fearns, Culshaw (2)
Sat Sep 20	Abram Colliery	A	Lge	W 2-1	T.Ashton, Merritt
Sat Sep 27	Atherton Reserves	H	Lge	W 4-1	
Sat Oct 4	Hindley Green	H	Lge	W 6-2	Culshaw (2), Merritt, T.Ashton (2), Pye
Sat Oct 11	Standish St. Wilfrids	A	Lge	W 3-0	T.Ashton, Culshaw, J.Ashton
Sat Oct 18	Skelmersdale Mission	H	Lge	W 4-2	Harry Ball, T.Ashton (2), Culshaw
Sat Nov 1	Atherton Reserves	A	Lge	D 1-1	Pye (2), T.Ashton
Sat Nov 8	Westhead	H	Friendly	W 2-0	
Sat Nov 15	Hindley Green	A	Lge	W 4-0	T.Ashton (3), O.G.
Sat Nov 22	Golborne United	H	Wigan Cup	W 3-1	Ball, T.Ashton (2)
Sat Dec 6	Standish St. Wilfrids	H	Lge	D 1-1	Pye
Sat Dec 13	Standish	A	Lge	D 1-1	T.Ashton
Sat Dec 20	Skelmersdale Mission	H	Wigan Cup	W 4-0	
Thu Dec 25	Ormskirk	A	Friendly	W 4-0	
Sat Dec 27	Hindley Green	H	Excelsior Cup	W 3-0	
Sat Jan 3	Earlestown Rovers	H	Liverpool Challenge Cup	W 5-1	
Sat Jan 10	Standish	H	Excelsior Cup	W 3-0	Culshaw (2), T.Ashton
Sat Jan 17	Skelmersdale Mission	A	Lge	D 0-0	
Sat Jan 24	South Liverpool	H	Friendly	L 3-4	
Sat Jan 31	Park Villa	A	Liverpool Challenge Cup	L 1-4	
Sat Feb 7	Golborne United	A	Lge	L 2-3	
Sat Feb 14	Standish St. Wilfrids	H	Excelsior Cup	W 2-1	
Sat Feb 21	Standish	A	Wigan Cup	W 1-0	
Sat Feb 28	Standish St. Wilfrids	A	Wigan Cup	L 1-3	
Sat Mar 7	Golborne United	H	Lge	W 3-1	Merritt (2), Pye (2)
Sat Mar 14	Golborne United	A	Excelsior Cup	L 1-2	Pye
Sat Mar 21	Hindley Green	A	Wigan Cup	W 2-0	Culshaw, Riding
Sat Mar 28	Skelmersdale Mission	A	Excelsior Cup	W 3-1	T.Ashton (3)
Sat Apr 4	Rest of League	H	Friendly	L 0-1	
Fri Apr 10	Tarleton	H	Friendly	W 6-1	T.Ashton (5), 1 unknown
Sat Apr 18	Standish St. Wilfrids	H	Excelsior Cup	W 6-0	
Sat Apr 25	Golborne United *at Hindley*		Wigan Cup Final	L 0-1	
Wed Apr 29	Standish *at Ormskirk*		Excelsior Cup Final	W 3-2	

1914/15 Season
Liverpool County Combination

Sat Sep 12	Clock Face	H	Lge	W 2-0
Sat Sep 19	Southport Park Villa	A	Lge	W 3-1
Sat Sep 26	Earlestown Rovers	A	Lge	D 1-1
Sat Oct 3	Borough of Wallasey	H	George Mahon Cup	W 3-1
Sat Oct 17	North Engineers	A	Lge	W 4-1
Sat Oct 24	Southport Park Villa	H	Lge	W 5-0
Sat Oct 31	Clock Face	H	George Mahon Cup	W 8-4
	George Mahon Cup abandoned due to War			
Sat Nov 7	Skelmersdale United	A	Lge	D 1-1
Sat Nov 14	Southport Central XI	H	Friendly	W 12-1
Sat Nov 28	North Engineers	H	Lge	W 9-0
Sat Dec 5	St. Helens Town	H	Lge	W 5-0
Sat Dec 12	South Liverpool	A	Lge	W 2-0
Sat Dec 19	South Liverpool	H	Lge	W 11-2
Fri Dec 25	Westhead	H	Friendly	W 3-0
Sat Dec 26	Skelmersdale United	H	Friendly	W 5-1
Fri Jan 1	Tarleton	H	Friendly	W 5-0
Sat Jan 23	Tranmere Rovers Res.	H	Liverpool Challenge Cup	W 1-0
Sat Feb 6	Borough of Wallasey	H	Lge	W 4-1
Sat Feb 13	Borough of Wallasey	A	Lge	W 2-1
Sat Feb 27	Dominion	H	Liverpool Challenge Cup	W 5-2
Sat Mar 6	Skelmersdale United	H	Lge	L 1-2
Sat Mar 13	Skelmersdale United	A	Liverpool Challenge Cup	D 0-0
	at Ormskirk		Semi-final	
Sat Mar 20	Skelmersdale United	H	Liverpool Challenge Cup	W 4-0
	at Ormskirk		Semi-final replay	
Mon Apr 5	Southport Park Villa		Liverpool Challenge Cup	D 1-1
	at Goodison Park		Final	
Sat Apr 10	St. Helens Town	A	Lge	L 0-1
Sat Apr 24	Southport Park Villa		Liverpool Challenge Cup	W 3-1
	at Goodison Park		Final replay	

1919/20 Season
Ormskirk & District Amateur League

Date	Opponent	H/A	Competition	Result	Scorers
Thu Sep 4	Burscough Town	H	Friendly	W 10-0	
Sat Sep 6	Ormskirk D.S.& S.	H	Friendly	L 1-2	
Wed Sep 10	Burscough Ordnance	H	Friendly	W 9-1	
Sat Sep 13	Ormskirk D.S.& S.	A	Friendly	L 1-3	
Sat Sep 20	Ormskirk Comrades	H	Friendly	L 2-3	
Sat Sep 27	Ormskirk Comrades	H	Friendly	W 3-1	
Sat Oct 4	Skelmersdale Rangers	A	Lge	L 1-10	
Sat Oct 11	Rainford Star	H	Lge	W 2-0	
Sat Oct 18	Ormskirk D.S.& S.	H	Lge	W 2-0	
Sat Oct 25	Ormskirk Comrades	A	Lge	W 4-1	
Sat Nov 1	Stormy Albion	A	Lge	D 1-1	
Sat Nov 8	Skelmersdale Rangers	H	Lge	L 0-2	
Sat Nov 15	Stormy Albion	H	Lge	W 3-0	Ike Jenkinson, James Ashton
Sat Nov 22	Westhead Juniors	H	Lge	W 4-0	Ireland, Jenkinson, Blundell (2)
Sat Nov 29	Ormskirk Juniors	H	Lge	W 5-1	
Sat Dec 6	Ormskirk D.S.& S.	A	Lge	W 7-2	Weston (2), Jenkinson (4), Jimmy Pye
Sat Dec 13	Westhead Juniors	A	Lge	W 4-0	Jenkinson (2), Ireland, H.Rimmer
Sat Dec 20	Skelmersdale Mission	H	Lge	D 2-2	
Thu Dec 25	Skelmersdale Rangers	H	Friendly	W 5-1	
Sat Dec 27	Rainford Star	A	Lge	W 1-0	
Thu Jan 1	Abbey Brick Works	H	Friendly	W 4-2	
Thu Jan 1	Ormskirk Juniors	H	Lge	W 9-1	
Sat Jan 3	Ormskirk Comrades	H	Lge	W 5-2	Jenkinson, J.Pye (2), George Merritt, Blundell
Sat Jan 10	Upholland	A	Lge	W 2-1	Jenkinson, Tommy Pye
Sat Jan 17	Skelmersdale Mission	A	Lge	D 2-2	Jenkinson, T.Pye
Sat Jan 24	Upholland	H	Lge	W 9-2	
Sat Jan 31	Ormskirk Juniors	H	Stanley Shield	W 10-0	
Sat Feb 7	Rainford Star	H	Stanley Shield	W 9-2	
Sat Feb 14	Ormskirk D.S.& S.	A	Stanley Shield	L 1-3	Pedder
Sat Feb 21	Clock Face	H	Liverpool Challenge Cup	W 4-1	
Sat Feb 28	Westhead Juniors	H	Stanley Shield	W 3-1	
Sat Mar 6	Stormy Albion	H	Stanley Shield		
	match abandoned with Rangers losing 3-1				
Sat Mar 13	Skelmersdale United	H	Liverpool Challenge Cup Semi-final	L 0-1	
	Attend: 2,500 - Gate £55				
Sat Mar 20	Upholland	A	Agricultural Cup	W 3-1	J.Pye, T.Pye, Pedder
Sat Mar 27	Upholland	A	Stanley Shield	L 0-1	
Sat Apr 3	Aughton Wanderers	A	Agricultural Cup	W 5-1	
Mon Apr 5	Stormy Albion		Agricultural Cup Semi-final	W 5-2	
	at Ormskirk				
Wed Apr 7	Skelmersdale Rangers	A	Stanley Shield	W 1-0	W.Aspinwall
Sat Apr 10	Skelmersdale Mission	A	Stanley Shield	D 4-4	
Sat Apr 17	Skelmersdale Rangers		Agricultural Cup Final	L 1-2	
	at Ormskirk				
Mon Apr 19	Stormy Albion	H	Stanley Shield	D 2-2	
Sat Apr 24	Skelmersdale Rangers		League Play-off	L 3-4	W.Aspinwall, T.Pye, Merritt
	at High Lane, Burscough - Gate: £27				
Sat May 1	Skelmersdale Rangers	A	Stanley Shield Semi-final	D 2-2	
	competition abandoned				

1920/21 Season
Liverpool County Combination

Date	Opponent	H/A	Competition	Result	Scorers
Sat Sep 4	Everton 'A'	H	Friendly	W 7-1	Manley (3), Blackburn (2), Billy Rigby, Jenkinson
Sat Sep 11	Sutton Manor	H	Lge	W 10-0	Blackburn (3), Jenkinson (2), Pedder (2), Manley, Billy Rigby, Rimmer
Sat Sep 18	Clock Face	H	Lge	D 1-1	Blackburn
Sat Sep 25	Whiston	A	Lge	L 0-2	
Sat Oct 2	Clock Face	A	Lge	W 5-1	Baron (4), Jack Rowbottom
Sat Oct 9	Frodsham	H	Lge	W 6-3	Rowbottom (2), Baron (4)
Sat Oct 16	Sutton Commercial	A	Lge	W 7-1	Jenkinson, 6 unknown
Sat Oct 23	Frodsham	A	George Mahon Cup	W 4-3	Billy Rigby (2), Rowbottom
	match replayed due to protest				
Sat Oct 30	Skelmersdale United	H	Lge	L 0-1	
	record gate: £99 18s 9d				
Sat Nov 6	Prescot	A	Lge	W 1-0	
Sat Nov 13	Prescot	H	Lge	W 5-1	Charlie Horton, Baron, Rowbottom
Sat Nov 20	Rainhill	H	Lge	W 9-0	
Sat Dec 4	Frodsham		George Mahon Cup	W 5-2	
	played at Skelmersdale		Replayed Tie		
Sat Dec 11	Chester Reserves	H	Lge	W 4-0	Rowbottom, Baron, Jenkinson (2)
Mon Dec 27	Sutton Commercial		George Mahon Cup	W 2-0	
	at Skelmersdale		Semi-final		
Sat Jan 8	Lancaster Town Reserves	H	Richardson Cup	W 8-2	
Sat Jan 15	Southport Vulcan	H	Richardson Cup	D 1-1	Billy Rigby
Sat Jan 22	Skelmersdale United	A	Lge	L 1-4	Rowbottom
Sat Jan 29	Croston	A	Richardson Cup	L 2-4	Rowbottom, Jones
Sat Feb 5	Rainhill	A	Lge	W 8-2	
Sat Feb 12	Sutton Manor	A	Liverpool Challenge Cup	L 0-1	
	Rangers awarded tie after protest				
Sat Feb 19	South Liverpool Reserves	A	Lge	W 5-0	Rowbottom (4), Pedder
Sat Feb 26	Whiston		George Mahon Cup Final	W 1-0	Billy Rigby
	at Sutton Commercial Ground, St.Helens				
Sat Mar 5	Prescot	A	Liverpool Challenge Cup	W 1-0	Pedder
	at Garston		Semi-final		
Sat Mar 12	Chester Reserves	A	Lge	D 2-2	Jenkinson, Woodhouse
Sat Mar 19	Frodsham	A	Lge	W 5-3	Rowbottom (2), Pedder, Jenkinson, Billy Rigby
Sat Mar 26	Sutton Commercial	H	Lge	W 3-1	
Mon Mar 28	Skelmersdale United		Liverpool Challenge Cup	L 1-4	Rowbottom
	at Anfield - gate £157		Final		
Sat Apr 2	Sutton Manor	A	Lge	L 2-6	Billy Rigby, Pedder
Sat Apr 9	Croston	H	Richardson Cup	L 1-3	OG
Tue Apr 12	Southport Vulcan	A	Richardson Cup	W 2-1	
Sat Apr 16	Whiston	H	Lge	W 1-0	Rowbottom
Sat Apr 23	Lancaster Town Reserves	A	Richardson Cup	D 0-0	
Sat Apr 30	South Liverpool Reserves	H	Lge	W 9-2	

1921/22 Season
Liverpool County Combination

Date	Opponent	H/A	Competition	Result	Scorers
Sat Sep 3	K.L.Allan & Co	H	Lge	W 4-2	Carr, Rowbottom, Jenkinson
Sat Sep 10	Southport Reserves	H	Friendly	W 5-1	
Sat Sep 17	Everton 'A'	H	Lge	D 2-2	Harold Rigby, Jenkinson
Sat Sep 24	Chorley	H	F.A.Cup	D 1-1	W.H.Rigby
	Attend: 'over 2,000'				
Wed Sep 28	Chorley	A	F.A.Cup replay	L 2-4	W.H.Rigby, Rowbottom
Sat Oct 1	New Brighton Reserves	A	Lge	W 3-0	W.H.Rigby (2), O.G.
	Attend: 3,000				
Sat Oct 8	Liverpool 'A'	A	Lge	W 2-1	Horton, W.H.Rigby
Sat Oct 15	Prescot Wire Works	H	Lancs Junior Cup	W 7-0	W.H.Rigby (2), W.Taylor (3), Jenkinson, Horton
Sat Oct 22	Frodsham	A	George Mahon Cup	L 1-2	Taylor
Sat Oct 29	K.L.Allan & Co.	A	Lge	W 5-0	Jackson (2), W.H.Rigby, Billy Rigby, Jenkinson
Sat Nov 5	Liverpool 'A'	H	Lge	W 4-2	Jenkinson, W.H.Rigby, 2 unknown
Sat Nov 12	New Brighton	H	Lancs Junior Cup	L 1-3	W.H.Rigby
	Gate: £48				
Sat Nov 19	Ormskirk & D Lge	H	Friendly	W 2-0	W.H.Rigby (2)
Sat Nov 26	Prescot	H	Lge	W 4-0	Taylor, Billy Rigby, W.H.Rigby, O.G.
Sat Dec 17	Prescot	A	Lge	D 1-1	Taylor
Sat Dec 24	Whiston Parish	H	Lge	W 5-4	Ashton, Sumner, Jenkinson, Taylor, Harold Rigby
Mon Dec 26	Wigan Borough Reserves	A	Lge	L 0-3	
Tue Dec 27	Croston	H	Friendly	L 2-3	
Sat Dec 31	Garston Gas Works	H	Lge	W 6-2	
Mon Jan 2	Wigan Borough Reserves	H	Lge	D 0-0	
Sat Jan 7	Everton 'A'	A	Lge	W 3-2	
Sat Jan 21	New Brighton Reserves	H	Lge	W 2-1	
Sat Jan 28	Ormskirk	H	Lge	W 3-1	Tommy Pye (2), O.G.
Sat Feb 4	Sutton Commercial	A	Lge	W 4-3	T.Pye (4)
Sat Feb 11	New Brighton Reserves	A	Liverpool Challenge Cup	L 1-2	T.Pye
Sat Feb 18	Frodsham	H	Lge	L 0-2	
Sat Feb 25	Garston Gas Works	A	Lge	D 0-0	
Sat Mar 4	Burnley 'A'	H	Friendly	W 2-0	Benson, Taylor
Sat Mar 18	St. Helens Junction	A	Lge	W 1-0	Benson
Sat Mar 25	Sutton Commercial	H	Lge	W 5-1	T.Pye (3), Benson, Hughes
Sat Apr 1	Bolton Wanderers 'A'	A	Friendly	L 2-4	Hughes (2)
Sat Apr 8	Whiston Parish	A	Lge	D 2-2	Benson, T.Pye
Fri Apr 14	Bolton Smithills	H	Friendly	W 5-2	
Mon Apr 17	Skelmersdale United	A	Friendly	L 2-5	T.Pye (2)
	Gate: £55				
Sat Apr 22	Frodsham	A	Lge	W 2-0	T.Pye, Tootle
Sat Apr 29	Ormskirk	A	Lge	W 5-0	Flannagan (3), Taylor, Horton
Tue May 2	Everton 'A'	H	Hall Walker Cup S/F	W 3-0	
Thu May 4	Frodsham	A	Hall Walker Cup Final	W 2-1	T.Pye, Tootle
	at Sandheys Park, New Brighton				
Sat May 6	St. Helens Junction	H	Lge	W 1-0	Benson

Rangers circa 1914. Back left to right: Tom Gregson (Trainer), Unknown, Charlie Welding, Unknown, Billy Aspinwall, Halsall, Popplewell, Rimmer, Unlnown. Front left to right: James Ashton, John Culshaw, Tommy Ashton, Jimmy Pye, Riding.
This photograph was taken in the goalmouth at the Mart Lane end. Part of Martland's Mill can be seen in the top right corner indicating the goal was then situated near where the Barons' Club now stands. Photograph kindly loaned by Danny Hunter.

Rangers 1926-27 Season. Standing left to right: Billy Snape, Billy Ashurst, Archie Kemp, Eddie Chatburn, George Cunningham, Unknown, Unknown, Billy Green, Unknown (possibly Owen). Seated left to right: Tommy Pye, Billy Bennett, Nat Rawlins. Photograph kindly loaned by Marlene Guy.

1922/23 Season
Liverpool County Combination

Date	Opponent	H/A	Competition	Result	Scorers
Sat Sep 2	Graysons Garston	H	Lge	W 3-1	Taylor, Bill Ashurst (2)
Sat Sep 16	New Brighton Reserves	A	Lge	L 1-2	W.Smith
Sat Sep 23	Dick Kerrs	H	F.A.Cup	L 2-7	
Sat Sep 30	Graysons Garston	A	Lge	W 2-1	Nat Rawlins, Taylor
Sat Oct 7	Everton 'A'	A	Lge	D 1-1	
Sat Oct 14	Skelmersdale United	A	Lancs Junior Cup	L 1-5	Taylor
	Gate: £74 - Rangers won after protest				
Sat Oct 21	Liverpool 'A'	H	Lge	W 5-1	Tootle, O.G., Ashurst (2), Brennan
Sat Oct 28	Prescot	H	George Mahon Cup	D 2-2	Rawlins, Ashurst
Sat Nov 11	Croston	A	Lancs Junior Cup	D 1-1	Tootle
Sat Nov 18	Skelmersdale United	H	Liverpool Challenge Cup	L 1-3	Frank Barlow
Sat Nov 25	Croston	H	Lancs Junior Cup replay	L 0-1	
	Gate: 'over £100'				
Sat Dec 2	St. Helens Junction	H	Lge	W 1-0	Hartley
Sat Dec 9	Prescot	A	George Mahon Cup replay	L 1-2	
Sat Dec 16	New Brighton Res.	A	Lge	D 1-1	Ashurst
Sat Dec 23	Prescot	A	Lge	L 0-2	
Mon Dec 25	Ormskirk	A	Lge	W 2-1	Rawlins, Taylor
Tue Dec 26	Wigan Borough Reserves	H	Lge	D 1-1	
Mon Jan 1	Ormskirk	H	Lge	W 2-1	W.H.Rigby (2)
	Gate: £55				
Sat Jan 6	Skelmersdale Utd Res.	H	Lge	W 2-0	W.H.Rigby (2)
Sat Jan 13	Everton 'A'	H	Lge	W 1-0	Rawlins
Sat Jan 20	Whiston	A	Lge	D 0-0	
Sat Jan 27	Liverpool 'A'	A	Lge	L 2-3	Rawlins, 1 unknown
Sat Feb 3	Prescot	H	Lge	W 3-1	W.H.Rigby (2), Taylor
Sat Feb 17	Monks Hall	H	Lge	W 1-0	Rawlins
Sat Feb 24	Frodsham	A	Lge	W 8-4	W.H.Rigby (4), Rawlins (2), Ashurst, Mather
Sat Mar 3	Monks Hall	A	Lge	D 0-0	
Sat Mar 10	Rainford	H	Lge	W 14-0	W.H.Rigby (6), Rawlins (4), Taylor (2), Ashurst, Mather
Sat Mar 17	Frodsham	H	Lge	W 2-1	Taylor, W.H.Rigby
Sat Mar 24	St. Helens Junction	A	Lge	W 3-0	Rawlins, W.H.Rigby (2),
Sat Mar 31	Wigan Borough Reserves	A	Lge	L 1-5	Rawlins
Mon Apr 2	Chester Reserves	H	Lge	W 4-2	Rawlins, W.H.Rigby (2), Jenkinson
Sat Apr 7	Skelmersdale Utd Res.	A	Lge	L 0-3	
Sat Apr 14	Chester Reserves	A	Lge	L 1-4	
Sat Apr 21	Rainford	A	Lge	W 6-1	Taylor, W.H.Rigby (2), Billy Martindale (2), Jenkinson
Sat Apr 28	Whiston	H	Lge	W 4-1	

1923/24 Season
Liverpool County Combination

Sat Aug 25	Liverpool 'A'	H	Lge	D 1-1	Pilkington
Sat Sep 1	Everton 'A'	H	Lge	D 4-4	Johnson, Jones, Rawlins, Cooper
Sat Sep 8	Skelmersdale Mission	A	Lge	L 2-3	Rawlins, Jones
Sat Sep 15	Whiston	H	Lge	W 3-0	Mather, Rawlins, Kirkman
Sat Sep 22	Marine	H	F.A.Cup	W 1-0	Hughes
Sat Sep 29	Everton 'A'	A	Lge	W 3-1	Rawlins, Hughes, Huyton
Sat Oct 6	Garston Gas Works	A	F.A.Cup	L 2-4	Rawlins, Hughes
Sat Oct 13	Skelmersdale United	H	Lancs Junior Cup	W 5-0	Payne (2), W.Aspinwall, Cooper, Pilkington
	Attend: 'over 3,000'				
Sat Oct 20	Everton 'A'	H	George Mahon Cup	W 2-1	Jones, Barlow
Sat Oct 27	Prescot	A	Lge	W 1-0	Balfour
Sat Nov 3	New Brighton Reserves	A	Lge	L 3-4	
Sat Nov 10	Rossendale United	H	Lancs Junior Cup	L 1-3	W.Aspinwall
Sat Nov 17	Prescot	H	George Mahon Cup	D 1-1	Pilkington
Sat Nov 24	Seaforth Fellowship	A	Liverpool Challenge Cup	L 1-5	
Sat Dec 1	Prescot	A	George Mahon Cup replay	D 3-3	Payne, Pilkington
Sat Dec 8	New Brighton Reserves	H	Lge	D 2-2	Payne, Rawlins
Sat Dec 15	Sutton Manor	H	Lge	W 3-1	Rawlins, Pilkington (2)
Sat Dec 22	Croston	H	Friendly	D 2-2	
Tue Dec 25	Ormskirk	A	Lge		
	abandoned with Ormskirk leading 2-1				
Tue Jan 1	Ormskirk	H	Lge	D 2-2	
Sat Jan 5	Liverpool 'A'	A	Lge	W 3-2	
Sat Jan 12	Prescot	A	George Mahon Cup 2nd replay	L 1-4	
Sat Jan 19	Sutton Manor	A	Lge	L 1-3	
Sat Jan 26	Ormskirk	A	Lge	L 2-6	Bert Rigsby, W.Aspinwall
Sat Feb 2	Port Sunlight	A	Lge	W 4-1	Rigsby (3), Barlow
Sat Feb 9	Newton Common Recs	H	Lge	W 1-0	Rawlins
Sat Feb 16	Frodsham	A	Lge	D 1-1	Rigsby
Sat Mar 1	Hoylake	H	Lge	W 3-1	Rigsby, Balfour, Pilkington
Sat Mar 8	Newton Common Recs	A	Lge	W 3-0	Rigsby, Joe Harrison, Pilkington
Sat Mar 15	Frodsham	H	Lge	W 6-1	Rigsby (4), Pilkington, Merritt
Sat Mar 22	Whiston	A	Lge	D 2-2	Rigsby, Pilkington
Sat Apr 5	Ellesmere Port	H	Lge	W 3-1	Merritt, Rawlins, Rigsby
Fri Apr 18	Skelmersdale Mission	H	Lge	W 5-1	Balfour, Rawlins, Rigsby (3)
Mon Apr 21	Hoylake	A	Lge	D 1-1	Merritt
Sat Apr 26	Prescot	H	Lge	W 4-1	Rigsby (2), Pilkington, Rawlins
Wed Apr 30	Port Sunlight	H	Lge	W 4-0	
Sat May 3	Ellesmere Port	A	Lge	L 2-5	

1924/25 Season
Liverpool County Combination

Date	Opponent	H/A	Competition	Result	Scorers
Sat Sep 6	Newton Common Recs	H	Lge	W 2-0	Rawlins (2)
Sat Sep 13	Liverpool A	H	Lge	W 5-1	Rawlins (2), Billy Snape (2), Gerrard
Sat Sep 20	Youlgrave	A	F.A.Cup	W 5-0	Gerrard (2), Rawlins, Snape (2)
Sat Sep 27	Newton Common Recs	A	Lge	L 1-3	
Sat Oct 4	Skelmersdale United	A	F.A.Cup	D 0-0	
Wed Oct 8	Skelmersdale United	H	F.A.Cup replay	W 5-0	Merritt, Rawlins, Snape (2), Beesley
Sat Oct 11	Breightmet United	A	Lancs Junior Cup	L 3-5	Beesley, Rawlins, Snape
Sat Oct 18	Glossop	A	F.A.Cup	L 2-3	
	Gate: £53				
Sat Nov 1	Port Sunlight	H	Lge	W 4-0	Barlow, Snape (2), Rawlins
Sat Nov 8	Port Sunlight	A	Lge	D 2-2	Snape, Rawlins
Sat Nov 15	Skelmersdale United	H	Liverpool Challenge Cup	W 2-1	
Sat Nov 22	Whiston	H	Lge	W 3-0	
Sat Nov 29	Prescot	A	George Mahon Cup	D 2-2	
Sat Dec 6	Ormskirk	H	Lge	W 3-0	
Sat Dec 13	Seaforth Albion	H	Liverpool Challenge Cup	D 3-3	
Sat Dec 20	Seaforth Albion	A	Liverpool Challenge Cup Replay	W 2-0	
Thu Dec 25	Ormskirk	A	Lge	L 0-1	
Sat Dec 27	Prescot	H	George Mahon Cup replay	W 1-0	Tommy Wyper
Thu Jan 1	Newton Common Recs	H	George Mahon Cup	W 7-4	Wyper (3), Snape, Ashurst, Rawlins, Balfour
Sat Jan 3	Skelmersdale United	H	Lge	W 2-0	Billy Green, Wyper
Sat Jan 17	Fairries	H	Liverpool Challenge Cup	L 2-3	Rawlins, Snape
Sat Jan 24	Prescot	A	Lge	W 5-0	Rawlins (4), Snape
Sat Jan 31	Whiston	A	Lge	L 0-1	
Sat Feb 14	Skelmersdale United	A	Lge	L 2-6	W.Aspinwall, Ashurst
Sat Feb 21	Everton A	A	Lge	L 2-3	Snape (2)
Sat Feb 28	Everton A	H	Lge	W 4-2	Rigsby (3), Snape
Sat Mar 7	Hoylake	H	Lge	W 5-0	Rawlins (2), Balfour (2), Rigsby
Sat Mar 14	Port Sunlight	H	George Mahon Cup Semi-final	W 2-0	Wyper, O.G.
Sat Mar 21	Everton A	H	Hall Walker Cup	W 1-0	Rigsby
Sat Mar 28	Prescot	H	Lge	W 3-0	Snape (2), Rigsby
Sat Apr 4	Poulton Rovers	A	Lge	L 0-1	
Sat Apr 11	Hoylake	A	Lge	D 1-1	George Cunningham
Mon Apr 13	Ormskirk	H	Hall Walker Cup	D 1-1	Snape
Sat Apr 18	Skelmersdale United	A	Hall Walker Cup	W 2-0	Snape (2)
Wed Apr 22	Skelmersdale United at Ravenscroft, Ormskirk		George Mahon Cup Final	D 1-1	
Sat Apr 25	Liverpool A	A	Lge	W 3-1	Cunningham, Snape (2)
Wed Apr 29	Skelmersdale United at Ravenscroft, Ormskirk		George Mahon Cup Final Replay	L 0-1	
Sat May 2	Poulton Rovers	H	Lge	W 4-1	

1925/26 Season
Liverpool County Combination

Date	Opponent	H/A	Competition	Result	Scorers
Sat Sep 5	Ormskirk	A	Lge	W 4-1	Rawlins, Billy Martindale (2), Tommy Pye
Sat Sep 12	Marine	H	Lge	W 3-1	Rawlins (2), Martindale
Sat Sep 19	Coppull	A	F.A. Cup	W 3-2	Pye (3)
Sat Sep 26	Poulton Rovers	H	Lge	W 4-1	Rawlins, Turner (2), Pye
Sat Oct 3	Darwen	A	F.A. Cup	L 1-2	Pye
Sat Oct 10	Skelmersdale United	A	Lancs Junior Cup	W 2-1	Bonney (2)
	Attend: 'about 2,000'				
Sat Oct 17	Marine	A	Lge	W 3-2	Rawlins, Walle (2)
Sat Oct 24	Liverpool 'A'	H	Lge	W 5-2	Turner (2), Eddie Chatburn, Pye, Walle
Sat Oct 31	Harlandic	A	Lge	D 2-2	Pye, Turner
Sat Nov 14	Prescot	A	Lancs Junior Cup	W 4-3	Rawlins, Jim Cookson, Pye (2)
Sat Nov 21	Bootle St. James	H	Liverpool Challenge Cup	W 5-1	Pye, Martindale (4)
Sat Nov 28	Leyland	A	Lancs Junior Cup	W 4-0	Rawlins, Pye, Martindale
Sat Dec 5	Bootle Celtic	A	Liverpool Challenge Cup	L 0-5	
Sat Dec 12	Ormskirk	H	Lge	W 4-1	Billy Green, Cunningham, Pye, Walle
Sat Dec 19	Chorley	H	Lancs Junior Cup	D 2-2	Green, Pye
	Gate: £23				
Fri Dec 25	Southport Reserves	A	Friendly	W 4-3	
Sat Dec 26	Whiston	A	George Mahon Cup	W 8-3	Rawlins, Walle, Tommy Downey (3), Chatburn (2), Pye
Sat Jan 2	Chorley	A	Lancs Junior Cup replay	L 1-2	Walle
Sat Jan 9	Newton Common Recs	H	Lge	W 5-0	Walle, Pye, Rawlins, Chatburn, Ashurst
Sat Jan 16	Liverpool 'A'	A	Lge	W 4-2	Pye (2), Cookson, Rawlins
Sat Jan 23	Prescot	H	Lge	W 5-0	Walle, Pye (3), Billy Bennett
Sat Jan 30	Everton 'A'	H	Lge	W 3-0	Bennett (2), Rawlins
Sat Feb 6	Harlandic	H	Lge	W 4-1	Bennett (2), Chatburn, W.Aspinwall
Sat Feb 13	Port Sunlight	A	Lge	W 7-0	Rawlins (2), Pye (3), Bennett (2)
Sat Feb 20	St. Helens Town	A	Lge	W 3-0	Pye, Walle, Chatburn
Sat Feb 27	Skelmersdale United	A	Lge	W 2-1	Walle, Bennett
	Gate: £41				
Sat Mar 6	Whiston	H	Lge	L 1-3	Pye
Sat Mar 13	Whiston	A	Lge	D 1-1	Rawlins
Sat Mar 20	Poulton Rovers	A	Lge	W 4-0	Chatburn (2), Walle, Bennett
Sat Mar 27	St. Helens Town	A	Lge	W 2-1	Bennett, Rawlins
Sat Apr 3	Everton 'A'	H	George Mahon Cup	W 6-1	Pye (3), Bennett, Walle, Rawlins
Mon Apr 5	Port Sunlight	H	Lge	W 4-1	Rawlins (2), Bennett, Walle
Sat Apr 10	Prescot	A	Lge	W 2-1	Rawlins, Bennett
Sat Apr 17	Skelmersdale United	A	George Mahon Cup Semi-final	D 2-2	Cookson, Chatburn
Wed Apr 21	Skelmersdale United	H	George Mahon Cup Semi-final replay	W 4-1	Cookson, Bennett (2), Ashurst
Sat Apr 24	Harlandic		George Mahon Cup Final	W 1-0	Chatburn
	at Whiston				
Thu Apr 29	Skelmersdale United	H	Lge	W 3-0	Pye, Bennett, Rawlins
Sat May 1	Everton 'A'	A	Lge	W 4-0	W.Aspinwall, Bennett, Rawlins, Pye

1926/27 Season
Liverpool County Combination

Date	Opponent	H/A	Competition	Result	Scorers
Sat Sep 4	Hindley Green Athletic	A	F.A.Cup	W 5-2	Rawlins (3), Pye, Bennett
Sat Sep 11	Everton 'A'	H	Lge	W 5-3	O.G., Rawlins (2), Bennett, Walle
Sat Sep 18	St. Helens Town	H	F.A.Cup	W 5-3	Bennett (2), Pye, Chatburn, Rawlins
Sat Sep 25	Prescot	A	Lge	L 2-3	Pye, Walle
Sat Oct 2	Great Harwood	H	F.A.Cup	W 2-0	Rawlins, Chatburn
Sat Oct 9	New Brighton Reserves	A	Lge	W 2-1	Rawlins, Bob Hargreaves
Sat Oct 16	Chorley	A	F.A.Cup	W 3-2	Harry Green, Snape, Pye
Sat Oct 23	Horwich RMI	H	Lancs Junior Cup	L 0-4	
Sat Oct 30	Lancaster Town	A	F.A.Cup	L 1-6	Pye
	Attend: 4,366				
Sat Nov 6	Skelmersdale Mission	H	Liverpool Challenge Cup	W 7-1	Pye (3), Snape (2), Rawlins, Bonney
Sat Nov 13	Skelmersdale United	A	Liverpool Challenge Cup		
	abandoned after 55 minutes with Skem leading 1-0 (waterlogged pitch)				
Sat Nov 20	Poulton Rovers	H	George Mahon Cup	W 4-0	Pye (2), Bennett, Rawlins
Sat Nov 27	Bootle Celtic	H	George Mahon Cup	W 4-0	Rawlins, Pye (2), Bennett
Sat Dec 4	Skelmersdale United	A	Liverpool Challenge Cup Replayed Tie	D 2-2	Mulholland, Snape
Sat Dec 11	Skelmersdale United	H	Liverpool Challenge Cup Replay	W 3-2	Snape, Walle, Bennett
	Gate: £44				
Sat Dec 18	Bootle Celtic	H	Lge	L 2-3	Bennett, Chatburn
Sat Dec 25	Orwell Wednesday	H	Friendly	W 2-1	
Mon Dec 27	St. Helens Town	A	Lge	W 2-1	Owen, Bennett
Sat Jan 1	Skelmersdale United	A	Lge	W 3-0	Bennett, Pye, Snape
Sat Jan 8	Liverpool 'A'	A	Lge	W 5-1	Pye (3), Rawlins, Bennett
Sat Jan 15	Skelmersdale United	H	Lge	D 2-2	Snape, Chatburn
Sat Jan 22	Liverpool 'A'	H	Lge	W 10-1	Pye (2), Rawlins (3), Bennett (4), 1 unknown
Sat Jan 29	Everton 'A'	A	Lge	W 4-0	Bennett, Pye (2), Snape
Sat Feb 5	Bootle CYMS	H	Liverpool Challenge Cup	W 6-0	Bennett (2), O.G., Pye (2), Chatburn
Sat Feb 12	Poulton Rovers	H	Lge	W 7-1	Chatburn (2), Pye, Rawlins, Owen, Bennett (2)
Sat Feb 19	Bootle Celtic	A	Lge	D 4-4	Chatburn, Snape, Bennett, Owen
Sat Feb 26	Bootle Boro	A	Lge	D 3-3	Cunningham, Chatburn (2)
Sat Mar 5	Marine	A	George Mahon Cup	L 2-3	Rawlins, Bennett
Sat Mar 12	Bootle Boro	H	Lge	W 4-1	Bennett (2), Pye, Rawlins
Sat Mar 19	Garston Royal	A	Lge	W 2-1	Pye, Rawlins
Sat Mar 26	New Brighton Reserves	A	Liverpool Challenge Cup Semi-final	W 4-1	Rawlins, Pye, Chatburn, Bennett
	at Cadby Hall				
Sat Apr 2	Poulton Rovers	A	Lge	W 5-1	Bennett (2), Snape, Pye, 1 unknown
Sat Apr 9	Whiston	H	Lge	W 4-1	Pye, Chatburn, Owen, Rawlins
Sat Apr 16	St. Helens Town	H	Lge	W 9-2	Rawlins (2), Pye (2), Chatburn, Snape (4)
Mon Apr 18	Bootle Celtic		Liverpool Challenge Cup Final	W 1-0	Pye
	at Anfield				
Sat Apr 23	Garston Royal	H	Lge	W 6-1	Bennett, Owen, Pye (3), 1 unknown
Mon Apr 25	Prescot	H	Lge	W 5-0	H.Green, Pye (2), Trevana
Wed Apr 27	Marine	H	Lge	W 3-1	
Sat Apr 30	Whiston	A	Lge	W 3-2	Pye, Rawlins, Bennett
Thu May 5	Marine	A	Lge	W 1-0	
Sat May 7	New Brighton Reserves	H	Lge	W 7-1	Bennett, Pye (3), Chatburn, Rawlins (2)
Tue May 10	Southport	H	Hospitals Charity	L 1-2	

1927/28 Season
Lancashire Combination

Date	Opponent	H/A	Comp	Result	Scorers
Sat Aug 27	Hindley Green	H	Lge	L 3-4	Rawlins, Forshaw (2)
Wed Aug 31	Nelson Reserves	H	Lge	D 4-4	
Sat Sep 3	Rossendale United	A	Lge	W 1-0	Forshaw
Wed Sep 7	Atherton	H	Lge	W 3-2	Rawlins (2), Forshaw
Sat Sep 10	Accrington Stanley Res.	A	Lge	L 1-3	'Sniggie' Graham
Wed Sep 14	Morecambe	H	Lge	L 1-2	
Sat Sep 17	Skelmersdale United	A	F.A.Cup	W 4-1	Hogan, Rawlins (2), Chatburn
	lost on a protest				
Sat Sep 24	Dick Kerrs	A	Lge	L 2-4	Bennett, Rawlins
Tue Sep 27	Southport Reserves	A	Combination Cup	W 3-0	
Sat Oct 1	Atherton	A	Lge	D 3-3	Billy Little, Bennett (2)
Sat Oct 8	Great Harwood	H	Lge	W 4-3	Bennett (2), Billy Little, Billy Glover
Sat Oct 15	Accrington Stanley Res.	H	Lge	D 2-2	Rawlins, Glover
Sat Oct 22	Skelmersdale United	H	Lancs Junior Cup	W 4-0	Bennett (4)
Sat Oct 29	Darwen	A	Lge	W 5-4	Bennett (2), Rawlins (3)
Sat Nov 5	Dick Kerrs	A	Lancs Junior Cup	W 3-1	Rawlins, Hogan, Bennett
Sat Nov 12	Nelson Reserves	A	Lge	D 2-2	Rawlins, Billy Little
Sat Nov 19	Rossendale United	A	Lancs Junior Cup	L 1-3	Bennett
Sat Nov 26	Bacup Borough	H	Lge	W 4-0	Rawlins (2), Bennett (2)
Sat Dec 3	Atherton	A	Combination Cup	W 4-2	Bennett, Glover, Graham, Hogan
Sat Dec 10	Chorley	A	Lge	L 0-2	
Sat Dec 17	Hindley Green	A	Lge	L 1-2	Glover
Sat Dec 24	Morecambe	A	Lge	W 3-2	Glover, Bennett (2)
Mon Dec 26	Southport Reserves	H	Lge	L 1-2	Glover
Tue Dec 27	Wigan Boro Res.	H	Lge	L 2-3	
Sat Dec 31	Bacup Borough	A	Lge	W 5-2	Jack Pears (2), Graham, Rawlins (2)
Mon Jan 2	Wigan Boro Reserves	A	Lge	D 1-1	Graham
Sat Jan 7	Chorley	H	Lge	W 2-0	Bennett, Job
Sat Jan 14	Rossendale United	H	Lge	W 3-1	Pears, Rawlins, Bennett
Sat Jan 21	Dick Kerrs	H	Lge	D 3-3	Glover, Pears, Rawlins
Sat Jan 28	Preston North End 'A'	A	Lge	L 1-6	Bennett
Sat Feb 4	Great Harwood	A	Lge	D 2-2	Bennett, Pears
Sat Feb 11	Clitheroe	H	Lge	W 4-2	Pears, Glover, Bennett (2)
Sat Feb 18	Horwich RMI	A	Lge	L 3-6	Glover, Graham (2)
Sat Feb 25	Horwich RMI	H	Lge	L 3-6	Rawlins (2), Glover
Sat Mar 3	Preston North End 'A'	H	Lge	W 2-0	Glover, Bennett
Sat Mar 10	Clitheroe	A	Lge	L 1-2	Rawlins
Sat Mar 17	Barnoldswick	A	Lge	L 0-5	
Sat Mar 24	Darwen	H	Lge	W 4-2	Bennett, Rawlins (3)
Sat Mar 31	Barnoldswick	H	Lge	D 4-4	Rawlins (2), Bennett (2)
Fri Apr 6	Hindley Green	H	Friendly	L 0-1	
Mon Apr 9	Southport Reserves	A	Lge	W 4-2	Bennett (2), Fletcher, Henshall
	Attend: '2,000'				
Sat Apr 14	Lancaster Town	A	Lge	L 0-1	
Wed Apr 18	Rossendale United	H	Combination Cup Semi-final	L 1-2	Bennett
Sat Apr 21	Prescot Cables	H	Lge	L 1-2	
Wed Apr 25	Lancaster Town	H	Lge	D 1-1	
Sat Apr 28	Wigan Boro Reserves	H	Friendly	W 5-2	Jimmy Little, Henshall, 3 unknown
Sat May 5	Prescot Cables	A	Lge	L 2-6	Job (2)
Sat May 12	Southport	H	Hospitals Charity	D 3-3	

1928/29 Season
Lancashire Combination

Date	Opponent	H/A	Competition	Result	Scorers
Sat Aug 25	Darwen	A	Lge	L 2-6	Fred Rogers, Cherry
Wed Aug 29	Nelson Reserves	H	Lge	W 3-2	Hagger, Edwards, Cherry
Sat Sep 1	Accrington Stanley Res	A	Lge	W 2-1	
Wed Sep 5	Wigan Boro Res.	H	Lge	W 3-1	
Sat Sep 8	Horwich RMI	H	Lge	L 1-3	Cherry
Wed Sep 12	Atherton	H	Lge	W 6-2	F.Rogers, Harry Banner, Edwards (2), Billy Green
Sat Sep 15	Dick Kerrs	A	F.A.Cup	L 2-4	F.Rogers (2)
Wed Sep 19	Accrington Stanley Res	H	Lge	L 2-6	Rawlins, Proctor
Sat Sep 22	Great Harwood	A	Lge	D 1-1	Green
Wed Sep 26	Atherton	A	Combination Cup	L 0-3	
Sat Sep 29	Clitheroe	A	Lge	L 1-4	O'Donnell
Sat Oct 6	Rossendale United	A	Lge	L 1-3	Coe
Sat Oct 13	Northern Nomads	H	Friendly	W 5-2	Cherry (3), Hurst, Kelsall
Sat Oct 20	Lancaster Town	H	Lge	L 0-2	
Sat Nov 3	Dick Kerrs	H	Lancs Junior Cup	D 1-1	Banner
Sat Nov 10	Dick Kerrs	A	Lancs Junior Cup replay	L 1-5	Ray Rogers
Sat Nov 17	Linacre Thermal	H	Liverpool Challenge Cup	W 7-2	Billy Little, Hurst (2), Birch, Cherry, Rawlins, O.G.
Sat Dec 1	Atherton	A	Lge	W 3-2	Banner (2), Rawlins
Sat Dec 8	Manchester Central	H	Lge	W 4-2	Rawlins (2), Crossthwaite (2)
Sat Dec 15	Prescot Cables	A	Lge	L 0-2	
Sat Dec 22	Clitheroe	H	Lge	L 0-3	
Tue Dec 25	Southport Reserves	H	Lge	W 1-0	
Wed Dec 26	Chorley	H	Lge	D 2-2	
Sat Dec 29	High Park	H	Liverpool Challenge Cup	D 1-1	Ashurst
Tue Jan 1	Wigan Boro Reserves	A	Lge	W 3-2	Cherry, Banner, Rawlins
Sat Jan 5	High Park	H	Liverpool Challenge Cup Replay	L 0-1	
Sat Jan 12	Preston North End 'A'	A	Lge	W 3-2	Bennett (2), Rawlins
Sat Jan 19	Great Harwood	H	Lge	W 3-1	Cherry, Billy Little, Houghton
Sat Feb 2	Rossendale United	H	Lge	W 2-1	
Sat Feb 9	Nelson Reserves	A	Lge	W 2-1	Cherry, Rawlins
Sat Feb 16	Darwen	H	Lge	L 0-2	
Sat Feb 23	Morecambe	A	Lge	L 0-3	
Sat Mar 2	Lancaster Town	A	Lge	D 2-2	Cherry (2)
Sat Mar 9	Barnoldswick Town	H	Lge	W 2-1	Banner, Little
Sat Mar 16	Morecambe	H	Lge	L 0-1	
Fri Mar 29	Chorley	A	Lge	L 2-3	Cherry, O'Donnell
	Attend: 3,000				
Sat Mar 30	Preston North End 'A'	H	Lge	D 3-3	Rawlins, O'Donnell, Cherry
Mon Apr 1	Southport Reserves	A	Lge	L 2-4	Houghton, Cherry
Sat Apr 6	Prescot Cables	H	Lge	D 1-1	Houghton
Sat Apr 13	Bacup Borough	H	Lge	W 1-0	Cherry
Tue Apr 16	Bacup Borough	A	Lge	D 2-2	Almond, Houghton
Sat Apr 20	Manchester Central	A	Lge	D 2-2	
Tue Apr 23	Dick Kerrs	H	Lge	D 1-1	Rawlins
Sat Apr 27	Barnoldswick Town	A	Lge	D 0-0	
Thu May 2	Dick Kerrs	A	Lge	W 1-0	
Sat May 4	Horwich RMI	A	Lge	L 2-4	Campbell, Cherry
Wed May 8	Southport	H	Hospitals Charity	D 2-2	

1929/30 Season
Lancashire Combination

Date	Opponent	H/A	Comp	Result	Scorers
Sat Aug 31	Lytham	H	Lge	W 2-1	Fred Rogers, Campbell
Sat Sep 7	Wigan Boro Reserves	A	Lge	L 1-2	F.Rogers
Wed Sep 14	Atherton	H	Lge	W 4-0	
Sat Sep 14	Manchester Central	A	Lge	L 2-4	F.Rogers (2)
Wed Sep 18	Atherton	A	Combination Cup	L 1-6	
Sat Sep 21	Great Harwood	H	F.A.Cup	W 6-3	F.Rogers (2), Haydock (2), Haggar, Little
Sat Sep 28	Barnoldswick Town	A	Lge	W 1-0	Lonsdale
Sat Oct 5	Adlington	H	F.A.Cup	D 4-4	F.Rogers (2), Haydock, Little
Wed Oct 9	Adlington	A	F.A.Cup replay	D 2-2	
Sat Oct 12	Great Harwood	H	Lancs Junior Cup	W 9-2	F.Rogers (4), Cookson (3), Bamford (2)
Mon Oct 14	Adlington at Chorley	A	F.A.Cup 2nd replay	W 4-2	O'Donnell (2), Lonsdale, F.Rogers
Sat Oct 19	Lytham	A	F.A.Cup	L 1-4	F.Rogers
Sat Oct 26	Darwen	H	Lge	W 2-1	Bamford, Lonsdale
Sat Nov 2	Great Harwood	A	Lge	D 2-2	Little, F.Rogers
Sat Nov 9	Lancaster Town	A	Lancs Junior Cup	L 0-2	
Sat Nov 16	Horwich RMI	H	Lge	W 2-1	Little (2)
Sat Nov 23	Accrington Stanley Res.	A	Lge	L 1-5	Bamford
Sat Nov 30	Accrington Stanley Res.	H	Lge	W 5-3	Drummond (2), F.Rogers (2), Lane
Sat Dec 7	Everton 'A'	H	Liverpool Challenge Cup	L 0-4	
Sat Dec 14	Nelson Reserves	A	Lge	L 1-3	Drummond
Sat Dec 21	Horwich RMI	A	Lge	L 2-4	Banner, Lonsdale
Wed Dec 25	Southport Reserves	H	Lge	W 5-0	Drummond (2), Lane, F.Rogers, Lonsdale
Thu Dec 26	Chorley	H	Lge	L 3-4	Drummond, F.Rogers, Banner
Sat Dec 28	Prescot Cables	A	Lge	L 0-4	
Wed Jan 1	Wigan Boro Reserves	H	Lge	L 1-3	
Sat Jan 4	Rossendale United	H	Lge	D 1-1	Bamford
Sat Jan 11	Lytham	A	Lge	L 2-5	F.Rogers, Banner
Sat Jan 18	Morecambe	H	Lge	W 4-0	Lonsdale (2), F.Rogers, Drummond
Sat Jan 25	Prescot Cables	H	Lge	D 2-2	O.G., F.Rogers
Sat Feb 1	Lancaster Town	A	Lge	L 0-4	
Sat Feb 8	Atherton	A	Lge	L 0-3	
Sat Feb 15	Dick Kerrs	H	Lge	L 0-1	
Sat Feb 22	Dick Kerrs	A	Lge	L 2-3	Hibbert (2)
Sat Mar 1	Bacup Borough	H	Lge	W 5-1	Reddyhough (3), Banner, Dickson
Sat Mar 8	Bacup Borough	A	Lge	L 2-6	Reddyhough, F.Rogers
Sat Mar 15	Clitheroe	A	Lge	L 3-4	F.Rogers, Reddyhough, Banner
Sat Mar 22	Clitheroe	H	Lge	W 2-0	Cordingley, Reddyhough
Sat Mar 29	Darwen	A	Lge	L 1-2	Bamford
Sat Apr 5	Manchester Central	H	Lge	D 1-1	F.Rogers
Sat Apr 12	Barnoldswick Town	H	Lge	L 2-3	Cordingley, Bamford
Mon Apr 14	Morecambe	A	Lge	L 1-4	
Fri Apr 18	Chorley	A	Lge	L 1-3	Ray Rogers
Sat Apr 19	Nelson Reserves	H	Lge	W 1-0	Bamford
Mon Apr 21	Southport Reserves	A	Lge	L 2-6	R.Rogers (2)
Wed Apr 23	Great Harwood	H	Lge	W 3-1	
Sat Apr 26	Lancaster Town	H	Lge	L 1-3	F.Rogers
Sat May 3	Rossendale United	A	Lge	L 1-2	F.Rogers

1930/31 Season
Lancashire Combination

Date	Opponent	H/A	Comp	Result	Scorers
Sat Aug 30	Bacup Borough	A	Lge	L 1-5	F.Rogers
Sat Sep 6	Chorley	H	Lge	W 2-0	F.Rogers, Arthur Hird
Wed Sep 10	Lancaster Town	H	Lge	L 1-3	F.Rogers
Sat Sep 13	Prescot Cables	A	Lge	L 0-3	
Sat Sep 20	Darwen	H	Lge	L 1-5	'Ginger' Smith
Sat Sep 27	Nelson Reserves	A	Lge	L 2-4	F.Rogers, Tommy Mandy
Sat Oct 4	Horwich RMI	A	F.A.Cup	L 1-5	Banner
Sat Oct 11	Skelmersdale United	H	Lancs Junior Cup	W 1-0	Tommy Downey
	Gate: £49				
Tue Oct 14	Southport Reserves	A	Combination Cup	L 1-3	Downey
Sat Oct 18	Great Harwood	A	Lge	L 0-6	
Sat Oct 25	Clitheroe	H	Lge	L 2-3	Mandy (2)
Sat Nov 1	Manchester Central	A	Lge	L 1-5	Gaskell
Sat Nov 8	Prescot Cables	A	Lancs Junior Cup	L 1-2	F.Rogers
Sat Nov 15	Barnoldswick Town	H	Lge	L 2-3	R.Rogers (2)
Sat Nov 22	Dick Kerrs	A	Lge	L 1-3	Skiffington
Sat Nov 29	Rochdale Reserves	H	Lge	W 2-0	R.Rogers (2)
Sat Dec 13	Horwich RMI	H	Lge	W 2-1	Downey, Bamford
Sat Dec 20	Wigan Boro Reserves	H	Lge	W 3-1	Skiffington, R.Rogers, Mandy
Thu Dec 25	Lytham	H	Lge	W 3-0	Rawlins, Skiffington (2)
	Gate: £30				
Fri Dec 26	Lytham	A	Lge	L 0-3	
Sat Dec 27	Bacup Borough	H	Lge	W 4-2	Skiffington, Rawlins, Flanagan (2)
Thu Jan 1	Rossendale United	H	Lge	W 3-2	Downey, Flanagan (2)
Sat Jan 3	Chorley	A	Lge	L 1-2	Rawlins
	Attend: 2,500				
Sat Jan 10	Accrington Stanley Res.	H	Lge	L 3-5	Jack Potter, Skiffington (2)
Sat Jan 17	Prescot Cables	H	Lge	W 2-1	Flanagan, McKenna
Sat Jan 24	Darwen	A	Lge	L 0-3	
Sat Jan 31	Nelson Reserves	H	Lge	W 6-1	Hird (3), McKenna, R.Rogers, Skiffington
Sat Feb 7	Southport Reserves	H	Lge	W 3-2	Flanagan (3)
Sat Feb 14	Rossendale United	A	Lge	L 4-5	Flanagan (2), Downey, Bamford
Sat Feb 21	Great Harwood	H	Lge	W 5-1	R.Rogers (2), Flanagan (2), McKenna
Sat Mar 7	Manchester Central	H	Lge	W 3-0	Flanagan (2), Bamford
	Gate: £8 18s				
Sat Mar 14	Morecambe	A	Lge	L 1-6	Skiffington
Wed Mar 18	Accrington Stanley Res.	A	Lge	W 5-3	Hird, Rawlins, Skiffington, Flanagan, R.Rogers
Sat Mar 21	Barnoldswick Town	A	Lge	W 3-2	Skiffington, Flanagan (2)
Sat Mar 28	Dick Kerrs	H	Lge	W 3-1	Skiffington, Flanagan, Banner
Fri Apr 3	Lancaster Town	A	Lge	W 2-1	Skiffington, Flanagan
	Attend: 3,000				
Sat Apr 4	Rochdale Reserves	A	Lge	W 2-0	Flanagan, Skifington
Mon Apr 6	Barrow Reserves	A	Friendly	D 1-1	
Tue Apr 14	Southport Reserves	A	Lge	L 1-3	Skiffington
Sat Apr 18	Horwich RMI	A	Lge	W 3-1	Downey, Hird, Rawlins
Wed Apr 22	Morecambe	H	Lge	W 3-2	Skiffington, Wally Haslam, Flanagan
Sat Apr 25	Wigan Boro Reserves	A	Lge	L 2-3	Hird, Downey
Mon Apr 27	Clitheroe	A	Lge	L 2-5	Skiffington (2)

1931/32 Season
Lancashire Combination

Date	Opponent	H/A	Competition	Result	Scorers
Sat Aug 29	Lytham	H	Lge	D 0-0	
Wed Sep 2	Lancaster Town	H	Lge	L 3-4	
Sat Sep 5	Barrow Reserves	A	Lge	L 0-4	
Tue Sep 8	Bacup Borough	A	Lge	L 1-3	
Sat Sep 12	Clitheroe	H	Lge	L 0-2	
Wed Sep 16	Bacup Borough	H	Lge	D 2-2	
Sat Sep 19	Fleetwood	A	Lge	L 3-7	Williams (2), Tommy Downey
Wed Sep 23	Prescot Cables	H	Combination Cup	L 1-2	
Sat Sep 26	Southport Reserves	H	Lge	L 1-2	Albert Pape
Sat Oct 3	Darwen	A	F.A.Cup	D 2-2	Williams, Downey
	Rangers drawn at home - game switched to Darwen				
Tue Oct 6	Darwen	A	F.A.Cup replay	L 3-5	Williams (2), Ray Rogers
Sat Oct 10	Skelmersdale United	A	Lancs Junior Cup	L 0-1	
Sat Oct 17	Wigan Boro Reserves	H	Lge	W 1-0	Downey
	Wigan Boro res. later resigned from League				
Sat Oct 24	Prescot Cables	A	Lge	L 0-5	
Sat Oct 31	Rossendale United	H	Lge	W 3-2	R.Rogers (2), Downey
Sat Nov 14	Dick Kerrs	A	Lge	L 0-5	
Sat Nov 21	Accrington Stanley Res.	H	Lge	W 5-1	Taylor, Rawlins (2), R.Rogers
Sat Nov 28	Liverpool 'A'	H	Liverpool Challenge Cup	D 1-1	
Sat Dec 5	Darwen	A	Lge	L 2-3	
Wed Dec 9	Liverpool 'A'	H	Liverpool Challenge Cup Replay	D 1-1	R.Rogers
Sat Dec 12	Chorley	H	Lge	L 0-2	
Sat Dec 19	Great Harwood	A	Lge	L 1-3	O.G.
Fri Dec 25	Barnoldswick Town	H	Lge	W 1-0	Pape
Fri Jan 1	Liverpool 'A'	H	Liverpool Challenge Cup 2nd replay	W 3-1	Rawlins, Baybutt (2)
Sat Jan 9	Kirkdale	H	Liverpool Challenge Cup	W 3-1	Baybutt, Taylor (2)
Sat Jan 16	Barrow Reserves	H	Lge	D 2-2	Pape (2)
Sat Jan 23	Clitheroe	A	Lge	D 1-1	Whitehead
Sat Jan 30	Fleetwood	H	Lge	D 2-2	R.Rogers, Mayson
Sat Feb 6	Garston	A	Liverpool Challenge Cup	W 3-0	Mayson, Rawlins, Baybutt
Sat Feb 13	Horwich RMI	H	Lge	D 4-4	Pape (2), Baybutt (2)
Sat Feb 20	Lancaster Town	A	Lge	L 0-1	
Sat Feb 27	Nelson	H	Lge	W 4-1	Flanagan (2), Jack Ingram, Taylor
Sat Mar 5	Earle	A	Liverpool Challenge Cup Semi-final	L 2-3	Baybutt (2)
Sat Mar 12	Rossendale United	A	Lge	D 2-2	Taylor, Mayson
Sat Mar 19	Lytham	A	Lge	W 3-2	Flanagan, Pape, Mayson
Fri Mar 25	Horwich RMI	A	Lge	W 2-1	Ingram, Taylor
Sat Mar 26	Dick Kerrs	H	Lge	W 3-0	Flanagan (2), Kay
Mon Mar 28	Nelson	A	Lge	L 1-5	Pape
Sat Apr 2	Accrington Stanley Res.	A	Lge	W 2-1	Flanagan, Bamford
Sat Apr 9	Morecambe	H	Lge	W 5-1	Flanagan (2), Bamford (2), Kay
Sat Apr 16	Darwen	H	Lge	L 1-4	Waters
Wed Apr 20	Barnoldswick Town	A	Lge	W 3-0	
Sat Apr 23	Chorley	A	Lge	D 1-1	Taylor
Wed Apr 27	Prescot Cables	H	Lge	L 0-5	
Sat Apr 30	Great Harwood	H	Lge	L 1-3	Unsworth
Tue May 3	Southport Reserves	A	Lge	L 0-1	
Sat May 7	Morecambe	A	Lge	W 1-0	Flanagan

1932/33 Season
Lancashire Combination

Date	Opponent	H/A	Competition	Result	Scorers
Sat Aug 27	Barrow Reserves	A	Lge	L 1-4	Nat Taylor
Sat Sep 3	Fleetwood	H	Lge	D 3-3	N.Taylor, J.Gastall, Jack Ingram
Thu Sep 8	Southport Reserves	H	Combination Cup	W 1-0	
Sat Sep 10	Barnoldswick Town	H	Lge	W 4-1	Ingram (2), Pilkington, Paddy Freeman
Sat Sep 17	Southport Reserves	A	Lge	L 1-2	Ingram
Sat Sep 24	Bacup Borough	H	Lge	W 4-3	Brown (3), Mayson
Tue Sep 27	Rochdale Reserves	A	Combination Cup	L 2-4	Cecil McCaughey, Bird
Sat Oct 1	Horwich RMI	A	F.A.Cup	L 1-4	N.Taylor
Sat Oct 8	Horwich RMI	A	Lge	L 1-6	Ingram
Sat Oct 15	Rochdale Reserves	H	Lge	L 0-1	
Sat Oct 22	Dick Kerrs	H	Lge	D 3-3	Ingram, Hills, N.Taylor
Sat Nov 5	Lancaster Town	H	Lge	D 0-0	
Sat Nov 12	Great Harwood	H	Lge	W 4-0	Ingram, Williams (2), Halsall
Sat Nov 19	Lytham	A	Lge	D 1-1	Ingram
Sat Nov 26	Prescot Cables	H	Lge	L 0-3	
Sat Dec 3	Darwen	A	Lge	L 0-4	
Sat Dec 10	Clitheroe	H	Lge	W 4-3	
Sat Dec 17	Chorley	A	Lge	L 0-6	
Sat Dec 24	Morecambe	A	Lge	D 1-1	Gastall
Mon Dec 26	Rossendale United	H	Lge	W 3-2	Ingram, Frank Ridings, Taberon
Sat Dec 31	Barrow Reserves	H	Lge	W 4-2	
Mon Jan 2	Rossendale United	A	Lge	D 1-1	
Sat Jan 7	Fleetwood	A	Lge	L 1-3	Kay
Sat Jan 14	Barnoldswick Town	A	Lge	L 1-3	N.Taylor
Sat Jan 21	Bacup Borough	A	Lancs Junior Cup	L 1-3	Ingram
Sat Jan 28	Southport Reserves	H	Lge	L 2-4	Pilkington, Taberon
Sat Feb 4	Garston	A	Liverpool Challenge Cup	L 1-5	N.Taylor
Sat Feb 18	Horwich RMI	H	Lge	W 2-1	McCaughey, Pilkington
Sat Mar 4	Dick Kerrs	A	Lge	L 3-6	Ingram, Ted Taylor
Sat Mar 11	Accrington Stanley Res.	H	Lge	L 0-2	
Sat Mar 18	Lancaster Town	A	Lge	L 1-3	Gastall
Sat Mar 25	Great Harwood	A	Lge	L 0-2	
Sat Apr 1	Lytham	H	Lge	D 2-2	Gastall, N.Taylor
Sat Apr 8	Prescot Cables	A	Lge	L 0-7	
Mon Apr 10	Morecambe	H	Lge	W 2-1	
Fri Apr 14	Nelson	H	Lge	W 3-0	
Sat Apr 15	Darwen	H	Lge	L 2-4	Gastall, Kenyon
Mon Apr 17	Nelson	A	Lge	L 0-4	
Wed Apr 19	Rochdale Reserves	A	Lge	D 0-0	
Sat Apr 22	Clitheroe	A	Lge	L 0-3	
Sat Apr 29	Chorley	H	Lge	L 2-4	N.Taylor, Roach
Mon May 1	Accrington Stanley Res.	A	Lge	D 2-2	Garvey, 1 unknown
Sat May 6	Bacup Borough	A	Lge	L 1-3	O.G.

1933/34 Season
Lancashire Combination

Sat Aug 26	Rossendale United	A	Lge	L 0-4	
Tue Aug 29	Rochdale Reserves	A	Lge	L 1-5	
Sat Sep 2	Leyland Motors	A	Lge	L 2-5	
Sat Sep 9	Lytham	H	Lge	L 1-2	Albert Gore
Sat Sep 23	Fleetwood	A	Combination Cup	L 0-1	

resigned from Lancs Comb - joined West Lancs League

West Lancashire League

Sat Oct 14	Whiston	H	Friendly	W 4-3	Keegan (3), Gore
Sat Oct 21	Nelson Reserves	H	Lge	L 1-2	Keegan
Sat Oct 28	Garston Royal	H	Liverpool Challenge Cup	W 2-1	Gore, Johnny Porter
Sat Nov 4	Westhoughton	H	Lge	W 5-1	Joe Sleight, Rasburn (3), Tommy Downey
Sat Nov 11	Nelson Reserves	A	Lge	L 2-3	Keegan, Rasburn
Sat Nov 18	Leyland Motors Reserves	H	Lge	W 2-1	Gore, Porter
Sat Nov 25	Peasley Cross	H	Liverpool Challenge Cup	W 3-0	Fred Rogers, Rasburn, Harry Sinclair
Sat Dec 2	Fleetwood Reserves	H	Lge	D 2-2	Lindsay, Downey
Sat Dec 9	Darwen Reserves	H	Lge	W 4-3	Downey (2), Southers, Smith
Sat Dec 16	Wigan Athletic Reserves	H	Lge	W 4-2	Downey (2), Lindsay, Southers
Sat Dec 23	Calderstones	A	Lge	Lost	Score unknown
Mon Dec 25	Lancaster Town Res.	A	Lge	W 2-0	
Tue Dec 26	Bolton Wanderers 'A'	H	Lge	Drew	Score unknown
Sat Dec 30	Earlestown White Star	H	Liverpool Challenge Cup	L 1-2	Gore
Mon Jan 1	Westhoughton *morning kick-off*	A	Lge	W 3-2	Rogers (2), Gore
Mon Jan 1	Lancaster Town Reserves *afternoon kick-off*	H	Lge	W 4-2	Rogers, Clayton, Southers (2)
Sat Jan 6	Chorley Reserves	H	Lge	W 4-1	Snelgrove (2), Quayle (2)
Sat Jan 20	Peasley Cross	H	Lancs Junior Cup	W 3-0	Quayle (2), Lewis
Sat Jan 27	Calderstones	H	Lge	D 2-2	Quayle (2)
Sat Feb 3	Nelson Reserves	A	Richardson Cup	W 4-0	Rogers, Quayle, Sleight, Snelgrove
Sat Feb 10	Darwen	H	Lancs Junior Cup	L 1-3	Quayle
Sat Feb 17	Bolton Wanderers 'A'	A	Richardson Cup	W 3-2	Quayle, Southers (2)
Sat Feb 24	Whittingham	A	Lge	L 0-5	
Sat Mar 3	Chorley Reserves	A	Lge	L 2-4	Quayle (2)
Sat Mar 10	Whittingham	H	Lge	W 3-1	Southers, Gore (2)
Sat Mar 17	Blackburn Rovers 'A'	A	Lge	L 3-7	Snelgrove, Quayle, 1 unknown
Sat Mar 24	Fleetwood Reserves	A	Lge	D 2-2	Quayle, Gore
Fri Mar 30	Blackburn Rovers 'A'	H	Lge	L 2-4	
Sat Mar 31	Bolton Wanderers 'A'	A	Lge	L 0-2	
Sat Apr 7	Leyland Motors Reserves	A	Lge	W 3-1	Baldwin, Gore (2)
Sat Apr 21	Darwen Reserves	A	Lge	W 2-0	Cothliff (2)
Mon Apr 23	Darwen Reserves *at Wigan*		Richardson Cup Semi-final	L 0-1	
Sat Apr 28	Breightmet United	H	Lge	W 5-0	Downey (2), W.H.Jones, Rogers (2)
Mon Apr 30	Wigan Athletic Reserves	A	Lge	W 5-1	Billy Orritt (2), Baldwin (2), Hall
Sat May 5	Breightmet United	A	Lge	D 2-2	Orritt (2)

217

1934/35 Season
West Lancashire League

Date	Opponent	H/A	Competition	Result	Scorers
Sat Sep 1	Bolton Wanderers 'A'	H	Lge	L 0-3	
Sat Sep 8	Fleetwood Reserves	A	Lge	L 0-3	
Sat Sep 22	Barnoldswick Town	H	Lge	L 1-2	Manville
Sat Sep 29	Nelson Reserves	H	Lge	W 3-1	Arthur Bird, Maguire, Wilson
Sat Oct 6	Calderstones	H	Lge Cup	D 1-1	Maguire
Sat Oct 13	Barnoldswick Town	A	Lge	L 3-6	Wilson, Wally Holt, Maguire
Sat Oct 20	Calderstones	A	Lge Cup Replay	L 2-4	Maguire, Bird
Sat Oct 27	Darwen Reserves	H	Lge	D 2-2	Maguire, Shepherd
Sat Nov 3	Chorley Reserves	A	Lge	L 0-3	
Sat Nov 10	Chorley Reserves	H	Lge	W 2-1	Bird, Shepherd
Sat Dec 1	Blackburn Rovers 'A'	H	Lge	L 0-1	
Sat Dec 8	Aigburth Parish Church	H	Liverpool Challenge Cup	W 3-2	Bird (2), Shepherd
Sat Dec 15	Burnley 'A'	H	Lge	W 2-1	Porter, Holt
Sat Dec 22	Wigan Athletic Reserves	H	Lge	W 1-0	Kavanagh
Tue Dec 25	Bury 'A'	H	Lge	L 1-3	Wilson
Sat Jan 5	Garston Protestant Reformers	H	Liverpool Challenge Cup	W 2-1	Maguire, Shepherd
Sat Jan 12	Whittingham	A	Lge	L 1-9	Shepherd
Sat Jan 26	Fleetwood Reserves	H	Lge	W 1-0	Sleight
Sat Feb 2	Burnley 'A'	A	Lge	L 2-3	Maguire, Shepherd
Sat Feb 9	Northern Nomads	A	Liverpool Challenge Cup	D 1-1	Holt
Sat Feb 16	Northern Nomads	H	Liverpool Challenge Cup	L 2-3	Jack Crowell (2)

Burscough Rangers folded

BURSCOUGH RANGERS F.C.

Season	P	W	D	L	F	A	Pos.	Highlights
Southport & District Amateur League (Second Division)								
1906-07	23	13	4	6	59	34	3	
Southport & District Amateur League (Senior Division)								
1907-08	35	20	5	10	101	64	5	Southport 2nd Senior Charity Cup winners
1908-09	30	18	4	8	96	58	4	Southport League Medals Competition winners
1909-10*	35	19	6	10	86	49	1	Southport League Champions
1910-11	29	18	7	4	87	43	4	
1911-12	29	13	7	9	64	48	6	

* also played in Ormskirk League

Season	P	W	D	L	F	A	Pos.	Highlights
Lancashire Alliance								
1912-13	37	25	4	8	128	54	2	Wigan Cup winners
1913-14	33	21	5	7	88	39	1	Winners Lancashire Alliance & Excelsior Cup, Wigan Cup finalists
Liverpool County Combination								
1914-15	26	20	4	2	100	22	2	Liverpool Challenge Cup winners, George Mahon Cup finalists
Ormskirk & District Amateur League								
1919-20	42	26	6	10	152	70	2	Agricultural Cup finalists

Liverpool County Combination

1920-21	34	22	4	8	119	51	2	George Mahon Cup winners, Liverpool Challenge Cup finalists
1921-22	39	24	6	9	102	57	1	County Combination Champions & Hall Walker Cup winners
1922-23	35	17	7	11	79	58	3	
1923-24	36	17	10	9	89	69	3	
1924-25	38	21	7	10	92	47	2	George Mahon Cup finalists
1925-26	38	30	4	4	126	49	1	County Combination Champions & George Mahon Cup winners
1926-27	41	31	4	6	152	63	1	County Combination Champions & L'pool Challenge Cup winners

Lancashire Combination

1927-28	48	19	10	19	116	113	11	
1928-29	47	17	12	18	85	99	12	
1929-30	47	15	6	26	98	121	16	
1930-31	43	20	1	22	89	107	12	
1931-32	47	15	11	21	80	99	16	
1932-33	43	10	9	24	65	116	18	
1933-34	5	0	0	5	4	17		

West Lancashire League

1933-34	35	20	4	11	88	70	5	Richardson Cup semi-finalists
1934-35	22	7	3	12	29	61		

| TOTAL | 932 | 485 | 153 | 294 | 2406 | 1709 | | |

BURSCOUGH A.F.C.

1946 - 1996

1946/47 Season
Liverpool County Combination (Division One)

Date	Opponent	H/A	Competition	Result	Scorers
Sat Aug 31	Prescot B.I. Social	A	Lge	L 2-5	Ray Monk, Geo. Davenport
Sat Sep 7	Prescot B.I. Social	H	Lge	W 4-3	Davenport (2), Seddon (2)
Sat Sep 14	Newton Y.M.C.A.	H	Lge	W 4-1	Bill Draper (3), O.G.
Sat Sep 21	Earlestown	H	Lge	L 3-4	Draper, Norman James, Davenport
Sat Sep 28	South Liverpool Reserves	A	Lge	W 1-0	Davenport
Sat Oct 5	Runcorn Reserves	A	Lge	L 1-3	Smith
Sat Oct 12	Runcorn Reserves	H	Lge	W 3-1	James, Davenport, Smith
Sat Oct 19	Liverpool 'A'	H	George Mahon Cup	L 1-2	Davenport
Sat Oct 26	Haydock Reserves	A	Liverpool Challenge Cup	W 1-0	Davenport
Sat Nov 2	Earlestown	A	Lge	D 1-1	Scorer unknown
Sat Nov 9	Skelmersdale United	H	Lge	D 0-0	
	Gate: £85				
Sat Nov 23	U.G.B. (St. Helens)	A	Liverpool Challenge Cup	W 3-1	Harry Bergin, Davenport, 1 unknown
Sat Nov 30	Formby	A	Lge	W 8-1	Scorers unknown
Sat Dec 7	Skelmersdale United	A	Lge	W 3-1	Tommy Saunders (3)
Sat Dec 14	Everton 'A'	A	Lge	L 1-2	Jimmy Aspinall
Sat Dec 21	South Liverpool Reserves	H	Lge	W 4-1	Bergin, Saunders, 2 O.G.
Sat Jan 4	Everton 'A'	H	Lge	W 3-1	Bergin (2), Frank Makeating
Sat Jan 11	Prescot B.I. Social	A	Liverpool Challenge Cup	L 2-3	Saunders, Billy McGrae
Sat Jan 18	U.G.B. (St. Helens)	A	Lge	W 5-3	Makeating (4), Bergin
Sat Feb 1	Ellesmere Port	A	Lge	D 2-2	Bergin (2)
Sat Feb 22	Ellesmere Port	H	Lge	W 3-0	Makeating (2), Saunders
Sat Mar 22	U.G.B. (St. Helens)	H	Lge	W 3-1	Saunders, Joe Vose, 1 unknown
Sat Mar 29	Earle	H	Lge	W 5-2	Makeating, Saunders, Bergin (2), McGrae
Fri Apr 4	Liverpool 'A'	A	Lge	D 1-1	Bonnette
Sat Apr 5	Newton Y.M.C.A.	A	Lge	W 4-0	Scorers unknown
Mon Apr 7	Liverpool 'A'	H	Lge	D 0-0	
Sat Apr 12	Haydock	A	Lge	W 4-2	Scorers unknown
Wed Apr 16	Orrell	A	Lge	W 3-1	Scorers unknown
Sat Apr 19	Earle	A	Lge	W 3-0	Wesley Bridge, Makeating, McGrae
Mon Apr 21	Formby	H	Lge	L 1-2	Saunders
Wed Apr 23	Orrell	H	Lge	L 1-2	Scorer unknown
Sat Apr 26	Haydock	H	Lge	D 1-1	Saunders

1947/48 Season
Liverpool County Combination (Division One)

Date	Opponent	H/A	Competition	Result	Scorers
Sat Aug 23	Formby	A	Lge	L 2-3	Makeating, Aspinall
Wed Aug 27	Orrell	H	Lge	D 2-2	Saunders, 1 unknown
Sat Aug 30	Everton 'A'	A	Lge	W 2-1	Joe Kelly (2)
Wed Sep 3	Orrell	A	Lge	L 3-4	Scorers unknown
Sat Sep 6	U.G.B. (St.Helens)	A	Lge	W 4-3	Wilf London, Makeating (3)
Sat Sep 13	Prescot B.I.	H	Lge	W 5-3	Matt Brennan, Bridge (3), Makeating
Sat Sep 20	Bangor City	H	F.A.Cup Prelim. Rd	W 3-1	Bridge (2), Makeating
Sat Sep 27	U.G.B. (St.Helens)	H	George Mahon Cup	W 2-0	Brennan, Saunders
Sat Oct 4	Rhyl	H	F.A. Cup 1st Qual. Rd	L 0-3	
	Attendance: 2,404 - Gate: £115				
Sat Oct 11	Skelmersdale United	A	Lge	L 2-3	Saunders, Aspinall
	Gate: £111				
Sat Oct 18	Ellesmere Port Town	A	Lge	L 2-8	Scorers unknown
Sat Oct 25	Earle	H	Lge	W 4-2	Connick, Johnny Buckley, Brennan (2)
Sat Nov 1	Runcorn Reserves	H	Lge	L 1-2	Frank Postlethwaite
Sat Nov 8	St. Helens Town	A	Lge	D 2-2	Scorers unknown
Sat Nov 22	Southport Reserves	H	Lancs Junior Cup	W 3-1	Bridge (2), Buckley
Sat Nov 29	U.G.B. (St.Helens)	H	Liverpool Challenge Cup	W 8-1	Postlethwaite, Buckley, Bridge (3), Saunders, Brennan, London
Sat Dec 6	South Liverpool Reserves	A	Lge	W 6-3	Bridge (6)
Sat Dec 13	Prescot B.I.	A	Lge	W 3-2	Bridge (3)
Sat Dec 20	Atherton Collieries	H	Lancs Junior Cup	W 4-1	Kelly, Reg Lunt, Saunders, Bridge
Thu Dec 25	Cromptons Recs	H	Lge	W 4-2	Scorers unknown
Fri Dec 26	Liverpool 'A'	A	George Mahon Cup	W 4-0	Scorers unknown
Sat Dec 27	U.G.B. (St.Helens)	H	Lge	D 1-1	Scorer unknown
Thu Jan 1	Cromptons Recs	A	Lge	W 5-3	Scorers unknown
Sat Jan 3	Formby	H	Lge	W 5-1	Alan Woolley, Bridge (2), Lunt, 1 unknown
Sat Jan 10	Formby	A	Liverpool Challenge Cup	W 3-1	Kelly, Woolley, Lunt
Sat Jan 17	Clitheroe	H	Lancs Junior Cup	W 7-1	Bridge (2), Saunders (2), Woolley (2), Kelly
Sat Jan 24	Everton 'A'		Liverpool Challenge Cup Semi-final	W 2-0	Kelly, Bridge
	at Anfield				
Sat Feb 7	Skelmersdale United	H	Lge	D 1-1	Bridge
	Attendance: 2,569 - Gate: £84				
Sat Feb 14	Barrow Reserves	H	Lancs Junior Cup S/F	W 2-0	Woolley, Postlethwaite
Sat Feb 21	Everton 'A'	H	Lge	W 5-1	Kelly (2), Lunt, Postlethwaite, Woolley
Sat Feb 28	St. Helens Town	H	Lge	W 4-1	Saunders (2), Postlethwaite, Bridge
Sat Mar 6	Ellesmere Port Town	H	Lge	W 7-0	Bridge (4), Saunders, 2 unknown
Sat Mar 13	Fleetwood		Lancashire Junior Cup Final	W 2-1	Kelly, Woolley
	at Blackpool - Attend: 6,726				
Sat Mar 27	Earlestown	A	Lge	L 1-2	Scorer unknown
Mon Mar 29	South Liverpool Reserves	H	Lge	W 5-3	Bridge (4), 1 unknown
Wed Mar 31	Ellesmere Port Town		George Mahon Cup Semi-Final	W 4-3	Bridge, Postlethwaite, Kelly, Buckley
	at South Liverpool				
Sat Apr 3	English Electric	A	Lge	W 4-1	Buckley (2), Bridge, London
Wed Apr 7	Newton Y.M.C.A.	A	Lge	W 2-1	Scorers unknown
Sat Apr 10	Earlestown		George Mahon Cup Final	W 2-0	Woolley, Buckley
	at South Liverpool - Attend: 4,280				
Fri Apr 16	English Electric	H	Lge	W 6-4	Bridge (4), Gant, Woolley
Sat Apr 17	Newton Y.M.C.A.	H	Lge	W 4-1	Bridge (2), London, Kelly
Mon Apr 19	Liverpool 'A'	A	Lge	D 3-3	Bridge (2), 1 unknown
Wed Apr 21	Haydock	H	Lge	D 1-1	Harrison
Fri Apr 23	Earlestown	H	Lge	L 1-4	Bridge
Sat Apr 24	Runcorn Reserves	A	Lge	D 0-0	
Mon Apr 26	Liverpool 'A'	H	Lge	L 0-3	
Wed Apr 28	Haydock	A	Lge	L 1-3	Scorer unknown
Sat May 1	Earle	A	Lge	W 6-3	Bridge (2), Saunders (2), 2 unknown
Sat May 8	Skelmersdale United		Liverpool Challenge Cup Final	W 4-1	Bridge (3), Woolley
	at Southport				
	Attend: 8,046 - Gate: £624				

1947-48 Season. Pictured with the Lancashire Junior Cup & Supporters' Club Officials.
Back left to right; Bob Pate (Chairman), Tom Rimmer, Wilf London, Frank Postlethwaite, George Langley, Harry Sutton, Jimmy Aspinall, Matt Brennan, Bill Robinson, Bob Walsh. Front left to right; Tom Martland, Alan Woolley, Wesley Bridge, Joe Kelly (Captain), Dorothy Johnson (Supporters' Club Queen), Reg Lunt, Tommy Saunders, Bill Eastwood.

LIVERPOOL COUNTY COMBINATION - DIVISION ONE
1946-47 SEASON
[Top Three only]

	P	W	D	L	F	A	Pts
Liverpool 'A'	28	19	8	1	96	36	46
Skelmersdale United	28	18	2	8	105	55	38
Burscough	**28**	**16**	**6**	**6**	**74**	**41**	**38**

LIVERPOOL COUNTY COMBINATION - DIVISION ONE
1947-48 SEASON

	P	W	D	L	F	A	Pts
Earlestown	34	25	3	6	115	54	53
Formby	34	21	7	6	129	59	49
Prescot B.I.	34	20	5	9	90	68	45
Skelmersdale United	34	17	11	6	79	60	45
Burscough	**34**	**18**	**7**	**9**	**104**	**77**	**43**
Ellesmere Port	34	18	3	13	80	77	39
Liverpool 'A'	34	16	6	12	79	57	38
Everton 'A'	34	15	7	12	86	68	37
Runcorn Reserves	34	14	6	14	71	62	34
St. Helens Town	34	13	8	13	83	80	34
South Liverpool Reserves	34	15	3	16	67	76	33
Earle	34	10	10	14	84	84	30
Orrell	34	11	8	15	61	87	30
Haydock	34	12	5	17	66	85	29
U.G.B. St. Helens	34	9	10	15	56	87	28
English Electric	34	6	5	23	49	97	17
Newton Y.M.C.A.	34	4	7	23	50	110	15
Crompton's Recs	34	3	7	24	50	117	13

LIVERPOOL COUNTY COMBINATION - DIVISION ONE
1949-50 SEASON

	P	W	D	L	F	A	Pts
Burscough	**34**	**25**	**4**	**5**	**96**	**35**	**54**
Skelmersdale United	34	25	3	6	141	60	53
Liverpool 'A'	34	20	3	11	66	33	43
Everton 'A'	34	19	2	3	101	49	40
Earle	34	15	9	10	91	74	39
Hindsford	34	15	8	11	73	75	38
Formby	34	14	9	11	90	71	37
Prescot B.I.	34	15	7	12	63	64	37
South Liverpool	34	14	6	14	79	71	34
Runcorn Reserves	34	13	8	13	66	69	34
Haydock	34	14	4	16	88	76	32
Hoylake Athletic	34	15	2	17	86	90	32
Cromptons Recs	34	15	2	17	87	96	32
Bootle Reserves	34	12	5	17	53	75	29
Liverpool Police	34	11	3	20	68	108	25
Newton Y.M.C.A.	34	8	6	20	76	108	22
Marine Reserves	34	8	3	23	58	89	19

1948/49 Season
Liverpool County Combination (Division One)

Date	Opponent	H/A	Competition	Result	Scorers
Sat Aug 21	English Electric	A	Lge	W 2-0	Kelly, Bridge
Wed Aug 25	Cromptons Recs	H	Lge	W 10-0	Bridge (3), Saunders (4), Kelly, Lunt, Tait
Sat Aug 28	U.G.B. (St.Helens)	A	Lge	W 9-1	Scorers unknown
Wed Sep 1	Cromptons Recs	A	Lge	W 9-0	Scorers unknown
Sat Sep 4	Liverpool Police	H	Lge	W 5-1	Woolley (2), Saunders, Bridge, 1 unknown
Wed Sep 8	South Liverpool Reserves	H	Lge	W 2-1	Saunders, Lunt
Sat Sep 11	Newton Y.M.C.A.	A	Lge	W 2-1	Lunt, Bridge
Sat Sep 18	Marine	H	F.A. Cup 1st Qual. Rd	W 4-1	Saunders, Bridge (2), Lunt
Sat Sep 25	Skelmersdale United	H	Lge	W 3-1	Woolley, Bridge (2)
	Attend: estimated 3,800 - Gate: £128				
Sat Oct 2	Bangor City	A	F.A. Cup 2nd Qual. Rd	L 2-4	Bridge (2)
	Attend: 4,300				
Sat Oct 9	St. Helens Town	A	Lge	L 1-2	Saunders
Sat Oct 16	Earlestown	A	Lge	L 0-9	
Sat Oct 23	Formby	A	Lge	L 3-8	Bridge (2), Postlethwaite
Sat Oct 30	Orrell	A	Lge	W 4-2	Bergin (2), Bridge (2)
Sat Nov 6	Runcorn Reserves	H	Lge	L 2-3	Saunders, Bridge
Sat Nov 13	Prescot B.I.	A	Lge	L 2-3	Kelly, Bergin
Sat Nov 20	Barrow Reserves	A	Lancs Junior Cup	L 0-2	
Sat Dec 4	Prescot B.I.	A	Liverpool Challenge Cup	W 4-2	Bergin, Woolley, Bridge, Ken Waterhouse
Sat Dec 11	Everton 'A'	H	Lge	D 2-2	Bridge, Bergin
Sat Dec 18	Haydock C & B	A	Lge	L 2-3	Bergin, Bridge
Mon Dec 27	Earlestown	H	George Mahon Cup	W 4-0	Scorers unknown
Sat Jan 1	Formby	H	Lge	W 4-1	Bridge (2), Bergin (2)
Sat Jan 8	Earlestown	H	Liverpool Challenge Cup	W 2-0	Woolley, Bridge
	game ordered to be replayed - Burscough fielded ineligible player				
Sat Jan 15	Newton Y.M.C.A.	H	Lge	W 4-0	Gant, Kelly, Buckley (2)
Sat Jan 22	U.G.B. (St.Helens)	H	Lge	D 1-1	Bridge
Sat Jan 29	Skelmersdale United	A	Lge	L 0-4	
	Attend: 2,800 - Gate: £113				
Sat Feb 5	Everton 'A'	A	Lge	W 3-2	Bridge, Bergin, Woolley
Sat Feb 12	Orrell	H	Lge	W 1-0	Bergin
Sat Feb 19	St. Helens Town	H	Lge	W 4-2	Bridge (3), Kelly
Sat Feb 26	Earlestown	H	Liverpool Challenge Cup Replayed Tie	L 1-2	Bridge
Sat Mar 5	Liverpool 'A'	A	Lge	D 1-1	Bridge
Sat Mar 12	Prescot B.I.	H	Lge	W 6-3	Bridge (2), Wiston, Buckley, London, Seddon
Sat Mar 19	Runcorn Reserves.	A	Lge	L 2-4	Bergin, London
Sat Mar 26	Everton 'A'	A	George Mahon Cup	W 2-0	Tommy Roberts, Colclough
Sat Apr 2	Liverpool Police	A	Lge	W 3-2	Colclough, Bergin, London
Wed Apr 6	Haydock C & B	H	Lge	W 2-0	Scorers unknown
Sat Apr 9	Liverpool 'A'	H	Lge	L 1-2	Kelly
Sat Apr 16	St. Helens Town		George Mahon Cup Semi-final	L 0-2	
	at Skelmersdale				
Wed Apr 20	Earlestown	H	Lge	L 1-2	Bridge
Sat Apr 23	South Liverpool Reserves	A	Lge	D 3-3	Bridge (3), Kelly
Mon Apr 25	Earle	H	Lge	D 1-1	Scorer unknown
Wed May 4	English Electric	H	Lge	W 5-1	London, Roberts, Bergin (2), Bridge
Sat May 7	Earle	A	Lge	L 1-3	Bridge

1949/50 Season
Liverpool County Combination (Division One)

Date	Opponent	H/A	Competition	Result	Scorers
Sat Aug 20	Liverpool 'A'	A	Lge	L 1-2	Bergin
Wed Aug 24	Everton 'A'	H	Lge	W 4-1	Johnson (2), Bergin, Jones
	Attend: 2,000				
Sat Aug 27	U.G.B. (St.Helens)	A	Lge	L 2-5	Bridge (2)
Wed Aug 31	Everton 'A'	A	Lge	W 1-0	Brennan
Sat Sep 3	Cromptons Recs	H	Lge	W 6-0	Bridge (4), London, Brennan
Wed Sep 7	Earle	A	Lge	W 2-0	Scorers unknown
Sat Sep 10	Newton Y.M.C.A.	A	Lge	W 2-1	Howard, Bridge
Wed Sep 14	Earle	H	Lge	L 1-4	Jones
Sat Sep 17	Marine	H	F.A.Cup Prelim. Rd	W 2-1	Bridge, Roberts
Sat Sep 24	Bootle Reserves	H	Lge	W 3-0	Kelly (3)
Sat Oct 1	Wigan Athletic	A	F.A.Cup 1st Qual. Rd	D 1-1	Roberts
	Attend: 7,000 - Gate: £344				
Sat Oct 8	Wigan Athletic	H	F.A.Cup replay	L 1-5	Kelly
	Attend: 4,128 - Gate: £215				
Sat Oct 15	Bootle Reserves	H	George Mahon Cup	L 2-3	Kelly, Bridge
	Gate: £40				
Sat Oct 29	Haydock C & B	H	Lge	W 3-0	Bridge (2), Bergin
Sat Nov 5	Hindsford	H	Lge	W 4-2	Aspinall, Bridge (2), Bergin
Sat Nov 12	Prescot B.I.	H	Lge	W 3-0	Harry Penkeyman, Bergin, Aspinall
Sat Nov 19	Rossendale United	A	Lancs Junior Cup 1st Rd	D 0-0	
	Gate: £67				
Sat Nov 26	Rossendale United	H	Lancs Junior Cup replay	W 4-0	Penkeyman, Joe Simpkin, Bridge, Bergin
	Gate: £71				
Sat Dec 3	Larkhill	H	Liverpool Challenge Cup	W 9-0	Simpkin, Bridge (5), Bergin, Chris Lynn, Penkeyman
	Gate: £27				
Sat Dec 10	Lancaster City	A	Lancs Junior Cup	W 5-3	Jones, Bridge (2), Simpkin, Penkeyman
	Attend: 1,525 - Gate: £86				
Sat Dec 17	Runcorn Reserves	A	Lge	D 0-0	
Mon Dec 26	Formby	H	Lge	W 2-1	Bridge (2)
Tue Dec 27	Formby	A	Lge	D 3-3	Aspinall (2), Bridge
Sat Dec 31	Liverpool 'A'	H	Lge	D 1-1	Bridge
Mon Jan 2	Skelmersdale United	A	Lge	W 6-2	Jones, Bridge (2), London, Bergin, Penkeyman
	Attend: 3,000 - Gate: £107				
Sat Jan 7	Earlestown	H	Liverpool Challenge Cup	W 6-1	Penkeyman (3), Jones, Bridge, Bergin
	Gate: £93				
Sat Jan 14	Stubshaw Cross Rovers	H	Lancs Junior Cup 3rd Rd	W 5-0	Bridge, Penkeyman, Jones, Bergin, London
	Attend: 2,500 - Gate: £95				
Sat Jan 21	U.G.B. (St.Helens)	H	Lge	W 8-0	Penkeyman (2), Bergin, Bridge (3), Jones, Kelly
Sat Jan 28	Prescot B.I.	A	Lge	W 3-0	Bridge, Kelly, Bergin
Sat Feb 4	Marine Reserves	A	Lge	W 3-0	Kelly, Bergin (2)
Sat Feb 11	Hoylake Athletic	H	Lge	W 4-2	Bridge (2), Penkeyman, O.G.
Sat Feb 18	Netherfield	H	Lancs Junior Cup Semi-final	W 1-0	Stan Jones
	Gate: £145				
Sat Feb 25	South Liverpool Reserves		Liverpool Challenge Cup Semi-final	L 3-4	Bridge, Kelly, Gill Houghton
	Attend: 2,175 at Skelmersdale				
Sat Mar 4	Hoylake Athletic	A	Lge	D 4-4	Saunders, Penkeyman, Bridge (2)
Sat Mar 11	Bootle Reserves	A	Lge	W 1-0	Stan Jones
Sat Mar 18	Haydock C & B	A	Lge	W 1-0	Bridge
Sat Mar 25	Marine Reserves	H	Lge	L 0-1	
Sat Apr 1	South Liverpool Reserves	H	Lge	W 1-0	Lynn
Sat Apr 8	Hindsford	A	Lge	W 4-0	Jimmy Graves, Penkeyman, Simpkin, Martin
Mon Apr 10	Liverpool Police	H	Lge	W 4-1	Bridge, Kelly, Bergin, Lynn
Sat Apr 15	Skelmersdale United	H	Lge	L 2-3	Bridge, Kelly
	Attend: 'over 3,000' - Gate: £120				
Tue Apr 18	Liverpool Police	A	Lge	W 3-1	Bridge, Bergin, Simpkin
Sat Apr 22	Newton Y.M.C.A.	H	Lge	W 5-0	Bridge (2), Stan Jones, Kelly, Penkeyman
	Gate: £35				
Thu Apr 27	Nelson		Lancs Junior Cup Final	W 2-1	Bridge (2)
	at Ewood Park, Blackburn - Attend: 12,077 - Gate: £854				
Sat Apr 29	Runcorn Reserves	H	Lge	W 3-0	Bridge, Kelly, Simpkin
Thu May 4	South Liverpool Reserves	A	Lge	W 3-0	Bridge (2), Kelly
Sat May 6	Cromptons Recs	A	Lge	W 3-1	Simpkin, Bridge, Jones

1949-50 Season. Back left to right: Ronnie Barker (Secretary), Matt Brennan, Bill Morris, Wif London, Frank Postlethwaite, Harry Sutton, Gill Houghton, Jimmy Aspinall. Front left to right: Chris Lynn, Joe Simpkin, Joe Kelly, Wesley Bridge, Tommy Roberts, Stan Jones, Ned Gregson (Trainer). Pictured at Victoria Park on Saturday 8th October 1949 in front of 4,128 spectators prior to an F.A. Cup Tie with Wigan Athletic.

LIVERPOOL COUNTY COMBINATION - DIVISION ONE 1950-51 SEASON	P	W	D	L	F	A	Pts
Skelmersdale United	32	23	3	6	101	43	49
Everton 'A'	32	21	6	5	110	41	48
Liverpool 'A'	32	21	4	7	78	42	46
Crompton's Recs	32	20	4	8	94	54	44
Earle	32	17	8	7	74	51	42
Burscough	**32**	**16**	**6**	**10**	**88**	**46**	**38**
Formby	32	15	5	12	80	66	35
Haydock	32	14	6	12	89	79	34
Hoylake Athletic	32	13	6	13	78	83	32
Ellesmere Port	32	13	4	15	66	86	30
Prescot B.I.	32	12	4	16	49	70	28
South Liverpool	32	11	5	16	54	73	27
Liverpool Police	32	11	5	16	61	85	27
Bootle Reserves	32	7	8	17	46	74	22
Marine Reserves	32	6	6	20	65	93	18
Prescot	32	4	5	23	40	109	13
Newton-le-Willows	32	4	3	25	48	126	11

LIVERPOOL COUNTY COMBINATION - DIVISION ONE 1951-52 SEASON	P	W	D	L	F	A	Pts
Skelmersdale United	30	20	5	5	96	44	45
Formby	30	21	2	7	94	49	44
Everton 'A'	30	17	6	7	86	32	40
Ellesmere Port T Res.	30	16	5	9	70	67	37
Stork	30	16	4	10	68	54	36
Liverpool 'A'	30	15	6	9	64	60	36
Cromptons Recs	30	16	3	11	72	61	35
Haydock	30	13	8	9	78	59	34
Burscough	**30**	**11**	**6**	**13**	**71**	**65**	**28**
Prescot B.I.	30	11	4	15	48	53	26
Earle	30	11	4	15	68	79	26
Marine Reserves	30	10	2	18	62	83	22
Bootle Reserves	30	8	4	18	56	81	20
Hoylake Athletic	30	8	4	18	52	88	20
South Liverpool Res.	30	7	3	20	44	77	17
Liverpool Police	30	6	2	22	45	122	14

1950/51 Season
Liverpool County Combination (Division One)

Date	Opponent	H/A	Competition	Result	Scorers
Sat Aug 19	Earle	A	Lge	L 1-2	Kelly
Sat Aug 26	Bootle Reserves	A	Lge	W 2-0	Stan Jones, Woolley
Sat Sep 2	St. Helens Town	H	F.A.Cup Extra Prelim. Rd	W 3-1	Kelly, Steve Jones, Lynn
Sat Sep 9	Liverpool 'A'	A	Lge	L 1-2	Gerrard
Sat Sep 16	Haydock C & B	A	F.A.Cup Prelim. Rd	W 3-1	Bridge (2), Stan Jones
Sat Sep 23	Haydock C & B	H	Lge	W 6-1	Bridge (6)
Sat Sep 30	Bootle	H	F.A.Cup 1st Qual. Rd	W 2-0	Bridge, Kelly
	Attend: 1,467 - Gate: £73				
Sat Oct 7	Skelmersdale United	H	Lge	L 0-1	
	Attend: 'over 3,000' - Gate: £136				
Sat Oct 14	Skelmersdale United	H	F.A.Cup 2nd Qual. Rd	W 3-2	Bridge (2), Stan Jones
	Attend: 3,526 - Gate: £168				
Sat Oct 21	Liverpool 'A'	H	Lge	L 0-2	
	Attend: 1,107 - Gate: £50				
Sat Oct 28	Wigan Athletic	H	F.A.Cup 3rd Qual. Rd	L 0-2	
	Attend: 4,798 - Gate: £280				
Sat Nov 4	Bootle Reserves	H	George Mahon Cup	W 3-1	Woolley, Bridge, Stan Jones
	Attend: 734 - Gate:£ 37				
Sat Nov 11	Skelmersdale United	A	Lge	D 3-3	Dom McGrail, Bridge (2)
Sat Nov 18	Cromptons Recs	H	Lge	W 4-1	Steve Jones, McGrail, Stan Jones, Graves
Sat Nov 25	Prescot Cables Reserves	H	Liverpool Challenge Cup	D 3-3	McGrail, Bridge, Bergin
	Attend: 802 - Gate: £39				abandoned in extra time
Sat Dec 2	Prescot Cables Reserves	H	Liverpool Challenge Cup Replayed Tie	W 5-0	McGrail (2), Bridge (3)
	Attend: 702				
Sat Dec 9	Prescot B.I.	H	Lge	W 6-1	Bergin (3), Graves, McGrail, Stan Jones
Sat Dec 16	Cromptons Recs	H	Lancs Junior Cup	W 4-0	McGrail, Bridge (2), Massey
	Attend: 687 - Gate: £32				
Mon Dec 25	Formby	A	Lge	L 1-3	Arthur Green
Tue Dec 26	Formby	H	Lge	D 1-1	McGrail
	Attend: 883 - Gate: £40				
Mon Jan 1	Skelmersdale United	H	Lpool Senior Non-lge Cup	W 2-0	Bergin, Brennan
	Attend: 1,238				
Sat Jan 6	Cromptons Recs	H	Liverpool Challenge Cup	D 1-1	London
					abandoned in extra-time (bad light)
Sat Jan 13	Leyland Motors	A	Lancs Junior Cup	L 3-4	Bergin (2), Green
Sat Jan 20	Cromptons Recs	H	Liverpool Challenge Cup Replayed tie	W 3-0	Bernie Woods (3)
	Attend: 664				
Sat Jan 27	Newton-le-Willows	H	Lge	W 5-0	McGrail (3), Woods (2)
	Attend: 508				
Sat Feb 3	Marine Reserves	A	Lge	W 3-1	McGrail, Bergin (2)
Sat Feb 10	Earle	H	George Mahon Cup	W 3-2	Jones (2), Billy Morrey
Sat Feb 17	South Liverpool Reserves	H	Lge	W 6-1	Vickers, Jones, Bergin (2), McGrail, Woods
Sat Feb 24	South Liverpool Reserves	A	Lge	W 6-2	Jones, Woods (3), Bergin (2)
Sat Mar 3	Liverpool Police	A	Lge	D 3-3	Woods (2), McGrail
Sat Mar 10	Marine Reserves	H	Lge	W 4-2	Woods, McGrail, London, Brennan
Sat Mar 17	Prescot Cables Reserves	A	Lge	D 1-1	Bergin
Sat Mar 24	Cromptons Recs	A	Lge	D 1-1	Jones
Mon Mar 26	Liverpool 'A'	A	Liverpool Challenge Cup Semi-final	W 4-0	Bergin, Woods (2), McGrail
	at Anfield				
Sat Mar 31	Haydock C & B	A	Lge	W 6-2	McGrail (2), Woods (2), Smith, Jones
Sat Apr 7	Everton 'A'	H	Lge	L 0-1	
Mon Apr 9	Bootle Reserves	H	Lge	L 0-1	
Sat Apr 14	Ellesmere Port Town Res.	H	Lge	W 8-1	Turner (3), Bergin (4), McGrail
	Attend: 412				
Wed Apr 18	Hoylake Athletic at South Liverpool		George Mahon Cup Semi-final	L 0-2	
Sat Apr 21	Hoylake Athletic	H	Lge	W 5-1	Woods (3), Jim Martland, McGrail
	Attend: 512				
Mon Apr 23	Bootle at Bootle Stadium	A	Lpool Senior Non-lge Cup Semi-final	D 0-0	abandoned in extra-time (bad light)
Tue Apr 24	Prescot B.I.	A	Lge	L 1-3	Harry Waugh
Wed Apr 25	Earle	H	Lge	L 0-1	
Sat Apr 28	Everton 'A'	A	Lge	L 1-2	London
Thu May 3	Newton-le-Willows	A	Lge	W 3-0	Lewin (3)
Sat May 5	Ellesmere Port Town Res.	A	Lge	W 3-1	Chick Heath (2), Jones
Mon May 7	Bootle	H	Lpool Senior Non-lge Cup Semi-final replay	L 1-2	Lynn
Tue May 8	Liverpool Police	H	Lge	W 3-2	Brennan, Lewin (2)
Thu May 10	Prescot Cables Reserves	H	Lge	D 2-2	Aspinall, Kelly
Sat May 12	Hoylake Athletic	A	Lge	W 2-1	Sutton (2)
Mon May 14	St. Helens Town at Wigan - Attend: 3,000		Liverpool Challenge Cup Final	W 3-1	Aspinall, Kelly, Woods

229

1950-51 Season. Back left to right: Wally Stone, Wilf London, Dom McGrail, Harry Sutton, Matt Brennan, Steve Jones, Johnny Baldwin (Trainer).

Front left to right: Jimmy Aspinall, Bernie Woods, Chris Lynn, Chick Heath, Stan Jones.

1952-53 Season. Back left to right: David Craig, Ronnie Wright, Wally Stone, Harry Sutton, Chris Lynn, Bill Parker, Harry Lowe (Trainer).

Front left to right: Jim Smith, Powell, Billy Thompson, Stan Jones, Tommy Tallon.

1951/52 Season
Liverpool County Combination (Division One)

Date	Opponent	H/A	Competition	Result	Scorers
Sat Aug 18	Prescot B.I.	H	Lge	W 2-1	Kelly, McGrail
	Attend: 697				
Wed Aug 22	Earle	H	Lge	W 7-1	Kelly (2), Lynn (2), McGrail, Jones, O.G.
Sat Aug 25	Skelmersdale United	A	Lge	L 2-3	Thomas, McGrail
	Attend: 2,180				
Wed Aug 29	Cromptons Recs	H	Lge	W 4-2	Jones (2), Thomas (2)
	Attend: 688				
Sat Sep 1	Everton 'A'	H	Lge	D 2-2	Kelly, Murphy
Sat Sep 8	Liverpool 'A'	A	Lge	W 4-2	Johnny Wishart, McGrail, Kelly, Lewin
Sat Sep 15	Haydock C & B	H	Lge	W 4-3	Woods (2), Jones, McGrail
Sat Sep 22	Stork	A	Lge	L 1-3	Kelly
Sat Sep 29	Morecambe	H	F.A. Cup 1st Qual. Rd	D 2-2	Kelly, Lewin
	Attend: 1,184				
Wed Oct 3	Morecambe	A	F.A. Cup replay	W 1-0	McGrail
Sat Oct 6	Bootle Reserves	A	Lge	L 1-2	O.G.
Sat Oct 13	Netherfield	A	F.A. Cup 2nd Qual. Rd	L 2-4	London, O.G.
	Attend: 2,115				
Sat Oct 20	Ellesmere Port Town Res.	H	Lge	W 6-0	Jones, McGrail, Waugh (2), O.G., Wishart
Sat Oct 27	Cromptons Recs	A	Lge	L 1-4	London
Sat Nov 3	Hoylake Athletic	A	George Mahon Cup	W 3-0	Waugh, Murphy, McGrail
Sat Nov 10	Hoylake Athletic	A	Lge	D 2-2	Penkeyman (2)
Sat Nov 17	Great Harwood	H	Lancs Junior Cup	W 5-2	O.G., Kelly (2), Powell, Penkeyman
Sat Nov 24	Larkhill	H	Liverpool Challenge Cup	W 3-1	London, Stan Jones, Penkeyman
	Attend: 650				
Sat Dec 1	Marine Reserves	H	Lge	W 5-0	Penkeyman (4), McGrail
	Attend: 666				
Sat Dec 8	Everton 'A'	A	Lge	D 2-2	Kelly, Stan Jones
Sat Dec 15	Prescot Cables	A	Lancs Junior Cup	W 2-0	Kelly, Penkeyman
Sat Dec 22	Haydock	A	Lge	L 1-4	Lynn
Tue Dec 25	Formby	H	Lge	D 1-1	McGrail
	Attend: 830				
Wed Dec 26	Formby	A	Lge	L 1-4	Jones
Sat Dec 29	Bootle Reserves	H	Lge	L 1-2	McGrail
Tue Jan 1	Liverpool 'A'	H	Lge	W 3-0	Kelly (3)
Sat Jan 5	Liverpool Police	A	Lge	D 1-1	Penkeyman
Sat Jan 12	Stork	H	Lge	L 3-4	McGrail, Penkeyman, Kelly
Sat Jan 19	South Liverpool Reserves	H	Lge	W 4-1	Penkeyman (3), McGrail
Sat Feb 2	Everton 'A'	A	Liverpool Challenge Cup 2nd Round	L 0-1	
	at Goodison Park				
	Attend: 'over 4,000'				
Sat Feb 9	Formby	A	George Mahon Cup	L 1-2	Bobby Thistlewood
	Attend: 'over 1,000'				
Sat Feb 16	Bootle	H	Lancs Junior Cup	L 1-6	Stan Jones
Sat Feb 23	Earle	A	Lge	L 1-2	Kelly
Sat Mar 1	Hoylake Athletic	H	Lge	W 4-1	Powell, Patterson (2), Thistlewood
Sat Mar 8	Ellesmere Port Town Res.	A	Lge	L 0-5	
Sat Mar 15	South Liverpool	A	L'pool Senior Non-lge Cup 2nd Rd	W 2-0	Thistlewood, Stan Jones
Sat Mar 22	Marine Reserves	A	Lge	L 0-1	
Sat Mar 29	Liverpool Police	H	Lge	W 6-3	Eddie Cliffe (2), Aspinall, Edmondson (2), Kirwan
Sat Apr 5	Prescot B.I.	A	Lge	L 0-5	
Mon Apr 21	Skelmersdale United	H	Lge	D 2-2	McGrail, Stan Jones
	Gate: £74				
Thu Apr 24	Prescot Cables	A	L'pool Senior Non-lge Cup Semi-final	L 0-3	
Sat Apr 26	South Liverpool Reserves	A	Lge	L 0-2	

1952/53 Season
Liverpool County Combination (Division One)

Date	Opponent	H/A	Competition	Result	Scorers
Sat Aug 23	Ellesmere Port Town Res. Attend: 1,500	A	Lge	W 4-3	Stan Jones (2), Tommy Tallon, David Craig
Sat Aug 30	Marine Reserves	H	Lge	W 6-2	Tallon (3), Craig (3)
Sat Sep 6	Everton 'A'	A	Lge	L 2-3	Tallon, Jim Smith
Mon Sep 8	Bootle Attend: 1,043,	H	Lpool Senior Non-lge Cup	D 2-2	Billy Hodge, Tallon
Sat Sep 13	Penrith	A	F.A.Cup Prelim. Rd	D 4-4	Craig (3), Tallon
Wed Sep 17	Penrith Gate: £61	H	F.A.Cup replay	W 3-1	Craig (2), Stan Jones
Sat Sep 20	Prescot B.I.	A	Lge	W 4-1	Stan Jones, Moylan, Smith, Tallon
Sat Sep 27	Lancaster City Attend: 1,528 - Gate: £81	H	F.A.Cup 1st Qual. Rd	W 1-0	Tallon
Sat Oct 4	Skelmersdale United Attend: 2,320 - Gate: £115	H	Lge	D 0-0	
Sat Oct 11	Netherfield Attend: 1,572 - Gate: £84	H	F.A.Cup 2nd Qual. Rd	L 2-4	Tallon, Stan Jones
Wed Oct 15	Bootle	A	Lpool Senior Non-lge Cup replay	L 0-3	
Sat Oct 18	Liverpool 'A'	A	Lge	L 1-3	Waugh
Sat Oct 25	Bootle Reserves	H	Lge	W 3-1	Thistlewood, Craig, Stan Jones
Sat Nov 1	Southport Trinity	H	Liverpool Challenge Cup	W 8-0	Louis Bimpson (7), Stan Jones
Sat Nov 8	Earle Gate: £26	H	Lge	W 3-0	Tallon, Bimpson (2)
Sat Nov 15	Stork	A	Lge	L 3-4	O.G., Bimpson, Wynne
Sat Nov 22	Hoylake Athletic Gate: £23	H	Lge	W 4-2	Morrey, Bill Pilson, Tallon (2)
Sat Nov 29	Maghull	A	Liverpool Challenge Cup	W 2-1	Tallon, Pilson
Sat Dec 6	Marine Reserves	A	Lge	L 1-3	Wally Stone
Sat Dec 13	Clitheroe Gate: £37	H	Lancs Junior Cup 2nd Rd	D 3-3	Moylan, Stan Jones, Bimpson
Sat Dec 20	Clitheroe	A	Lancs Junior Cup replay	L 2-5	Tallon, Bimpson
Thu Dec 25	Formby	A	Lge	L 2-4	Stan Jones, Bimpson
Fri Dec 26	Formby	H	Lge	L 0-1	
Sat Jan 3	Prescot B.I.	H	Lge	W 5-1	Bimpson (3), Billy Thompson, O.G.
Sat Jan 10	Liverpool 'A'	H	Lge	W 6-0	Stan Jones, Bimpson (4), Tallon
Sat Jan 17	Bootle Reserves	A	Lge	W 3-2	Thompson, Bimpson (2)
Sat Jan 24	Crossens played at Burscough	A	Liverpool Challenge Cup	W 5-2	Stan Jones, Pilson, Tallon, Bimpson (2)
Sat Jan 31	Hoylake Athletic	A	Lge	W 4-3	Bill Parker (3), Tallon
Sat Feb 7	Fleetwood Hesketh	H	Lge	W 1-0	Thompson
Sat Feb 14	Ellesmere Port Town Res.	H	George Mahon Cup	W 5-1	Lofthouse, Stan Jones (4)
Sat Feb 21	Everton 'A'	H	Lge	L 0-4	
Sat Feb 28	Haydock	A	Lge	D 1-1	Thompson
Sat Mar 7	Haydock Gate: £35	H	George Mahon Cup	W 2-0	Bill McLean, Thompson
Sat Mar 14	Skelmersdale United Attend: 'nearly 2,000' - Gate: £68	A	Lge	L 1-3	Stan Jones
Sat Mar 28	Earle	A	Lge	L 1-4	Thompson
Fri Apr 3	Ellesmere Port Town Res.	H	Lge	W 3-2	Lofthouse, Thompson, Wally Burnett
Mon Apr 6	Fleetwood Hesketh	A	Lge	L 1-2	Burnett
Sat Apr 11	Stork	H	Lge	L 1-2	Thompson
Sat Apr 18	Everton 'A' at Skelmersdale		Liverpool Challenge Cup Semi-final	L 0-6	
Wed Apr 22	Bootle Reserves at Skelmersdale		George Mahon Cup Semi-final	D 2-2	Lofthouse (2)
Fri Apr 24	Bootle Reserves	H	Geo. Mahon Cup replay	L 0-2	
Sat Apr 25	Haydock	H	Lge	W 5-1	Lofthouse (2), Thompson (3)

1953/54 Season
Lancashire Combination (Division Two)

Date	Opponent	H/A	Competition	Result	Scorers
Wed Aug 19	Lomax	H	Lge	W 5-0	Tom Galvin (2), Johnny Vincent (3)
Sat Aug 22	Astley Bridge	H	Lge	W 4-0	Ronnie Wilson (2), Vincent (2)
Thu Aug 27	St. Helens Town	A	Lge	D 3-3	Vincent, O.G., John Disley
Sat Aug 29	Chorley Reserves	A	Lge	W 5-1	Morrey, Vincent (2), Wilson, Galvin
Wed Sep 2	St. Helens Town	H	Lge	D 0-0	
Sat Sep 5	Clitheroe	H	Lge	W 7-1	McGrail (3), Vincent, Wilson, Burnett, Jim Cookson
Mon Sep 7	New Brighton *Gate: £54*	H	Lancs Comb Cup	W 4-0	Wilson, McGrail (2), Disley
Wed Sep 9	Nelson Reserves	H	Lge	W 5-0	Vincent (2), Disley (2), Burnett
Sat Sep 12	Nelson Reserves	A	Lge	W 2-1	Burnett, Disley
Wed Sep 16	Marine	A	Lpool Senior Non-lge Cup	W 2-1	Disley, Thompson
Sat Sep 19	Lytham	H	Lge	W 7-0	Burnett, Vincent (4), Disley, Cookson
Sat Sep 26	Bacup Borough	H	F.A.Cup 1st Qual. Rd	W 4-1	Burnett, Vincent (3)
Mon Sep 28	Prescot Cables *Gate: £84*	A	Lancs Comb Cup 2nd Rd	D 1-1	Galvin
Sat Oct 3	Great Harwood *Gate: £47*	H	Lge	W 6-2	Burnett (2), Vincent, McGrail (2), Cookson
Sat Oct 10	Lancaster City *Attend: 1,951 - Gate: £97*	H	F.A.Cup 2nd Qual. Rd	W 2-1	Burnett, Disley
Wed Oct 14	Prescot Cables *Gate: £50*		Lancs Comb Cup	L 1-2	Vincent
Sat Oct 17	Stubshaw Cross	A	Lge	W 3-1	Disley, Burnett, Vincent
Sat Oct 24	Morecambe *Gate: £122*	A	F.A.Cup 3rd Qual. Rd	W 1-0	Wilson
Sat Oct 31	Barnoldswick Town	A	Lge	L 0-2	
Sat Nov 7	Wigan Athletic *Attend: 6,060 - Gate: £279*	A	F.A.Cup 4th Qual. Rd	L 1-2	Vincent
Sat Nov 21	Blackpool 'B' *Gate: £55*	H	Lge	W 3-1	Cookson (2), Thompson
Sat Nov 28	Darwen Reserves	A	Lge	D 1-1	Thompson
Sat Dec 5	Leyland Motors	H	Lge	W 5-1	Thompson, Vincent, O.G., Disley, Wilson
Sat Dec 12	Lomax	A	Lge	W 6-1	Len Wilkinson, Cookson (3), Vincent, Burnett
Sat Dec 19	Astley Bridge	A	Lge	D 2-2	Wilkinson (2)
Fri Dec 25	Earlestown *Gate: £55*	H	Lge	W 3-2	Vincent, Cookson, Wilkinson
Sat Dec 26	Earlestown	A	Lge	W 3-0	Vincent, Wilson, Wilkinson
Fri Jan 1	Skelmersdale United	A	Liverpool Senior Non-lge Cup Semi-final	W 3-0	Vincent (2), Michael Feegan
Sat Jan 2	Chorley Reserves	H	Lge	W 8-0	Vincent (4), Wilson (3), Burnett
Sat Jan 9	Droylesden	A	Lge	W 3-0	Wilson, Vincent, Wilkinson
Sat Jan 16	Clitheroe	A	Lge	W 4-1	Vincent, Wilkinson, Burnett
Sat Jan 23	St. Helens Town	A	Lancs Junior Cup	W 4-0	Wilkinson (2), O.G., Vincent
Sat Jan 30	Droylesden	H	Lge	L 0-2	
Sat Feb 13	Northern Nomads *Attend: 1,213 - Gate: £62*	H	Lancs Junior Cup 2nd Rd	W 2-0	Vincent, Wilkinson
Sat Feb 20	Great Harwood	A	Lge	W 4-1	Vincent, Wilkinson, Burnett (2)
Sat Feb 27	Burnley 'A'	A	Lge	L 0-4	
Sat Mar 6	Stubshaw Cross	H	Lge	W 9-1	Feegan (2), Burnett, Vincent (2), Bobby Warren, Disley (2), Cookson
Sat Mar 13	Bacup Borough	A	Lge	W 5-0	Burnett, Vincent (2), Wilkinson (2)
Sat Mar 20	Horwich RMI	H	Lancs Junior Cup 3rd Rd	L 0-2	
Sat Mar 27	Prescot Reserves	A	Lge	W 4-3	Vincent (2), Wilkinson, Disley
Sat Apr 3	Padiham	H	Lge	W 5-0	Vincent (2), Thompson (2), Joe Hart
Sat Apr 10	Blackpool 'B'	A	Lge	W 1-0	Burnett
Mon Apr 12	Prescot Reserves	H	Lge	W 4-0	Vincent (2), Warren (2)
Wed Apr 14	Wigan Athletic Reserves	H	Lge	W 5-1	Thompson, Vincent, Cookson, Hart, O.G.
Fri Apr 16	Cromptons Recs *Gate: £49*	H	Lge	W 5-0	Thompson (2), Vincent, Hart (2)
Sat Apr 17	Darwen Reserves	H	Lge	W 4-1	Disley (2), Vincent, Hart
Mon Apr 19	Cromptons Recs	A	Lge	L 1-2	Burnett
Wed Apr 21	Lytham	A	Lge	W 2-0	Thompson, Burnett
Thu Apr 22	Wigan Athletic Reserves	A	Lge	W 3-0	Thompson, Martland, Vincent
Sat Apr 24	Leyland Motors	A	Lge	L 1-2	Disley
Mon Apr 26	Padiham	A	Lge	W 4-0	Vincent (3), Hart
Wed Apr 28	Bacup Borough	H	Lge	W 3-0	Vincent (2), Disley
Fri Apr 30	Burnley 'A' *Gate: £48*	H	Lge	W 4-0	Thompson, Hart, Vincent (2)
Sat May 1	Barnoldswick Town	H	Lge	W 6-1	Vincent (2), Burnett, Hart (3)
Sat May 8	South Liverpool *at Anfield - Attend: 3,000*		Liverpool Senior Non-lge Cup Final	L 0-1	

1953-54 Season. Back left to right: Johnny Baldwin (Trainer), Wally Burnett, Arthur Green, Stan Hurst, Joe Brazier, Johnny Vincent, Charlie Jones (Manager).
Front left to right: Dom McGrail, Ronnie Wilson, Billy Morrey, Jim Cookson, Billy Thompson, John Disley. Jim Cookson died in 1993. He had been born in the Tailor's Arms, Litherland, where his father was 'mine host'. His father, also Jim Cookson, had played for Burscough Rangers in the 1920s.

1954-55 Season. Back left to right: Johnny Baldwin (Trainer), George Higgins, Joe Brazier, Arthur Green, Stan Hurst, Bobby Warren, Charlie Jones (Manager).
Front left to right: Billy Pilson, Joe Hart, Wally Burnett, Bill Hounslea, Ronnie Wilson, Johnny Disley.

1954/55 Season
Lancashire Combination (Division One)

Date	Opponent	H/A	Competition	Result	Scorers
Sat Aug 21	Bolton Wanderers 'B'	H	Lge	W 2-0	Jim Nuttall, Martland
	Gate: £51				
Mon Aug 23	Marine	H	Lpool Senior Non-lge Cup	L 1-2	Nuttall
	Gate: £57				
Wed Aug 25	Horwich RMI	A	Lge	W 2-0	Hart, Bill Hounslea
Sat Aug 28	Lancaster City	A	Lge	D 1-1	Pilson
Wed Sep 1	Horwich RMI	H	Lge	W 2-0	Hounslea, Burnett
Sat Sep 4	Netherfield	H	Lge	W 3-0	Hounslea, Burnett, Hart
	Gate: £50				
Mon Sep 6	Ashton United	A	Lge	W 4-1	Warren, Hounslea, Hart (2)
	Attend: 1,500				
Wed Sep 8	Ashton United	H	Lge	W 1-0	Hounslea
Sat Sep 11	Accrington Stanley Res.	A	Lge	L 1-2	Burnett
	Attend: 5,000				
Wed Sep 15	Leyland Motors	H	Lancs Comb Cup 2nd Rd	D 2-2	Pilson, Aspinall
Sat Sep 18	Accrington Stanley Res.	H	Lge	L 0-2	
Sat Sep 25	Penrith	H	F.A.Cup 1st Qual. Rd	W 4-0	Burnett, Hart, Disley, Hounslea
	Gate: £57				
Mon Sep 27	Leyland Motors	H	Lancs Comb Cup replay	W 7-0	Hounslea (2), Warren, Burnett (3), Green
Sat Oct 2	Darwen	A	Lge	D 2-2	Burnett (2)
	Gate: £80				
Sat Oct 9	Lancaster City	A	F.A.Cup 2nd Qual. Rd	W 3-2	Pilson, Burnett (2)
	Attend: 2,788 - Gate: £163				
Sat Oct 16	Nelson	H	Lge	W 4-2	Hounslea (2), Green, Hart
	Gate: £45				
Sat Oct 23	Netherfield	H	F.A.Cup 3rd Qual. Rd	L 0-1	
	Gate: £77				
Sat Oct 30	Oldham Athletic Reserves	H	Lge	W 2-1	Burnett, Pilson
Sat Nov 6	Marine	A	Lge	L 0-2	
Sat Nov 13	New Brighton	H	Lge	W 1-0	Burnett
Sat Nov 20	Rochdale Reserves	A	Lge	W 7-0	Tommy Cronin (3), Burnett (3), Hart
Sat Nov 27	Morecambe	H	Lge	W 1-0	Hounslea
Sat Dec 4	Southport Reserves	A	Lge	L 0-2	
Sat Dec 11	Chorley	H	Lge	D 1-1	Hart
Sat Dec 18	Bolton Wanderers 'B'	A	Lge	L 0-3	
Sat Dec 25	Wigan Athletic	H	Lge	W 2-1	Disley, Cronin
	Gate: £100				
Mon Dec 27	Wigan Athletic	A	Lge	L 1-4	Cronin
Sat Jan 1	Lancaster City	H	Lge	L 1-2	Ray Williams
Sat Jan 8	Chorley	A	Lancs Comb Cup 3rd Rd	W 1-0	Williams
	Attend: 1,228				
Sat Jan 15	Netherfield	A	Lge	W 3-2	Hart, Williams, Pilson
Sat Jan 22	Morecambe	A	Lancs Junior Cup 1st Rd	D 1-1	Cronin
	Attend: 1,628 - Gate: £89				
Sat Jan 29	Morecambe	H	Lancs Junior Cup replay	W 1-0	Joe Brine
	Attend: 1,017 - Gate: £55				
Sat Feb 5	Blackpool 'B'	A	Lge	W 2-0	Wilkinson (2)
Sat Feb 12	Wigan Athletic	A	Lancs Junior Cup 2nd Rd	L 1-3	Wilkinson
	Attend: 3,805 - Gate: £244				
Sat Mar 5	Nelson	A	Lge	L 1-4	Disley
Sat Mar 12	Rossendale United	H	Lge	W 3-1	Bob McAdam, Wright, Martland
Sat Mar 19	Oldham Athletic Reserves	A	Lge	L 0-2	
Sat Mar 26	Marine	H	Lge	W 6-1	Wright, Bridge (2), Wilson, Hart, Aspinall
Sat Apr 2	New Brighton	A	Lge	D 0-0	
Fri Apr 8	South Liverpool	H	Lge	W 3-0	Hart, Warren, Wesley Bridge
Sat Apr 9	Barrow Reserves	H	Lge	W 2-1	Bridge, Warren
Mon Apr 11	South Liverpool	A	Lge	W 2-0	Bridge, Disley
Wed Apr 13	Fleetwood	H	Lge	L 0-3	
Sat Apr 16	Morecambe	A	Lge	L 1-2	Bridge
Mon Apr 18	Blackpool 'B'	H	Lge	L 0-1	
Tue Apr 19	Accrington Stanley Res.	A	Lancs Comb Cup 3rd Rd	L 1-3	McAdam
Wed Apr 20	Fleetwood	A	Lge	D 0-0	
Sat Apr 23	Southport Reserves	H	Lge	W 3-1	Hart, Disley, Bridge
Mon Apr 25	Rochdale Reserves	H	Lge	D 0-0	
Wed Apr 27	Rossendale United	A	Lge	D 2-2	Hart, McAdam
Sat Apr 30	Chorley	A	Lge	D 2-2	Hart, Wilkinson
Mon May 2	Darwen	H	Lge	W 4-1	Wright, Disley, Pilson, McAdam
Sat May 7	Barrow Reserves	A	Lge	W 3-0	Aspinall, Disley, Hart

LANCASHIRE COMBINATION - DIVISION TWO
1953-54 SEASON

	P	W	D	L	F	A	Pts
Burscough	42	33	4	5	155	38	70
Blackpool 'B'	42	29	6	7	132	53	64
Burnley 'A'	42	29	4	9	146	66	62
Earlestown	42	26	8	8	121	74	60
Droylesden	42	26	7	9	116	50	59
Nelson Reserves	42	25	4	13	101	85	54
Barnoldswick	42	21	8	13	120	95	50
Bacup Borough	42	20	8	14	99	86	48
Clitheroe	42	21	4	17	113	107	46
Leyland Motors	42	20	3	19	87	84	43
Lytham	42	17	9	16	66	78	43
Cromptons Recs.	42	19	3	20	88	111	41
Darwen Reserves	42	18	3	21	90	94	39
Prescot Cables Reserves	42	16	6	20	101	90	38
St. Helens Town	42	16	6	20	86	98	38
Chorley Reserves	42	12	8	22	81	111	32
Wigan Athletic Reserves	42	12	7	23	83	107	31
Padiham	42	12	3	27	60	118	27
Great Harwood	42	10	6	26	82	120	26
Lomax	42	12	1	29	73	139	25
Astley Bridge	42	7	4	31	65	160	18
Stubshaw Cross Rovers	42	4	2	36	51	152	10

LANCASHIRE COMBINATION - DIVISION ONE
1954-55 SEASON

	P	W	D	L	F	A	Pts
Accrington Stanley Res.	42	29	10	3	110	46	68
Rossendale United	42	24	6	12	123	84	54
Wigan Athletic	42	21	10	11	93	56	52
Burscough	42	22	8	12	75	50	52
Oldham Athletic Reserves	42	21	10	11	98	74	52
Fleetwood	42	19	11	12	73	69	49
Blackpool 'B'	42	21	6	15	95	59	48
Horwich RMI	42	20	8	14	81	62	48
Morecambe	42	18	9	15	68	59	45
Marine	42	19	5	18	91	84	43
Netherfield	42	20	3	19	92	94	43
Darwen	42	15	13	14	65	80	43
Chorley	42	17	7	18	78	91	41
Lancaster City	42	16	9	17	68	84	41
Barrow Reserves	42	14	9	19	88	90	37
Nelson	42	14	8	20	79	83	36
Ashton United	42	13	9	20	75	107	35
Southport Reserves	42	12	9	21	74	79	33
Bolton Wanderers 'B'	42	12	8	22	53	69	32
South Liverpool	42	12	8	22	67	105	32
Rochdale Reserves	42	8	9	25	58	92	25
New Brighton	42	6	3	33	48	147	15

LIVERPOOL COUNTY COMBINATION - DIVISION TWO
1953-54 SEASON

	P	W	D	L	F	A	Pts
Burscough Reserves	28	24	2	2	109	28	49
Liverpool 'B'	28	21	1	6	107	38	43
Everton 'B'	28	20	3	5	82	39	43
Skelmersdale Utd Res.	28	16	3	9	93	49	35
Automatic 'B'	28	16	3	9	93	69	35
Aintree S.S.	28	16	3	9	80	64	35
Dunlop (Speke)	28	12	3	13	68	71	27
Liverpool Transport	28	10	5	13	74	88	25
Marlborough	28	9	5	14	60	81	23
Napiers	28	9	5	14	50	74	23
New Brighton Res.	28	8	6	14	54	56	22
Earle Reserves	28	5	6	17	58	75	16
Stork Reserves	28	7	1	20	59	120	15
Fleetwood Hesketh Res.	28	6	3	19	37	114	15
I.C.I (Widnes)	28	3	4	21	47	108	10

LANCASHIRE COMBINATION - DIVISION ONE
1955-56 SEASON

	P	W	D	L	F	A	Pts
Burscough	38	26	7	5	96	37	59
Horwich R.M.I.	38	24	9	5	104	49	57
Accrington Stanley Res.	38	20	10	8	87	56	50
Netherfield	38	21	7	10	95	55	49
Lancaster City	38	19	11	8	83	59	49
Wigan Athletic	38	18	10	10	80	56	48
New Brighton	38	18	8	12	78	57	44
Prescot Cables	38	19	6	13	102	93	44
Chorley	38	17	5	16	78	68	39
Marine	38	14	8	16	71	83	36
Southport Reserves	38	13	9	16	54	60	35
Ashton United	38	14	7	17	62	75	35
Darwen	38	13	8	17	66	85	34
Fleetwood	38	12	8	18	65	79	32
Nelson	38	12	8	18	60	89	32
Morecambe	38	10	9	19	59	74	29
Bacup Borough	38	12	5	21	68	94	29
South Liverpool	38	12	3	23	69	98	27
Rossendale United	38	8	9	21	61	89	25
St. Helens Town	38	3	3	32	34	110	9

1955/56 Season
Lancashire Combination (Division One)

Date	Opponent	H/A	Comp	Result	Scorers
Sat Aug 20	New Brighton *Attend: 'over 1,000'*	A	Lge	W 3-0	Disley (2), John Hendry
Wed Aug 24	Morecambe *Attend: 'over 1,000'*	H	Lge	W 2-1	Hendry (2)
Sat Aug 27	Bacup Borough *Gate: £31*	H	Lge	W 5-2	Disley, Billy Birchall, Hart (2), Hendry
Wed Aug 31	Morecambe	A	Lge	W 4-0	Hendry (2), Hart (2)
Sat Sep 3	Chorley *Attend: 'over 2,000' - Gate: £124*	A	Lge	W 2-1	Hendry, Stan Jessop
Mon Sep 5	Marine	A	Lancs Comb Cup 1st Rd	D 1-1	Disley
Sat Sep 10	Nelson	H	Lge	W 5-0	Hart, Bob Millington, Disley, Jessop (2)
Mon Sep 12	South Liverpool	H	Lpool Senior Non-lge Cup	W 5-0	Aspinall, Jessop, Hart, Disley, Hendry
Sat Sep 17	Rossendale United	A	Lge	D 1-1	Hendry
Mon Sep 19	Marine *Attend: 1,400 - Gate: £63*	H	Lancs Comb Cup replay	W 4-0	Hart (2), Hendry, Jessop
Sat Sep 24	Lancaster City *Attend: 2,237 - Gate: £137*	A	F.A. Cup 1st Qual. Rd	L 0-2	
Sat Oct 1	South Liverpool	A	Lge	W 2-0	Jessop, Bobby Murdoch
Sat Oct 8	St. Helens Town	A	Lge	W 2-1	Jessop, Dennis Walmsley
Sat Oct 15	Accrington Stanley Res. *Gate: £45*	H	Lge	W 3-0	Hart (2), Hendry
Sat Oct 22	Wigan Athletic	A	Lge	D 2-2	Hart, Hendry
Sat Oct 29	Fleetwood	H	Lge	W 5-0	Hart (3), Disley, Walmsley
Sat Nov 5	Darwen	A	Lge	D 1-1	Brine
Sat Nov 12	Horwich RMI *Gate: £60*	H	Lge	W 3-1	Jessop (2), Wilson
Sat Nov 26	Ashton United	H	Lge	W 3-0	Green, Tommy Scroggins, Jessop
Sat Dec 3	Lancaster City *Attend: 1,604 - Gate: £94*	A	Lge	D 2-2	Millington, Disley
Sat Dec 10	Marine	H	Lge	W 5-0	Disley, Scroggins, Hart (3)
Sat Dec 17	New Brighton	H	Lge	L 0-1	
Mon Dec 26	Prescot Cables	H	Lge	W 3-0	Disley (2), Hendry
Tue Dec 27	Prescot Cables	A	Lge	L 2-5	Jessop, Hendry
Sat Dec 31	Chorley *Gate: £47*	H	Lge	W 4-1	Hendry, Scroggins, Green, Hart
Sat Jan 7	Rossendale United	H	Lge	W 1-0	Disley
Sat Jan 21	Lancaster City *Attend: 1,042 - Gate: £79*	A	Lancs Junior Cup	W 1-0	Millington
Sat Feb 4	Marine	A	Lge	D 1-1	Hart
Sat Feb 11	Skelmersdale United *Attend: 2,484 - Gate: £109*	A	Lancs Junior Cup	D 1-1	Green
Sat Feb 18	Skelmersdale United *Attend: 2,317*	H	Lancs Junior Cup replay	W 3-0	Green, Disley, McAdam
Sat Feb 25	Accrington Stanley Res.	A	Lge	L 0-2	
Sat Mar 3	Wigan Athletic *Gate: £112*	H	Lge	W 3-2	Hart (2), Millington
Sat Mar 10	Prescot Cables *Gate: £80*	A	Lancs Junior Cup	L 1-4	Hart
Sat Mar 17	Bacup Borough	A	Lge	W 3-1	Disley, Hart, Walmsley
Wed Mar 21	New Brighton	A	Lancs Comb Cup	W 2-1	Disley, Millington
Sat Mar 24	Horwich RMI *Attend; 1,500 - Gate: £86*	A	Lge	W 1-0	Disley
Fri Mar 30	Southport Reserves	A	Lge	L 1-2	Hendry
Sat Mar 31	Netherfield	H	Lge	W 2-0	Millington, Disley
Mon Apr 2	Southport Reserves	H	Lge	W 2-1	Disley, Millington
Sat Apr 7	Ashton United *Attend: 1,380 - Gate: £81*	A	Lge	W 2-1	Hart (2)
Wed Apr 11	St. Helens Town	H	Lge	W 2-0	Hart (2)
Thu Apr 12	Ashton United	H	Lancs Comb Cup	D 2-2	Walmsley, Hendry
Sat Apr 14	Lancaster City	H	Lge	W 7-1	Walmsley (2), Jessop, Disley (3), Hart
Mon Apr 16	Ashton United	A	Lancs Comb Cup replay	L 1-2	Brine
Wed Apr 18	Wigan Athletic *Gate: £75*	H	Liverpool Senior Non-lge Cup Semi-final	W 3-0	Disley (2), Hart
Sat Apr 21	Darwen	H	Lge	W 1-0	Jessop
Wed Apr 25	South Liverpool	H	Lge	W 6-0	Jessop (2), Hart (2), Dodds (2)
Sat Apr 28	Netherfield	A	Lge	L 2-4	Hendry, Aspinall
Wed May 2	Fleetwood	A	Lge	D 2-2	Walmsley (2)
Fri May 4	Nelson	A	Lge	D 1-1	Hart
Sat May 12	New Brighton *at Goodison Park*		Liverpool Senior Non-lge Cup Final	W 1-0	Aspinall

237

Above: 1955-56 Season. Back left to right: Ronnie Wilson, George Higgins, Stan Hurst, Brian Finnigan, Jimmy Aspinall, Arthur Green. Front left to right: Stan Jessop, John Hendry, Johnny Disley, Bobby Murdoch, Bob Millington. Bobby Murdoch, the former Liverpool player, only had a brief stay at Burscough.

Below: 1956-57 Season. Back left to right: Charlie Jones (Manager), George Higgins, John Glover, Arthur Green, Ronnie Wilson, Bobby Warren, Frank Richmond (Trainer).
Front left to right: Brian Finnigan, A.Murphy, Joe Hart, Johnny Disley, Des Steele, Len Wilkinson. Photograph kindly loaned by Bobby Warren.

1956/57 Season
Lancashire Combination (Division One)

Date	Opponent	H/A	Competition	Result	Scorers
Sat Aug 18	South Liverpool	A	Lge	W 2-0	Hart (2)
	Attend: 440 - Gate: £19				
Wed Aug 22	Morecambe	A	Lge	L 1-6	Disley
Sat Aug 25	Chorley	H	Lge	D 1-1	Williams
	Gate: £40				
Thu Aug 30	St. Helens Town	A	Lancs Comb Cup	W 6-4	Disley, Hart (4), Jessop
Sat Sep 1	Droylesden	A	Lge	W 3-1	Hart, Williams, Wilson
	Attend: 1,218 - Gate: £53				
Mon Sep 3	Skelmersdale United	A	Lpool Senior Non-lge Cup	L 1-4	Scroggins
	Attend: 2,110				
Wed Sep 5	Morecambe	H	Lge	D 1-1	Jessop
Sat Sep 8	Darwen	H	Lge	W 3-1	Jessop (2), Scroggins
Wed Sep 12	Prescot Cables	H	Lge	D 1-1	Des Steele
Sat Sep 15	Fleetwood	A	Lge	L 2-4	Wilson, Jessop
Sat Sep 22	Milnthorpe Corinthians	A	F.A. Cup 1st Qual. Rd	L 1-2	Jessop
Wed Sep 26	New Brighton	H	Lancs Comb Cup	L 2-4	Green, Steele
Sat Oct 6	Lancaster City	A	Lge	L 0-2	
	Attend: 1,007 - Gate: £59				
Sat Oct 13	Wigan Athletic	A	Lge	L 0-1	
	Attend: 4,109 - Gate: £240				
Sat Oct 20	Skelmersdale United	H	Lge	W 3-1	Warren, Disley, Jessop
	Gate: £78				
Sat Oct 27	Netherfield	A	Lge	L 0-2	
	Attend: 1,200 - Gate: £61				
Sat Nov 3	Accrington Stanley Res.	H	Lge	W 4-1	Disley, Warren, Worsley
Sat Nov 10	Nelson	A	Lge	L 0-4	
Sat Nov 17	Prescot Cables	A	Lge	W 1-0	Hart
Sat Nov 24	Bacup Borough	A	Lge	W 4-2	Wilkinson (2), Scroggins, Steele
Sat Dec 1	Lancaster City	H	Lge	W 6-1	Wilkinson (3), Hart (2), Disley
Sat Dec 15	South Liverpool	H	Lge	W 5-2	Scroggins, Hart (2), Green, Disley
Sat Dec 22	Chorley	A	Lge	L 0-1	
Tue Dec 25	Southport Reserves	A	Lge	D 0-0	
Sat Dec 29	Droylesden	H	Lge	W 7-0	Hart (3), Murphy (3), Wilkinson
Sat Jan 5	Ashton United	H	Lge	L 2-3	Wilkinson, Disley
Sat Jan 12	Darwen	A	Lge	W 3-1	Disley (2), Hart
Sat Jan 19	Wigan Athletic	A	Lancs Junior Cup	W 4-1	Hart (3), Steele
Sat Jan 26	Ashton United	A	Lge	L 1-4	Wilson
	Attend: 1,500 - Gate: £88				
Sat Feb 9	Marine	H	Lge	W 5-1	Hart (2), Disley (2), Green
Sat Feb 23	Leyland Motors	H	Lancs Junior Cup	L 0-2	
Sat Mar 2	Skelmersdale United	A	Lge	W 3-2	Hart (2), Steele
	Attend: 1,545 - Gate: £68				
Sat Mar 9	Netherfield	H	Lge	W 3-1	Scroggins, Disley, Hart
Sat Mar 16	Accrington Stanley Res.	A	Lge	L 1-4	Steele
Sat Mar 23	Nelson	H	Lge	W 3-0	Hart (3)
Sat Mar 30	New Brighton	A	Lge	D 2-2	Coupe, Green
Wed Apr 3	New Brighton	H	Lge	W 5-1	Disley (4), Green
Sat Apr 6	Bacup Borough	H	Lge	D 1-1	Steele
Mon Apr 8	Wigan Athletic	H	Lge	W 2-1	Wilkinson, Disley
Sat Apr 13	Fleetwood	H	Lge	D 0-0	
Fri Apr 19	Horwich RMI	H	Lge	W 3-0	Hart, Disley (2)
Sat Apr 20	Southport Reserves	H	Lge	W 6-1	Green, Hart (3), Steele (2)
Mon Apr 22	Horwich RMI	A	Lge	L 0-2	
Fri Apr 26	Marine	A	Lge	L 2-3	Disley, Wilkinson

1957/58 Season
Lancashire Combination (Division One)

Date	Opponent	H/A	Competition	Result	Scorers
Sat Aug 24	Darwen	H	Lge	W 3-0	Charlie Whiteside (3)
Mon Aug 26	South Liverpool	A	Lge	L 1-2	Whiteside
Sat Aug 31	Chorley	A	Lge	L 3-5	Hart, Whiteside (2)
	Attend: 1,919 - Gate: £99				
Mon Sep 2	South Liverpool	H	Lge	D 1-1	Steele
Thu Sep 5	Marine	H	Lpool Senior Non-lge Cup	W 3-2	Whiteside (2), Green
Sat Sep 7	New Brighton	H	Lge	D 1-1	Whiteside
Mon Sep 9	Marine	H	Lancs Comb Cup	W 4-1	Disley, Hart, Whiteside, Wilson
Sat Sep 14	Horwich RMI	H	Lge	L 1-2	Hart
Wed Sep 18	Horwich RMI	A	Lge	L 1-5	O.G.
Sat Sep 21	Fleetwood	H	F.A.Cup 1st Qual. Rd	W 4-3	Hart, Whiteside, Aspinall, Wilson
Sat Sep 28	Morecambe	H	Lge	L 0-1	
Sat Oct 5	Netherfield	A	F.A.Cup 2nd Qual. Rd	W 2-0	Steele (2)
Sat Oct 12	Southport Reserves.	H	Lge	W 2-1	Hart (2)
Sat Oct 19	Morecambe	A	F.A.Cup 3rd Qual. Rd	L 2-6	Wilson, Scroggins
Sat Oct 26	Rossendale United	H	Lge	W 7-3	Disley, Hart, Whiteside (4), Scroggins
Sat Nov 2	Bacup Borough	A	Lge	L 0-2	
Sat Nov 9	New Brighton	H	Lge	D 1-1	Hart
Sat Nov 16	Accrington Stanley Res.	A	Lge	D 2-2	Disley, Steele
Sat Nov 23	Lancaster City	H	Lge	L 1-3	Steele
Sat Nov 30	Ashton United	A	Lge	W 4-3	Steele (2), Wilson, Hart
Sat Dec 14	Prescot Cables	A	Lge	L 1-4	Steele
Sat Dec 21	Darwen	A	Lge	W 6-0	Disley, Hendry (3), Whiteside, Wilson
Wed Dec 25	Skelmersdale United	A	Lge	W 3-2	Wilson, Hendry, Scroggins
	Gate: £52				
Thu Dec 26	Skelmersdale United	H	Lge	W 6-2	Steele, Scroggins, O.G., Warren, Whiteside, Hendry
	Gate: £51				
Sat Dec 28	Chorley	H	Lge	D 2-2	Green, Hendry
	Gate: £63				
Wed Jan 1	Wigan Athletic	A	Lpool Senior Non-Lge Cup Semi-final	D 2-2	Whiteside, Wilson
	Attend: 1,248 - Gate: £88				
Sat Jan 4	Marine	A	Lge	L 1-2	Wilson
Sat Jan 18	Darwen	H	Lancs Junior Cup	W 2-1	Disley, Wilson
Sat Feb 1	Droylesden	H	Lge	L 1-2	Hendry
Sat Feb 8	Morecambe	A	Lge	L 0-5	
Sat Feb 15	Netherfield	H	Lge	L 0-1	
Sat Feb 22	Wigan Athletic	A	Lancs Junior Cup	D 0-0	
Sat Mar 1	Wigan Athletic	H	Lancs Junior Cup replay	W 3-2	Disley (2), Scroggins
Sat Mar 8	Rossendale United	A	Lge	D 1-1	Hart
Thu Mar 13	South Liverpool	A	Lancs Comb Cup	W 2-1	Hendry, Scroggins
Sat Mar 15	New Brighton	H	Lancs Junior Cup	W 1-0	Hart
Sat Mar 22	Netherfield	A	Lge	L 0-1	
Tue Mar 25	Ashton United	H	Lge	W 1-0	Wilson
Sat Mar 29	Accrington Stanley Res.	H	Lge	L 2-4	Disley, Woolley
Mon Mar 31	Wigan Athletic	H	L'pool Senior Non-Lge Cup replay	L 2-3	Jeff Aughton, Steele
Fri Apr 4	Fleetwood	A	Lge	W 2-1	Hart, Woolley
Sat Apr 5	Lancaster City	A	Lge	L 1-2	Hendry
Mon Apr 7	Fleetwood	H	Lge	W 4-2	Warren, Hart, Aspinall, Hendry
Thu Apr 10	Marine	H	Lge	W 8-0	Steele (2), Disley (4), Scroggins (2)
Sat Apr 12	Horwich	A	Lancs Junior Cup	L 0-1	
Mon Apr 14	Morecambe	H	Lancs Comb Cup	W 2-0	John Melling, O.G.
Tue Apr 15	Southport Reserves	A	Lge	D 0-0	
Thu Apr 17	Nelson	A	Lge	L 0-3	
Sat Apr 19	Wigan Athletic	A	Lge	W 2-1	Scroggins, Hart
Mon Apr 21	Droylesden	A	Lge	L 1-2	Scorer unknown
Wed Apr 23	Cromptons Recs	A	Lge	L 1-3	Brian Finnigan
Thu Apr 24	Nelson	H	Lge	L 1-2	Steele
Fri Apr 25	Fleetwood	A	Lancs Comb Cup Semi-final	W 2-1	Aughton (2)
Sat Apr 26	Prescot Cables	H	Lge	D 1-1	Aughton
Mon Apr 28	Cromptons Recs	H	Lge	W 2-0	Kenny Spencer, Steele
Tue Apr 29	Bacup Borough	H	Lge	L 1-2	Aughton
Thu May 1	Wigan Athletic	H	Lge	W 4-1	Steele (2), Spencer, Scroggins
Sat May 3	New Brighton	H	Lancs Comb Cup Final	L 0-2	

1957-58 Season. Back left to right: Charlie Jones (Manager), Charlie Whiteside, Brian Finnigan, Alan Buttons, Bobby Warren, Arthur Green, Percy Steele, Frank Richmond (Trainer). Front left to right: Tommy Scroggins, Joe Hart, Ronnie Wilson, John Disley, Unknown. Charlie Whiteside died in 1988, his career included one Football League appearance for Swindon Town. Percy Steele was only at Victoria Park for a short period. He had spent more than 10 years with Tranmere Rovers, making over 300 first team appearances.

LANCASHIRE COMBINATION - DIVISION TWO
1955-56 SEASON

	P	W	D	L	F	A	Pts
Skelmersdale United	34	21	9	4	110	54	51
Droylesden	34	23	4	7	110	71	50
Wigan Athletic Reserves	34	21	6	7	102	44	48
Burscough Reserves	**34**	**23**	**1**	**10**	**91**	**49**	**47**
Crompton's Recs	34	20	7	7	94	54	47
Lytham	34	19	7	8	81	44	45
Clitheroe	34	19	4	11	82	69	42
Lomax	34	15	2	17	81	91	32
Chorley Reserves	34	11	6	17	59	76	28
Earlestown	34	10	6	18	60	77	26
Leyland Motors	34	10	6	18	65	87	26
Prescot Cables Reserves	34	11	4	19	60	99	26
Nelson Reserves	34	11	4	19	72	102	26
Great Harwood	34	9	7	18	65	74	25
St. Annes	34	10	5	19	63	97	25
Rolls Royce	34	10	4	20	77	109	24
Padiham	34	9	5	20	63	101	23
Darwen Reserves	34	6	9	19	42	79	21

LANCASHIRE COMBINATION - DIVISION ONE
1956-57 SEASON

	P	W	D	L	F	A	Pts
Prescot Cables	38	26	5	7	123	52	57
New Brighton	38	25	4	9	94	50	54
Morecambe	38	20	7	11	81	53	47
Horwich RMI	38	22	3	13	93	70	47
Burscough	**38**	**19**	**7**	**12**	**86**	**58**	**45**
Accrington Stanley Res.	38	18	8	12	82	61	44
Ashton United	38	19	5	14	89	74	43
Chorley	38	15	8	15	74	74	38
Netherfield	38	15	8	15	73	73	38
Wigan Athletic	38	17	3	18	73	61	37
Lancaster City	38	14	8	16	71	91	36
Bacup Borough	38	12	11	15	80	88	35
Nelson	38	15	5	18	53	59	35
Skelmersdale United	38	14	6	18	67	82	34
South Liverpool	38	14	5	19	71	82	33
Fleetwood	38	13	7	18	56	70	33
Marine	38	12	8	18	62	84	32
Southport Reserves	38	12	7	19	62	88	31
Darwen	38	11	5	22	62	88	27
Droylesden	38	4	6	28	59	153	14

1958/59 Season
Lancashire Combination (Division One)

Date	Opponent	H/A	Competition	Result	Scorers
Sat Aug 23	Fleetwood	A	Lge	L 0-1	
Wed Aug 27	Prescot Cables	H	Lge	L 2-3	Ted Green, Tony Rimmer
Sat Aug 30	Clitheroe	H	Lge	W 3-1	O.G., Rimmer, Steele
Mon Sep 1	Prescot Cables	A	Lge	D 1-1	Green
Wed Sep 3	Wigan Athletic	A	Lpool Senior Non-lge Cup	L 1-3	Green
Sat Sep 6	Darwen	A	Lge	D 2-2	Green, Rimmer
Wed Sep 10	New Brighton	H	Lge	L 1-5	Rimmer
Sat Sep 13	Skelmersdale United	H	Lancs Comb Cup	L 1-3	Aughton
	Gate: £66				
Wed Sep 17	Darwen	H	Lge	L 1-2	Melling
Sat Sep 20	Netherfield	H	F.A.Cup 1st Qual. Rd	D 2-2	Green (2)
Mon Sep 22	Netherfield	A	F.A.Cup replay	L 1-2	Green
Wed Sep 24	Rossendale United	H	Lge	W 2-0	Rimmer, Aughton
Sat Sep 27	South Liverpool	H	Lge	W 4-2	Green (2), Spencer, Rimmer
Wed Oct 1	Lancaster City	A	Lge	D 1-1	Spencer
Sat Oct 4	Marine	H	Lge	W 3-2	Rimmer, O.G., Green
Sat Oct 11	Skelmersdale United	A	Lge	L 0-1	
	Attend: 1,458 - Gate: £78				
Sat Oct 18	Bacup Borough	H	Lge	W 3-1	Green, Steele, Porter
Sat Oct 25	Droylesden	A	Lge	L 1-2	Green
Sat Nov 1	Horwich RMI	H	Lge	D 1-1	Porter
Sat Nov 8	Wigan Athletic	A	Lge	D 1-1	Dennis Walmsley
Sat Nov 15	Nelson	H	Lge	L 1-2	Green
Sat Nov 22	Chorley	A	Lge	W 2-0	Green, Steele
Sat Nov 29	Oldham Athletic Reserves	H	Lge	W 2-1	Green, Hart
Sat Dec 6	Rossendale United	A	Lge	L 0-1	
Sat Dec 13	Lancaster City	H	Lge	L 0-2	
Sat Dec 20	Fleetwood	H	Lge	L 1-3	Green
Fri Dec 26	Southport Reserves	H	Lge	W 2-1	Green, Gerry Joyce
Sat Dec 27	Southport Reserves	A	Lge	W 3-2	Walmsley (2), Hart
Sat Jan 3	Clitheroe	A	Lge	L 1-2	Porter
Sat Jan 24	South Liverpool	H	Lancs Junior Cup	W 4-2	Green (3), Steele
Sat Jan 31	New Brighton	A	Lge	L 1-8	Hart
	Attend: 2,000				
Sat Feb 7	Ashton United	H	Lge	L 1-2	Green
Sat Feb 14	South Liverpool	A	Lge	D 1-1	Kenny
Sat Feb 21	Lytham	H	Lancs Junior Cup	D 1-1	Green
Sat Feb 28	Lytham	A	Lancs Junior Cup replay	L 1-4	Green
Sat Mar 7	Bacup Borough	A	Lge	D 2-2	Stan Polk, Rimmer
Sat Mar 14	Droylesden	H	Lge	W 2-1	Robinson, Hart
Sat Mar 21	Marine	A	Lge	D 1-1	Hart
Fri Mar 27	Netherfield	A	Lge	L 0-3	
Sat Mar 28	Wigan Athletic	H	Lge	W 1-0	Steele
Mon Mar 30	Netherfield	H	Lge	W 2-1	Steele, Robinson
Sat Apr 4	Nelson	A	Lge	L 0-1	
Sat Apr 11	Chorley	H	Lge	W 2-0	Rimmer, O.G.
Mon Apr 13	Morecambe	H	Lge	W 2-0	Hart, Rimmer
Wed Apr 15	Horwich RMI	A	Lge	L 1-2	Steele
Sat Apr 18	Oldham Athletic Reserves	A	Lge	L 1-2	Robinson
Mon Apr 20	Morecambe	A	Lge	L 0-3	
Sat Apr 25	Ashton United	A	Lge	W 3-0	Robinson (3)
Wed Apr 29	Skelmersdale United	H	Lge	D 2-2	Hart, Robinson

1958-59 Season. Back left to right: P.J.Geran (Manager), Walsh, Parry, Gerry Joyce, Harry Smelt, Brian Finnigan, Bobby Warren, Frank Richmond (Trainer).
Front left to right: Mooney, Des Steele, Ted Green, George Duncalf, Tony Rimmer.

1959-60 Season. Back left to right: Ray Prentice, Tony Greenwood, Albert Ashurst, Don Baker, Gerry Joyce, Arthur Rowley, Charlie Jones (Manager).
Front left to right: Frank Richmond (Trainer), Dennis Walmsley, Arthur Green, Des Steele, Joe Hart, H.Holt.

1959/60 Season
Lancashire Combination (Division One)

Date	Opponent	H/A	Competition	Result	Scorers
Sat Aug 22	Marine	H	Lge	W 4-0	Arthur Rowley (3), Walmsley
Mon Aug 24	Skelmersdale United Gate: £74	A	Lancs Comb Cup	D 1-1	H.Holt
Wed Aug 26	Earlestown	H	Lge	W 6-0	Hart (3), Rowley (3)
Sat Aug 29	Southport Reserves	A	Lge	W 3-2	O.G., Walmsley, Rowley
Wed Sep 2	Earlestown	A	Lge	W 7-1	Rowley (2), Hart (2), Joyce, Steele, O.G.
Sat Sep 5	Fleetwood	H	Lge	W 2-1	Rowley, Walmsley
Mon Sep 7	Skelmersdale United	H	Lancs Comb Cup replay	W 1-0	Rowley
Sat Sep 12	Darwen	A	Lge	D 2-2	Walmsley, Rowley
Mon Sep 14	Skelmersdale United	H	Lpool Senior Non-lge Cup	W 2-1	Rowley (2)
Wed Sep 16	Lytham	A	Lge	W 3-0	Rowley, Steele, O.G.
Sat Sep 19	Lancaster City	H	F.A.Cup 1st Qual. Rd	W 4-1	Walmsley (2), Rowley (2)
Sat Sep 26	Horwich RMI	A	Lge	L 1-3	Walmsley
Sat Oct 3	Netherfield	H	F.A.Cup 2nd Qual. Rd	W 4-1	Jimmy Jones (2), 'Snowie' Snelgrove, Rowley
Sat Oct 10	Ashton United	H	Lge	L 1-2	Jones
Sat Oct 17	Clitheroe	A	F.A.Cup 3rd Qual. Rd	W 2-1	Jones, Walmsley
Sat Oct 24	Wigan Athletic	H	Lge	D 1-1	Rowley
Sat Oct 31	Ellesmere Port Town Attend: 3,807	A	F.A.Cup 4th Qual. Rd	W 2-1	Hart, Walmsley
Sat Nov 7	Nelson	H	Lge	W 5-1	Steele (3), Walmsley, Hart
Sat Nov 14	Crewe Alexandra Attend: 4,200 - Gate: £412	H	F.A.Cup 1st Round	L 1-3	Jones
Sat Nov 21	Chorley Gate: £80	H	Lge	W 2-0	Rowley, Walmsley
Sat Nov 28	Netherfield	A	Lge	W 2-1	Hart, Steele
Sat Dec 5	Prescot Cables	H	Lge	D 2-2	Ray Prentice, Hart
Sat Dec 12	Lancaster City	A	Lge	L 1-2	Rowley
Sat Dec 19	Marine	A	Lge	L 2-4	Snelgrove, Hart
Sat Dec 26	New Brighton Gate: £60	H	Lge	L 1-3	Snelgrove
Mon Dec 28	New Brighton	A	Lpool Senior Non-lge Cup	L 1-3	Rowley
Sat Jan 2	Southport Reserves	H	Lge	W 7-3	Rowley (3), Snelgrove (2), Spencer, Steele
Sat Jan 9	Morecambe	A	Lge	L 1-3	Joyce
Sat Jan 16	Leyland Motors	A	Lancs Junior Cup 1st Rd	W 7-0	Rowley (3), Tony Greenwood (2), Steele (2)
Sat Jan 23	Darwen	H	Lge	D 1-1	Rowley
Sat Jan 30	Morecambe	H	Lge	W 2-1	Johnny Vincent, Rowley
Sat Feb 6	Lytham	A	Lge	L 1-6	Rowley
Sat Feb 13	Chorley	H	Lancs Junior Cup 2nd Rd	L 1-2	Rowley
Sat Feb 20	South Liverpool	A	Lge	D 3-3	Don Baker, Walmsley (2)
Sat Feb 27	Ashton United	A	Lge	W 3-0	O.G., Spencer, Joyce
Sat Mar 5	Oldham Athletic Reserves	H	Lge	D 1-1	Spencer
Sat Mar 12	Wigan Athletic	A	Lge	L 1-4	Steele
Sat Mar 26	Nelson	A	Lge	L 0-3	
Tue Mar 29	Rossendale United	A	Lge	L 1-4	Rowley
Sat Apr 2	Rossendale United	H	Lge	D 3-3	Spencer, Rowley (2)
Wed Apr 6	Fleetwood	A	Lge	L 0-3	
Mon Apr 11	Southport Reserves	A	Lancs Comb Cup Semi-final	L 1-4	Robinson
Wed Apr 13	Chorley	A	Lge	L 0-3	
Fri Apr 15	Skelmersdale United	A	Lge	L 1-2	Hart
Sat Apr 16	Netherfield	H	Lge	W 2-0	Rowley (2)
Mon Apr 18	Skelmersdale United	H	Lge	W 2-1	Spencer, Walmsley
Thu Apr 21	South Liverpool	H	Lge	W 5-0	Vincent (2), Rowley, Joyce, Dalton
Sat Apr 23	Prescot Cables	A	Lge	W 3-1	O.G., Vincent, Spencer
Tue Apr 26	New Brighton	A	Lge	L 0-2	
Thu Apr 28	Bacup Borough	A	Lge	D 2-2	Rowley, Baker
Sat Apr 30	Lancaster City	H	Lge	W 5-0	Gregson, Vincent (3), Rowley
Mon May 2	Bacup Borough	H	Lge	W 1-0	Rowley
Wed May 4	Oldham Athletic Reserves	A	Lge	W 1-0	O.G.
Fri May 6	Horwich RMI	H	Lge	W 3-2	Rowley, Spencer, Gregson

1960-61 Season. Back left to right: Pat Murphy (Manager), Gerry Joyce, Joe Hart, Farrell, Don Baker, Arthur Green, Tony Greenwood. Front left to right: Dennis Walmsley, Des Steele, Harry Lyon, McMictall, Martin.

1961-62 Season. Back left to right: Roberts, Gerry Joyce, Albert Ashurst, Tony Greenwood, Joe Hart, Wilf Charlton, Pat Murphy (Manager). Front left to right: Des Steele, Harry Lyon, Arthur Green, Arthur Rowley, Tony Rimmer. Wilf Charlton was a North Easterner, who came from the famous Milburn/Charlton family. After playing in the Football League for Southport and Tranmere Rovers, he spent a brief period at Burscough during the final stages of his playing career.

1960/61 Season
Lancashire Combination (Division One)

Date	Opponent	H/A	Comp	Result	Scorers
Sat Aug 20	Netherfield	H	Lge	L 1-3	McCallum
Thu Aug 25	Skelmersdale United	A	Lge	L 2-3	Steele, Martin
Sat Aug 27	Bacup Borough	A	Lge	D 0-0	
Mon Aug 29	South Liverpool	H	Lancs Comb Cup	D 1-1	Joyce
Wed Aug 31	Skelmersdale United	H	Lge	D 0-0	
Sat Sep 3	Oldham Athletic Reserves	H	Lge	W 1-0	Rowley
Tue Sep 6	South Liverpool	A	Lancs Comb Cup replay	D 3-3	Barry Brookfield (3)
Thu Sep 8	Nelson	A	Lge	L 0-5	
Sat Sep 10	Milnthorpe Corinthians	H	F.A.Cup 1st Qual. Rd	W 2-1	Walmsley, Brookfield
Mon Sep 12	South Liverpool	A	Lpool Senior Non-lge Cup	L 0-2	
Thu Sep 15	South Liverpool	A	Lancs Comb Cup 2nd replay	L 3-5	Walmsley, Joyce, O.G.
Sat Sep 17	Rossendale United	H	Lge	L 2-4	Martin, Harry Lyon
Mon Sep 19	Oldham Athletic Reserves	A	Lge	W 4-0	Murphy, Lyon, Rowley, Steele
Sat Sep 24	Morecambe	A	F.A.Cup 2nd Qual. Rd	D 2-2	Lyon (2)
	Gate: £128				
Wed Sep 28	Morecambe	H	F.A.Cup replay	L 1-2	Steele
Sat Oct 1	Chorley	H	Lge	W 3-0	Joyce, Spencer, Lyon
Sat Oct 8	Lancaster City	H	Lge	W 2-0	Lyon (2)
Sat Oct 15	Ashton United	A	Lge	W 1-0	Lyon
Sat Oct 22	Marine	A	Lge	D 1-1	Rowley
Sat Oct 29	Prescot Cables	A	Lge	L 0-2	
Sat Nov 5	Darwen	H	Lge	W 2-1	Lyon (2)
Sat Nov 12	Lytham	A	Lge	W 2-1	Greenwood (2)
Sat Nov 19	Fleetwood	H	Lge	W 4-2	Lyon (2), Walmsley (2)
Sat Dec 3	Marine	H	Lge	W 2-1	Lyon, Rowley
Sat Dec 10	Horwich RMI	A	Lge	L 0-2	
Sat Dec 24	Droylesden	H	Lge	W 1-0	Rowley
Sat Dec 31	Bacup Borough	H	Lge	W 4-0	Lyon, Walmsley (3)
Sat Jan 7	Morecambe	H	Lge	W 2-1	Lyon, Martin
Sat Jan 21	Marine	A	Lancs Junior Cup	D 0-0	
Sat Jan 28	Marine	H	Lancs Junior Cup replay	L 0-1	
Sat Feb 4	Rossendale United	A	Lge	D 3-3	Lyon (2), Walmsley
Sat Feb 11	Darwen	H	Lge	W 5-0	Lyon (3), Steele, Walmsley
Sat Feb 18	Chorley	A	Lge	D 0-0	
	Attend: 1,611 - Gate: £87				
Sat Feb 25	Lancaster City	A	Lge	L 1-2	Greenwood
Sat Mar 4	Ashton United	H	Lge	W 4-0	Steele, Lyon, O.G., Walmsley
Sat Mar 11	Clitheroe	A	Lge	W 1-0	O.G.
Sat Mar 18	Prescot Cables	H	Lge	D 1-1	Green
Mon Mar 27	Morecambe	A	Lge	W 3-2	Lyon (2), Walmsley
Fri Mar 31	Earlestown	H	Lge	W 2-1	Steele (2)
Sat Apr 1	Lytham	H	Lge	W 1-0	Martin
Mon Apr 3	Earlestown	A	Lge	D 1-1	Lyon
Wed Apr 5	Wigan Athletic	A	Lge	W 2-0	Lyon (2)
	Attend: 1,078				
Sat Apr 8	Fleetwood	A	Lge	L 3-5	Lyon, Steele, Roberts
Tue Apr 11	New Brighton	A	Lge	W 2-0	Lyon, Walmsley
Thu Apr 13	Droylesden	A	Lge	W 2-1	Lyon, Keith Reeder
Sat Apr 15	Clitheroe	H	Lge	W 2-0	Lyon, Roberts
Thu Apr 20	Netherfield	A	Lge	W 3-2	Lyon (2), Walmsley
Mon Apr 24	New Brighton	H	Lge	D 2-2	Lyon, Greenwood
Thu Apr 27	Wigan Athletic	H	Lge	W 2-1	Melling, Walmsley
Sat Apr 29	Horwich RMI	H	Lge	W 1-0	Steele
Wed May 3	Nelson	H	Lge	L 1-2	Roberts

LANCASHIRE COMBINATION - DIVISION ONE
1957-58 SEASON

	P	W	D	L	F	A	Pts
Horwich RMI	42	28	7	7	109	47	63
Prescot Cables	42	26	9	7	117	49	61
Wigan Athletic	42	22	10	10	95	60	54
New Brighton	42	23	8	11	85	61	54
Accrington Stanley Res.	42	23	6	13	92	71	52
Netherfield	42	20	9	13	85	68	49
Rossendale United	42	19	10	13	104	88	48
Morecambe	42	18	12	12	66	50	48
Chorley	42	20	7	15	123	85	47
Marine	42	18	7	17	74	103	43
Nelson	42	18	6	18	65	71	42
Ashton United	42	17	5	20	96	108	39
Southport Reserves	42	16	5	21	69	102	37
Burscough	42	14	8	20	80	79	36
South Liverpool	42	15	6	21	94	102	36
Skelmersdale United	42	15	6	21	77	92	36
Lancaster City	42	14	7	21	74	93	35
Darwen	42	14	6	22	71	104	34
Droylesden	42	13	7	22	75	99	33
Fleetwood	42	11	10	21	57	82	32
Bacup Borough	42	12	8	22	88	115	32
Crompton's Recs	42	5	6	31	51	118	16

LANCASHIRE COMBINATION - DIVISION ONE
1959-60 SEASON

	P	W	D	L	F	A	Pts
Chorley	42	31	5	6	133	48	67
Wigan Athletic	42	27	6	9	101	51	60
New Brighton	42	28	4	10	103	54	60
Morecambe	42	28	2	12	103	54	58
Rossendale United	42	21	7	14	115	95	49
Burscough	42	20	8	14	94	73	48
Nelson	42	22	4	16	78	68	48
Netherfield	42	20	7	15	88	70	47
Marine	42	19	6	17	92	98	44
Horwich RMI	42	17	8	17	82	76	42
Prescot Cables	42	16	9	17	74	68	41
Oldham Athletic Res.	42	16	7	19	64	66	39
Ashton United	42	13	12	17	61	86	38
Fleetwood	42	16	5	21	63	71	37
Bacup Borough	42	11	12	19	71	99	34
Lancaster City	42	12	9	21	73	107	33
Earlestown	42	13	7	22	79	113	33
Lytham	42	10	12	20	60	88	32
Skelmersdale United	42	13	6	23	60	96	32
Darwen	42	10	11	21	57	86	31
Southport Reserves	42	9	10	23	57	91	28
South Liverpool	42	7	9	26	54	102	23

LANCASHIRE COMBINATION - DIVISION ONE
1958-59 SEASON

	P	W	D	L	F	A	Pts
New Brighton	42	29	6	7	127	53	64
Prescot Cables	42	27	6	9	111	57	60
Horwich RMI	42	25	9	8	95	57	59
Skelmersdale United	42	22	10	10	107	69	54
Morecambe	42	22	9	11	77	44	53
Chorley	42	22	7	13	109	82	51
Netherfield	42	22	5	15	91	73	49
Bacup Borough	42	19	10	13	104	88	48
Nelson	42	19	9	14	82	74	47
Fleetwood	42	20	4	18	72	87	44
Marine	42	16	8	18	80	97	40
Burscough	42	15	9	18	60	69	39
South Liverpool	42	16	6	20	81	94	38
Darwen	42	16	6	20	75	93	38
Lancaster City	42	13	12	17	69	95	38
Rossendale United	42	16	5	21	88	89	37
Oldham Athletic Res.	42	13	8	21	80	96	34
Wigan Athletic	42	12	7	23	60	84	31
Ashton United	42	12	6	24	69	103	30
Southport Reserves	42	10	8	24	70	104	28
Clitheroe	42	11	3	28	71	105	25
Droylesden	42	6	5	31	43	106	17

LANCASHIRE COMBINATION - DIVISION ONE
1960-61 SEASON

	P	W	D	L	F	A	Pts.
Chorley	42	31	7	4	125	33	69
Nelson	42	29	7	6	106	47	65
Wigan Athletic	42	25	8	9	108	56	58
Burscough	42	25	8	9	76	49	58
Netherfield	42	24	8	10	123	71	56
Morecambe	42	23	5	14	96	76	51
Lancaster City	42	17	14	11	75	53	48
Prescot Cables	42	20	7	15	70	78	47
New Brighton	42	20	6	16	80	65	46
Marine	42	17	10	15	79	75	44
Clitheroe	42	17	7	18	84	88	41
Ashton United	42	18	5	19	78	88	41
Horwich R.M.I.	42	14	7	21	75	94	35
Lytham St. Annes	42	13	8	21	69	85	34
Skelmersdale United	42	12	9	21	71	85	33
Rossendale United	42	13	7	22	92	139	33
Oldham Athletic Reserves	42	13	6	23	71	84	32
Earlestown	42	12	8	22	74	103	32
Bacup Borough	42	11	9	22	76	96	31
Fleetwood	42	12	5	25	82	110	29
Droylesden	42	10	5	27	73	132	25
Darwen	42	7	2	33	45	121	16

1961/62 Season
Lancashire Combination (Division One)

Date	Opponent	H/A	Competition	Result	Scorers
Sat Aug 19	Darwen	H	Lge	W 6-1	Tony Rimmer (2), Roberts, Lyon (2), Rowley
Tue Aug 22	Oldham Athletic Reserves	A	Lge	L 0-2	
Sat Aug 26	Skelmersdale United	A	Lge	W 5-2	Lyon (4), Roberts
Mon Aug 28	Oldham Athletic Reserves	H	Lge	W 6-0	Rowley (2), Hart, Lyon (2), Rimmer
Sat Sep 2	Hyde United	A	Inter-league Cup 1st Rd.	L 0-1	
	Gate: £105				
Mon Sep 4	New Brighton	H	Lge	W 2-1	Lyon (2)
	Gate: £34				
Sat Sep 9	Lancaster City	H	F.A.Cup 1st Qual. Rd	W 2-0	Lyon, Steele
Wed Sep 13	New Brighton	A	Lge	D 1-1	Rowley
Sat Sep 16	Morecambe	A	Lge	L 1-3	Lyon
Mon Sep 18	St. Helens Town	H	Lpool Senior Non-lge Cup	W 3-1	Lyon, Roberts, O.G.
Sat Sep 23	Fleetwood	A	F.A.Cup 2nd Qual. Rd	D 1-1	Lyon
	Attend: 992 - Gate: £62				
Wed Sep 27	Fleetwood	H	F.A.Cup replay	W 5-2	Reeder, Steele, Green (2), Lyon
	Gate: £55				
Sat Sep 30	Netherfield	A	Lge	W 4-1	Rowley (2), Steele, Lyon
Sat Oct 7	Morecambe	H	F.A.Cup 3rd Qual. Rd	L 1-8	Rowley
	Gate: £121				
Sat Oct 14	Leyland Motors	A	Lge	W 3-2	Lyon (2), Wilf Charlton
Sat Oct 21	Padiham	H	Lge	D 2-2	Lyon (2)
Sat Oct 28	Prescot Cables	A	Lge	D 2-2	Lyon, Steele
Sat Nov 4	Bacup Borough	H	Lge	W 3-1	Lyon (3)
Sat Nov 11	Marine	A	Lge	W 4-1	Lyon (2), Lydon (2)
Sat Nov 18	Earlestown	H	Lge	W 3-0	Lyon, Rowley, Walmsley
Sat Nov 25	Lancaster City	A	Lge	L 2-5	Lyon, Lydon
Sat Dec 2	Horwich RMI	H	Lge	W 3-2	Steele, Walmsley, Rowley
Sat Dec 9	Rossendale United	H	Lge	W 5-3	Lyon (2), Walmsley, Greenwood, Steele
Sat Dec 16	Darwen	A	Lge	D 2-2	Steele, Rowley
Sat Dec 23	Skelmersdale United	H	Lge	W 4-0	Rowley, Lyon (2), Walmsley
Tue Dec 26	Southport Reserves	A	Lge	W 3-1	Lyon (2), Rowley
Sat Dec 30	Southport Reserves	H	Lge	D 4-4	Walmsley, O.G., Lyon, Steele
Mon Jan 1	Chorley	A	Lge	L 1-2	Rowley
Sat Jan 6	Fleetwood	H	Lge	D 0-0	
Sat Jan 13	Chorley	H	Lge	W 4-1	Walmsley, Lyon, Spencer, Rowley
	Gate: £30				
Sat Jan 20	Netherfield	A	Lancs Junior Cup 1st Rd	L 1-4	Lydon
Sat Feb 3	Morecambe	H	Lge	W 3-1	Walmsley, Lyon (2)
Sat Feb 17	Netherfield	H	Lge	W 3-1	Lyon (2), Rowley
Sat Feb 24	Nelson	A	Lge	D 2-2	Rowley, Bill Norcross
Sat Mar 3	Leyland Motors	H	Lge	W 3-1	Walmsley, Lyon (2)
Sat Mar 10	Padiham	A	Lge	L 2-3	Lyon (2)
Sat Mar 17	Prescot Cables	H	Lge	W 2-1	Lyon, Rowley
Sat Mar 24	Bacup Borough	A	Lge	W 5-1	Lyon (2), Steele, Roberts, Walmsley
Wed Mar 28	Clitheroe	A	Lge	L 2-3	Lyon, Steele
Sat Mar 31	Marine	H	Lge	D 1-1	Walmsley
Sat Apr 7	Earlestown	A	Lge	W 3-2	Steele, Spencer, Lyon
Mon Apr 9	Clitheroe	H	Lge	W 3-1	Lyon (2), Roberts
Thu Apr 12	Wigan Athletic	H	L'pool Senior Non-lge Cup Semi-final	L 0-4	
	Gate: £65				
Sat Apr 14	Lancaster City	H	Lge	W 5-2	Walmsley, Steele (2), Rowley, Lyon
Tue Apr 17	Fleetwood	A	Lge	W 3-2	Lyon (2), Steele
Fri Apr 20	Lytham	A	Lge	W 2-1	Walmsley, Steele
Sat Apr 21	Horwich RMI	A	Lge	L 1-3	Walmsley
Mon Apr 23	Lytham	H	Lge	W 6-1	Rowley (2), Walmsley (3), Roberts
Sat Apr 28	Rossendale United	A	Lge	L 1-3	Steele
Thu May 3	Nelson	H	Lge	W 5-0	Lyon (2), Rowley, Greenwood, Albert Ashurst

1962/63 Season
Lancashire Combination (Division One)

Date	Opponent	H/A	Competition	Result	Scorers
Sat Aug 18	Skelmersdale United	A	Lge	L 0-1	
Mon Aug 20	South Liverpool	A	Lge	L 2-6	Rowley, Walker
Sat Aug 25	Marine	H	Lge	L 1-4	Colin Vizard
Mon Aug 27	South Liverpool	H	Lge	W 2-0	Rowley, Joyce
Thu Aug 30	Marine	H	Lpool Senior Non-lge Cup	W 3-2	Rowley (2), Vizard
Sat Sep 1	Congleton Town	H	Inter-league Cup	D 2-2	O.G., Tinker
Tue Sep 4	New Brighton	A	Lge	L 0-3	
Thu Sep 6	Congleton Town	A	Inter-league Cup	W 1-0	Greenwood
Sat Sep 8	Fleetwood	H	F.A.Cup 1st Qual. Rd	L 1-4	Joe Porter
Mon Sep 10	Fleetwood	H	Lge	L 0-1	
Sat Sep 15	Lytham St.Annes	A	Lge	L 0-3	
Mon Sep 17	Stafford Rangers	H	Inter-league Cup 2nd Rd	L 3-7	Parkinson, Greenwood, Walmsley
Sat Sep 22	Darwen	H	Lge	W 2-0	Vizard (2)
Tue Sep 25	Fleetwood	A	Lge	L 1-3	Rich
Sat Sep 29	Earlestown	A	Lge	W 3-1	Vizard, Steele (2)
Sat Oct 13	Liverpool 'A'	H	Liverpool Challenge Cup	L 4-5	Walmsley, Vizard, Rowley (2)
Sat Oct 20	Leyland Motors	A	Lge	W 4-3	Walmsley (3), Joyce
Sat Oct 27	Nelson	H	Lge	D 3-3	Rowley, Walmsley, O.G.
Sat Nov 3	Chorley	A	Lge	L 2-6	Roy Rees, Walmsley
Sat Nov 10	Rossendale United	H	Lge	D 3-3	Underwood, Rowley (2)
Sat Nov 17	Horwich RMI	A	Lge	L 0-4	
Sat Nov 24	Bacup Borough	H	Lge	L 3-4	Walmsley, Rowley (2)
Sat Dec 1	Prescot Cables	A	Lge	L 1-2	Tinker
Sat Dec 8	Morecambe	H	Lge	L 0-3	
Sat Dec 15	Skelmersdale United	H	Lge	W 1-0	Tinker
Sat Dec 22	Marine	A	Lge	W 1-0	Walmsley
Wed Dec 26	Southport Reserves	A	Lge	D 2-2	Walmsley (2)
Sat Jan 19	Chorley	A	Lancs Junior Cup 1st Rd	L 1-5	Hart
Sat Mar 2	Ashton United	A	Lge	L 1-3	Porter
Sat Mar 9	Leyland Motors	H	Lge	W 1-0	Martin
Sat Mar 16	Morecambe	A	Lge	L 0-2	
Sat Mar 23	Chorley	H	Lge	L 0-2	
Mon Mar 25	Nelson	A	Lge	L 1-3	Albert Finley
Thu Mar 28	Horwich RMI	H	Lge	W 1-0	Finley
Sat Mar 30	Rossendale United	A	Lge	W 5-2	Steele, Lou Rigby (3), Martin
Mon Apr 1	Southport Reserves	H	Lge	L 2-3	Rigby (2)
Thu Apr 4	South Liverpool	A	Lpool Senior Non-lge Cup Semi-final	D 1-1	Diggle
Mon Apr 8	Ashton United	H	Lge	D 2-2	Diggle, Walmsley
Wed Apr 10	South Liverpool	H	Lpool Senior Non-lge Cup Semi-final replay	D 2-2	Greenwood, Rigby
Fri Apr 12	Lancaster City	A	Lge	L 1-2	Scorer unknown
Sat Apr 13	Bacup Borough	A	Lge	L 0-3	
Mon Apr 15	Lancaster City	H	Lge	L 1-2	Walmsley
Thu Apr 18	Netherfield	A	Lge	L 0-8	
Sat Apr 20	Prescot Cables	H	Lge	W 3-2	Diggle, Rigby (2)
Mon Apr 22	Clitheroe	H	Lge	L 1-2	Finley
Thu Apr 25	Lytham St Annes	H	Lge	W 5-1	Finley (3), Rigby, Jackson
Mon Apr 29	New Brighton	H	Lge	W 2-0	Finley (2)
Sat May 4	Darwen	A	Lge	W 1-0	Jackson
Mon May 6	Netherfield	H	Lge	D 1-1	Rigby
Wed May 8	Earlestown	H	Lge	W 6-2	Diggle, Finley (2), Spencer, Rigby
Sat May 11	Clitheroe	A	Lge	W 4-1	Rigby, Finley (2), Spencer
Thu May 16	South Liverpool	H	Lpool Senior Non-lge Cup Semi-final 2nd replay	L 2-3	Finley, Diggle

1962-63 Season. Back left to right: Joe Hart, Bob Jones, Gerry Joyce, Linaker, Woods, Tony Greenwood. Front left to right: Roberts, Des Sreele, Arthur Rowley, Walker, Colin Vizard.

1963-64 Season. Back left to right: Roy Rees, John Melling, Les Dumbell, Gerry Joyce, Bob Jones, Barry Todd. Front left to right: Cec Eyres, Dennis Walmsley, Bill Norcross, Kenny Spencer, Des Steele.

1963/64 Season
Lancashire Combination (Division One)

Sat Aug 24	Barrow Reserves	H	Lge	L 2-3	George Glover (2)
Mon Aug 26	Prescot Cables	A	Lge	W 3-0	Glover, Finley (2)
Sat Aug 31	Skelmersdale United	H	Lancs Comb Cup	D 1-1	Glover
Mon Sep 2	Skelmersdale United	H	Lge	W 5-1	Finley (3), Glover, Murphy
Sat Sep 7	Horwich RMI	A	F.A.Cup 1st Qual. Rd	W 3-0	Glover, Bob Jones, Finley
Wed Sep 11	Marine	A	Lge	L 2-3	Finley, Steele
Sat Sep 14	Horwich RMI	H	Lge	L 0-3	
Mon Sep 16	Wigan Athletic	A	L'pool Senior Non-lge Cup	L 1-2	Cec Eyres
Tue Sep 17	Skelmersdale United	A	Lancs Comb Cup replay	L 1-3	T.Spencer
Sat Sep 21	Netherfield	A	F.A.Cup 2nd Qual. Rd	L 0-2	
Mon Sep 23	New Brighton	H	Lge	D 2-2	Barry Todd, Wallace
Sat Sep 28	Nelson	H	Lge	L 1-2	Rees
Sat Oct 5	Leyland Motors	A	Lge	L 0-2	
Sat Oct 12	South Liverpool	A	Lge	W 2-1	Steele, Norcross
Sat Oct 19	Clitheroe	H	Lge	L 2-4	Spencer, Wallace
Sat Oct 26	Fleetwood	A	Lge	W 2-1	Norcross, Walmsley
Sat Nov 2	Chorley	H	Lge	L 1-2	Rees
Sat Nov 9	Southport Reserves	A	Lge	D 1-1	Steele
Sat Nov 16	Droylesden	H	Lge	D 1-1	Eyres
Sat Nov 23	Cromptons Recs	A	Lge	L 2-3	Eyres, Norcross
Sat Nov 30	Morecambe	H	Lge	D 2-2	Rees, Norcross
Sat Dec 14	Barrow Reserves	A	Lge	W 4-1	Rees (3), Norcross
Sat Dec 21	Prescot Cables	H	Lge	D 3-3	Farrell, Rees, Norcross
Thu Dec 26	Bacup Borough	H	Lge	W 3-1	Spencer, Norcross, Todd
Sat Dec 28	Bacup Borough	A	Lge	L 1-3	Louis Bimpson
Wed Jan 1	Marine	H	Lge	W 3-1	Norcross, Rees, Bimpson
Sat Jan 4	Lancaster City	H	Lge	W 2-1	Rees, Norcross
Sat Jan 11	Skelmersdale United	A	Lge	D 2-2	Spencer, Norcross
Sat Jan 18	Skelmersdale United	A	Lancs Junior Cup	W 2-0	Rees, Bimpson
Sat Feb 1	Rossendale United	H	Lge	W 4-1	Rees, Spencer, Norcross, Canavan
Sat Feb 8	Great Harwood	A	Lancs Junior Cup	D 3-3	Bimpson, Rees (2)
Sat Feb 15	Great Harwood	H	Lancs Junior Cup replay	L 0-2	
Tue Feb 18	Chorley	A	Lge	L 0-4	
Sat Feb 22	South Liverpool	H	Lge	D 2-2	Norcross (2)
Sat Feb 29	Clitheroe	A	Lge	L 1-2	Murphy
Sat Mar 7	Fleetwood	H	Lge	W 5-0	Rich, Rees (2), Eyres (2)
Thu Mar 19	Netherfield	A	Lge	L 0-2	
Sat Mar 21	Southport Reserves	H	Lge	L 1-2	Norcross
Fri Mar 27	Ashton United	A	Lge	D 1-1	Norcross
Sat Mar 28	Droylesden	A	Lge	L 0-1	
Mon Mar 30	Ashton United	H	Lge	W 6-1	Walmsley (3), Canavan (2), Murphy
Sat Apr 4	Cromptons Recs	H	Lge	D 2-2	Bimpson, Norcross
Wed Apr 8	Lancaster City	A	Lge	L 0-2	
Sat Apr 11	Morecambe	A	Lge	L 0-4	
Tue Apr 14	Rossendale United	A	Lge	D 2-2	Bimpson, Murphy
Sat Apr 18	Netherfield	H	Lge	L 4-5	Rich, Murphy (2), Bimpson
Mon Apr 20	Horwich RMI	A	Lge	L 2-3	Walmsley (2)
Wed Apr 22	Leyland Motors	H	Lge	D 2-2	Murphy (2)
Sat Apr 25	New Brighton	A	Lge	L 0-2	
Tue Apr 28	Nelson	A	Lge	L 2-3	Norcross, Walmsley

1964/65 Season
Lancashire Combination (Division One)

Date	Opponent	H/A	Competition	Result	Scorers
Sat Aug 22	Clitheroe	A	Lge	D 1-1	Murphy
Thu Aug 27	Skelmersdale United	A	Lancs Comb Cup	L 2-3	O.G., Foster
Sat Aug 29	Chorley	H	Lge	L 1-2	Walmsley
Wed Sep 2	Lancaster City	A	Lge	L 1-2	Scorer unknown
Sat Sep 5	Lancaster City	A	F.A.Cup 1st Qual. Rd	D 1-1	Norcross
Mon Sep 7	Lancaster City	H	Lge	L 1-2	Jimmy Hammell
Wed Sep 9	Lancaster City	H	F.A.Cup replay	L 1-2	Hammell
Sat Sep 12	Fleetwood	H	Lge	L 0-2	
Tue Sep 15	Great Harwood	A	Lge	L 0-3	
Thu Sep 17	Marine	H	L'pool Senior Non-lge Cup	W 2-1	Norcross (2)
Sat Sep 19	Prescot Town	A	Lge	W 6-1	Brian Murphy (4), Hughes, Hammell
Tue Sep 22	Morecambe	A	Lge	L 1-4	O.G.
Sat Sep 26	New Brighton	H	Lge	L 0-2	
Sat Oct 3	Horwich RMI	A	Lge	L 1-4	Hammell
Sat Oct 10	Prescot Town	H	Lge	W 5-0	Murphy (2), Wolfe (2), Rees
Sat Oct 17	Barrow Reserves	A	Lge	L 1-4	Rees
Sat Oct 24	Nelson	H	Lge	L 1-3	Greenwood
Sat Oct 31	Rossendale United	A	Lge	L 1-4	Hammell
Sat Nov 7	Leyland Motors	H	Lge	D 2-2	Rees, Sharples
Sat Nov 14	Bacup Borough	A	Lge	W 3-0	Hammell (2), Walmsley
Sat Nov 21	Netherfield	H	Lge	L 1-2	Walmsley
Sat Nov 28	Droylesden	A	Lge	L 0-2	
Sat Dec 5	Skelmersdale United *Attend: 250*	H	Lge	W 3-2	Walmsley (2), Greenwood
Sat Dec 12	Clitheroe	H	Lge	L 1-2	Rees
Sat Dec 19	Chorley	A	Lge	L 0-2	
Sat Dec 26	Southport Reserves	A	Lge	W 3-2	Clarke, Hammell, Lol Lister
Sat Jan 2	Great Harwood	H	Lge	W 6-0	Hammell (2), Walmsley (2), Hughes, Greenwood
Sat Jan 9	Marine	H	Lge	W 2-1	Walmsley, Hammell
Sat Jan 16	Blackpool Mechanics.	H	Lancs Junior Cup 1st Rd	W 6-0	Greenwood (2), Lister (2), Hammell, Hughes
Sat Jan 23	South Liverpool	H	Lge	L 1-2	Clarke
Sat Feb 6	Ashton United	A	Lancs Junior Cup 2nd Rd	L 5-7	Hammell (2), Hughes (2), Todd
Tue Feb 16	South Liverpool	A	Lge	L 1-3	Todd
Tue Feb 23	New Brighton	A	Lge	L 1-2	Smith
Sat Feb 27	Barrow Reserves	H	Lge	L 0-2	
Sat Mar 6	Nelson	A	Lge	D 2-2	Hughes (2)
Sat Mar 13	Rossendale United	H	Lge	L 0-2	
Sat Mar 20	Leyland Motors	A	Lge	L 3-4	Hughes (2), O.G.
Wed Mar 24	Wigan Athletic	A	L'pool Senior Non-lge Cup	L 1-2	Hammell
Sat Mar 27	Bacup Borough	H	Lge	L 1-4	Walmsley
Mon Mar 29	Horwich RMI	H	Lge	L 0-3	
Mon Apr 5	Netherfield	A	Lge	L 3-6	McGowan (2), Johnson
Sat Apr 10	Droylesden	H	Lge	W 1-0	Lister
Fri Apr 16	Accrington Stanley Res.	A	Lge	L 1-2	O.G.
Sat Apr 17	Skelmersdale United	A	Lge	L 0-2	
Mon Apr 19	Accrington Stanley Res.	H	Lge	W 5-1	Lister (3), Hammell, Tommy Forbes
Thu Apr 22	Southport Reserves	H	Lge	W 2-1	Johnson, Forbes
Sat Apr 24	Morecambe	H	Lge	W 2-1	O.G., Greenwood
Mon Apr 26	Marine	A	Lge	L 2-3	Johnson, McGowan
Tue Apr 29	Fleetwood	A	Lge	L 1-2	Hammell

1965-66 Season. Back left to right: Tommy Forbes, Graham Walton, Dave Parker, Barry Todd, Bob Jones, John Melling. Front left to right: Kenny Hodge, Jimmy Hammell, Dennis Walmsley, Tony Greenwood, Kenny Worden. This was Tony Greenwood's final season after 10 years service with Burscough.

LANCASHIRE COMBINATION - DIVISION ONE
1961-62 SEASON

	P	W	D	L	F	A	Pts
Morecambe	42	32	6	4	143	51	70
Netherfield	42	27	10	5	143	67	64
Horwich RMI	42	26	9	7	110	48	61
Burscough	**42**	**26**	**8**	**8**	**122**	**68**	**60**
Chorley	42	24	9	9	107	71	57
Rossendale United	42	22	6	14	114	89	50
Oldham Athletic Reserves	42	21	8	13	89	71	50
New Brighton	42	23	3	16	105	57	49
Lancaster City	42	18	12	12	75	65	48
Southport Reserves	42	18	9	15	102	77	45
Nelson	42	20	5	17	86	71	45
Clitheroe	42	18	9	15	85	83	45
Earlestown	42	17	6	19	89	102	40
Marine	42	15	7	20	94	99	37
Prescot Cables	42	14	9	19	66	83	37
Fleetwood	42	11	11	20	84	89	33
Skelmersdale United	42	12	7	23	62	103	31
Lytham St. Annes	42	9	7	26	67	127	25
Darwen	42	8	9	25	56	119	25
Leyland Motors	42	6	8	28	67	126	20
Bacup Borough	42	6	4	32	52	149	16
Padiham	42	4	8	30	51	154	16

LANCASHIRE COMBINATION - DIVISION ONE
1962-63 SEASON

	P	W	D	L	F	A	Pts
Morecambe	42	31	6	5	153	40	68
Chorley	42	31	6	5	137	59	68
Ashton United	42	25	8	9	101	57	58
Horwich RMI	42	25	5	12	107	59	55
Netherfield	42	23	7	12	125	69	53
Lancaster City	42	23	6	13	96	61	52
Marine	42	22	6	14	92	73	50
Nelson	42	22	4	16	95	81	48
Fleetwood	42	23	1	18	97	71	47
South Liverpool	42	20	3	19	76	65	43
New Brighton	42	18	5	19	83	76	41
Southport Reserves	42	17	7	18	80	76	41
Clitheroe	42	17	6	19	80	81	40
Rossendale United	42	17	6	19	103	138	40
Skelmersdale United	42	15	5	22	73	90	35
Burscough	**42**	**15**	**5**	**22**	**68**	**93**	**35**
Bacup Borough	42	14	6	22	81	110	34
Earlestown	42	14	3	25	88	132	31
Prescot Cables	42	13	5	24	71	108	31
Leyland Motors	42	9	7	26	54	106	25
Darwen	42	5	6	31	41	117	16
Lytham	42	5	3	34	34	173	13

1965/66 Season
Lancashire Combination (Division One)

Date	Opponent	H/A	Competition	Result	Scorers
Sat Aug 21	Great Harwood	H	Lge	W 3-2	Hammell, Lister, Brown
Mon Aug 23	St. Helens Town	H	Lancs Comb Cup	L 1-2	Lister
Sat Aug 28	Fleetwood	A	Lge	L 0-1	
Mon Aug 30	Chorley	H	Lge	L 1-6	Brown
Sat Sep 4	Horwich RMI	A	F.A.Cup 1st Qual. Rd	L 1-2	Arnold
Tue Sep 7	Chorley	A	Lge	L 1-2	Walmsley
Sat Sep 11	Guinness Exports	A	Lge	L 3-4	Kenny Hodge, Arnold, Brown
Tue Sep 14	Skelmersdale United	A	Lpool Senior Non-lge Cup	W 4-1	Hodge (2), Kenny Worden, Greenwood
Mon Sep 20	Clitheroe	H	Lge	W 4-1	Jones, Greenwood (2), Forbes
Sat Sep 25	Skelmersdale United	A	Lge	L 1-3	Forbes
Sat Oct 2	Netherfield	A	Lge	L 1-3	Worden
Sat Oct 9	Horwich RMI	H	Lge	L 0-5	
Sat Oct 16	Bacup Borough	A	Lge	L 1-2	Greenwood
Sat Oct 23	Nelson	H	Lge	L 0-1	
Sat Oct 30	Leyland Motors	A	Lge	D 3-3	Micky Worswick, Hodge, Walmsley
Sat Nov 6	Rossendale United	H	Lge	W 3-0	Forbes, Hammell, Worden
Sat Nov 13	Droylesden	A	Lge	D 1-1	Tony Fitzgerald
Sat Nov 20	Southport Reserves	H	Lge	W 1-0	Greenwood
Sat Nov 27	Prescot Town	A	Lge	L 0-3	
Sat Dec 4	Morecambe	H	Lge	W 5-0	Worswick, Fitzgerald (2), Greenwood, Walmsley
Sat Dec 11	Barrow Reserves	A	Lge	L 1-5	Fitzgerald
Sat Dec 18	Bacup Borough	H	Lge	W 6-1	Greenwood (2), Hammell, Walmsley, Worswick (2)
Mon Dec 27	Lancaster City	H	Lge	D 1-1	Walmsley
Tue Dec 28	Lancaster City	A	Lge	D 0-0	
Sat Jan 1	Horwich RMI	A	Lge	D 3-3	Fitzgerald, Worswick, Walmsley
Tue Jan 4	South Liverpool	A	Lpool Senior Non-lge Cup Semi-final	L 1-2	Greenwood
Sat Jan 8	Leyland Motors	H	Lge	L 1-2	Worden
Sat Jan 15	Rossendale United	H	Lancs Junior Cup	W 3-1	Hodge, Hammell, Fitzgerald
Sat Jan 22	Nelson	A	Lge	W 3-0	Worswick (3)
Sat Jan 29	Great Harwood	A	Lge	L 0-1	
Sat Feb 5	Skelmersdale United	A	Lancs Junior Cup	W 3-2	Hammell, Hodge, Forbes
Sat Feb 12	South Liverpool	A	Lge	L 1-3	Fitzgerald
Sat Feb 19	Clitheroe	A	Lge	L 1-2	Hodge
Sat Feb 26	Guinness Exports	H	Lge	W 3-0	Fitzgerald, Hammell, Jones
Sat Mar 5	South Liverpool	H	Lge	W 2-1	Hodge (2)
Sat Mar 12	Morecambe	A	Lancs Junior Cup	L 0-2	
Sat Mar 19	Skelmersdale United	H	Lge	L 1-6	Worswick
Sat Mar 26	Netherfield	H	Lge	D 3-3	Jones, Fitzgerald, Worswick
Wed Mar 30	Fleetwood	H	Lge	L 1-3	Seanor
Fri Apr 8	Marine	A	Lge	L 1-4	Worden
Sat Apr 9	Barrow Reserves	H	Lge	W 5-1	Hammell (3), Forbes, Fitzgerald
Mon Apr 11	Marine	H	Lge	L 2-3	Jones, Hodge
Sat Apr 16	Southport Reserves	A	Lge	L 1-5	Fitzgerald
Mon Apr 18	St. Helens Town	A	Lge	L 1-2	Scorer unknown
Sat Apr 23	Prescot Town	H	Lge	W 6-1	Fitzgerald (3), Worswick (2), Worden
Thu Apr 28	Rossendale United	A	Lge	W 2-1	Scorers unknown
Sat Apr 30	Morecambe	A	Lge	L 0-2	
Mon May 2	St. Helens Town	H	Lge	L 0-1	
Sat May 7	Droylesden	H	Lge	W 3-1	Fitzgerald (2), Worswick

1966/67 Season
Lancashire Combination (Division One)

Date	Opponent	H/A	Competition	Result	Scorers
Sat Aug 20	Morecambe	A	Lge	L 0-2	
Tue Aug 23	Chorley	H	Lge	L 1-4	Hammell
Sat Aug 27	St. Helens Town	H	Lge	D 1-1	Fitzgerald
Mon Aug 29	Guinness Exports	H	Lancs Comb Cup	D 1-1	Fitzgerald
Thu Sep 1	Guinness Exports	A	Lancs Comb Cup replay	W 1-0	Scorer unknown
Sat Sep 3	Rossendale United	H	F.A.Cup 1st Qual. Rd	L 2-3	Hodge, Hammell
Mon Sep 5	Kirkby Town	A	Lpool Senior Non-lge Cup	W 2-1	Alan Tordoff, Nicholls
Thu Sep 8	Skelmersdale United	A	Lge	L 0-6	
Sat Sep 10	Droylesden	A	Lge	L 0-1	
Tue Sep 13	Chorley	A	Lge	L 0-2	
Sat Sep 17	Leyland Motors	H	Lge	W 3-1	Nicholls, Forbes, Charlie Daniels
Sat Sep 24	Rossendale United	A	Lge	W 2-1	Forbes, O.G.
Tue Sep 27	Skelmersdale United	A	Lancs Comb Cup	D 1-1	Scorer unknown
Sat Oct 1	Bacup Borough	H	Lge	W 3-1	Forbes, Murray, Hammell
Tue Oct 4	Skelmersdale United	H	Lancs Comb Cup replay	L 0-2	
Sat Oct 8	Wigan Rovers	H	Lge	D 0-0	
Sat Oct 15	Lancaster City	A	Lge	L 2-5	Hodge, Forbes
Sat Oct 22	Barrow Reserves	H	Lge	W 1-0	Terry Finlay
Sat Oct 29	South Liverpool	A	Lge	L 0-3	
Sat Nov 5	Fleetwood	H	Lge	L 0-3	
Sat Nov 12	Great Harwood	A	Lge	L 1-3	Fitzgerald
Sat Nov 19	Horwich RMI	H	Lge	D 1-1	Forbes
Sat Nov 26	Southport Reserves	A	Lge	L 0-4	
Sat Dec 3	Darwen	H	Lge	W 4-2	Daniels, Hodge, Fitzgerald, O.G.
Sat Dec 10	Clitheroe	A	Lge	L 1-4	Hammell
Sat Dec 17	Morecambe	H	Lge	W 1-0	Hodge
Sat Dec 24	Marine	H	Lge	L 2-3	Forbes, Fitzgerald
Mon Dec 26	Marine	A	Lge	L 1-4	Hammell
Sat Jan 14	Rossendale United	A	Lancs Junior Cup 1st Rd	D 1-1	Tony Corbett
Sat Jan 21	Rossendale United	H	Lancs Junior Cup replay	W 2-0	Hammell, Forbes
Sat Jan 28	Droylesden	H	Lge	W 1-0	Corbett
Sat Feb 4	Wigan Athletic	H	Lancs Junior Cup 2nd Rd	D 1-1	Corbett
	Gate: £125				
Sat Feb 11	Wigan Athletic	A	Lancs Junior Cup replay	W 2-1	Hodge, Corbett
Sat Feb 18	Netherfield	A	Lge	L 1-4	Corbett
Sat Feb 25	Wigan Rovers	A	Lge	L 0-4	
Sat Mar 4	Lancaster City	H	Lge	W 2-1	Fitzgerald, Corbett
Sat Mar 11	Clitheroe	H	Lancs Junior Cup 3rd Rd	W 3-2	Hammell (2), Hodge
Sat Mar 18	Barrow Reserves	A	Lge	D 2-2	O.G., Tordoff
Fri Mar 24	Guinness Exports	A	Lge	W 1-0	Daniels
Sat Mar 25	South Liverpool	H	Lge	L 0-1	
Mon Mar 27	Guinness Exports	H	Lge	W 3-0	Corbett, Hammell (2)
Sat Apr 1	Chorley	A	Lancs Junior Cup Semi-final	D 1-1	Hammell
	Attend: 1,000 - Gate: £116				
Mon Apr 3	Skelmersdale United	H	Lge	W 2-1	Fitzgerald, Mick Phoenix
Thu Apr 6	Netherfield	H	Lge	D 0-0	
Sat Apr 8	Chorley	H	Lancs Junior Cup replay	D 1-1	Daniels
Mon Apr 10	St. Helens Town	A	Lge	L 0-2	
Fri Apr 14	Chorley	A	Lancs Junior Cup 2nd Replay	W 2-1	Corbett, Hammell
	Gate: £129				
Sat Apr 15	Horwich RMI	A	Lge	L 0-4	
Mon Apr 17	Bacup Borough	A	Lge	L 0-4	
Wed Apr 19	Rossendale United	H	Lge	L 0-1	
Thu Apr 20	Wigan Athletic	H	Lpool Senior Non-lge Cup Semi-final	L 1-3	Finlay
Sat Apr 22	Southport Reserves	H	Lge	W 4-1	Clayton, Phoenix, Roy Johnson (2)
Mon Apr 24	Fleetwood	A	Lge	L 1-6	Tordoff
Wed Apr 26	South Liverpool at Springfield Park, Wigan		Lancs Junior Cup Final	W 1-0	O.G.
Sat Apr 29	Darwen	A	Lge	W 2-1	Scorers unknown
Mon May 1	Leyland Motors	A	Lge	W 2-0	Scorers unknown
Wed May 3	Great Harwood	H	Lge	W 6-1	Hammell (2), Daniels, Fitzgerald, Corbett, Finlay
Sat May 6	Clitheroe	H	Lge	W 4-1	Hodge, Hammell (2), Fitzgerald

LANCASHIRE COMBINATION - DIVISION ONE
1963-64 SEASON

	P	W	D	L	F	A	Pts
Chorley	42	27	7	8	114	51	61
Netherfield	42	26	8	8	123	64	60
New Brighton	42	24	10	8	83	45	58
Horwich RMI	42	24	8	10	91	51	56
Ashton United	42	20	10	12	91	65	50
Lancaster City	42	21	8	13	90	69	50
Droylesden	42	21	7	14	80	58	49
Nelson	42	23	3	16	84	73	49
South Liverpool	42	19	9	14	88	62	47
Morecambe	42	19	8	15	93	71	46
Skelmersdale United	42	21	4	17	88	76	46
Southport Reserves	42	17	6	19	68	75	40
Bacup Borough	42	17	5	20	59	68	39
Marine	42	15	8	19	73	83	38
Burscough	**42**	**11**	**11**	**20**	**80**	**84**	**33**
Fleetwood	42	10	13	19	54	88	33
Rossendale United	42	12	9	21	70	114	33
Prescot Cables	42	11	9	22	66	98	31
Clitheroe	42	10	10	22	59	88	30
Leyland Motors	42	11	7	24	57	118	29
Barrow Reserves	42	8	9	25	56	109	25
Cromptons Recs	42	8	5	29	58	115	21

LANCASHIRE COMBINATION - DIVISION ONE
1965-66 SEASON

	P	W	D	L	F	A	Pts
South Liverpool	42	29	6	7	128	56	64
Chorley	42	24	12	6	121	56	60
Skelmersdale United	42	28	4	10	120	62	60
Marine	42	27	4	11	129	66	58
Horwich RMI	42	26	3	13	100	58	55
Netherfield	42	20	13	9	104	70	53
Morecambe	42	19	12	11	105	65	50
Lancaster City	42	19	10	13	77	59	48
Clitheroe	42	20	8	14	77	73	48
Great Harwood	42	18	10	14	81	73	46
Barrow Reserves	42	19	8	15	88	85	46
Droylesden	42	15	12	15	80	78	42
Fleetwood	42	18	5	19	95	101	41
Guinness Exports	42	14	5	23	74	103	33
Leyland Motors	42	14	5	23	52	99	33
Burscough	**42**	**13**	**6**	**23**	**76**	**89**	**32**
St. Helens Town	42	11	5	26	65	125	27
Rossendale United	42	9	9	24	48	97	27
Bacup Borough	42	11	5	26	57	126	27
Southport Reserves	42	9	7	26	65	98	25
Nelson	42	10	5	27	55	121	25
Prescot Town	42	8	8	26	66	104	24

LANCASHIRE COMBINATION - DIVISION ONE
1964-65 SEASON

	P	W	D	L	F	A	Pts
Netherfield	42	30	6	6	143	53	66
Chorley	42	27	9	6	130	55	63
Morecambe	42	30	2	10	132	50	62
Horwich RMI	42	24	13	5	128	53	61
South Liverpool	42	27	5	10	97	67	59
Droylesden	42	23	6	13	81	67	52
New Brighton	42	21	9	11	82	46	51
Marine	42	21	6	15	90	69	48
Barrow Reserves	42	19	9	14	80	77	47
Great Harwood	42	19	7	16	85	83	45
Lancaster City	42	18	6	18	75	65	42
Fleetwood	42	14	12	16	68	93	40
Nelson	42	15	7	20	68	108	37
Skelmersdale United	42	15	6	21	83	84	36
Bacup Borough	42	16	2	24	61	94	34
Leyland Motors	42	13	7	22	74	103	33
Rossendale United	42	13	6	23	75	114	32
Clitheroe	42	13	6	23	60	90	32
Southport Reserves	42	11	5	26	51	99	27
Burscough	**42**	**11**	**3**	**28**	**68**	**90**	**25**
Accrington Stanley	42	7	4	34	48	123	18
Prescot Town	42	4	6	32	44	132	14

LANCASHIRE COMBINATION - DIVISION ONE
1966-67 SEASON

	P	W	D	L	F	A	Pts
Morecambe*	41	30	9	2	90	24	69
Horwich RMI	42	27	9	6	88	37	63
Netherfield	42	27	8	7	122	54	62
Chorley	42	23	9	10	97	59	55
Fleetwood	42	22	10	10	103	62	54
South Liverpool	42	24	6	12	94	61	54
Marine	42	20	9	13	84	69	49
Wigan Rovers	42	16	15	11	78	64	47
Skelmersdale United*	41	20	5	16	99	77	45
Lancaster City	42	18	6	18	66	72	42
Southport Reserves	42	16	8	18	72	77	40
Bacup Borough	42	15	9	18	53	57	39
Droylesden	42	14	9	19	59	68	37
Burscough	**42**	**16**	**5**	**21**	**55**	**85**	**37**
St. Helens Town	42	13	9	20	66	76	35
Guinness Exports	42	12	11	19	62	87	35
Barrow Reserves	42	13	8	21	80	84	34
Rossendale United	42	12	8	22	64	90	32
Clitheroe	42	10	10	22	56	93	30
Great Harwood	42	11	5	26	56	101	27
Darwen	42	6	12	24	56	102	24
Leyland Motors	42	4	4	34	28	129	12

* Skelmersdale United v. Morecambe not played

Opposite: 1966-67 Season. Back left to right: Larry Carberry, Alan Tordoff, Alan Swift, John Coates, Tommy Ball, Charlie Daniels. Front left to right: Kenny Hodge, Jimmy Hammell, Bob Jones, Alan Cocks, Paul Fairclough. Larry Carberry, now a Burscough resident, was the former Ipswich Town full-back. He had spent 10 years as a professional at Portman Road. Under manager Alf Ramsey, Larry had the unique distinction of winning First, Second and Third Division Championship medals. Alan Cocks, then 18 years old, was signed as an apprentice professional by Chelsea in October 1967 for a reported £100 donation. He had been recommended by Verdi Godwin, a former professional player with an eye for spotting promising talent, who has quietly influenced developments at Victoria Park ever since. Two years later, when Cocks was selected for Chelsea's first team, a further donation of £25 was sent, a sum described in the local press as 'disgusting'.

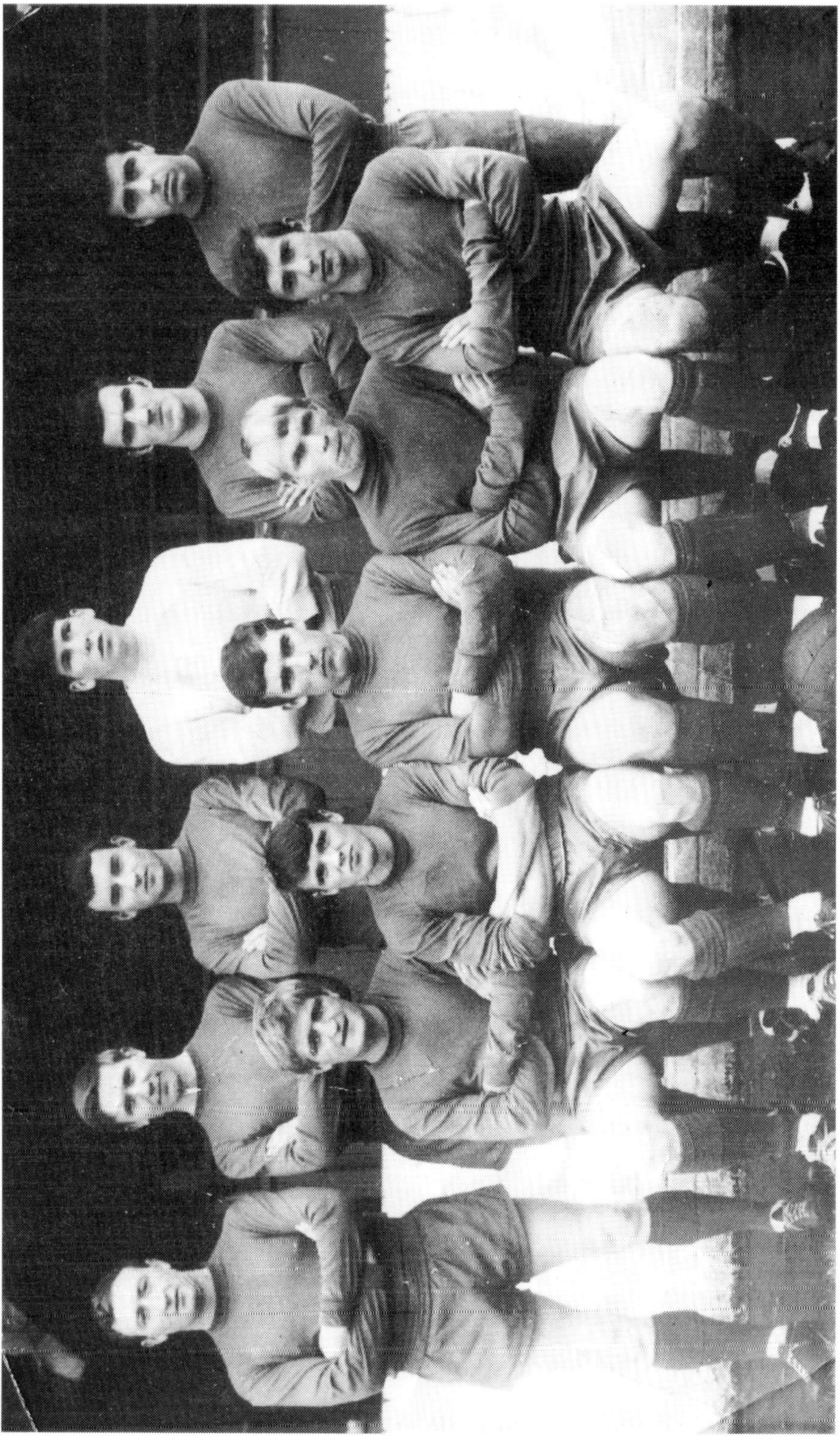

1967/68 Season
Lancashire Combination (Division One)

Date	Opponent	H/A	Competition	Result	Scorers
Sat Aug 19	Clitheroe	A	Lge	W 1-0	Hammell
Mon Aug 21	Prescot Town	H	Lancs Comb Cup	L 0-3	
Thu Aug 24	Guinness Exports	A	Lpool Senior Non-lge Cup	L 0-3	
Sat Aug 26	Great Harwood	H	Lge	D 1-1	Hodge
Thu Aug 31	Skelmersdale United	A	Lge	L 1-2	Forbes
Sat Sep 2	Fleetwood	A	Lge	L 0-2	
Sat Sep 9	South Liverpool	H	Lge	W 1-0	Hammell
Tue Sep 12	Kirkby Town	A	Lge	L 0-1	
Sat Sep 16	Droylesden	A	F.A.Cup 1st Qual. Rd	D 1-1	Alan Swift
Thu Sep 21	Droylesden	H	F.A.Cup replay	W 5-2	Swift, Daniels, Hammell, O.G., Ball
Sat Sep 30	Stalybridge Celtic	A	F.A.Cup 2nd Qual. Rd	D 1-1	Swift
Thu Oct 5	Stalybridge Celtic	H	F.A.Cup replay	W 3-1	Alan Cocks, Swift, Hammell
	Attend: 400				
Sat Oct 7	Southport Res.	H	Lge	L 0-1	
Sat Oct 14	Ellesmere Port Town	A	F.A.Cup 3rd Qual. Rd	L 2-3	Daniels (2)
Sat Oct 21	Wigan Rovers	H	Lge	W 2-1	Keith Reeder (2)
Sat Oct 28	Rossendale United	A	Lge	W 2-1	Hodge, Hammell
Sat Nov 4	Rossendale United	H	Lge	W 2-0	Hammell, Daniels
Sat Nov 11	Chorley	A	Lge	L 1-3	Duncan
Sat Nov 18	Droylesden	H	Lge	W 2-1	Hammell, Hickson
Sat Nov 25	Barrow Reserves	A	Lge	W 4-0	Reeder (3), Tordoff
Sat Dec 2	Morecambe	H	Lge	W 2-1	Reeder (2)
Sat Dec 16	Clitheroe	H	Lge	W 3-0	Hodge, Hickson (2)
Tue Dec 26	Horwich RMI	H	Lge	W 3-1	Hammell, Hodge, Hickson
Sat Dec 30	Horwich RMI	A	Lge	D 2-2	Fitzgerald, Hodge
Sat Jan 6	Fleetwood	H	Lge	D 1-1	Hickson
Sat Jan 20	Barrow Reserves	H	Lge	L 1-2	Hickson
Sat Jan 27	Droylesden	A	Lge	L 0-2	
Sat Feb 3	Guinness Exports	H	Lge	L 0-3	
Sat Feb 10	Lancaster City	A	Lge	D 1-1	Reeder
Tue Feb 13	Netherfield	A	Lge	D 2-2	Hodge (2)
Sat Feb 17	Prestwich Heys	H	Lancs Junior Cup 1st Rd	D 2-2	Frank Riding, Fitzgerald
Sat Feb 24	Prestwich Heys	A	Lancs Junior Cup replay	W 3-2	Reeder (2), Hodge
Sat Mar 2	Maghull	H	Lancs Junior Cup 2nd Rd	W 4-3	Swift, Fitzgerald, Reeder (2)
Sat Mar 9	Morecambe	A	Lancs Junior Cup 3rd Rd	L 0-1	
Tue Mar 12	Southport Reserves	A	Lge	D 1-1	Scorer unknown
Sat Mar 16	Wigan Rovers	A	Lge	L 0-2	
Tue Mar 19	South Liverpool	A	Lge	W 1-0	Scorer unknown
Tue Mar 26	Guinness Exports	A	Lge	L 0-1	
Sat Apr 6	Chorley	H	Lge	D 3-3	Reeder, Hammell, Swift
Tue Apr 9	Prescot Town	H	Lge	W 2-1	Hodge, Reeder
Fri Apr 12	St. Helens Town	H	Lge	L 1-3	O.G.
Sat Apr 13	Skelmersdale United	H	Lge	D 2-2	Riding, Reeder
	Attend: 1,000 - Gate: £105				
Mon Apr 15	St. Helens Town	A	Lge	L 0-1	
Mon Apr 22	Lancaster City	H	Lge	D 1-1	Scorer unknown
Thu Apr 25	Bacup Borough	H	Lge	L 1-3	Scorer unknown
Sat Apr 27	Morecambe	A	Lge	L 0-2	
Tue Apr 30	Great Harwood	A	Lge	L 0-5	
Thu May 2	Bacup Borough	A	Lge	L 0-1	
Sat May 4	Netherfield	H	Lge	L 1-2	Swift
Tue May 7	Kirkby Town	H	Lge	D 1-1	Scorer unknown
Thu May 9	Marine	H	Lge	W 4-2	Scorers unknown
Sat May 11	Prescot Town	A	Lge	L 1-2	Fitzgerald
Mon May 13	Marine	A	Lge	L 2-3	Scorers unknown

1968/69 Season
Lancashire Combination (Division One)

Date	Opponent	H/A	Competition	Result	Scorers
Sat Aug 17	Rossendale United	H	Lge	D 2-2	Brian Robinson, Paul Fairclough
Tue Aug 20	Formby	H	Lancs Comb Cup	W 4-2	Fairclough (2), Kenny Jarvis, C.Murphy
Sat Aug 24	Wigan Ath. Reserves	A	Lge	W 4-1	Robinson, Jarvis, Fairclough, Murphy
Mon Aug 26	Dukinfield Town	A	Lge	W 1-0	Robinson
Sat Aug 31	Prescot Town	H	Lancs Comb Cup	W 3-1	Fairclough, Kenny Miller, Jarvis
	Attend: 350				
Tue Sep 3	Nelson	H	Lge	W 10-0	Robinson (5), Fairclough (2), Jarvis (2), Miller
Sat Sep 7	Leyland Motors	A	Lge	W 2-0	Jarvis, Fairclough
Wed Sep 11	Marine	A	Lge	W 2-0	Scorers unknown
Sat Sep 14	Bacup Borough	H	Lge	W 7-0	Robinson (3), Jarvis, Fairclough, Murphy, Graham Glover
Tue Sep 17	Wigan Rovers	A	Lge	W 3-0	Robinson (3)
Sat Sep 21	Ellesmere Port Town	H	F.A.Cup 1st Qual. Rd	W 3-1	Robinson (3)
Sat Sep 28	Barrow Reserves	A	Lge	W 2-0	Robinson (2)
Tue Oct 1	Dukinfield Town	H	Lge	D 2-2	Scorers unknown
Sat Oct 5	Stalybridge Celtic	A	F.A.Cup 2nd Qual. Rd	D 2-2	Murphy, Fairclough
Thu Oct 10	Stalybridge Celtic	H	F.A.Cup replay	L 2-4	Robinson, Miller
	Attend: 600				
Sat Oct 12	Formby	H	Lge	D 1-1	Robinson
Sat Oct 19	Prescot Town	A	Lge	L 0-2	
Sat Oct 26	Darwen	H	Lge	W 4-0	Miller, Swift (3)
Sat Nov 9	Great Harwood	H	Lge	W 3-0	Swift, Robinson (2)
Sat Nov 16	Blackpool Mechanics	A	Lge	D 3-3	Swift (3)
Sat Nov 23	Clitheroe	H	Lge	W 3-0	Swift, Daniels, Robinson
Sat Nov 30	Lytham St. Annes	A	Lge	W 5-0	Robinson (3), Murphy, Jarvis
Sat Dec 7	Lancaster City	H	Lge	D 3-3	Fairclough (2), O.G.
Sat Dec 14	Formby	A	Lge	D 1-1	Swift
Sat Dec 21	Prescot Town	H	Lge	W 2-1	Robinson, Fairclough
Thu Dec 26	Prestwich Heys	A	Lge	L 2-4	Scorers unknown
Sat Dec 28	Prestwich Heys	H	Lge	D 1-1	Swift
Wed Jan 1	Leyland Motors	H	Lancs Comb Cup	W 4-0	Robinson (3), 1 unknown
Sat Jan 4	Kirkby Town	H	Lge	L 2-3	Robinson (2)
Sat Jan 11	Darwen	A	Lancs Junior Cup 1st Rd	L 1-3	Fairclough
Sat Jan 25	St. Helens Town	H	Lge	W 3-2	Scorers unknown
Sat Jan 18	Great Harwood	A	Lge	L 2-3	Robinson, Swift
Sat Feb 1	Blackpool Mechanics	H	Lge	D 2-2	Scorers unknown
Sat Feb 22	Lancaster City	A	Lge	W 3-2	Fairclough, Swift (2)
Mon Feb 24	Skelmersdale United	A	Lpool Senior Non-lge Cup	L 2-6	Swift, Robinson
Sat Mar 1	Clitheroe	A	Lge	L 1-3	Barry Ravenscroft
Thu Mar 6	Wigan Athletic Reserves	A	Lancs Comb Cup Semi-final	W 1-0	Robinson
Sat Mar 8	Rossendale United	A	Lge	W 6-0	Robinson (4), 2 unknown
Sat Mar 15	Wigan Athletic Reserves	H	Lge	D 1-1	Miller
Tue Mar 18	Kirkby Town	A	Lge	D 1-1	Scorer unknown
Sat Mar 22	Nelson	A	Lge	W 4-1	Ravenscroft, Fairclough (2), Daniels
Sat Mar 29	Leyland Motors	H	Lge	W 3-0	O.G., Fairclough (2)
Fri Apr 4	Radcliffe Borough	A	Lge	L 1-3	Ravenscroft
Sat Apr 5	Bacup Borough	A	Lge	W 4-0	Daniels, Fairclough (2), Robinson
Mon Apr 7	Radcliffe Borough	H	Lge	W 2-0	Jarvis, Robinson
Thu Apr 10	Marine	H	Lge	D 3-3	Jarvis, Robinson, Miller
Sat Apr 12	Wigan Rovers	H	Lge	W 4-1	Jarvis (2), Robinson, Fairclough
Thu Apr 17	Lytham St. Annes	H	Lge	W 1-0	Robinson
Sat Apr 19	Barrow Reserves	A	Lge	L 1-2	Robinson
Sat Apr 26	Marine	A	Lancs Comb Cup Final 1st Leg	L 1-2	Scorer unknown
Mon Apr 28	St.Helens Town	A	Lge	W 2-0	Robinson, Fairclough
Thu May 1	Darwen	A	Lge	L 1-2	Scorer unknown
Tue May 6	Marine	H	Lancs Comb Cup Final 2nd Leg	D 4-4	Swift, Jones, Jarvis, Daniels

Above: 1968-69 Season. Back left to right: Alan Tordoff, Kenny Miller, Kenny Jarvis, Frank Riding, Bob Jones, Charlie Daniels. Front left to right: Barry Ravenscroft, Graham Glover, Paul Fairclough, Brian Robinson, Alan Swift, Roy Hart. Brian Robinson scored 150 goals during his four years at Burscough, putting him second only to Wesley Bridge's 188 goals. Brian lives in the Chorley area, his main interests are now bowls and amateur dramatics. He describes his spell at Victoria Park as 'my happiest time in football.'
Below: 1969-70 Season. Lancashire Combination Division One Champions. Back left to right: Bob Bolton, Rodney Webb, Larry Madgin, Peter Wassall, Kenny Miller, Bob Jones, Chris Booth. Front left to right: Kenny Jarvis, Barry Ravenscroft, Brian Robinson, Graham Glover, Kenny Dumican, Ivor Swarbrick, Frank Riding.

1969/70 Season
Lancashire Combination (Division One)

Date	Opponent	H/A	Comp	Result	Scorers
Sat Aug 9	Wigan Athletic Reserves	H	Lge	D 1-1	Robinson
Tue Aug 12	Chorley	H	Lge	W 3-2	Harry Miller, K.Miller, Jarvis
Sat Aug 16	Blackpool Mechanics	A	Lge	W 3-0	H.Miller, Jarvis, Ivor Swarbrick
Tue Aug 19	Clitheroe	H	Lge	W 8-1	Robinson (3), 5 unknown
Sat Aug 23	Wigan Rovers	H	Lge	W 6-1	Swarbrick (2), Robinson (3), Jarvis
Tue Aug 26	Chorley	A	Lge	D 1-1	Robinson
Sat Aug 30	St. Helens Town	A	Lancs Comb Cup	L 1-2	Swarbrick
Sat Sep 6	Lytham St.Annes	H	Lge	W 2-0	Swarbrick(2)
Sat Sep 13	Wigan Athletic Reserves	A	Lge	D 2-2	Jarvis, Robinson
Tue Sep 16	Dukinfield Town	H	Lge	W 3-0	K.Miller (2), Robinson
Sat Sep 20	Leyland Motors	H	F.A.Cup 1st Qual. Rd	W 5-2	Robinson (3), Jarvis, O.G.
Sat Sep 27	Wigan Rovers	A	Lge	D 3-3	Robinson, Kenny Dumican, H.Miller
Sat Oct 4	Hyde United	A	F.A.Cup 2nd Qual. Rd	W 1-0	Robinson
Sat Oct 11	Darwen	A	Lge	L 2-3	Swarbrick, H.Miller
Sat Oct 18	Wigan Athletic	A	F.A.Cup 3rd Qual. Rd	D 1-1	Robinson
Thu Oct 23	Wigan Athletic	H	F.A.Cup replay	L 2-3	Dumican, Robinson
Sat Oct 25	Radcliffe Borough	H	Lge	W 6-1	Robinson, Ravenscroft (3), H.Miller (2)
Sat Nov 1	Rossendale United	A	Lge	W 2-0	Dumican, Robinson
Sat Nov 8	St. Helens Town	A	Lge	W 1-0	H.Miller
Sat Nov 15	Nelson	H	Lge	W 4-1	Robinson (3), H.Miller
Sat Nov 22	Leyland Motors	A	Lge	W 3-1	Dumican (3)
Sat Nov 29	Lytham St.Annes	A	Lge	W 5-0	Dumican, H.Miller (2), Ravenscroft, Swarbrick
Sat Dec 6	Bacup Borough	A	Lge	W 2-0	Robinson, Dumican
Sat Dec 13	Blackpool Mechanics	H	Lge	W 3-0	Robinson, Dumican, H.Miller
Fri Dec 26	Formby	A	Lge	W 8-1	H.Miller (2), Glover (2), Ravenscroft, Jarvis, Robinson, Dumican
Sat Jan 3	Prescot Town	H	Lge	W 3-1	Robinson (2), H.Miller
Wed Jan 14	Macclesfield Town	A	F.A. Trophy	L 0-1	
Sat Jan 17	Maghull	H	Lancs Challenge Trophy	W 4-1	Robinson, Glover (2), Dumican
Sat Jan 24	Formby	H	Lge	W 6-1	Dumican (3), Robinson (2), Glover
Sat Jan 31	Clitheroe	A	Lge	W 2-1	Robinson, Jarvis
Sat Feb 7	Rossendale United	H	Lancs Challenge Trophy	L 0-1	
Sat Feb 28	Kirkby Town	H	Lge	L 1-2	Glover
Sat Mar 14	Nelson	A	Lge	W 5-0	Ravenscroft (3), Jarvis, Robinson
Tue Mar 17	Kirkby Town	A	Lge	W 2-0	Dumican, Robinson
Sat Mar 21	Bacup Borough	H	Lge	W 6-1	Jarvis, Dumican, Robinson (3), Ravenscroft
Wed Mar 25	Guinness Exports	A	Lpool Senior Non-lge Cup	L 1-2	Riding
Fri Mar 27	Lancaster City	A	Lge	W 1-0	Dumican
Mon Mar 30	Lancaster City	H	Lge	L 0-3	
Sat Apr 4	Rossendale United	H	Lge	W 3-0	Jarvis (2), Ravenscroft
Tue Apr 7	Darwen	H	Lge	W 2-0	Swarbrick, Robinson
Tue Apr 14	St. Helens Town	H	Lge	W 1-0	Dumican
Thu Apr 16	Prescot Town	A	Lge	W 3-1	Ravenscroft, Robinson (2)
Sat Apr 18	Prestwich Heys	H	Lge	W 1-0	Dumican
Tue Apr 21	Prestwich Heys	A	Lge	L 0-7	
Tue Apr 28	Leyland Motors	H	Lge	W 6-0	Ravenscroft, Robinson, Riding (2), Chris Booth (2)
Sat May 2	Radcliffe Borough	A	Lge	W 2-1	Dumican, Robinson
Thu May 7	Dukinfield Town	A	Lge	W 4-0	Booth, Jarvis (2), Robinson

1970-71 Season. Back left to right: Ivor Swarbrick, Eddie Lawson (Committee), Rodney Webb, Bob Jones (Asst. Manager), Kenny Jarvis, Bob Langton (Manager), Kenny Dumican, Chris Mahood (Secretary), Peter Wassall, John Draper (Committee), Roy Hart, Bill Martland (Chairman), Brian Bannister, Jim Bridge (Committee), Terry Kelly (Treasurer). Front left to right: Bill Ward (Committee), Alan Swift, Graham Glover, Brian Robinson, Kenny Miller, Leo Skeete, Frank Riding. Leo Skeete was the Club's Player of the Year. He went on to play for Rochdale, then captain Mossley at Wembley Stadium in the 1979-80 F.A. Trophy Final.

LANCASHIRE COMBINATION - DIVISION ONE 1967-68 SEASON

	P	W	D	L	F	A	Pts
Morecambe	42	28	9	5	112	41	65
Guinness Exports	42	29	6	7	85	37	64
Skelmersdale United	42	23	10	9	94	49	56
Fleetwood	42	22	10	10	72	43	54
Marine	42	21	10	11	78	60	52
Great Harwood	42	20	11	11	71	50	51
South Liverpool	42	21	7	14	76	53	49
Netherfield	42	20	9	13	103	88	49
Horwich RMI	42	19	9	14	79	52	47
Lancaster City	42	18	11	13	72	67	47
Chorley	42	17	9	16	72	65	43
St. Helens Town	42	16	8	18	68	65	40
Kirkby Town	42	13	13	16	54	60	39
Burscough	**42**	**13**	**10**	**19**	**53**	**64**	**36**
Droylesden	42	13	10	19	52	84	36
Wigan Rovers	42	14	6	22	56	69	34
Clitheroe	42	14	6	22	58	86	34
Southport Reserves	42	12	9	21	59	66	33
Barrow Reserves	42	13	4	25	55	78	30
Prescot Town	42	12	1	29	53	109	23
Bacup Borough	42	8	6	28	34	105	22
Rossendale United	42	6	6	30	50	115	18

LANCASHIRE COMBINATION - DIVISION ONE 1968-69 SEASON

	P	W	D	L	F	A	Pts
Great Harwood	42	33	6	3	115	35	72
Kirkby Town	42	27	11	4	126	36	65
Lancaster City	42	28	3	11	120	58	59
Burscough	**42**	**23**	**11**	**8**	**110**	**51**	**57**
Prestwich Heys	42	24	7	11	109	58	55
St. Helens Town	42	22	10	10	84	44	54
Marine	42	22	9	11	95	48	53
Darwen	42	17	9	16	59	64	43
Blackpool Mechanics	42	16	10	16	76	68	42
Formby	42	17	7	18	82	72	41
Wigan Rovers	42	17	7	18	68	82	41
Radcliffe Borough	42	16	8	18	86	72	40
Rossendale United	42	16	8	18	68	83	40
Clitheroe	42	15	8	19	68	74	38
Wigan Athletic Reserves	42	13	9	20	73	80	35
Prescot Town	42	12	11	19	49	80	35
Barrow Reserves	42	11	10	21	51	82	32
Nelson	42	12	8	22	66	110	32
Dukinfield Town	42	9	11	22	63	98	29
Leyland Motors	42	9	11	22	44	90	29
Bacup Borough	42	9	3	30	33	109	21
Lytham St. Annes	42	3	5	34	23	174	11

1970/71 Season
Cheshire County League

Date	Opponent	H/A	Comp	Result	Scorers
Sat Aug 15	Ashton United	H	Lge	W 3-1	Kenny Miller, 2 unknown
Wed Aug 19	New Brighton	A	Lge	W 3-1	Robinson, Dumican, Swarbrick
Sat Aug 22	Horwich RMI	A	Lge	W 2-1	Jarvis, Dumican
Tue Aug 25	Witton Albion	H	League Cup	L 2-4	Dumican, Madgin
Sat Aug 29	Oswestry Town	H	Lge	D 2-2	Booth, Dumican
Thu Sep 3	South Liverpool	H	Lpool Senior Non-lge Cup	L 0-1	
Tue Sep 8	Winsford United	H	Lge	W 4-2	Skeete (3), Robinson
Sat Sep 12	Hyde United	H	Lge	D 3-3	Robinson (3)
Mon Sep 14	Witton Albion	A	Lge	W 3-2	Scorers unknown
Wed Sep 16	Winsford United	A	Lge	L 1-2	Scorer unknown
Sat Sep 19	Prestwich Heys	A	F.A.Cup 1st Qual. Rd	W 3-2	Leo Skeete (2), Swarbrick
Thu Sep 24	Skelmersdale United	H	Lge	L 0-4	
	Attend: 1,500 - Gate: £250				
Sat Sep 26	Buxton	A	Lge	W 4-2	Dumican, Skeete (3)
Tue Sep 29	Droylesden	H	Lge	W 4-1	Booth (2), Robinson (2)
Sat Oct 3	Ashton United	A	Lge	W 3-1	Robinson (2), Dumican
Sat Oct 10	South Liverpool	H	F.A.Cup 2nd Qual. Rd	L 0-3	
Sat Oct 17	Horwich RMI	H	Lge	W 3-1	Skeete, Miller, Robinson
Sat Oct 24	Oldham Athletic Reserves	H	Lge	W 5-3	Skeete (3), Swarbrick, Robinson
Sat Oct 31	Buxton	H	Lge	W 3-1	Skeete, Swarbrick, Dumican
Sat Nov 7	Oldham Athletic Reserves	A	Lge	L 2-3	Skeete (2)
Sat Nov 14	Mossley	A	Lge	L 1-5	Skeete
Sat Nov 21	Sandbach Ramblers	H	Lge	W 5-2	Swarbrick (3), Skeete, Dumican
Wed Nov 25	Wigan Athletic	A	Lancs Challenge Trophy	L 2-5	Glover, Skeete
Sat Nov 28	Nantwich	A	Lge	D 2-2	Campbell, Robinson
Sat Dec 5	Port Vale Reserves	H	Lge	W 4-0	Skeete (2), Robinson (2)
Sat Dec 12	Stalybridge Celtic	A	Lge	W 2-1	Swarbrick, Dumican
Sat Dec 19	Nantwich	H	Lge	D 1-1	Dumican
Sat Dec 26	Marine	H	Lge	D 1-1	Miller
Mon Dec 28	Marine	A	Lge	D 2-2	O.G., Dumican
Sat Jan 2	Stalybridge Celtic	H	Lge	W 2-1	Skeete (2)
Sat Jan 9	Sandbach Ramblers	A	Lge	W 3-1	Skeete, Dumican, Riding
Sat Jan 16	Great Harwood	A	F.A.Trophy	W 3-2	Dumican, Miller, Skeete
Sat Jan 23	Port Vale Reserves	A	Lge	L 1-2	Glover
Sat Jan 30	Rossendale United	H	Lge	W 3-0	Skeete, Dumican, Robinson
Sat Feb 6	Chorley	A	F.A. Trophy	L 0-1	
Sat Feb 13	Droylesden	A	Lge	W 4-1	Skeete (4)
Sat Feb 27	Ellesmere Port	H	Lge	D 3-3	Skeete, Miller, Dumican
Sat Mar 6	Mossley	H	Lge	W 4-3	O.G., Roy Hart, Dumican (2)
Sat Mar 13	Rhyl	H	Lge	W 4-1	Skeete (2), Dumican, Robinson
Sat Mar 27	Rossendale United	A	Lge	D 0-0	
Wed Mar 31	Ellesmere Port	A	Lge	D 1-1	Skeete
Sat Apr 3	Oswestry Town	A	Lge	D 0-0	
Tue Apr 6	Skelmersdale United	A	Lge	W 5-1	Robinson (3), Skeete (2)
Fri Apr 9	Ormskirk	A	Lge	W 4-0	Scorers unknown
Sat Apr 10	Witton Albion	H	Lge	W 2-0	Robinson, Dumican
Mon Apr 12	Ormskirk	H	Lge	D 1-1	Scorer unknown
Thu Apr 15	Rhyl	A	Lge	D 0-0	
Sat Apr 17	Hyde United	A	Lge	L 0-2	
Sat Apr 24	New Brighton	H	Lge	W 6-0	Skeete, Robinson (5)

263

1971/72 Season
Cheshire County League

Date	Opponent	H/A	Competition	Result	Scorers
Sat Aug 14	Oldham Athletic Reserves	H	Lge	D 0-0	
Tue Aug 17	Formby	A	Lge	L 1-2	Skeete
Sat Aug 21	Witton Albion	A	Lge	L 2-3	Jarvis, Miller
Tue Aug 24	Formby	H	Lge	W 3-1	Jarvis (2), Robinson
Thu Aug 26	Prescot Town	H	Lpool Senior Non-lge Cup	W 4-0	Glover, Jarvis, Swarbrick, Robinson
Sat Aug 28	Buxton	H	Lge	L 0-4	
Mon Aug 30	Ormskirk	H	League Cup	W 5-2	John Rogers (3), Skeete, Robinson
Tue Sep 7	New Brighton	H	Lge	W 4-1	Skeete, Miller, Rogers, Robinson
Sat Sep 11	Ashton United	H	Lge	W 5-1	Robinson (2), Hart (2), Miller
Tue Sep 14	Horwich RMI	A	Lge	L 0-4	
Sat Sep 18	Radcliffe Borough	A	F.A.Cup 1st Qual. Rd	W 3-2	Skeete (2), Glover
Wed Sep 22	New Brighton	A	Lge	D 1-1	Rogers
Sat Sep 25	Stalybridge Celtic	A	Lge	L 1-2	Rogers
Mon Sep 27	Sandbach Ramblers	A	Lge	L 1-2	Robinson
Sat Oct 2	Hyde United	A	Lge	W 1-0	Rogers
Sat Oct 9	Chorley	H	F.A.Cup 2nd Qual. Rd	W 2-1	Robinson, Dumican
Sat Oct 16	Nantwich Town	A	Lge	L 0-2	
Sat Oct 23	Ellesmere Port Town	H	F.A.Cup 3rd Qual. Rd	L 0-1	
Sat Oct 30	Mossley	A	Lge	L 1-2	Robinson
Sat Nov 6	Prestwich Heys	H	Lge	D 3-3	Robinson, Rogers (2)
Sat Nov 13	Radcliffe Borough	A	Lge	D 1-1	Rogers
Tue Nov 16	Lancaster City	H	Lancs Challenge Trophy	W 4-2	Glover, Robinson (2), Dumican
	played at Chorley				
Sat Nov 20	Witton Albion	H	Lge	W 1-0	Glover
Sat Nov 27	Rhyl	A	Lge	W 1-0	Robinson
Sat Dec 4	Horwich RMI	H	Lge	W 4-0	Miller (2), Swarbrick, Robinson
Sat Dec 11	Buxton	A	Lge	D 1-1	Robinson
Sat Dec 18	Rossendale United	H	Lge	W 2-1	Skeete (2)
Mon Dec 27	Marine	A	Lge	D 0-0	
Tue Dec 28	Marine	H	Lge	L 1-2	Skeete
Sat Jan 1	Stalybridge Celtic	H	Lge	W 1-0	Robinson
Tue Jan 4	Morecambe	A	Lancs Challenge Trophy	L 1-2	Dumican
Sat Jan 8	Oldham Athletic Reserves	A	Lge	W 2-1	Dave Parry (2)
Sat Jan 15	Sandbach Ramblers	H	Lge	W 2-1	Dumican (2)
Sat Jan 22	South Liverpool	A	F.A.Trophy	D 2-2	Robinson, Skeete
Thu Jan 27	South Liverpool	H	F.A.Trophy replay	D 1-1	Dumican
Sat Jan 29	Radcliffe Borough	H	Lge	W 3-2	Dumican, Glover, Rogers
Mon Feb 1	South Liverpool	H	F.A.Trophy 2nd replay	L 1-2	Robinson
	at Haig Avenue, Southport				
Sat Feb 5	Rossendale United	A	Lge	L 1-2	Robinson
Sat Feb 12	Hyde United	H	Lge	W 5-0	Skeete (4), Swarbrick
Sat Feb 19	Oswestry Town	A	Lge	L 1-2	O.G.
Sat Feb 26	Nantwich Town	H	Lge	W 3-0	Skeete, Miller, Robinson
Sat Mar 4	Prestwich Heys	A	Lge	L 2-3	Skeete, Swarbrick
Thu Mar 9	Oswestry Town	H	Lge	W 3-1	Dumican (2), Skeete
Sat Mar 11	Droylesden	A	Lge	L 0-1	
Mon Mar 13	Oswestry Town	A	League Cup	L 1-3	Glover
Thu Mar 16	Skelmersdale United	H	Lpool Senior Non-lge Cup Semi-final	W 3-0	Parry, Skeete, Melling
Sat Mar 18	Mossley	H	Lge	W 2-1	Dumican, Brian Bannister
Thu Mar 23	Rhyl	H	Lge	W 2-1	Robinson, Sutton
Sat Mar 25	Droylesden	H	Lge	D 0-0	
Fri Mar 31	Ormskirk	A	Lge	W 2-1	Robinson (2)
Sat Apr 1	Winsford United	A	Lge	L 3-4	Glover (2), Riding
Mon Apr 3	Ormskirk	H	Lge	D 1-1	Dumican
Fri Apr 7	Winsford United	H	Lge	W 4-2	Skeete (3), Robinson
Wed Apr 19	Formby	H	Lpool Senior Non-lge Cup Final	W 4-1	Robinson, Skeete, Parry, Dumican
Sat Apr 22	Ashton United	A	Lge	D 0-0	

1972/73 Season
Cheshire County League

Date	Opponent	H/A	Competition	Result	Scorers
Sat Aug 12	Oldham Athletic Reserves	A	Lge	W 2-0	Swift, Dumican
Thu Aug 17	Formby	H	Lge	D 1-1	Tommy Taylor
Sat Aug 19	Ashton United	H	Lge	W 3-2	Dumican, Miller, Hughes
Thu Aug 24	Marine	H	League Cup	W 1-0	David Wassall
Sat Aug 26	Sandbach Ramblers	A	Lge	D 3-3	Parry, Glover, Wassall
Sat Sep 2	Witton Albion	H	Lge	L 0-1	
Mon Sep 4	Skelmersdale Utd	H	Lpool Senior Non-lge Cup	L 0-2	
Thu Sep 7	Chorley	H	Lge	W 3-1	Wassall (2), Jackie Allen
Sat Sep 9	Stalybridge Celtic	A	Lge	W 2-0	Wassall (2)
Mon Sep 11	New Brighton	A	Lge	L 0-1	
Sat Sep 16	Wigan Rovers	H	F.A.Cup 1st Qual. Rd	W 2-0	Glover, Miller
Sat Sep 23	Rossendale United	H	Lge	D 0-0	
Thu Sep 28	Earle	H	Lancs Challenge Trophy	W 5-0	Wassall (3), Dumican (2)
Sat Sep 30	Buxton	H	Lge	D 0-0	
Sat Oct 7	Chorley	H	F.A.Cup 2nd Qual. Rd	D 1-1	Taylor
Tue Oct 10	Chorley	A	F.A.Cup replay	W 2-1	Dumican, Wassall
Thu Oct 12	Radcliffe Borough	H	Lge Cup 2nd Rd.	D 2-2	Allen, Ian Ledgard
Sat Oct 14	Hyde United	A	Lge	D 1-1	Allen
Sun Oct 15	Radcliffe Borough	A	Lge Cup replay	W 1-0	Allen
Sat Oct 21	Runcorn	H	F.A.Cup 3rd Qual. Rd	D 2-2	Miller, Wassall
Mon Oct 23	Runcorn	A	F.A.Cup replay	W 3-2	Scorers unknown
Thu Oct 26	Kirkby Town	H	Lancs Floodlit Trophy	W 4-2	Allen (4)
Sat Oct 28	Rhyl	H	Lge	L 1-3	Allen
Sat Nov 4	Wigan Athletic	H	F.A.Cup 4th Qual. Rd	L 1-3	Bannister
	Attend: 2,259 - Gate: £500				
Sat Nov 11	Prestwich Heys	H	Lge	W 4-0	Ledgard, Miller, Swift (2)
Sat Nov 18	Droylesden	A	Lge	D 1-1	Dumican
Thu Nov 23	Skelmersdale United	H	Lancs Floodlit Trophy	L 2-4	Riding, Allen
Sat Nov 25	Droylesden	H	Lge	W 4-2	Allen, Swift, Wassall
Sat Dec 2	Sandbach Ramblers	A	F.A.Trophy	L 1-3	Swarbrick
Sat Dec 9	Radcliffe Borough	H	Lge	D 1-1	Wassall
Sat Dec 16	Oldham Athletic Reserves	H	Lge	W 2-0	Glover, Swift
Mon Dec 18	Great Harwood	H	Lancs Challenge Trophy	L 2-3	Swift, Bannister
Fri Dec 22	Ashton United	A	Lge	W 2-1	Scorers unknown
Tue Dec 26	Marine	A	Lge	L 1-2	Parry
Wed Dec 27	Marine	H	Lge	W 1-0	Swift
Sat Dec 30	Sandbach Ramblers	H	Lge	W 1-0	Bannister
Sat Jan 6	Buxton	A	Lge	L 2-3	Glover, Parry
Thu Jan 11	Formby	H	League Cup	W 2-0	Scorers unknown
Sat Jan 13	Stalybridge Celtic	H	Lge	L 2-3	Scorers unknown
Sun Jan 14	Radcliffe Borough	A	Lge	D 1-1	Scorer unknown
Sat Jan 20	Oswestry Town	H	Lge	L 0-3	
Sat Jan 27	Chorley	A	Lge	L 0-1	
Sat Feb 3	Winsford United	A	Lge	D 2-2	Scorers unknown
Sat Feb 10	Oswestry Town	A	Lge	D 2-2	Swift (2)
Sat Feb 17	Horwich RMI	H	Lge	D 1-1	
Sat Feb 24	Rhyl	A	Lge	W 4-1	Billy Marsh (2), Wassall, Swift
Sat Mar 3	Witton Albion	A	Lge	W 1-0	Marsh
Sat Mar 10	Prestwich Heys	A	Lge	W 3-1	Glover, Marsh, Swift
Thu Mar 15	Winsford United	H	Lge	W 2-0	Scorers unknown
Sat Mar 17	New Brighton	H	Lge	L 0-2	
Sat Mar 24	Rossendale United	A	Lge	L 0-3	
Sat Mar 31	Hyde United	H	Lge	D 0-0	
Thu Apr 5	Buxton	H	League Cup Semi-final 1st leg	L 1-4	Swift
Sun Apr 8	Formby	A	Lge	L 2-4	Scorers unknown
Thu Apr 12	Buxton	A	League Cup Semi-final 2nd leg	L 0-1	
Sat Apr 14	Horwich RMI	A	Lge	D 1-1	Dumican
Fri Apr 20	Ormskirk	A	Lge	W 2-1	Miller, Swift
Sat Apr 21	Nantwich Town	H	Lge	W 3-1	Glover, Tim Winter (2)
Mon Apr 23	Ormskirk	H	Lge	W 2-0	Ledgard, Swift
Sat Apr 28	Nantwich Town	A	Lge	L 0-3	

1973/74 Season
Cheshire County League

Date	Opponent	H/A	Competition	Result	Scorers
Sat Aug 11	Chorley	A	Lge Cup 1st Rd 1st leg	W 3-0	Scorers unknown
Wed Aug 15	Formby	H	Lge	D 0-0	
Sat Aug 18	Chorley	H	Lge Cup 1st Rd 2nd leg	L 0-1	
Wed Aug 22	South Liverpool	H	Lpool Senior Non-lge Cup	W 2-0	O.G., Joey Flaherty
Sat Aug 25	Oldham Athletic Reserves	A	Lge	L 0-1	
Wed Aug 29	New Brighton	H	Lge	W 2-1	Miller, Flaherty
Sat Sep 1	Rossendale United	H	Lge	L 1-2	Swarbrick
Tue Sep 4	Prescot Town	H	Lpool Senior Non-lge Cup	W 3-0	Dumican, Bannister, Herbert
Sat Sep 8	Hyde United	A	Lge	W 1-0	Scorer unknown
Wed Sep 12	New Brighton	A	Lge	W 2-0	Allen (2)
Sat Sep 15	Formby	H	F.A.Cup 1st Qual. Rd	D 1-1	Flaherty
Tue Sep 18	Formby	A	F.A.Cup replay	L 1-4	Flaherty
Sat Sep 22	Witton Albion	A	Lge	W 4-2	Mick Clarke, O.G., Phil Spencer, Dumican
Wed Sep 26	Oswestry Town	A	Lge	L 2-5	Scorers unknown
Sat Sep 29	Radcliffe Borough	H	Lge	L 1-2	Spencer
Wed Oct 3	Maghull	H	Lancs Challenge Trophy	W 5-1	Flaherty (2), Clarke, Allen (2)
Sat Oct 6	Radcliffe Borough	A	Lge	W 3-0	Spencer (2), Allen
Wed Oct 10	Ormskirk	H	Lge	W 1-0	Dumican
Sat Oct 13	Sandbach Ramblers	H	Lge	D 2-2	Spencer (2)
Sat Oct 20	Droylesden	A	Lge	L 1-3	Flaherty
Wed Oct 24	Lancaster City	A	Lancs Floodlit Trophy	W 2-0	Dumican, Flaherty
Sat Oct 27	Winsford United	H	Lge	L 0-1	
Wed Oct 31	Ormskirk *played at Burscough*	A	Lge Cup 2nd Rd.	W 3-0	Spencer (2), Alan Swift
Sat Nov 3	Nantwich	A	Lge	W 2-0	Swift, Rodney Webb
Sat Nov 10	Prestwich Heys	H	Lge	W 4-2	Swift, Clarke, Dumican, Spencer
Sat Nov 17	Rossendale United	A	Lge	W 2-0	Flaherty, Spencer
Sat Nov 24	Hyde United	H	Lge	W 3-1	Swift, Allen, Webb
Sat Dec 8	Ashton United	H	Lge	W 4-2	Spencer (3), Flaherty
Sun Dec 16	Leek Town	A	Lge	L 1-3	Dumican
Sat Dec 22	Leek Town	H	Lge	W 2-0	Scorers unknown
Wed Dec 26	Marine	A	Lge	D 2-2	Ledgard, Spencer
Sat Dec 29	Winsford United	A	Lge	D 1-1	Flaherty
Tue Jan 1	Marine	H	Lge	L 0-3	
Sat Jan 5	Witton Albion	H	Lge	D 1-1	Lol Armstrong
Sun Jan 6	Morecambe	A	Lancs Challenge Trophy	L 2-3	Flaherty (2)
Sun Jan 13	Mossley	H	F.A.Trophy	W 2-0	Spencer, Flaherty
Sat Jan 19	Oldham Athletic Reserves	H	Lge	W 2-0	Flaherty, Spencer
Sat Jan 26	Horwich RMI	A	Lge	W 2-1	Dumican (2)
Sat Feb 2	South Shields	H	F.A.Trophy	D 1-1	Spencer
Sat Feb 9	South Shields	A	F.A.Trophy replay	L 0-1	
Sat Feb 16	Droylesden	H	Lge	D 1-1	Miller
Sat Feb 23	Rhyl	A	Lge	L 1-2	Frank Rigby
Sat Mar 2	Nantwich	H	Lge	L 1-2	Ledgard
Sun Mar 3	Marine	H	Lpool Senior Non-lge Cup Semi-final	W 2-0	Clarke, Flaherty
Sat Mar 9	Horwich RMI	H	Lge	D 1-1	Armstrong
Sat Mar 16	Ormskirk	A	Lge	W 2-0	Ledgard, Swift
Tue Mar 19	Marine	A	Lge Cup 3rd Rd.	D 1-1	Swift
Sat Mar 23	Oswestry Town	H	Lge	W 2-1	Swift, Spencer
Sun Mar 24	Ashton United	A	Lge	W 2-1	Swift, Flaherty
Sat Mar 30	Rhyl	H	Lge	D 1-1	Scorer unknown
Tue Apr 2	Marine	H	Lge Cup replay	W 3-2	Miller, Ledgard, Flaherty
Sat Apr 6	Sandbach Ramblers	A	Lge	D 2-2	Flaherty, Dumican
Mon Apr 8	Leek Town	H	Lge Cup Semi-final 1st leg	D 1-1	Scorer unknown
Wed Apr 10	Fleetwood	H	Lancs Floodlit Trophy	W 4-2	Swift, Flaherty (3)
Fri Apr 12	Chorley	H	Lge	W 5-0	Flaherty, Swift, Spencer, Dumican, Swarbrick
Sat Apr 13	Formby	A	Lge	L 0-3	
Mon Apr 15	Chorley	A	Lge	L 0-1	
Sat Apr 20	Stalybridge Celtic	H	Lge	D 2-2	Flaherty, Dumican
Tue Apr 23	Leek Town *Attend: 900*	A	Lge Cup Semi-final 2nd leg	W 2-0	Dumican, Spencer
Thu Apr 25	Skelmersdale United	H	Lpool Senior Non-lge Cup Final	L 1-2	Flaherty
Sat Apr 27	Prestwich Heys	A	Lge	W 3-0	Flaherty, Allen, Spencer
Tue Apr 30	Rossendale Utd	H	Lge Cup Final 1st leg	W 3-0	Flaherty, Swift, Dumican
Mon May 6	Rossendale Utd	A	Lge Cup Final 2nd leg	L 0-5	
Wed May 8	Stalybridge Celtic	A	Lge	L 0-1	
Sat May 11	Skelmersdale United	H	Lancs Floodlit Cup Semi-final	L 1-2	Allen

LANCASHIRE COMBINATION - DIVISION ONE
1969-70 SEASON

	P	W	D	L	F	A	Pts
Burscough	38	30	4	4	116	35	64
Prestwich Heys	38	28	5	5	127	46	61
Chorley	38	27	6	5	112	35	60
Kirkby Town	38	25	9	4	98	38	59
Radcliffe Borough	38	22	7	9	84	45	51
Lancaster City	38	22	6	10	84	43	50
Rossendale United	38	22	4	12	96	50	48
St. Helens Town	38	21	4	13	69	42	46
Blackpool Mechanics	38	20	4	14	78	56	44
Darwen	38	15	11	12	78	67	41
Bacup Borough	38	18	5	15	78	72	41
Formby	38	13	7	18	48	71	33
Wigan Athletic Reserves	38	10	9	19	44	61	29
Prescot Town	38	10	6	22	58	85	26
Dukinfield Town	38	6	11	21	49	96	23
Nelson	38	8	5	25	60	106	21
Clitheroe	38	6	7	25	40	107	19
Leyland Motors	38	5	8	25	37	96	18
Lytham St. Annes	38	6	4	28	29	109	16
Wigan Rovers	38	1	8	29	22	147	10

CHESHIRE COUNTY LEAGUE
1971-72 SEASON

	P	W	D	L	F	A	Pts
Rhyl	42	31	4	7	95	33	66
Rossendale United	42	26	5	11	90	65	57
Marine	42	23	9	10	72	48	55
Buxton	42	21	12	9	81	47	54
Oswestry Town	42	21	7	14	84	66	49
Mossley	42	20	7	15	74	55	47
Burscough	42	19	9	14	71	56	47
Hyde United	42	17	10	15	79	72	44
Droylesden	42	16	11	15	77	70	43
Oldham Athletic Res.	42	16	9	17	66	63	41
Stalybridge Celtic	42	16	9	17	68	65	41
Prestwich Heys	42	13	14	15	74	94	40
Horwich RMI	42	16	6	20	61	82	38
Witton Albion	42	17	3	22	75	82	37
Winsford United	42	16	5	21	57	82	37
Ormskirk	42	12	11	19	54	54	35
Sandbach Ramblers	42	11	13	18	51	68	35
Ashton United	42	14	7	21	57	79	35
Radcliffe Borough	42	11	10	21	65	82	32
Formby	42	11	10	21	61	92	32
New Brighton	42	11	8	23	58	96	30
Nantwich	42	12	5	25	59	88	29

CHESHIRE COUNTY LEAGUE
1970-71 SEASON

	P	W	D	L	F	A	Pts
Rossendale United	42	28	11	3	84	39	67
Burscough	42	24	12	6	106	61	60
Skelmersdale United	42	22	12	8	87	48	56
Mossley	42	24	6	12	81	51	54
Ellesmere Port Town	42	16	7	9	56	38	49
Stalybridge Celtic	42	20	7	15	74	59	47
Horwich RMI	42	16	12	14	67	55	44
Buxton	42	18	8	16	69	72	44
Marine	42	16	11	15	66	59	43
Ormskirk	42	17	8	17	62	64	42
Oswestry Town	42	15	12	15	75	81	42
Witton Albion	42	12	17	13	68	68	41
Ashton United	42	15	9	18	65	72	39
Rhyl	42	13	13	16	49	56	39
Sandbach Ramblers	42	14	10	18	54	67	38
Hyde United	42	12	13	17	69	80	37
Oldham Athletic Res.	42	13	9	20	64	74	35
Nantwich Town	42	11	13	18	56	70	35
Droylesden	42	9	16	17	59	72	34
Winsford United	42	10	14	18	55	80	34
Port Vale Reserves	42	7	10	25	39	88	24
New Brighton	42	7	6	29	35	85	20

CHESHIRE COUNTY LEAGUE
1972-73 SEASON

	P	W	D	L	F	A	Pts
Buxton	42	28	8	6	89	32	64
Marine	42	27	7	8	73	36	61
Hyde United	42	22	9	11	75	49	53
Stalybridge Celtic	42	17	19	6	77	55	53
Rossendale United	42	21	9	12	61	39	51
Sandbach Ramblers	42	19	10	13	66	55	48
Burscough	42	17	13	12	63	53	47
Formby	42	17	13	12	60	64	47
Chorley	42	18	9	15	69	50	45
Witton Albion	42	16	11	15	60	48	43
Oldham Athletic Res.	42	16	8	18	60	52	40
New Brighton	42	16	8	18	47	64	40
Oswestry Town	42	12	15	15	75	73	39
Ormskirk	42	12	14	16	53	60	38
Winsford United	42	13	12	17	56	71	38
Rhyl	42	9	16	17	49	70	34
Droylesden	42	11	11	20	62	75	33
Radcliffe Borough	42	11	11	20	58	72	33
Nantwich Town	42	10	12	20	44	69	32
Ashton United	42	12	6	24	61	86	30
Horwich RMI	42	6	16	20	57	83	28
Prestwich Heys	42	9	10	23	47	96	28

1974/75 Season
Cheshire County League

Date	Opponent	H/A	Competition	Result	Scorers
Sat Aug 17	Stalybridge Celtic	H	Lge	W 4-1	Spencer, Bannister (2), Flaherty
Tue Aug 20	Formby	A	Lge Cup 1st Rd.	W 1-0	Flaherty
Sat Aug 24	Rhyl	H	Lge	W 3-0	Allen, Flaherty, Miller
Wed Aug 28	Witton Albion	H	Lge	W 1-0	Dumican
Sat Aug 31	Nantwich	A	Lge	D 1-1	Tony Williams
Tue Sep 3	Horwich RMI	A	Lge	L 1-3	Flaherty
Thu Sep 5	Formby	H	Lpool Senior Non-lge Cup	W 4-0	Armstrong, Spencer (2), Dumican
Sat Sep 7	Winsford United	H	Lge	W 3-2	Bannister, Flaherty, Williams
Wed Sep 11	Formby	H	Lge	L 0-3	
Sat Sep 14	Lancaster City	H	F.A.Cup 1st Qual. Rd	L 0-1	
Sat Sep 21	Oldham Athletic Reserves	A	Lge	W 1-0	Miller
Sat Sep 28	Droylesden	H	Lge	W 5-1	Dumican (2), Williams (2), Spencer
Sat Oct 5	Prestwich Heys	H	Lge	W 5-1	Williams (3), Flaherty, Dumican
Tue Oct 8	Prescot Town	H	Lancs Challenge Trophy	W 4-2	Brian Stokes (2), Spencer, Dumican
Sat Oct 12	Stalybridge Celtic	A	Lge	L 0-1	
Wed Oct 23	Rossendale United	H	Lge	D 0-0	
Sat Oct 26	Witton Albion	A	Lge	W 2-1	Allen, Spencer
Wed Oct 30	Rhyl	H	Lge Cup 2nd Rd.	D 1-1	Spencer
Sat Nov 2	Hyde United	H	Lge	W 3-0	Dumican, Bannister, Williams
Sat Nov 9	Nantwich	H	Lge	W 2-0	Flaherty (2)
Tue Nov 12	Sandbach Ramblers	H	Lge	L 1-2	Flaherty
Sat Nov 16	Ashton United	H	Lge	W 2-0	Bannister, Flaherty
Wed Nov 27	Rhyl	A	Lge Cup replay	W 4-1	Flaherty (2), Dumican, O.G.
Sat Nov 30	Leek Town	H	Lge	D 3-3	Flaherty, Miller, Williams
Sat Dec 7	Radcliffe Borough	A	Lge	W 6-1	Dumican (3), Clarke, Flaherty (2)
Wed Dec 11	Oswestry Town	A	Lge	D 1-1	Spencer
Sat Dec 14	Formby	A	Lge	W 2-1	Spencer, Dumican
Mon Dec 16	South Liverpool	H	Lancs Floodlit Trophy	D 0-0	
Thu Dec 19	Atherton Collieries	H	Lancs Challenge Trophy	W 6-1	Spencer, Dumican (2), Bannister, Flaherty (2)
Sat Dec 21	New Brighton	H	Lge	D 0-0	
Thu Dec 26	Marine	A	Lge	L 0-1	
Sat Dec 28	Rhyl	A	Lge	W 3-0	Flaherty, Dumican, Stokes
Wed Jan 1	Marine	H	Lge	L 0-1	
Sat Jan 4	Oswestry Town	H	Lge	W 1-0	Dumican
Sat Jan 11	Bangor City	H	F.A.Trophy	D 1-1	Spencer
Wed Jan 15	Bangor City	A	F.A.Trophy replay	W 2-1	Spencer (2)
	Attend: 514				
Thu Jan 23	South Liverpool	A	Lancs Floodlit Trophy replay	W 2-1	Flaherty, Dumican
	played at Burscough				
Sat Jan 25	Droylesden	H	Lge	W 3-0	Williams, Dumican, Spencer
Sat Feb 1	Matlock Town	H	F.A.Trophy	D 1-1	Flaherty
Tue Feb 4	Matlock Town	A	F.A.Trophy replay	L 1-3	Spencer
	Attend: 1,085				
Sat Feb 8	Sandbach Ramblers	A	Lge	L 1-2	Miller
Mon Feb 10	Marine	H	Lancs Challenge Trophy	W 2-0	Flaherty (2)
Wed Feb 12	Skelmersdale United	H	Lpool Senior Non-lge Cup Semi-final	L 1-2	Flaherty
Sat Feb 15	Horwich RMI	H	Lge	D 1-1	Spencer
Sat Feb 22	Hyde United	A	Lge	W 3-1	Flaherty, Dumican, Spencer
Thu Feb 27	New Brighton	H	Lge Cup	W 1-0	Ledgard
Mon Mar 3	Lancaster City	A	Lancs Challenge Trophy Semi-final	L 1-2	Flaherty
Sat Mar 8	Ashton United	A	Lge	L 0-1	
Sun Mar 9	Skelmersdale United	H	Lancs Floodlit Trophy Semi-final	W 1-0	Swift
Wed Mar 12	New Mills	H	Lge Cup Semi-final 1st leg	W 2-1	Dumican, Flaherty
Sat Mar 15	New Mills	A	Lge Cup Semi-final 2nd leg	W 1-0	Dumican
Wed Mar 19	New Mills	H	Lge	W 2-0	Stokes, Flaherty
Sat Mar 22	Leek Town	A	Lge	L 1-2	Dumican
Tue Mar 25	New Mills	A	Lge	D 1-1	Stokes
Fri Mar 28	Chorley	A	Lge	L 1-3	Dave Shannon
Sat Mar 29	Radcliffe Borough	H	Lge	W 4-1	Spencer, Flaherty, Dumican, Miller
Mon Mar 31	Chorley	H	Lge	D 1-1	Dumican
Sat Apr 5	Oldham Athletic Reserves	H	Lge	D 0-0	
Wed Apr 9	Prestwich Heys	A	Lge	L 1-2	Dumican
Thu Apr 10	Great Harwood	H	Lancs Floodlit Trophy Final 1st leg	D 0-0	
Sat Apr 12	New Brighton	A	Lge	D 1-1	Spencer
Mon Apr 14	Marine	H	Lge Cup Final 1st leg	D 1-1	Spencer
Thu Apr 17	Great Harwood	A	Lancs Floodlit Trophy Final 2nd leg	L 3-5	Flaherty (2), Spencer
Sat Apr 19	Marine	A	Lge Cup Final 2nd leg	W 1-0	Flaherty
Tue Apr 22	Rossendale United	A	Lge	L 0-4	
Sat Apr 26	Winsford United	A	Lge	L 0-5	

1975/76 Season
Cheshire County League

Date	Opponent	H/A	Competition	Result	Scorers
Sat Aug 16	Middlewich Athletic	A	Lge	L 0-3	
Wed Aug 20	Formby	H	Lge Cup	D 0-0	
Sat Aug 23	Witton Albion	H	Lge	L 0-1	
Tue Aug 26	Formby	A	Lge	L 1-3	Shannon
Thu Aug 28	Formby	A	Lge Cup replay	W 3-1	John Foy, Spencer, Robinson
Sat Aug 30	Great Harwood	A	F.A.Cup Prelim. Rd	L 1-2	Foy
Wed Sep 3	Rhyl	A	Lge	D 2-2	O.G., Bannister
Sat Sep 6	Prestwich Heys	H	Lge	W 2-1	Spencer, Foy
Tue Sep 9	St. Helens Town	H	Lge	W 1-0	Spencer
Sat Sep 13	Middlewich Athletic	H	Lge	L 0-1	
Wed Sep 17	Formby	H	Lge	W 6-0	Foy, Spencer (2), John Davies, Miller, Dumican
Sat Sep 20	Winsford United	A	Lge	D 1-1	O.G.
Sat Sep 27	Ashton United	A	Lge	W 2-1	Foy, Dumican
Sat Oct 4	Stalybridge Celtic	H	Lge	W 2-1	Dumican, Davies
Wed Oct 8	Formby	H	Lpool Senior Non-lge Cup	W 2-1	Steve Evans, Dumican
Sat Oct 11	Droylesden	A	Lge	L 1-2	Bannister
Sat Oct 18	Horwich RMI	H	Lge	D 2-2	Dumican, Spencer
Sat Oct 25	New Mills	A	Lge	W 1-0	Evans
Sat Nov 1	Nantwich	A	Lge	L 2-4	Dumican, Miller
Sat Nov 8	St. Helens Town	A	Lge	L 1-5	Foy
Sat Nov 15	Hyde United	A	Lge	W 5-1	Spencer (2), Miller, Evans (2)
Sat Nov 22	Leek Town	H	Lge	L 0-3	
Sat Nov 29	Radcliffe Borough	H	Lge	W 4-2	Spencer (2), Dumican (2)
Wed Dec 3	Nantwich	H	Lge	W 3-2	Foy (2), Spencer
Sat Dec 6	New Brighton	A	Lge	D 2-2	Foy, Swift
Wed Dec 10	Rossendale United	H	Lge	D 2-2	Swift, Foy
Sat Dec 13	Darwen	A	Lge	D 2-2	Glover, Swift
Sat Dec 20	Winsford United	H	Lge	L 1-2	Swift
Fri Dec 26	Marine	A	Lge	L 0-3	
Thu Jan 1	Marine	H	Lge	L 0-1	
Sat Jan 3	Witton Albion	A	Lge	L 0-4	
Sat Jan 10	Stafford Rangers	A	F.A.Trophy	L 0-4	
	Attend: 2,300				
Sat Jan 17	Prestwich Heys	A	Lge	W 2-1	Dumican, Foy
Sat Jan 24	Ashton United	H	Lge	L 0-1	
Sat Jan 31	Rhyl	H	Lge	D 1-1	Spencer
Sat Feb 7	New Brighton	H	Lge	W 4-2	Evans, Miller, Spencer (2)
Sat Feb 14	Droylesden	H	Lge	L 1-3	Spencer
Sat Feb 21	Horwich RMI	A	Lge	D 1-1	Swift
Tue Feb 24	Stalybridge Celtic	A	Lge Cup	L 0-1	
Sat Feb 28	New Mills	H	Lge	W 1-0	Spencer
Sat Mar 6	Rossendale United	A	Lge	W 2-1	Kenny Crisp, Dumican
Tue Mar 9	Stalybridge Celtic	A	Lge	W 2-1	Tommy Cheetham, Spencer
Sun Mar 14	Marine	A	Lpool Senior Non-lge Cup Semi-final	L 1-2	Spencer
Wed Mar 17	Darwen	H	Lge	W 3-1	Spencer (2), Swift
Sat Mar 20	Hyde United	H	Lge	D 1-1	Dave Griffiths
Sat Mar 27	Leek Town	A	Lge	L 1-4	Cheetham
Sat Apr 3	Radcliffe Borough	A	Lge	W 3-2	John Beesley, Bannister, Dumican
Fri Apr 16	Chorley	A	Lge	D 0-0	
Mon Apr 19	Chorley	H	Lge	L 2-4	O.G., Spencer

CHESHIRE COUNTY LEAGUE 1973-74 SEASON

	P	W	D	L	F	A	Pts
Marine	42	28	8	6	79	26	64
Rossendale United	42	29	6	7	87	39	64
Chorley	42	23	11	8	68	39	57
Leek Town	42	23	11	8	75	49	57
Sandbach Ramblers	42	19	16	7	66	40	54
Burscough	**42**	**19**	**10**	**13**	**70**	**54**	**48**
Formby	42	17	12	13	62	53	46
Stalybridge Celtic	42	17	12	13	65	63	46
Witton Albion	42	14	17	11	57	48	45
Oldham Athletic Res.	42	15	11	16	53	49	41
Winsford United	42	12	16	14	51	51	40
Radcliffe Borough	42	12	15	15	57	67	39
Droylesden	42	13	12	17	57	68	38
New Brighton	42	16	6	20	52	63	38
Rhyl	42	14	10	18	67	82	38
Hyde United	42	14	8	20	65	67	36
Oswestry Town	42	12	12	18	61	78	36
Nantwich Town	42	8	13	21	57	82	29
Ashton United	42	11	7	24	59	97	29
Ormskirk	42	9	9	24	52	74	27
Horwich RMI	42	10	7	25	51	88	27
Prestwich Heys	42	7	11	24	54	88	25

CHESHIRE COUNTY LEAGUE 1975-76 SEASON

	P	W	D	L	F	A	Pts
Marine	42	28	8	6	94	34	64
Chorley	42	29	5	8	88	33	63
Leek Town	42	27	7	8	74	33	61
Winsford United	42	24	10	8	83	44	58
Witton Albion	42	20	14	8	71	37	54
Nantwich Town	42	23	8	11	88	54	54
Middlewich Athletic	42	20	8	14	61	51	48
Stalybridge Celtic	42	20	6	16	67	47	46
Droylesden	42	17	11	14	66	55	45
New Brighton	42	19	7	16	59	57	45
Rossendale United	42	17	9	16	69	62	43
Burscough	**42**	**16**	**10**	**16**	**68**	**73**	**42**
Hyde United	42	15	11	16	73	75	41
St. Helens Town	42	14	11	17	54	57	39
Formby	42	10	15	17	44	59	35
Ashton United	42	13	8	21	50	63	34
Radcliffe Borough	42	13	5	24	56	94	31
Horwich RMI	42	8	13	21	42	90	29
Rhyl	42	8	10	24	46	83	26
Darwen	42	9	7	26	49	89	25
New Mills	42	8	6	28	47	95	22
Prestwich Heys	42	6	7	29	39	103	19

CHESHIRE COUNTY LEAGUE 1974-75 SEASON

	P	W	D	L	F	A	Pts
Leek Town	42	27	9	6	92	49	63
Winsford United	42	26	9	7	108	58	61
Sandbach Ramblers	42	21	15	6	80	56	57
Oldham Athletic Res.	42	24	8	10	85	43	56
Marine	42	24	7	11	73	40	55
Chorley	42	19	11	12	86	68	49
Burscough	**42**	**19**	**10**	**13**	**70**	**49**	**48**
Rossendale United	42	17	13	12	77	64	47
Formby	42	16	13	13	55	55	45
Oswestry Town	42	16	10	16	56	52	42
Horwich RMI	42	17	7	18	60	59	41
New Mills	42	14	11	17	68	82	39
Stalybridge Celtic	42	14	10	18	66	69	38
Rhyl	42	14	10	18	72	78	38
New Brighton	42	12	14	16	53	60	38
Witton Albion	42	10	17	15	59	69	37
Droylesden	42	14	8	20	53	78	36
Nantwich Town	42	9	14	19	63	87	32
Ashton United	42	11	7	24	43	86	29
Hyde United	42	9	8	25	62	80	26
Radcliffe Borough	42	6	12	24	50	97	24
Prestwich Heys	42	8	7	27	48	100	23

CHESHIRE COUNTY LEAGUE 1976-77 SEASON

	P	W	D	L	F	A	Pts
Winsford United	42	31	8	3	98	41	70
Chorley	42	28	6	8	80	35	62
Witton Albion	42	27	6	9	91	32	60
Leek Town	42	24	10	8	91	37	58
Stalybridge Celtic	42	23	10	9	66	44	56
Nantwich	42	22	7	13	72	59	51
Marine	42	18	14	10	62	40	50
Horwich RMI	42	18	10	14	72	58	46
Formby	42	17	9	16	59	56	43
St. Helens Town	42	16	10	16	51	58	42
New Brighton	42	13	14	15	64	59	40
Ashton United	42	15	10	17	65	72	40
Prestwich Heys	42	16	8	18	56	63	40
Burscough	**42**	**12**	**15**	**15**	**60**	**65**	**39**
Rhyl	42	13	9	20	54	69	35
Droylesden	42	13	8	21	60	78	34
Hyde United	42	12	9	21	57	74	33
New Mills	42	10	10	22	47	67	30
Darwen	42	10	8	24	49	81	28
Rossendale United	42	9	10	23	48	85	28
Middlewich Athletic	42	9	4	29	48	108	22
Radcliffe Borough	42	4	9	29	44	113	17

1976/77 Season
Cheshire County League

Date	Opponent	H/A	Comp	Result	Scorers
Sat Aug 21	Droylesden	H	Lge	W 1-0	Beesley
Tue Aug 24	Formby	A	Lge	L 2-3	Stokes, Keith Barlow
Sat Aug 28	Winsford United	A	Lge	L 2-3	Barlow, Glover
Wed Sep 1	Darwen	H	Lge	D 1-1	Cheetham
Sat Sep 4	Horwich RMI	H	Lge	W 2-1	Beesley, Barlow
Tue Sep 7	St. Helens Town	A	League Cup	W 4-1	Stokes (3), Spencer
Sat Sep 11	Stalybridge Celtic	A	Lge	D 1-1	Barlow
Wed Sep 15	New Brighton	H	Lge	L 1-3	Jimmy Flanagan
Sat Sep 18	Winsford United	A	F.A.Cup 1st Qual. Rd	D 0-0	
Wed Sep 22	Winsford United	H	F.A.Cup replay	L 1-3	Flanagan
Sat Sep 25	Witton Albion	A	Lge	L 1-2	Jeff Larner
Sat Oct 2	Nantwich	A	Lge	L 0-2	
Sat Oct 9	Middlewich Athletic	H	Lge	D 1-1	Larner
Sat Oct 16	Ashton United	A	Lge	D 3-3	Spencer (2), Larner
Sat Oct 23	Leek Town	H	Lge	W 2-1	Stokes, Beesley
Sat Oct 30	Marine	A	Lge	L 1-3	Dumican
Wed Nov 17	Horwich RMI	H	Lancs Junior Cup	D 1-1	Steve Tickle
Sat Nov 20	Horwich RMI	A	Lancs Junior Cup replay	L 3-4	Beesley, Larner, Spencer
Wed Nov 24	New Brighton	H	Lpool Senior Non-lge Cup	L 3-4	Spencer, Barlow, John Quinn
Sat Nov 27	Hyde United	H	Lge	W 3-2	Dumican, Bannister, Tickle
Wed Dec 1	Prestwich Heys	H	Lge	W 3-2	Dumican (2), Larner
Wed Dec 8	New Mills	H	Lge	D 0-0	
Sat Dec 18	South Liverpool	A	F.A.Trophy	L 0-5	
Mon Dec 27	New Mills	A	Lge	W 2-0	Dumican, Stokes
Sat Jan 1	Darwen	A	Lge	W 1-0	Griffiths
Sat Jan 8	Droylesden	A	Lge	L 3-4	Stokes, Griffiths (2)
Sat Jan 15	Radcliffe Borough	A	Lge	D 3-3	Bannister, Dumican, Griffiths
Sat Jan 22	Horwich RMI	A	Lge	W 2-1	Glover, Griffiths
Sat Jan 29	New Brighton	A	Lge	W 4-1	Bannister, Stokes (3)
Sat Feb 5	Nantwich	H	Lge	D 1-1	Stokes
Sat Feb 12	Middlewich Athletic	A	Lge	W 4-0	Glover, Bannister (2), Hutchinson
Tue Feb 15	Marine	H	Lge	L 0-2	
Sat Feb 19	Ashton United	H	Lge	L 0-1	
Tue Feb 22	Winsford United	H	Lge	D 1-1	Griffiths
Sat Feb 26	Leek Town	A	Lge	L 1-3	Stokes
Wed Mar 2	Formby	H	Lge	D 1-1	Stokes
Sat Mar 5	Witton Albion	H	Lge	L 0-1	
Wed Mar 9	Radcliffe Borough	H	Lge	D 2-2	Jeff Stanton, Glover
Sat Mar 19	Prestwich Heys	A	Lge	L 1-2	Bannister
Wed Mar 23	Darwen	H	League Cup Q/F	L 0-1	
Sat Mar 26	Rossendale United	H	Lge	D 1-1	Flanagan
Tue Mar 29	Rhyl	A	Lge	D 1-1	Tickle
Sat Apr 2	Hyde United	A	Lge	L 0-1	
Tue Apr 5	Chorley	A	Lge	L 0-3	
Sat Apr 9	Rossendale United	A	Lge	D 0-0	
Mon Apr 11	Chorley	H	Lge	W 1-0	Dumican
Sat Apr 16	Stalybridge Celtic	H	Lge	W 2-1	Bannister, Flanagan
Sat Apr 23	Rhyl	H	Lge	D 2-2	O.G., Beesley
Tue Apr 26	St. Helens Town	H	Lge	L 1-3	Dave Watson
Sat May 7	St. Helens Town	A	Lge	D 2-2	Beesley (2)

1976-77 Season. Back left to right: Unknown, Ian Crossley, Geoff Clarke (Secretary), Bob Jones (Manager), Frank Parr (Chairman), Charlie Bannister, Jeff Stanton, Kenny Dumican, Unknown.
Front left to right: Graham Glover, Brian Stokes, Unknown, Kenny Miller, Steve Tickle, Micky Deitz, Unknown.

1977-78 Season. Back left to right: Billy Jaycock, John Durnin, Al Bowen, Tony Metcalfe, Mike Lawson, Vinny McGrady, Jeff Stanton, Tony Shallcross, George Rooney (Manager).
Front left to right: Larry Garrity, Graham Glover, Unknown, Alex Blakeman, Unknown.

1977/78 Season
Cheshire County League

Date	Opponent	H/A	Comp	Result	Scorers
Sat Aug 20	Darwen	H	Lge	D 1-1	Billy Jaycock
Tue Aug 23	Horwich RMI	A	Lge	L 2-5	Jaycock, Larry Garrity
Sat Aug 27	Middlewich Athletic	H	Lge	W 3-0	Tony Shallcross (2), Jaycock
Wed Aug 31	Formby	A	Lge	D 0-0	
Sat Sep 3	Rhyl	A	Lge	W 2-0	Garrity, Jaycock
Tue Sep 6	Formby	H	Lge	D 0-0	
Sat Sep 10	St. Helens Town	A	Lge	L 0-1	
Wed Sep 14	New Brighton	H	Lge	L 0-1	
Sat Sep 17	Accrington Stanley	H	F.A.Cup 1st Qual. Rd	D 2-2	Garrity (2)
Wed Sep 21	Accrington Stanley	A	F.A.Cup replay	W 1-0	Garrity
Sat Sep 24	New Mills	H	Lge	D 0-0	
Sat Oct 1	Hyde United	A	Lge	D 1-1	Charlie Bannister
Sat Oct 8	Great Harwood	A	F.A.Cup 2nd Qual. Rd	W 1-0	Garrity
Sat Oct 15	New Brighton	A	F.A.Trophy	L 0-1	
Sat Oct 22	Chorley	H	F.A.Cup 3rd Qual. Rd	W 3-0	Jaycock (2), Garrity
	Attend: 625				
Wed Oct 26	Nantwich	H	Lge	D 1-1	Griffiths
Sat Oct 29	Radcliffe Borough	H	Lge	W 3-1	Jaycock, Griffiths, Shallcross
Sat Nov 5	Morecambe	H	F.A.Cup 4th Qual. Rd	D 0-0	
Tue Nov 8	Morecambe	A	F.A.Cup replay	W 1-0	Jaycock
	Attend: 540				
Sat Nov 12	Rossendale United	H	Lge	W 3-0	John Durnin, O.G., Garrity
Tue Nov 15	Stalybridge Celtic	H	Lge	W 3-1	Jaycock (2), Ronnie Madine
Sat Nov 26	Blyth Spartans	A	F.A.Cup 1st Round	L 0-1	
Sat Dec 3	Prescot Town	A	Liverpool Senior Cup	W 1-0	Durnin
Sat Dec 10	Ashton United	A	Lge	L 0-3	
Sat Dec 17	Witton Albion	H	Lge	D 3-3	Shallcross, Jaycock, Garrity
Mon Dec 26	Marine	A	Lge	L 1-2	Jaycock
Tue Dec 27	St. Helens Town	H	Lge	W 2-1	
Sat Dec 31	Middlewich Athletic	A	Lge	L 2-4	Scorers unknown
Mon Jan 2	Marine	H	Lge	D 1-1	Garrity
	Attend: 400				
Sat Jan 7	New Mills	A	Lge	L 1-2	O.G.
Sat Jan 14	Rhyl	H	Lge	D 2-2	John Moran, Jaycock
Tue Jan 17	St. Helens Town	H	Liverpool Senior Cup	W 2-0	Jaycock, Stokes
Sat Jan 21	Nantwich	A	Lge	L 2-4	Scorers unknown
Tue Feb 7	St. Helens Town	H	Lge Cup 1st Rd	L 2-3	Garrity, Jaycock
Sat Feb 18	Hyde United	H	Lge	D 1-1	Moran
Tue Feb 21	Ashton United	H	Lge	L 1-2	O'Connor
Sat Feb 25	Stalybridge Celtic	A	Lge	L 0-2	
Sat Mar 4	Rossendale United	A	Lge	W 2-0	Scorers unknown
Mon Mar 6	Droylesden	A	Lge	L 1-3	Scorer unknown
Sat Mar 11	Radcliffe Borough	A	Lge	W 1-0	Moran
Fri Mar 24	Chorley	H	Lge	W 3-2	Moran, Jaycock, Wilson
Sat Mar 25	New Brighton	A	Lge	W 1-0	Scorer unknown
Mon Mar 27	Chorley	A	Lge	L 1-3	Moran
Wed Mar 29	Winsford United	H	Lge	L 1-3	Scorer unknown
Sat Apr 1	Horwich RMI	H	Lge	W 2-0	Russ Thomas (2)
Sat Apr 8	Darwen	A	Lge	D 1-1	Moran
Mon Apr 10	Prestwich Heys	A	Lge	L 0-1	
Thu Apr 13	Formby	H	Liverpool Senior Cup Semi-final	L 0-1	
Sat Apr 15	Droylesden	H	Lge	L 0-1	
Mon Apr 17	Winsford United	A	Lge	L 0-2	
Sat Apr 22	Leek Town	H	Lge	W 3-0	Turner, Moran, Jaycock
Tue Apr 25	Leek Town	A	Lge	L 0-4	
Sat Apr 29	Witton Albion	A	Lge	D 2-2	Scorers unknown
Thu May 4	Prestwich Heys	H	Lge	W 3-2	Scorers unknown

Another 1977-78 line-up. Back left to right: Billy Jaycock, Larry Garrity, Amby Clarke, Mike Lawson, Al Bowen, John Moran, Vinny McGrady. Front left to right: Dave Griffiths, John Durnin, Graham Glover, Ronnie Madine, Tony Shallcross, Barry Beesley. Amby Clarke made almost 200 Football League appearances for Southport prior to joining Burscough. Barry Beesley managed the Burscough Youth team in 1995-96 season.

CHESHIRE COUNTY LEAGUE 1977-78 SEASON

	P	W	D	L	F	A	Pts
Marine	42	26	10	6	101	48	62
Stalybridge Celtic	42	23	12	7	75	47	58
Witton Albion	42	21	14	7	98	54	56
Hyde United	42	21	13	8	68	37	55
Winsford United	42	24	7	11	80	51	55
Ashton United	42	20	13	9	88	56	53
Horwich RMI	42	19	14	9	62	50	52
Leek Town	42	20	10	12	62	45	50
Chorley	42	19	11	12	69	48	49
Formby	42	18	11	13	71	57	47
Middlewich Athletic	42	15	15	12	67	66	45
St. Helens Town	42	15	15	12	53	55	45
Droylesden	42	15	10	17	54	56	40
Burscough	**42**	**13**	**12**	**17**	**56**	**63**	**38**
Darwen	42	14	6	22	50	68	34
Nantwich Town	42	9	13	20	56	69	31
Rhyl	42	10	10	22	44	67	30
New Brighton	42	10	10	22	35	69	30
New Mills	42	9	9	24	42	72	27
Rossendale United	42	11	4	27	51	110	26
Prestwich Heys	42	6	9	27	42	88	21
Radcliffe Borough	42	7	6	29	46	94	20

CHESHIRE COUNTY LEAGUE - DIVISION ONE 1978-79 SEASON

	P	W	D	L	F	A	Pts
Horwich RMI	42	35	2	5	89	45	72
Witton Albion	42	30	4	8	114	38	64
Marine	42	29	5	8	104	38	63
Stalybridge Celtic	42	25	5	12	93	47	55
Burscough	**42**	**19**	**15**	**8**	**59**	**31**	**53**
Winsford United	42	21	11	10	74	49	53
Chorley	42	21	8	13	66	43	50
Formby	42	20	9	13	73	57	49
Leek Town	42	19	10	13	62	43	48
Droylesden	42	18	9	15	62	61	45
Nantwich Town	42	18	8	16	76	72	44
Fleetwood Town	42	17	10	15	70	68	44
Hyde United	42	15	12	15	59	57	42
St. Helens Town	42	16	9	17	59	57	41
Darwen	42	15	9	18	52	53	39
Rhyl	42	15	8	19	53	60	38
Ashton United	42	13	5	24	63	94	31
New Mills	42	9	11	22	58	82	29
Rossendale United	42	11	6	25	51	108	28
Radcliffe Borough	42	4	7	31	37	115	15
New Brighton	42	3	5	34	36	115	11
Middlewich Athletic	42	3	4	35	43	120	10

274

1978/79 Season
Cheshire County League (Division One)

Date	Opponent	H/A	Comp	Result	Scorers
Sat Aug 19	Horwich RMI	A	Lge	L 1-2	Jaycock
Tue Aug 22	Fleetwood	A	Lge	W 2-1	Scorers unknown
Sat Aug 26	Rhyl	A	Lge	W 2-0	Scorers unknown
Tue Aug 29	Formby	A	Lge	W 1-0	Tony Duffy
Sat Sep 2	Mossley	A	F.A.Cup Prelim. Rd	L 1-2	Scorer unknown
Tue Sep 5	Darwen	A	Lge	D 0-0	
Sat Sep 9	Darwen	H	Lge Cup 1st Rd	L 1-2	Scorer unknown
Tue Sep 12	Radcliffe Borough	H	Lge	W 5-1	Jaycock (4), Duffy
Sat Sep 16	Nantwich	A	Lge	W 1-0	Scorer unknown
Tue Sep 19	New Brighton	H	Lge	W 2-1	Ronnie Moogan, Dave Pearson
Sat Sep 23	Middlewich Athletic	H	Lge	W 3-2	Pearson, Jaycock, Moogan
Tue Sep 26	Hyde United	H	Lge	W 3-1	Jaycock (3)
Sat Sep 30	Ashton United	A	Lge	L 1-2	Duffy
Sat Oct 7	Nantwich	H	Lge	D 0-0	
Sat Oct 14	Rhyl	H	F.A.Trophy	W 1-0	Bannister
Sat Oct 21	New Mills	A	Lge	D 2-2	Jaycock (2)
Tue Oct 24	Leek Town	A	Lge	D 0-0	
Sat Oct 28	Hyde United	A	Lge	D 1-1	Jaycock
Sat Nov 4	Rossendale United	H	Lge	W 6-0	Alex Blakeman, Syl Nolan (2), 3 unknown
Sat Nov 11	Barrow	H	F.A.Trophy	L 2-3	Jaycock (2)
Tue Nov 14	St. Helens Town	H	Lge	D 0-0	
Sat Nov 18	Kirkby Town	H	Liverpool Senior Cup	L 1-4	O.G.
Sat Nov 25	Winsford United	H	Lge	D 1-1	Moran
Sat Dec 16	Radcliffe Borough	A	Lge	W 1-0	Scorer unknown
Tue Dec 26	Marine	H	Lge	D 0-0	
Sat Dec 30	Leek Town	H	Lge	D 2-2	Scorers unknown
Sat Feb 3	Droylesden	H	Lge	L 1-3	Nolan
Tue Feb 20	Darwen	H	Lge	W 3-0	John Shergold (2), Nolan
Sat Feb 24	Fleetwood	H	Lge	W 4-1	Nolan, Duffy (2), Graham Tobin
Tue Feb 27	Ashton United	H	Lge	L 1-2	Duffy
Sat Mar 3	New Mills	H	Lge	W 3-1	Moogan (2), Doherty
Tue Mar 6	Formby	H	Lge	L 0-1	
Sat Mar 10	St. Helens Town	A	Lge	D 0-0	
Wed Mar 14	Winsford United	A	Lge	D 1-1	Scorer unknown
Sat Mar 24	Droylesden	A	Lge	W 2-0	Jaycock, Doherty
Sat Mar 31	Horwich RMI	H	Lge	L 0-1	
Tue Apr 3	Stalybridge Celtic	H	Lge	D 0-0	
Sat Apr 7	Stalybridge Celtic	A	Lge	W 1-0	Moran
Fri Apr 13	Marine	A	Lge	W 1-0	Duffy
Sat Apr 14	Witton Albion	H	Lge	D 1-1	Nolan
Mon Apr 16	Chorley	H	Lge	L 0-1	
Sat Apr 21	Rhyl	H	Lge	D 0-0	
Tue Apr 24	Rossendale United	A	Lge	D 1-1	Scorer unknown
Thu Apr 26	Chorley	A	Lge	W 2-0	Nolan, Doherty
Sat Apr 28	Middlewich Athletic	A	Lge	W 2-1	Jaycock, Tickle
Wed May 2	New Brighton	A	Lge	W 1-0	Duffy
Sat May 5	Witton Albion	A	Lge	L 1-2	Duffy

1979/80 Season
Cheshire County League (Division One)

Date	Opponent	H/A	Competition	Result	Scorers
Sat Aug 18	Formby	A	Lge	W 1-0	Scorer unknown
Tue Aug 21	Droylesden	H	Lge	W 3-1	Andy Gray, Jaycock, Nolan
Sat Aug 25	Chorley	H	Lge	D 1-1	Jaycock
Sat Sep 1	Bootle	A	Lge	L 1-2	Scorer unknown
Tue Sep 4	Leek Town	H	Lge	W 4-1	Jaycock (2), Steve Taylor, Ronnie Ellis
Sat Sep 8	Nantwich	H	Lge	D 0-0	
Sat Sep 15	Chorley	H	F.A.Cup 1st Qual. Rd.	W 6-1	Moran (2), Jimmy Lundon, Jaycock, Nolan, Ellis
Sat Sep 22	Rossendale United	A	Lge Cup 2nd Rd.	W 1-0	Ellis
Sat Sep 29	Hyde United	H	Lge	D 1-1	Keith Garland
Sat Oct 6	Netherfield	A	F.A.Cup 2nd Qual. Rd.	W 2-0	Jaycock, Duffy
Sat Oct 13	Workington	H	F.A.Trophy	L 0-1	
Sat Oct 20	Rossendale United	A	F.A.Cup 3rd Qual. Rd	W 4-0	Taylor, Jaycock, Steve Tickle, Nolan
Sat Oct 27	St. Helens Town	A	Lge	D 0-0	
Sat Nov 3	Horden Colliery Welfare	A	F.A.Cup 4th Qual. Rd.	W 2-0	Moran, Tommy Reed
Sat Nov 10	Curzon Ashton	H	Lge	D 2-2	Tickle, 1 unknown
Sat Nov 17	Kirkby Town	H	Lpool Senior Cup	W 3-2	Taylor, Nolan, Moran
Sat Nov 24	Sheffield United		F.A.Cup 1st Round	L 0-3	
	switched to Bramall Lane				
	Attend: 14,209 - Gate £18,000				
Sat Dec 1	Rhyl	A	Lge	D 1-1	Flaherty
Tue Dec 4	St. Helens Town	H	Lge	W 4-3	Flaherty, O.G., Lundon, Ellis
Tue Dec 11	Stalybridge Celtic	A	Lge	W 4-1	Flaherty, Lundon, Ellis, Moran
Sat Dec 15	Nelson	A	Lancs Junior Cup	W 5-0	Ellis, Lundon, Taylor (2), Blakeman
	played at Burscough				
Sat Dec 29	Bootle	H	Lge	L 1-2	Taylor
Sat Jan 5	Marine	A	Lancs Junior Cup	L 0-1	
Tue Jan 15	Ashton United	H	Lge	W 3-1	Duffy, Ellis, Jaycock
Tue Jan 22	Horwich RMI	H	Lge	W 2-0	Taylor, Nolan
Sat Jan 26	Hyde United	A	Lge	D 3-3	Ellis, Reed (2)
Tue Jan 29	Chorley	A	Lge	L 0-2	
Sat Feb 2	New Mills	H	Lge	L 1-2	O.G.
Sat Feb 9	Leek Town	A	Lge	L 1-3	Scorer unknown
Sat Mar 1	Droylesden	A	Lge	L 1-4	Scorer unknown
Tue Mar 4	Everton	H	Lpool Senior Cup 2nd Rd	D 0-0	
Sat Mar 8	Darwen	A	Lge	W 3-0	Scorers unknown
Tue Mar 11	Radcliffe Borough	H	Lge	W 2-0	Duffy, Ellis
Sat Mar 15	Curzon Ashton	A	Lge Cup 3rd Rd.	W 3-2	Scorers unknown
Tue Mar 18	Everton		Lpool Senior Cup replay	W 3-1	Duffy, Ellis, Taylor
Thu Mar 20	Rossendale United	H	Lge	W 3-1	Scorers unknown
Sat Mar 22	Nantwich	A	Lge	W 3-1	Scorers unknown
Tue Mar 25	Stalybridge Celtic	H	Lge	L 2-3	Ellis, Nolan
Thu Mar 27	Rossendale United	A	Lge	W 5-0	Scorers unknown
Tue Apr 1	Chorley	A	Lge Cup 4th Rd.	L 0-2	
Fri Apr 4	Winsford United	A	Lge	D 1-1	Carroll
Sat Apr 5	Horwich RMI	A	Lge	D 0-0	
Mon Apr 7	Darwen	H	Lge	W 2-1	Duffy, Nolan
Sat Apr 12	Winsford United	H	Lge	W 1-0	Scorer unknown
Tue Apr 15	Liverpool	H	Liverpool Senior Cup Semi-Final	L 1-2	Blakeman
Sat Apr 19	Fleetwood	A	Lge	L 0-3	
Sat Apr 26	New Mills	A	Lge	L 0-4	
Wed Apr 30	Formby	H	Lge	L 1-2	Scorer unknown
Sat May 3	Radcliffe Borough	A	Lge	W 6-2	Scorers unknown
Mon May 5	Curzon Ashton	A	Lge	W 1-0	Scorer unknown
Sat May 10	Fleetwood	H	Lge	L 0-3	
	Rhyl	H	Lge	D 1-1	Scorer unknown
	Ashton United	A	Lge	D 2-2	Scorers unknown

CHESHIRE COUNTY LEAGUE - DIVISION ONE
1979-80 SEASON

	P	W	D	L	F	A	Pts
Stalybridge Celtic	38	26	7	5	94	46	59
Winsford United	38	23	6	9	72	41	52
Chorley	38	20	11	7	60	35	51
Ashton United	38	15	15	8	71	65	45
Burscough	**38**	**16**	**11**	**11**	**67**	**54**	**43**
Hyde United	38	16	10	12	60	48	42
Droylesden	38	15	10	13	63	45	40
Horwich RMI	38	13	12	13	53	52	38
Curzon Ashton	38	11	14	13	48	55	36
Darwen	38	12	12	14	41	52	36
Rossendale United	38	12	12	14	48	73	36
St. Helens Town	38	10	15	13	59	55	35
Bootle	38	14	7	17	50	53	35
Nantwich Town	38	14	7	17	53	62	35
New Mills	38	11	13	14	44	57	35
Formby	38	13	7	18	50	58	33
Fleetwood Town	38	10	11	17	51	63	31
Leek Town	38	10	9	19	45	66	29
Rhyl	38	10	7	21	54	66	27
Radcliffe Borough	38	6	10	22	45	82	22

CHESHIRE COUNTY LEAGUE - DIVISION ONE
1981-82 SEASON

	P	W	D	L	F	A	Pts
Hyde United	38	27	8	3	91	34	62
Chorley	38	23	9	6	70	34	55
Burscough	**38**	**21**	**10**	**7**	**70**	**39**	**52**
Winsford United	38	21	9	8	68	43	51
Rossendale United	38	18	10	10	62	44	46
Glossop	38	13	19	6	52	30	45
Darwen	38	16	10	12	63	62	40*
Curzon Ashton	38	12	15	11	57	50	39
Prescot Cables	38	16	8	14	51	45	38*
Stalybridge Celtic	38	14	9	15	71	66	37
Fleetwood Town	38	12	13	13	42	55	37
Formby	38	12	11	15	42	55	35
Accrington Stanley	38	11	11	16	40	57	33
Nantwich Town	38	10	13	15	48	49	31*
Leek Town	38	10	11	17	39	45	31
Horwich RMI	38	12	7	19	58	72	31
Bootle	38	11	12	15	49	47	30*
St. Helens Town	38	7	11	20	34	71	25
Ashton United	38	8	6	24	38	77	22
Droylesden	38	3	4	31	26	96	10

* denotes points deducted

CHESHIRE COUNTY LEAGUE - DIVISION ONE
1980-81 SEASON

	P	W.	D	L	F	A	Pts
Nantwich Town	38	28	6	6	87	34	58
Hyde United	38	23	9	6	75	27	55
Winsford United	38	20	10	8	75	38	50
Formby	38	21	7	10	65	39	49
Stalybridge Celtic	38	16	15	7	62	50	47
Chorley	38	17	11	10	65	48	45
Bootle	38	18	7	13	68	53	43
Prescot Cables	38	16	9	13	60	46	41
Horwich RMI	38	15	9	14	53	49	39
Leek Town	38	15	9	14	50	47	39
Ashton United	38	12	12	14	70	73	36
Curzon Ashton	38	14	8	16	48	63	36
St. Helens Town	38	14	7	17	63	82	35
Fleetwood Town	38	9	13	16	33	53	31
Rossendale United	38	9	12	17	49	69	30
Burscough	**38**	**11**	**6**	**21**	**52**	**62**	**28**
Darwen	38	8	10	20	46	74	26
Droylesden	38	9	8	21	49	82	26
Kirkby Town	38	6	11	21	30	65	23
New Mills	38	8	7	23	34	80	23

NORTH WEST COUNTIES LEAGUE - DIVISION ONE
1982-83 SEASON

	P	W	D	L	F	A	Pts
Burscough	**38**	**26**	**7**	**5**	**93**	**45**	**59**
Rhyl	38	23	11	4	76	30	57
Horwich RMI	38	22	10	6	78	35	54
Stalybridge Celtic	38	17	15	6	60	32	49
Winsford United	38	18	10	10	72	48	46
Darwen	38	17	12	9	68	46	46
Lancaster City	38	17	11	10	69	54	45
Congleton Town	38	13	14	11	52	35	40
Penrith	38	17	6	15	68	61	40
Accrington Stanley	38	13	12	13	56	55	38
Leek Town	38	14	9	15	42	44	37
Curzon Ashton	38	14	8	16	46	47	36
Ashton United	38	13	10	15	55	69	36
Bootle	38	14	6	18	55	79	34
Prescot Cables	38	9	13	16	50	60	31
Formby	38	10	8	20	48	68	28
Leyland Motors	38	7	10	21	34	74	24
Glossop	38	6	11	21	29	67	23
St. Helens Town	38	5	10	23	29	80	20
Nantwich Town	38	6	5	27	43	93	17

1980/81 Season
Cheshire County League (Division One)

Date	Opponent	H/A	Competition	Result	Scorers
Sat Aug 16	St. Helens Town	A	Lge	L 2-4	Stokes, Frank Gamble
Tue Aug 19	Darwen	H	Lge	L 1-2	Scorer unknown
Sat Aug 23	Stalybridge Celtic	H	Lge	L 2-4	Blakeman, Gamble
Tue Aug 27	Formby	A	Lge	L 1-2	Scorer unknown
Sat Aug 30	Leek Town	A	Lge	L 0-2	
Tue Sep 2	Kirkby Town	H	Lge	W 3-1	Gray, Jaycock (2)
Sat Sep 6	Horwich RMI	H	Lge	L 0-2	
Tue Sep 10	Fleetwood Town	A	Lge	L 0-1	
Sat Sep 13	Prestwich Heys	H	F.A.Cup 1st Qual. Rd	W 2-1	Jaycock, 1 unknown
Tue Sep 16	Formby	H	Lge	L 0-3	
Sat Sep 20	Accrington Stanley	H	Lge Cup 2nd Rd.	L 2-3	Jaycock, Blakeman
Sat Sep 27	New Mills	A	Lge	L 1-2	Scorer unknown
Sat Oct 4	Hyde United	A	F.A.Cup 2nd Qual. Rd	W 2-1	Jaycock (2)
Sat Oct 11	Southport	A	F.A.Trophy	L 0-1	
	Attend: 241				
Sat Oct 18	Prescot Town	H	F.A.Cup 3rd Qual. Rd	W 4-0	Stokes, Gamble (2), Durnin
Sat Oct 25	Kirkby Town	A	Lge	W 2-1	Durnin, Gamble
Sat Nov 1	Morecambe	H	F.A.Cup 4th Qual. Rd	W 2-0	Gamble, Jaycock
Sat Nov 8	Stalybridge Celtic	A	Lge	L 2-3	Jaycock (2)
Sat Nov 15	Formby	H	Lpool Senior Cup	L 0-1	
Sat Nov 22	Altrincham	H	F.A.Cup 1st Rd.	L 1-2	Parry
	Attend: 1,207				
Sat Nov 29	Nantwich	H	Lge	W 1-0	Jaycock
Sat Dec 6	Wren Rovers	H	Lancs Junior Cup 1st Rd	D 2-2	Durnin, Blakeman
Sat Dec 13	Wren Rovers	A	Lancs Junior Cup replay	W 3-1	Blakeman (2), Stokes
Sat Dec 20	Darwen	A	Lge	W 2-1	Al Bowen, P.McFerran
Sat Dec 27	Hyde United	A	Lge	L 0-1	
Thu Jan 1	Chorley	H	Lge	L 2-3	Gamble, Durnin
Sat Jan 10	Ashton United	H	Lge	L 3-5	O.G., Durnin, Jaycock
Tue Jan 20	South Liverpool	A	Lancs Junior Cup 2nd Rd	D 1-1	Jaycock
	played at Burscough				
Thu Jan 22	South Liverpool	H	Lancs Junior Cup replay	L 2-4	Scorers unknown
Wed Jan 28	Prescot Cables	H	Lge	D 2-2	Jaycock (2)
Sat Feb 7	Leek Town	H	Lge	D 0-0	
Tue Feb 10	Curzon Ashton	H	Lge	L 0-1	
Sat Feb 14	Rossendale United	A	Lge	W 6-1	Scorers unknown
Tue Feb 17	Bootle	H	Lge	W 2-1	Gamble, Stokes
Sat Feb 21	Hyde United	H	Lge	D 0-0	
Sat Feb 28	New Mills	H	Lge	W 6-1	O.G., Les Brown (3), Blakeman (2)
Tue Mar 3	St. Helens Town	H	Lge	W 1-0	Blakeman
Sat Mar 7	Winsford United	A	Lge	D 2-2	Scorers unknown
Sat Mar 14	Fleetwood Town	H	Lge	L 0-2	
Tue Mar 17	Winsford United	H	Lge	D 1-1	Gamble
Tue Mar 24	Rossendale United	H	Lge	W 2-1	Stokes, Blakeman
Sat Mar 28	Droylesden	H	Lge	W 2-1	Stokes, McFerran
Tue Mar 31	Horwich RMI	A	Lge	L 0-1	
Sat Apr 4	Bootle	A	Lge	L 0-1	
Wed Apr 8	Prescot Cables	A	Lge	L 0-2	
Sat Apr 11	Curzon Ashton	A	Lge	D 0-0	
Mon Apr 13	Droylesden	A	Lge	L 1-2	Scorer unknown
Thu Apr 16	Chorley	A	Lge	L 0-3	
Sat Apr 18	Nantwich	A	Lge	L 0-2	
Sat Apr 25	Ashton United	A	Lge	W 5-2	Dave Carberry (2), Jaycock (3)

1981/82 Season
Cheshire County League (Division One)

Date	Opponent	H/A	Competition	Result	Scorers
Sat Aug 15	Nantwich Town	A	Lge	L 2-3	MikeTickle, Jaycock
Tue Aug 18	Prescot Cables	H	Lge	W 2-1	John Brady (2)
Sat Aug 22	Ashton United	H	Lge Cup 2nd Rd.	D 1-1	Brady
Wed Aug 26	Ashton United	A	Lge Cup replay	W 5-0	Scorers unknown
Sat Aug 29	Formby	A	Lge	D 2-2	Ged McKenna, Nolan
Tue Sep 1	Rossendale United	H	Lge	W 1-0	Brady
Sat Sep 5	Glossop	A	Lge	L 0-1	
Wed Sep 9	Bootle	A	Lge	W 1-0	Scorer unknown
Sat Sep 12	Stalybridge Celtic	H	Lge	W 3-1	Jaycock, Moran, Brady
Tue Sep 16	Formby	H	Lge	D 0-0	
Sat Sep 19	Darwen	H	F.A.Cup 1st Qual. Rd	W 4-0	Scorers unknown
Tue Sep 22	St. Helens Town	H	Lge	W 4-0	Scorers unknown
Sat Sep 26	Winsford United	H	Lge	D 1-1	Wright
Sat Oct 3	Telford United	A	F.A.Cup 2nd Qual. Rd	L 0-3	
Tue Oct 6	Leek Town	A	Lge	W 3-1	Scorers unknown
Sat Oct 10	Nantwich Town	H	Lge	W 1-0	Jaycock
Sat Oct 17	Leek Town	H	Lge	D 0-0	
Sat Oct 24	South Bank	A	F.A.Trophy	W 2-1	Scorers unknown
Sat Oct 31	Glossop	H	Lge	D 0-0	
Tue Nov 3	Bootle	H	Liverpool Senior Cup	D 1-1	Nolan
	ordered to be replayed at Burscough - no extra-time played				
Sat Nov 7	Winsford United	A	Lge	L 0-7	
Sat Nov 14	Hyde United	H	Lge	L 1-3	Carberry
Sat Nov 21	Curzon Ashton	A	Lge	D 3-3	Scorers unknown
Tue Nov 24	Bootle	H	Liverpool Senior Cup Replayed Tie	W 4-1	John Connor, Brady, Mike Fagan, McKenna
Sat Nov 28	Whitby Town	H	F.A.Trophy	W 3-1	McKenna (3)
Sat Dec 5	Blackpool Mechanics	H	Lancs Junior Cup	W 2-0	Fagan, Brady
Sat Jan 2	Horden Colliery Welfare	H	F.A.Trophy	L 1-3	Carberry
Sat Jan 23	Fleetwood Town	H	Lancs Junior Cup	W 2-1	Mckenna (2)
Sat Jan 30	Lancaster City	A	Lancs Junior Cup	D 0-0	
Tue Feb 2	Lancaster City	H	Lancs Junior Cup replay	W 1-0	Fagan
Sat Feb 6	Stalybridge Celtic	A	Lge	L 1-2	Scorer unknown
Tue Feb 9	Darwen	H	Lge	W 3-1	Carberry (2), Beesley
Sat Feb 13	Accrington Stanley	H	Lge	W 4-0	Fagan, Nolan, Brady (2)
Mon Feb 15	Horwich RMI	A	Lge	W 3-1	Peter Doyle, Fagan (2)
Sat Feb 20	Droylesden	A	Lge	W 5-1	Carberry (3), Brady, McKenna
Sat Feb 27	Ashton United	A	Lge	W 2-1	Scorers unknown
Mon Mar 1	Formby	H	Liverpool Senior Cup	W 2-0	Brady (2)
Sat Mar 6	Chorley	H	Lancs Junior Cup Semi-final	L 0-1	
Sat Mar 13	Curzon Ashton	H	Lge	W 2-1	Blakeman, Carberry
Sat Mar 20	Hyde United	A	Lge	L 1-2	Blakeman
Tue Mar 23	Droylesden	H	Lge	W 5-0	Bobby Pascoe (3), Brady, Hulme
Sat Mar 27	Prescot Cables	A	Lge Cup 3rd Rd.	W 1-0	O.G.
Tue Mar 30	Everton	H	Liverpool Senior Cup Semi-final	L 0-1	
Thu Apr 1	Horwich RMI	H	Lge	W 3-1	Doyle, Fagan (2)
Sat Apr 3	Fleetwood Town	A	Lge	D 1-1	Scorer unknown
Mon Apr 5	Accrington Stanley	A	Lge	L 0-1	
Fri Apr 9	Chorley	A	Lge	D 1-1	Nolan
Sat Apr 10	St. Helens Town	A	Lge	W 2-0	Brady (2)
Mon Apr 12	Chorley	H	Lge	W 1-0	Doyle
Wed Apr 14	Prescot Cables	A	Lge	W 2-1	Scorers unknown
Sat Apr 17	Hyde United	H	Lge Cup 4th Rd	L 1-4	Mortimer
Tue Apr 20	Rossendale United	A	Lge	D 1-1	Scorer unknown
Sat Apr 24	Ashton United	H	Lge	W 5-0	Pascoe (3), Brady, Paul Conchie
Mon Apr 26	Fleetwood Town	H	Lge	W 2-1	Scorers unknown
Thu Apr 29	Bootle	H	Lge	D 1-1	Scorer unknown
Sat May 1	Darwen	A	Lge	W 1-0	Pascoe

1982/83 Season
North West Counties Football League (Division One)

Date	Opponent	H/A	Competition	Result	Scorers
Sat Aug 14	Winsford United	H	Lge	W 2-1	John Veacock, Fagan
Tue Aug 17	Glossop	A	Lge	W 3-0	Pascoe (2), Doyle
Sat Aug 21	Leek Town	A	Lge	W 3-0	Nolan (2), Pascoe
Tue Aug 24	Prescot Cables	H	Lge	L 0-4	
Sat Aug 28	Curzon Ashton	H	Lge	W 2-1	Connor, Veacock
Mon Aug 30	Penrith	A	Lge	W 3-1	Veacock (2), Brady
Sat Sep 4	Stalybridge Celtic	A	F.A.Cup Prelim. Rd	D 1-1	Scorer unknown
Tue Sep 7	Stalybridge Celtic	H	F.A.Cup replay	W 4-1	Nolan (3), Brady
Sat Sep 11	Lancaster City	A	Lge	W 5-0	Veacock (2), Nolan, Brady
Tue Sep 14	Leyland Motors	H	Lge	W 5-0	Nolan (2), Richie Woosey, Veacock, Brady
Sat Sep 18	Oswestry Town	A	F.A.Cup 1st Qual. Rd	L 1-2	Scorer unknown
Tue Sep 21	St. Helens Town	H	Lge	W 5-1	Brady (2), Veacock (2), Nolan
Sat Sep 25	Congleton Town	A	Lge	D 1-1	Brady
Sat Oct 2	Nantwich	H	Lge	W 4-1	Veacock (2), Doyle, Brady
Sat Oct 9	Darwen	A	Lge	D 2-2	Robbie Griffiths, Brady
Sat Oct 16	Darwen	H	Lge	D 2-2	Fagan, Pascoe
Sat Oct 23	Netherfield	A	F.A.Trophy	W 2-1	Pascoe, Carberry
Sat Oct 30	Nantwich	A	Lge	D 3-3	Pascoe, Fagan, Jimmy Horrocks
Tue Nov 2	Bootle	H	Liverpool Senior Cup	W 3-1	Scorers unknown
Sat Nov 6	Formby	A	Lge	W 3-2	Moogan, Brady (2)
Sat Nov 13	Prestwich Heys	A	League Cup 3rd Rd.	L 2-3	Fagan, Carberry
Sat Nov 20	Rhyl	A	Lge	L 3-4	Fagan, Veacock (2)
Sat Nov 27	Workington	A	F.A.Trophy	D 0-0	
Tue.Nov 30	Workington	H	F.A.Trophy replay	W 2-0	O.G., Carberry
Sat Dec 4	Bootle	A	Lge	W 4-1	Veacock (2), Brady, Moogan
Sat Dec 18	Lancaster City	H	F.A.Trophy	W 4-1	Nolan (2), Brady, Veacock
Tue Dec 21	Accrington Stanley	H	Lge	W 3-2	Brady (2), Veacock
Mon Dec 27	Winsford United	A	Lge	W 3-2	Brady (2), Veacock
Thu Dec 30	Ashton United	H	Lge	W 4-1	Brady (2), Fagan, Nolan
Sat Jan 1	Leek Town	H	Lge	W 1-0	Fagan
Sat Jan 8	Formby	H	Lge	W 5-0	Nolan (3), Brady, Veacock
Sat Jan 15	Ashington	A	F.A.Trophy 1st Rd	L 0-1	
Tue Jan 18	Horwich RMI	H	Lge	L 1-2	Veacock
Sat Jan 22	South Liverpool	H	Lancs Junior Cup 2nd Rd	L 0-1	
Sat Jan 29	Glossop	H	Lge	L 1-2	Fagan
Sat Feb 5	Congleton Town	H	Lge	W 2-1	Alan Donnelly, Brady
Tue Feb 8	St. Helens Town	H	Liverpool Senior Cup	W 2-1	Donnelly, Fagan
Sat Feb 19	Lancaster City	H	Lge	D 2-2	Johnston, Brady
Sat Feb 26	Stalybridge Celtic	H	Lge	W 1-0	Dave Pennell
Sat Mar 5	St. Helens Town	A	Lge	W 2-1	Pennell, Donnelly
Sat Mar 12	Ashton United	A	Lge	W 2-1	Pennell, O.G.
Sat Mar 19	South Liverpool	H	Liverpool Senior Cup Semi-final	D 1-1	Brady
Sat Mar 26	Leyland Motors	A	Lge	W 2-0	Fagan, Donnelly
Tue Mar 29	South Liverpool	A	L'pool Senior Cup replay	L 1-3	Nolan
Sat Apr 2	Rhyl	H	Lge	D 2-2	Donnelly, O.G.
Mon Apr 4	Stalybridge Celtic	A	Lge	D 1-1	Donnelly
Sat Apr 9	Curzon Ashton	A	Lge	W 1-0	Donnelly
Tue Apr 12	Bootle	H	Lge	W 3-0	Brady (2), Conchie
Tue Apr 19	Accrington Stanley	A	Lge	W 2-1	Donnelly, Brady
Sat Apr 23	Horwich RMI	A	Lge	L 0-2	
Tue Apr 26	Penrith *Attend: 204*	H	Lge	W 3-1	Redmond, Donnelly, Brady
Sat May 7	Prescot Cables	A	Lge	W 2-0	Doyle, Horrocks

1982-83 Season. Back left to right: Mike McKenzie (Asst. Manager), Robbie Griffiths, Alex Blakeman, John O'Brien, Jimmy Horrocks, Peter Doyle, Shaun Teale, John Veacock.
Front left to right: Mike Fagan, Syl Nolan, Richie Woosey, John Brady, John Connor, Tommy Barry, Paul Conchie. John Brady signed for Southport at the end of the season, while young Shaun Teale eventually achieved fame with Aston Villa. Richie Woosey died in 1995.

NORTH WEST COUNTIES LEAGUE - DIVISION ONE
1983-84 SEASON

	P	W	D	L	F	A	Pts
Stalybridge Celtic	38	26	8	4	81	30	60
Penrith	38	23	9	6	88	39	55
Radcliffe Borough	38	26	3	9	79	41	55
Burscough	**38**	**22**	**8**	**8**	**87**	**47**	**52**
Curzon Ashton	38	21	5	12	74	51	47
Lancaster City	38	21	3	14	76	56	43*
Accrington Stanley	38	17	8	13	67	60	42
St. Helens Town	38	17	7	14	69	55	41
Congleton Town	38	18	5	15	64	50	41
Prescot Cables	38	17	6	15	72	45	40
Leek Town	38	14	10	14	56	64	38
Winsford United	38	12	12	14	49	54	36
Formby	38	14	7	17	48	61	35
Caernarfon Town	38	11	12	15	46	55	34
Glossop	38	11	11	16	38	61	33
Bootle	38	11	7	20	46	69	27*
Leyland Motors	38	9	9	20	44	79	27
Netherfield	38	5	11	22	27	73	21
Ashton United	38	7	9	22	47	86	19*
Darwen	38	2	2	34	29	111	6

* denotes points deducted

NORTH WEST COUNTIES LEAGUE - DIVISION ONE
1984-85 SEASON

	P	W	D	L	F	A	Pts
Radcliffe Borough	38	24	10	4	67	33	58
Caernarfon Town	38	23	9	6	73	40	55
Burscough	**38**	**23**	**7**	**8**	**81**	**46**	**53**
Stalybridge Celtic	38	21	10	7	89	40	52
Eastwood Hanley	38	20	12	6	72	42	52
Curzon Ashton	38	21	6	11	85	60	48
Winsford United	38	20	7	11	58	37	47
Fleetwood Town	38	18	8	12	84	57	44
Leek Town	38	16	11	11	52	38	43
Congleton Town	38	13	11	14	43	46	37
Leyland Motors	38	13	8	17	52	67	34
St. Helens Town	38	12	9	17	64	75	33
Prescot Cables	38	13	7	18	64	68	31*
Bootle	38	10	11	17	34	48	31
Accrington Stanley	38	11	8	19	45	59	30
Glossop	38	8	11	19	46	70	27
Formby	38	9	9	20	41	79	25*
Netherfield	38	7	9	22	42	80	23
Lancaster City	38	8	5	25	46	90	21
Penrith	38	4	4	30	36	99	12

* denotes points deducted

281

1983/84 Season
North West Counties Football League (Division One)

Date	Opponent	H/A	Competition	Result	Scorers
Sat Aug 13	Penrith	H	Lge	L 2-3	John Coleman, John Durnin
Tue Aug 16	Darwen	H	Champions v. Cup Winners	W 2-0	Durnin, T.Murphy
Sat Aug 20	Congleton Town	H	Lge	W 2-0	Fagan, Coleman
Tue Aug 23	Formby	A	Lge	W 3-2	Fagan, Smith, Peter Murphy
Sat Aug 27	Radcliffe Borough	H	Lge	W 3-1	P.Murphy, Coleman, Fagan
Tue Aug 30	St. Helens Town	A	Lge	D 0-0	
Sat Sep 3	Lancaster City	A	Lge	L 1-2	Coleman
Tue Sep 6	Bootle	H	Lge	W 4-2	Fagan, Coleman, Smith, Terry Darracott
Sat Sep 10	Stalybridge Celtic	H	Lge	D 0-0	
Sat Sep 17	Chorley	A	F.A.Cup 1st Qual. Rd	L 0-2	
Sat Sep 24	Curzon Ashton	H	Lge	L 0-1	
Tue Sep 27	Prescot Cables	H	Lge	L 0-2	
Sat Oct 1	Darwen	A	Lge	W 4-1	Coleman (2), P.Murphy, Chris Murphy
Sat Oct 8	Caernarfon Town	H	Lge	L 1-2	Coleman
Tue Oct 11	Formby	H	Liverpool Senior Cup	W 1-0	Fagan
Sat Oct 15	Netherfield	A	Lge	D 1-1	Fagan
Sat Oct 22	Goole Town	H	F.A.Trophy	D 3-3	Cole (2), Coleman
Tue Oct 25	Goole Town	A	F.A.Trophy replay	L 2-4	P.Murphy, Coleman
Sat Oct 29	Leek Town	A	Lge	W 2-1	Fagan, Coleman
Sat Nov 5	Ashton United	A	Lge	D 2-2	Steve Skeete, Fagan
Sat Nov 12	Curzon Ashton	A	League Cup	L 1-3	Skeete
Sat Nov 19	Glossop	A	Lge	D 2-2	Skeete, Fagan
Sat Nov 26	Leyland Motors	H	Lge	W 6-0	Coleman (2), Skeete (2), Fagan, Keith Ashton
Sat Dec 3	Accrington Stanley	A	Lge	W 4-2	Skeete (3), Duffy
Sat Dec 10	Fleetwood Town	A	Lancs Challenge Trophy	W 7-6	Skeete (2), Duffy (3), Coleman (2)
Sat Dec 17	Darwen	H	Lge	W 4-1	Duffy, Coleman, Skeete, Fagan
Tue Dec 27	Penrith	A	Lge	L 2-5	Scorers unknown
Sat Dec 31	Congleton Town	A	Lge	L 1-2	Coleman
Sat Jan 7	Radcliffe Borough	A	Lge	W 2-0	Durnin, Coleman
Sat Jan 14	Formby	H	Lge	W 2-0	Scorers unknown
Sat Jan 28	South Liverpool	H	Lancs Challenge Trophy	D 1-1	Coleman
Tue Jan 31	South Liverpool	A	Lancs Challenge Trophy Replay	L 0-1	
Sat Feb 4	Curzon Ashton	A	Lge	W 2-1	Coleman, Steve McNeilis
Sat Feb 11	Prescot Cables	A	Lge	D 1-1	Coleman
Tue Feb 14	St. Helens Town	H	Lge	D 0-0	
Sat Feb 18	Caernarfon Town	A	Lge	W 2-1	Murphy, Manifold
Tue Feb 21	Liverpool	H	Liverpool Senior Cup	L 0-1	
Sat Feb 25	Netherfield	H	Lge	W 3-0	Coleman, Veacock, Blakeman
Sat Mar 3	Bootle	A	Lge	W 4-0	Blakeman, Coleman, Fagan (2)
Tue Mar 6	Stalybridge Celtic	A	Lge	L 3-4	O.G., Duffy, Murphy
Sat Mar 10	Leek Town	H	Lge	W 4-1	Fagan (2), Blakeman, Duffy
Sat Mar 17	Ashton United	H	Lge	W 4-1	Fagan, Veacock, Duffy (2)
Tue Mar 27	Accrington Stanley	H	Lge	W 3-1	Blakeman, Coleman, Fagan
Sat Mar 31	Glossop	H	Lge	D 1-1	Coleman
Tue Apr 3	Winsford United	H	Lge	W 2-1	Duffy, Blakeman
Sat Apr 7	Leyland Motors	A	Lge	W 2-1	Coleman, McNeilis
Tue Apr 10	Lancaster City	H	Lge	W 3-2	Veacock, Coleman, Duffy
Sat Apr 21	Winsford United	A	Lge	W 5-0	Duffy (2), Fagan, Gray, Coleman

Above: 1983-84 Season. Back left to right: Peter Murphy, Brian Hayes, Dick Johnson, Willie Broom, Paul Henry, Chris Murphy. Front left to right: Mike McKenzie (Manager), Brian Stokes, John Coleman, Mike Fagan, John Durnin, Steve Rawlings. Pictured with the Champions v Cup-winners Challenge Trophy.
Below: 1984-85 Season. Back left to right: Mike McKenzie (Manager), Jimmy Comer, John Veacock, Brian Hayes, John O'Brien, Dave Ball, Alex Blakeman, Billy Jaycock (Asst. Manager). Front left to right: Steve McNeilis, John Coleman, Peter Murphy, Sponsor, Andy Gray, Adrian Pender, Tony Duffy.

1984/85 Season
North West Counties Football League (Division One)

Date	Opponent	H/A	Competition	Result	Scorers
Sat Aug 11	Radcliffe Borough	A	Lge	L 1-2	Coleman
Sat Aug 18	Eastwood Hanley	H	Lge	D 0-0	
Tue Aug 21	Bootle	H	Lge	W 2-1	Dave Ball, Coleman
Sat Aug 25	Fleetwood Town	A	Lge	W 5-2	O.G., Duffy (2), Coleman (2)
Tue Aug 28	Congleton Town	A	Lge	W 1-0	Jimmy Bell
Sat Sep 1	Emley	H	F.A.Cup Prelim. Rd	W 2-1	Coleman, Ball
Sat Sep 8	Winsford United	A	Lge	L 1-2	Ball
Tue Sep 11	Leyland Motors	H	Lge	W 1-0	Coleman
Sat Sep 15	Skelmersdale United	H	F.A.Cup 1st Qual. Rd	W 3-0	Coleman, Ball, Veacock
Sat Sep 22	St. Helens Town	A	Lge	D 2-2	Comer, Coleman
Wed Sep 26	Penrith	A	Lge	D 2-2	Scorers unknown
Sat Sep 29	Leek Town	H	F.A.Cup 2nd Qual. Rd	W 2-0	Veacock (2)
Sat Oct 6	Leek Town	A	Lge	W 2-1	Coleman (2)
Tue Oct 9	Skelmersdale United	H	Liverpool Senior Cup	L 1-2	Birkett
Sat Oct 13	Alfreton Town	H	F.A.Cup 3rd Qual. Rd	D 2-2	Ball, Coleman
Wed Oct 17	Alfreton Town	A	F.A.Cup replay	W 3-2	Duffy (2), Jimmy Comer
	Attend: 650				
Sat Oct 20	Peterlee	H	F.A.Trophy 1st Qual. Rd	L 0-1	
Sat Oct 27	Blue Star	A	F.A.Cup 4th Qual. Rd	D 0-0	
Wed Oct 31	Blue Star	H	F.A.Cup replay	L 0-4	
	Attend: 450				
Sat Nov 10	Glossop	H	Lge Cup 3rd Rd.	W 4-2	Blakeman, Coleman, Peter Murphy, O.G.
Sat Nov 17	Curzon Ashton	H	Lge	W 2-0	O.G., Coleman
Sat Nov 24	Formby	A	Lge	W 6-0	Veacock, Coleman (4), Duffy
Sat Dec 1	Prescot Cables	H	Lge	W 2-0	Coleman, Veacock
Sat Dec 8	Lancaster City	A	Lancs ATS Trophy	W 3-0	Ball, Coleman, Duffy
Sat Dec 15	Caernarfon Town	H	Lge	D 2-2	Murphy, Duffy
Sat Dec 22	Lancaster City	H	Lge	W 5-1	Coleman, McNeilis (2), Ball, Veacock
Sat Dec 29	Eastwood Hanley	A	Lge	L 1-4	Duffy
Tue Jan 1	Accrington Stanley	H	Lge	W 5-1	Coleman (3), Bell, 1 unknown
Sat Jan 26	Marine	H	Lancs ATS Trophy	W 3-1	Ball, Coleman, Duffy
Sat Feb 2	St. Helens Town	H	Lge	W 3-1	Bell (2), Duffy
Sat Feb 16	Leyland Motors	A	Lancs ATS Trophy	L 1-2	Blakeman
Sat Feb 23	Accrington Stanley	A	Lge	W 2-1	Coleman, Bell
Tue Mar 5	Formby	H	Lge	W 2-0	Donnelly
Sat Mar 9	Netherfield	A	Lge	W 3-2	Blakeman, Duffy (2)
Tue Mar 12	Leek Town	H	Lge	W 2-0	McNeilis, Bell
Sat Mar 16	Fleetwood Town	A	Lge Cup 4th Rd	W 3-2	Coleman, Gray, Blakeman
Tue Mar 19	Congleton Town	H	Lge	D 1-1	Blakeman
Sat Mar 23	Radcliffe Borough	H	Lge Cup 5th Rd	L 0-6	
Tue Mar 26	Radcliffe Borough	H	Lge	L 1-2	Coleman
Sat Mar 30	Curzon Ashton	A	Lge	L 0-1	
Tue Apr 2	Netherfield	H	Lge	D 1-1	Scorer unknown
Thu Apr 4	Fleetwood Town	H	Lge	W 2-1	Scorers unknown
Mon Apr 8	Prescot Cables	A	Lge	W 3-2	Wilkinson (2), Duffy
Sat Apr 13	Glossop	H	Lge	W 3-1	Coleman (3)
Tue Apr 16	Winsford United	H	Lge	W 3-1	Duffy, Gray, Coleman
Sat Apr 20	Caernarfon Town	A	Lge	L 1-2	Bell
Mon Apr 22	Lancaster City	A	Lge	D 1-1	Coleman
Thu Apr 25	Penrith	H	Lge	W 5-1	Duffy (2), Bell, Coleman, McNeilis
Sat Apr 27	Leyland Motors	A	Lge	L 0-1	
Wed May 1	Bootle	A	Lge	W 4-3	Scorers unknown
Sat May 4	Glossop	A	Lge	W 1-0	McNeilis
Tue May 7	Stalybridge Celtic	H	Lge	L 2-4	Ball, Coleman
Thu May 9	Stalybridge Celtic	A	Lge	W 1-0	Donnelly

1985/86 Season
North West Counties Football League (Division One)

Sat Aug 10	Accrington Stanley	A	Lge	W 1-0	Mark Barron
Wed Aug 14	Bootle	A	Lge	D 0-0	
Sat Aug 17	Stalybridge Celtic	A	Lge	D 2-2	Veacock, Donnelly
Tue Aug 20	Formby	A	Lge	W 4-0	Donnelly, Blakeman, Veacock (2)
Sat Aug 24	Winsford United	H	Lge	W 6-0	Ball, Donnelly (4), Gray
Tue Aug 27	St. Helens Town	A	Lge	D 1-1	Scorer unknown
Sat Aug 31	Clitheroe	A	Lge	D 1-1	Scorer unknown
Tue Sep 3	Bootle	H	Lge	L 0-1	
Sat Sep 7	Armthorpe Welfare	H	F.A.Cup 1st Qual. Rd	D 1-1	Duffy
Tue Sep 10	Armthorpe Welfare	A	F.A.Cup replay	W 1-0	Scorer unknown
Sat Sep 14	Irlam Town	A	Lge	L 1-2	Donnelly
Tue Sep 17	St.Helens Town	H	Lge	W 3-1	Duffy, Donnelly (2)
Sat Sep 21	Curzon Ashton	H	Lge	W 2-0	Donnelly (2)
Tue Sep 24	Formby	H	Lge	D 0-0	
Sat Sep 28	Mossley	H	F.A.Cup 2nd Qual. Rd	L 0-3	
Sat Oct 5	Southport	A	F.A.Trophy	L 1-2	Duffy
Sat Oct 12	Congleton Town	H	Lge	L 1-2	Donnelly
Tue Oct 15	Leyland Motors	A	Lge	L 0-2	
Sat Oct 19	Netherfield	A	Lge	W 2-0	Blakeman, McNeilis
Sat Oct 26	Eastwood Hanley	H	Lge	W 2-1	Donnelly, Steve Cowley
Sat Nov 2	Fleetwood Town	A	Lge	W 2-1	Donnelly (2)
Sat Nov 16	St. Helens Town	H	Lge Cup 2nd Rd.	W 2-1	Ball, Donnelly
Sat Nov 23	Glossop	A	Lge	W 3-1	O.G., Ashton, Donnelly
Tue Nov 26	Southport	H	Liverpool Senior Cup	D 2-2	Steve Nickson, Ball
Sat Nov 30	Netherfield	H	Lge	L 0-1	
Tue Dec 10	Southport	A	L'pool Senior Cup replay	L 0-1	
Sat Dec 14	Leek Town	H	Lge	W 2-0	Ball, 1 unknown
Sat Dec 21	Irlam Town	H	Lge	L 1-2	Donnelly
Thu Dec 26	Prescot Cables	H	Lge	W 3-0	Blakeman, Donnelly, Nickson
Sat Jan 11	Penrith	A	Lge	W 3-1	Nickson (2), Donnelly
Sat Jan 18	Congleton Town	A	Lge	L 1-2	Donnelly
Tue Jan 21	Morecambe	A	Lancs ATS Trophy 2nd Rd	D 1-1	Duffy
Sat Jan 25	Fleetwood Town	H	Lge	L 0-4	
Tue Jan 28	Morecambe	H	Lancs ATS Trophy replay	L 0-4	
Sat Feb 1	Clitheroe	H	Lge Cup 3rd Rd	L 2-3	Nickson, Veacock
Sat Feb 22	Clitheroe	H	Lge	D 0-0	
Sat Mar 1	Penrith	H	Lge	D 0-0	
Sat Mar 8	Glossop	H	Lge	W 1-0	Mick Potter
Sat Mar 15	Eastwood Hanley	A	Lge	W 1-0	Scorer unknown
Tue Mar 18	Leyland Motors	H	Lge	L 0-2	
Sat Mar 22	Radcliffe Borough	A	Lge	D 0-0	
Tue Mar 25	Accrington Stanley	H	Lge	D 0-0	
Sat Mar 29	Radcliffe Borough	H	Lge	L 0-2	
Mon Mar 31	Prescot Cables	A	Lge	L 0-2	
Sat Apr 5	Curzon Ashton	A	Lge	W 1-0	Tommy Fanning
Sat Apr 12	Stalybridge Celtic	H	Lge	D 1-1	Fanning
Sat Apr 19	Winsford United	A	Lge	L 0-1	
Sat Apr 26	Leek Town	A	Lge	L 0-2	

NORTH WEST COUNTIES LEAGUE - DIVISION ONE
1985-86 SEASON

	P	W	D	L	F	A	Pts
Clitheroe	38	20	14	4	61	30	54
Congleton Town	38	22	10	6	51	29	54
Eastwood Hanley	38	22	9	7	68	45	53
Stalybridge Celtic	38	21	10	7	62	39	52
Fleetwood Town	38	21	10	7	70	34	50*
Irlam Town	38	16	14	8	66	45	46
Leek Town	38	20	6	12	64	44	46
Curzon Ashton	38	18	9	11	52	50	45
Burscough	**38**	**15**	**10**	**13**	**45**	**35**	**40**
St. Helens Town	38	15	8	15	65	55	38
Accrington Stanley	38	13	11	14	62	60	37
Leyland Motors	38	13	8	17	62	67	34
Winsford United	38	14	6	18	55	68	34
Radcliffe Borough	38	12	9	17	48	49	33
Bootle	38	11	7	20	46	54	29
Penrith	38	9	8	21	46	63	26
Netherfield	38	8	10	20	38	76	26
Glossop	38	7	10	21	37	69	24
Prescot Cables	38	5	9	24	33	68	19
Formby	38	5	8	25	35	86	18

* denotes points deducted

NORTH WEST COUNTIES LEAGUE - DIVISION ONE
1986-87 SEASON

	P	W	D	L	F	A	Pts
Stalybridge Celtic	38	25	9	5	74	39	58
Accrington Stanley	38	19	15	4	63	32	53
Clitheroe	38	20	12	6	76	47	52
Kirkby Town	38	22	4	12	71	48	48
Bootle	38	19	10	9	52	38	48
St. Helens Town	38	19	9	10	65	37	47
Winsford United	38	19	8	11	55	39	46
Fleetwood Town	38	16	13	9	61	49	45
Penrith	38	16	10	12	62	59	42
Rossendale United	38	14	11	13	66	59	39
Congleton Town	38	13	11	14	38	39	37
Burscough	**38**	**11**	**11**	**16**	**58**	**54**	**33**
Leyland Motors	38	13	7	18	52	56	33
Eastwood Hanley	38	10	11	17	40	50	31
Radcliffe Borough	38	11	8	19	46	57	30
Leek Town	38	9	12	17	42	55	30
Netherfield	38	12	5	21	45	73	29
Irlam Town	38	4	13	21	36	74	21
Curzon Ashton	38	4	12	22	35	78	20
Glossop	38	5	8	25	33	87	18

1986-87 Season. Back left to right: Ray Coleman (Manager), Brendan Grant, Paul Moran, Geoff Thornton, Unknown, Steve Cowley, Chris Parkes ?, Dennis Smith (Asst. Manager).
Front left to right: Alex Blakeman, Steve Bleasdale, Steve McNeilis, Sponsor, Dave Bleasedale, John Moran, Nigel Halsall, George Ford (Trainer).

1986/87 Season
North West Counties Football League (Division One)

Date	Opponent	H/A	Competition	Result	Scorers
Sat Aug 9	Curzon Ashton	H	Lge	L 1-2	Karl Thomas
Wed Aug 13	Leyland Motors	A	Lge	D 0-0	
Sat Aug 16	Irlam Town	A	Lge	L 1-2	Scorer unknown
Tue Aug 19	Fleetwood Town	H	Lge	D 1-1	Brendan Grant
Sat Aug 23	Eastwood Hanley	H	Lge	W 3-0	John Moran, Grant (2)
Mon Aug 25	St. Helens Town	A	Lge	L 0-2	
Sat Aug 30	Kirkby Town	H	F.A.Cup Prelim. Rd	W 2-0	Grant (2)
Tue Sep 2	Leyland Motors	H	Lge	W 6-3	Grant (4), J.Moran, Steve Bleasdale
Sat Sep 6	Ellesmere Port & Neston	H	Lge Cup 3rd Rd	W 1-0	Blakeman
Wed Sep 10	Fleetwood Town	A	Lge	W 3-0	J.Moran, Grant, McNeilis
Sat Sep 13	Bootle	H	F.A.Cup 1st Qual. Rd	D 2-2	Grant, Thomas
Wed Sep 17	Bootle	A	F.A.Cup replay	L 1-2	Thomas
Sat Sep 20	Atherton L.R.	H	F.A.Vase Prelim. Rd	W 2-1	Thomas, Grant
Tue Sep 23	St. Helens Town	H	Lge	L 1-2	Grant
Sat Sep 27	Radcliffe Borough	H	Lge	L 1-2	Thomas
Sat Oct 4	Clitheroe	A	Lge	D 1-1	Blakeman
Sat Oct 11	Penrith	H	Lge	L 0-1	
Sat Oct 18	Guiseley	H	F.A.Vase 1st Rd	L 1-2	J.Moran
Sat Oct 25	Leek Town	A	Lge	W 2-0	Brady, Paul Moran
Sat Nov 1	Accrington Stanley	H	Lge	L 0-1	
Tue Nov 4	Kirkby Town	H	Liverpool Senior Cup	L 0-1	
Sat Nov 8	Winsford United	A	Lge	L 0-1	
Sat Nov 15	Rossendale United	H	Lge	W 4-0	Grant (2), Brady, Steve Robinson
Sat Nov 22	Glossop	A	Lge	W 3-0	Thomas, O.G., Brady
Sat Nov 29	Netherfield	H	Lge	W 4-1	Nigel Halsall, Grant (2), Robinson
Sat Dec 6	Leyland Motors	H	Lancs ATS Trophy 1st Rd	D 1-1	Bleasdale
Wed Dec 10	Leyland Motors	A	Lancs ATS Trophy replay	W 1-0	Scorer unknown
Sat Dec 13	Irlam Town	H	Lge	D 2-2	Brady, Grant
Fri Dec 26	Kirkby Town	H	Lge	W 2-1	Thomas (2)
Sat Dec 27	Netherfield	A	Lge	D 4-4	Brady, Thomas, Davies (2)
Sat Jan 3	Stalybridge Celtic	A	Lge	L 0-4	
Sat Jan 17	Leek Town	H	Lge	D 2-2	Carberry, Brady
Sat Jan 24	Accrington Stanley	A	Lge	D 0-0	
Sat Jan 31	Chorley	A	Lancs ATS Trophy	L 0-2	
Sat Feb 7	Stalybridge Celtic	H	Lge	L 0-1	
Sat Feb 14	Radcliffe Borough	A	Lge	L 2-3	Ashton, Gareth Drury
Sat Feb 21	Glossop	H	Lge	L 1-2	Carberry
Sat Feb 28	Penrith	A	Lge	L 2-3	Thomas, Robinson
Sat Mar 14	Curzon Ashton	A	Lge	W 2-0	Robinson, Thomas
Tue Mar 17	Winsford United	H	Lge	W 1-0	Halsall
Sat Mar 21	Bootle	A	Lge	L 0-1	
Tue Mar 24	Bootle	H	Lge	W 1-0	Ashton
Tue Mar 31	St. Helens Town	A	Lge Cup	W 5-3	Robinson (4), Ashton
Sat Apr 4	Ashton United	H	Lge Cup	L 1-2	Thomas
Wed Apr 8	Congleton Town	A	Lge	D 1-1	Scorer unknown
Sat Apr 11	Eastwood Hanley	A	Lge	D 0-0	
Tue Apr 14	Kirkby Town	A	Lge	L 2-5	Scorers unknown
Sat Apr 18	Rossendale United	A	Lge	L 3-4	McNeilis, Thomas (2)
Thu Apr 23	Clitheroe	H	Lge	D 2-2	Scorers unknown
Tue Apr 28	Congleton Town	H	Lge	D 0-0	

NORTH WEST COUNTIES LEAGUE - DIVISION ONE
1987-88 SEASON

	P	W	D	L	F	A	Pts
Colne Dynamoes	34	24	7	3	71	14	55
Rossendale United	34	24	7	3	68	23	55
Clitheroe	34	18	10	6	51	20	46
Colwyn Bay	34	20	7	7	60	42	45*
St. Helens Town	34	18	6	10	61	36	42
Ellesmere Port & N.	34	17	5	12	55	48	39
Darwen	34	14	10	10	55	45	38
Warrington Town	34	16	5	13	68	47	37
Kirkby Town	34	11	13	10	57	54	35
Burscough	**34**	**14**	**7**	**13**	**45**	**51**	**35**
Leyland Motors	34	10	11	13	53	53	31
Prescot Cables	34	10	11	13	34	45	29*
Bootle	34	12	5	17	43	61	29
Formby	34	6	10	18	32	63	22
Salford	34	8	6	20	33	66	22
Skelmersdale United	34	4	11	19	34	64	19
Atherton L.R.	34	4	7	23	31	78	15
Glossop	34	5	4	25	30	71	14

* denotes points deducted

NORTH WEST COUNTIES LEAGUE - DIVISION ONE
1988-89 SEASON

	P	W	D	L	F	A	Pts
Rossendale United	34	24	8	2	84	27	56
Knowsley United	34	21	8	5	85	43	50
St. Helens Town	34	20	8	6	60	25	48
Colwyn Bay	34	19	9	6	77	45	47
Darwen	34	19	9	6	64	36	47
Warrington Town	34	16	10	8	47	37	42
Flixton	34	15	8	11	61	44	38
Leyland Motors	34	15	8	11	53	44	38
Bootle	34	14	4	16	49	54	32
Burscough	**34**	**11**	**10**	**13**	**40**	**51**	**32**
Ellesmere Port	34	9	12	13	36	42	30
Clitheroe	34	8	12	14	38	41	28
Skelmersdale United	34	8	9	17	39	68	25
Atherton L.R.	34	9	6	19	47	74	24
Prescot Cables	34	7	9	18	36	60	23
Salford	34	7	8	19	33	70	22
Ashton United	34	7	6	21	37	72	18*
Formby	34	3	4	27	24	77	10

* denotes points deducted

1987-88 Season. Back left to right: Alvin McDonald (Asst. Manager), Peter Spencer, Paul Tomlinson, Steve Baker, John Evans, Paul Moran, Andy Rice, Mike Ryman (Manager). Front left to right: John Wright, Mark Wilson, Alan Donnelly, Jay Flannery, John Moran, Ged Peers ?. Paul Tomlinson was voted Player of the Year.

1987/88 Season
North West Counties Football League (Division One)

Date	Opponent	H/A	Competition	Result	Scorers
Sat Aug 15	Atherton L.R.	A	Lge	W 3-1	Donnelly (2), Tommy Doherty
Tue Aug 18	Formby	A	Lge	W 3-1	Doherty, Spellman, Donnelly
Sat Aug 22	Bootle	A	Lge	D 1-1	Donnelly
Sat Aug 29	Warrington Town at Haig Avenue, Southport	H	F.A.Cup Prelim. Rd	L 1-2	Donnelly
Mon Aug 31	Glossop	A	Lge	W 2-0	Peter Spencer, J.Moran
Sat Sep 5	Bradley Rangers	A	F.A.Vase Extra Prelim. Rd	W 1-0	Donnelly
Wed Sep 9	Prescot Cables	A	Lge	D 0-0	
Sat Sep 12	Kirkby Town	A	Lge	L 1-2	Paul Tomlinson
Sat Sep 19	Prescot Cables at St. Helens	H	F.A.Vase Prelim. Rd	W 2-0	Donnelly (2)
Tue Sep 22	Leyland Motors	A	Lge	L 2-4	Alan McDermott, P.Moran
Sat Sep 26	Formby	H	Lge	W 2-1	Jay Flannery, Andy Rice
Sat Oct 3	Great Harwood Town	A	Lge Cup	L 0-2	
Sat Oct 10	Warrington Town	A	Lge	L 2-4	McDermott, Steve Baker
Tue Oct 13	Darwen	H	Lge	L 1-3	S.Whittle
Sat Oct 17	Atherton Collieries	H	F.A.Vase 1st Rd	W 3-2	Donnelly (2), McDermott
Tue Oct 20	Colwyn Bay	H	Lge	L 0-2	
Sat Oct 24	St.Helens Town	A	Lge	W 1-0	Donnelly
Tue Oct 27	Skelmersdale United	H	Liverpool Senior Cup	L 0-1	
Sat Oct 31	Ellesmere Port & Neston	A	Lge	L 1-4	Whittle
Tue Nov 3	Colne Dynamoes	H	Lge	L 0-1	
Sat Nov 7	Uniasco	H	F.A.Vase 2nd Rd.	L 0-2	
Sat Nov 14	Clitheroe	A	Lge	L 0-2	
Sat Nov 21	Skelmersdale United	H	Lge	W 2-0	Mark Fletcher, Donnelly
Wed Nov 25	Horwich RMI	H	Lancs ATS Trophy	L 0-1	
Sat Dec 5	Colwyn Bay	A	Lge	W 3-2	Baker, Donnelly (2)
Sat Dec 12	Leyland Motors	H	Lge	W 3-1	Steve Burton, Baker, Fletcher
Tue Dec 15	St. Helens Town	H	Lge	D 0-0	
Sat Dec 19	Salford	A	Lge	W 1-0	Ronnie Williams
Mon Dec 28	Clitheroe	H	Lge	L 0-4	
Sat Jan 9	Atherton L.R.	H	Lge	W 1-0	Terry McDonough
Sat Jan 16	Prescot Cables	H	Lge	D 0-0	
Sat Jan 30	Bootle	H	Lge	D 2-2	Graham Green, McDonough
Sat Feb 6	Salford	H	Lge	W 2-1	Williams (2)
Sat Feb 13	Warrington Town	H	Lge	L 2-5	Jay Flannery, McDonough
Sat Feb 20	Darwen	A	Lge	L 0-2	
Sat Feb 27	Rossendale United	H	Lge	L 0-2	
Sat Mar 5	Glossop	H	Lge	W 4-1	Paul Clarke, Williams (2), Flannery
Sat Mar 12	Skelmersdale United	A	Lge	W 1-0	Williams
Sat Mar 26	Ellesmere Port & Neston	H	Lge	L 1-2	Tomlinson
Mon Apr 4	Kirkby Town	H	Lge	W 4-3	McDonough (2), Williams, Clarke
Sat Apr 9	Colne Dynamoes	A	Lge	D 0-0	
Sat Apr 16	Rossendale United	A	Lge	D 0-0	

1988/89 Season
North West Counties Football League (Division One)

Date	Opponent	H/A	Comp	Result	Scorers
Sat Aug 20	Warrington Town	A	Lge	L 0-1	
Sat Aug 27	Bootle	H	Lge	L 0-4	
Wed Aug 31	Prescot Cables	A	Lge	D 0-0	
Tue Sep 6	Colwyn Bay	H	Lge	L 1-3	McDonough
Sat Sep 10	Rossendale United	H	Lge	L 0-1	
Wed Sep 14	Leyland Motors	A	Lge	L 0-2	
Sat Sep 17	Emley	H	F.A.Cup 1st Qual. Rd	L 0-1	
Sat Sep 24	Atherton L.R.	H	Lge	W 4-2	Paul Moran, Goulding (2), Carberry
Sat Oct 1	Darwen	A	Lge	L 0-2	
Sat Oct 8	St. Dominics	H	F.A.Vase Prelim. Rd	W 3-1	Goulding (2), Alan Clark
Sat Oct 15	Skelmersdale United	A	Lge	D 0-0	
Tue Oct 18	Formby	H	Liverpool Senior Cup	W 3-0	Williams (3)
Sat Oct 22	Rossendale United	A	League Cup	L 1-7	Wood
Sat Oct 29	St. Helens Town	H	Lge	L 0-3	
Sat Nov 5	Rossendale United	A	F.A.Vase 1st Rd	L 1-6	Carberry
Sat Nov 12	Knowsley United	H	Lge	L 1-2	Johnson
Sat Nov 26	Ellesmere Port	A	Lge	D 0-0	
Sat Dec 3	Ashton United	A	Lge	W 1-0	Carberry
Sat Dec 10	Darwen	H	Lge	D 1-1	Dave Webster
Wed Dec 14	Rossendale United	A	Lge	L 1-9	Carberry
Sat Dec 17	Ellesmere Port	H	Lge	D 3-3	McDonough (2), Webster
Tue Dec 27	Leyland Motors	H	Lge	D 1-1	Mike Scott
Sat Jan 7	Bootle	A	Lge	W 4-0	Tomlinson, Shaun McIlwaine, Scott, Baker
Sat Jan 14	Prescot Cables	H	Lge	W 5-0	Byrne, Walbank, Scott, Carberry, McDonough
Sat Jan 21	Colwyn Bay	A	Lge	L 1-2	McDonough
Sat Jan 28	Salford	H	Lge	W 3-0	McIlwaine (2), Baker
Tue Jan 31	Marine	A	Liverpool Senior Cup	L 0-1	
Sat Feb 4	Atherton L.R.	A	Lge	W 1-0	Webster
Sat Feb 11	Ashton United	H	Lge	W 2-1	Webster, McDonough
Sat Feb 18	Clitheroe	A	Lge	W 3-2	Carberry (2), Baker
Sat Feb 25	Skelmersdale United	H	Lge	W 2-0	Byrne, Carberry
Sat Mar 4	St. Helens Town	A	Lge	W 2-1	Webster, McIlwaine
Tue Mar 7	Warrington Town	H	Lge	D 0-0	
Sat Mar 11	Formby	A	Lge	W 1-0	Baker
Sat Mar 18	Knowsley United	A	Lge	L 0-3	
Tue Mar 21	Clitheroe	H	Lge	D 2-2	Baker (2)
Sat Mar 25	Salford	A	Lge	L 0-1	
Mon Mar 27	Flixton	H	Lge	D 0-0	
Tue Apr 11	Formby	H	Lge	D 0-0	
Mon May 1	Flixton	A	Lge	L 1-5	Scott

1988-89 Season. Back left to right: Dave Walbank, Paul Carney, Paul Tomlinson, Paul Moran, John Burton, Paul Proctor, John McAdam.
Front left to right: Kevin Cullen, Steve Baker, Jay Flannery, Dave Fealey, Terry McDonough.

1989-90 Season. Back left to right: Physio, Kevin Humphries, Mark Cullen, Dave Walbank, Ally Anderson, Dave Webster, Paul Byrne, Tony Brookfield, Unknown.
Front left to right: Billy Buck (Asst. Manager), Paddy Baccino, Ian Hodgson, Mike Scott (Manager), Shaun McIlwaine, Colin Beck, Mike Baker, Joey Fay.

1989/90 Season
North West Counties Football League (Division One)

Date	Opponent	H/A	Competition	Result	Scorers
Sat Aug 19	Salford	H	Lge	W 5-0	McIlwaine, Fanning, Joey Dunn (3)
Tue Aug 22	Knowsley United	H	Lge	L 0-1	
Sat Aug 26	Chadderton	A	Lge	W 3-0	Paul Proctor, Mike Baker, Dunn
Mon Aug 28	Colwyn Bay	H	Lge	D 1-1	Baker
Sat Sep 2	Bootle	H	F.A.Cup Prelim. Rd	W 2-0	Tony Brookfield, Dunn
Tue Sep 5	Vauxhall GM	H	Lge	D 1-1	May
Sat Sep 9	Warrington Town	A	Lge	D 1-1	Brookfield
Wed Sep 13	Darwen	A	Lge	D 2-2	Dunn (2)
Sat Sep 16	Maine Road	H	F.A.Cup 1st Qual. Rd	L 1-2	McIlwaine
Sat Sep 23	Leyland Motors	A	Lge	L 2-4	Colin Beck, McIlwaine
Sat Sep 30	Prescot Cables	H	Lge	W 2-0	Blakeman, O.G.
Sat Oct 7	Rocester	H	F.A.Vase Prelim. Rd	L 0-2	
Sat Oct 14	Nantwich Town	A	Lge	D 0-0	
Sat Oct 21	Bootle	H	Lge	L 1-3	Beck
Sat Oct 28	Clitheroe	A	Lge	L 1-2	McAllister
Sat Nov 4	Skelmersdale United	H	Lge	W 3-1	Paul Byrne, Dave Walbank, Furlong
Sat Nov 11	Glossop	H	League Cup	W 4-1	McIlwaine, Williams, Furlong, O.G.
Sat Nov 18	Flixton	A	Lge	L 0-3	
Sat Nov 25	Atherton L.R.	H	Lge	W 3-0	McIlwaine, Webster, Baker
Sat Dec 2	Skelmersdale United	A	Lge	W 1-0	McIlwaine
Sat Dec 9	Bacup Borough	A	Lancs ATS Trophy	L 1-2	Byrne
Tue Dec 19	Marine	H	Liverpool Senior Cup	L 1-3	Baker
Sat Dec 23	Knowsley United	A	Lge	L 1-2	McIlwaine
Tue Dec 26	St. Helens Town	A	Lge	D 1-1	Dunn
Sat Dec 30	Colwyn Bay	A	Lge	L 0-2	
Mon Jan 1	St. Helens Town	H	Lge	D 1-1	Byrne
Sat Jan 13	Darwen	H	Lge	D 1-1	Brookfield
Sat Jan 20	Bootle	A	Lge	L 1-2	Baker
Sat Jan 27	Chadderton	H	Lge	W 2-1	Steve Cannon (2)
Sat Feb 3	Leyland Motors	A	League Cup	L 0-2	
Sat Feb 10	Leyland Motors	H	Lge	D 1-1	Baker
Sat Feb 17	Prescot Cables	A	Lge	L 1-2	O.G.
Sat Feb 24	Nantwich Town	H	Lge	L 0-1	
Sat Mar 3	Vauxhall GM	A	Lge	D 1-1	Cannon
Sat Mar 10	Clitheroe	H	Lge	L 0-1	
Tue Mar 13	Warrington Town	H	Lge	L 0-2	
Sat Mar 24	Flixton	H	Lge	D 0-0	
Sat Mar 31	Ashton United	A	Lge	L 1-3	Cannon
Sat Apr 7	Salford	A	Lge	W 1-0	Baker
Sat Apr 14	Atherton L.R.	A	Lge	D 0-0	
Mon Apr 16	Ashton United	H	Lge	L 0-1	

NORTH WEST COUNTIES LEAGUE - DIVISION ONE
1989-90 SEASON

	P	W	D	L	F	A	Pts
Warrington Town	34	22	6	6	69	31	72
Knowsley United	34	21	6	7	68	45	69
Colwyn Bay	34	16	12	6	79	50	60
Vauxhall GM	34	16	9	9	50	42	57
Clitheroe	34	17	6	11	48	47	57
Darwen	34	15	9	10	40	34	54
Nantwich Town	34	13	5	16	50	52	44
St. Helens Town	34	10	13	11	50	48	43
Ashton United	34	11	10	13	39	45	43
Prescot Cables	34	10	11	13	49	54	41
Bootle	34	11	8	15	44	58	41
Flixton	34	11	7	16	37	47	40
Leyland Motors	34	10	7	17	55	64	37
Atherton LR	34	8	13	13	43	58	37
Skelmersdale United	34	8	11	15	48	59	35
Salford	34	8	11	15	31	47	35
Burscough	**34**	**8**	**12**	**14**	**38**	**41**	**33***
Chadderton	34	7	12	15	39	55	33

* denotes points deducted

NORTH WEST COUNTIES LEAGUE - DIVISION TWO
1991-92 SEASON

	P	W	D	L	F	A	Pts
Bamber Bridge	34	25	3	6	97	39	78
Newcastle Town	34	23	6	5	69	26	75
Blackpool Mechanics	34	20	9	5	75	34	69
Burscough	**34**	**19**	**7**	**8**	**82**	**46**	**64**
Formby	34	17	5	12	49	39	56
Glossop	34	15	9	10	61	44	54
Salford City	34	14	9	11	57	41	51
Castleton Gabriels	34	14	9	11	54	43	51
Cheadle Town	34	15	6	13	53	50	51
Kidsgrove Athletic	34	14	7	13	44	45	49
Chadderton	34	14	6	14	50	48	48
Oldham Town	34	11	8	15	49	62	41
Atherton Collieries	34	12	4	18	51	64	40
Squires Gate	34	11	5	18	45	60	38
Holker Old Boys	34	10	6	18	37	53	36
Maghull	34	7	2	25	38	90	23
Ashton Town	34	4	7	23	47	101	19
Westhoughton Town	34	5	4	25	33	106	19

NORTH WEST COUNTIES LEAGUE - DIVISION TWO
1990-91 SEASON

	P	W	D	L	F	A	Pts
Great Harwood Town	34	27	5	2	81	22	86
Blackpool (Wren) Rovers	34	25	4	5	84	33	76*
Bradford Park Avenue	34	20	9	5	72	41	69
Bamber Bridge	34	20	6	8	78	46	66
Blackpool Mechanics	34	18	7	9	51	30	61
Newcastle Town	34	16	12	6	48	30	60
Cheadle Town	34	17	3	14	55	54	54
Glossop	34	12	10	12	47	42	46
Burscough	**34**	**12**	**8**	**14**	**39**	**51**	**44**
Westhoughton Town	34	11	10	13	50	64	43
Castleton Gabriels	34	11	9	14	42	47	42
Chadderton	34	10	6	18	51	61	36
Maghull	34	9	8	17	37	54	35
Kidsgrove Athletic	34	7	10	17	37	65	31
Ashton Town	34	9	2	23	43	86	29
Oldham Town	34	8	4	22	35	66	25*
Formby	34	5	9	20	46	63	24
Atherton Collieries	34	6	4	24	37	78	22

* denotes points deducted

NORTH WEST COUNTIES LEAGUE - DIVISION ONE
1992-93 SEASON

	P	W	D	L	F	A	Pts
Atherton LR	42	33	7	2	75	25	106
Bamber Bridge	42	24	11	7	81	37	83
Chadderton	42	24	11	7	99	64	83
Prescot	42	20	12	10	68	42	72
Newcastle Town	42	20	8	14	70	57	68
Bradford Park Avenue	42	19	8	15	54	43	65
Clitheroe	42	17	8	17	61	40	59
St. Helens Town	42	16	11	15	79	62	59
Salford City	42	15	13	14	58	61	58
Burscough	**42**	**16**	**10**	**16**	**58**	**68**	**58**
Flixton	42	14	15	13	50	42	57
Blackpool Rovers	42	16	9	17	66	64	57
Nantwich Town	42	14	15	13	60	60	57
Penrith	42	15	11	16	62	67	56
Bacup Borough	42	14	13	15	66	59	55
Glossop North End	42	16	9	17	70	67	54*
Darwen	42	14	10	18	54	61	52
Eastwood Hanley	42	14	10	18	45	57	52
Maine Road	42	12	9	21	55	63	45
Kidsgrove Athletic	42	9	8	25	53	94	35
Skelmersdale United	42	7	10	25	45	84	31
Blackpool Mechanics	42	2	4	36	27	137	10

293

1990/91 Season
North West Counties Football League (Division Two)

Date	Opponent	H/A	Competition	Result	Scorers
Sat Aug 18	Chadderton	H	Lge	L 0-2	
Tue Aug 21	Great Harwood Town	A	Lge	L 0-1	
Sat Aug 25	Bradford Park Avenue	A	Lge	D 2-2	O.G., Cannon
Mon Aug 27	Cheadle Town	H	Lge	W 1-0	Cannon
Sat Sep 1	Maine Road	H	F.A.Cup Prelim. Rd	L 0-3	
Sat Sep 8	Castleton Gabriels	A	Lamot Pils Trophy 1st leg	L 0-1	
Sat Sep 22	Blackpool Rovers	H	Lge	L 0-2	
Tue Sep 25	Castleton Gabriels	H	Lamot Pils Trophy 2nd leg	W 3-1	M.Brady, Richie Worsley, Cannon
Sat Sep 29	Blackpool Mechanics	H	Lge	L 0-2	
Sat Oct 6	Great Harwood Town	A	F.A.Vase Prelim. Rd	L 0-4	
Tue Oct 9	Formby	H	Liverpool Senior Cup	W 3-2	Cannon (2), Walbank
Sat Oct 13	Westhoughton Town	A	Lge	L 1-3	Lee Barrett
Sat Oct 20	Eastwood Hanley	A	League Cup	D 1-1	Joey Fay
Sat Oct 27	Maghull	H	Lge	W 3-2	Cannon (3)
Tue Oct 30	Eastwood Hanley	H	League Cup replay	W 3-0	Bayliss, Cannon (2)
Sat Nov 3	Ashton Town	A	Lge	W 3-1	Walbank, Jason Bridge, Cannon
Sat Nov 10	Oldham Town	H	Lge	W 3-0	McIlwaine, Barrett, Bayliss
Sat Nov 17	Castleton Gabriels	A	Lge	L 1-2	McIlwaine
Sat Nov 24	Kidsgrove Athletic	H	Lge	D 1-1	Liam Watson
Sat Dec 1	Bacup Borough	A	League Cup	D 1-1	Walbank
Tue Dec 4	Lancaster City	H	Lancs ATS Trophy	L 0-2	
Sat Dec 8	Bacup Borough	H	League Cup replay	W 1-0	Watson
Sat Dec 15	Newcastle Town	A	Lge	L 0-4	
Sat Dec 22	Ashton Town	H	Lge	W 2-0	Cannon, Watson
Sat Dec 29	Atherton Collieries	A	Lge	D 0-0	
Sat Jan 5	Atherton Collieries	H	Lge	D 0-0	
Sat Jan 12	Kidsgrove Athletic	A	Lge	W 1-0	McIlwaine
Sat Jan 19	Newcastle Town	H	Lge	L 0-1	
Sat Jan 26	Cheadle Town	A	Lge	L 1-2	McIlwaine
Sat Feb 16	Atherton Collieries	A	Lamot Pils Trophy 1st leg	L 2-3	Terry Roche, Cannon
Tue Feb 19	Bootle	A	Liverpool Senior Cup	W 1-0	Cannon
Sat Feb 23	Atherton Collieries	H	Lamot Pils Trophy 2nd leg	D 1-1	Roche
Sat Mar 2	Maine Road	A	League Cup	L 0-2	
Tue Mar 5	Formby	H	Lge	W 2-1	Bridge, Cannon
Sat Mar 9	Blackpool Mechanics	A	Lge	L 0-3	
Sat Mar 16	Westhoughton Town	H	Lge	D 2-2	Byrne, Baker
Tue Mar 19	Glossop	H	Lge	W 1-0	Cannon
Thu Mar 21	Southport	A	Liverpool Senior Cup	L 1-3	Scorer unknown
Sat Mar 23	Oldham Town	A	Lge	L 1-3	Roche
Mon Apr 1	Bamber Bridge	H	Lge	W 1-0	O.G.
Sat Apr 6	Castleton Gabriels	H	Lge	D 2-2	Baker, Cannon
Tue Apr 9	Blackpool Rovers	A	Lge	L 0-5	
Sat Apr 13	Glossop	A	Lge	W 2-0	Baker, Tommy Knox
Tue Apr 16	Bradford Park Avenue	H	Lge	L 0-1	
Sat Apr 20	Great Harwood Town	H	Lge	D 1-1	McIlwaine
Tue Apr 23	Bamber Bridge	A	Lge	L 1-5	Cannon
Sat Apr 27	Chadderton	A	Lge	W 4-1	McIlwaine (2), Cannon, Baker
Tue Apr 30	Formby	A	Lge	D 2-2	McIlwaine (2)
Sat May 4	Maghull	A	Lge	W 1-0	Bridge

1991/92 Season
North West Counties Football League (Division Two)

Date	Opponent	H/A	Competition	Result	Scorers
Sat Aug 24	Newcastle Town	H	Lge	D 1-1	Tony Quinn
Mon Aug 26	Castleton Gabriels	A	Lge	L 0-3	
Sat Aug 31	Formby	A	Lge	W 1-0	McIlwaine
Wed Sep 4	Squires Gate	H	Lge	W 2-0	Ian Hodge, Vinny Connelly
Sat Sep 7	Chadderton	H	Lge	W 1-0	McIlwaine
Tue Sep 10	Salford City	A	Lge	D 1-1	Connelly
Sat Sep 14	Buxton	A	F.A.Cup 1st Qual. Rd	L 2-4	Sean Boland (2)
Sat Sep 21	Westhoughton Town	H	Lge	W 4-0	McIlwaine, Hodge, Connelly, O.G.
Sat Sep 28	Oldham Town	A	Lge	D 1-1	Hodge
Wed Oct 2	Castleton Gabriels	H	Lge	L 1-2	Kevin Still
Sat Oct 5	St. Helens Town	A	F.A.Vase Prelim. Rd	W 3-2	Hodge (2), Quinn
Sat Oct 12	Maghull	A	Lge	W 6-1	Quinn, Hodge (2), Sean Togher, Still (2)
Tue Oct 15	Knowsley United	A	Liverpool Senior Cup	L 1-3	Dave Johnson
Sat Oct 19	Skelmersdale United	A	League Cup	W 2-0	McIlwaine, Still
Sat Oct 26	Holker Old Boys	A	Lge	W 1-0	McIlwaine
Sat Nov 2	Irlam Town	H	F.A.Vase 1st Rd	W 5-1	Hodge (2), Boland (2), Togher
Sat Nov 9	Bamber Bridge	A	Lge	W 3-2	Togher, Boland (2)
Sat Nov 16	Atherton Collieries	H	Lge	L 1-2	Hodge
Sat Nov 23	Rossendale United	H	F.A.Vase 2nd Rd	W 2-0	Boland, Hodge
Sat Nov 30	Glossop	A	League Cup	D 1-1	Togher
Wed Dec 4	Glossop	H	League Cup replay	W 3-2	Hodge, Togher, McIlwaine
Sat Dec 7	Newcastle Town	A	Lge	L 0-2	
Sat Dec 14	Newton Aycliffe	A	F.A.Vase 3rd Rd	W 4-2	Togher (3), Hodge
Tue Dec 17	Morecambe	A	Lancs ATS Trophy 1st Rd	L 0-3	
Sat Dec 21	Formby	H	Lge	L 1-3	Hodge
Thu Dec 26	Glossop	H	Lge	D 1-1	Walbank
Sat Dec 28	Cheadle Town	H	Lge	L 0-1	
Sat Jan 4	Maghull	A	Lamot Pils Trophy	W 1-0	McIlwaine
Sat Jan 11	Salford City	H	Lge	W 6-2	Hodge (3), Tony Rigby, Boland, Quinn
Sat Jan 18	Eastwood Hanley	H	F.A.Vase 4th Rd	L 0-1	
Sat Feb 1	Maine Road	H	League Cup	W 4-0	Still (2), Rigby (2)
Sat Feb 8	Maghull	H	Lamot Pils Trophy	L 1-4	Quinn
Sat Feb 15	Kidsgrove Athletic	A	Lge	D 1-1	Togher
Sat Feb 22	Oldham Town	H	Lge	W 9-2	Still (4), Hodge (3), Norman Owers (2)
Tue Feb 25	Blackpool Mechanics	H	Lge	W 1-0	Still
Sat Feb 29	Ashton Town	H	Lge	W 3-1	McIlwaine, Hodge (2)
Sat Mar 7	Squires Gate	A	Lge	W 4-3	Still, Quinn, Rigby, Boland
Sat Mar 14	Bamber Bridge	H	Lge	L 1-2	O.G.
Tue Mar 17	Kidsgrove Athletic	H	Lge	W 4-1	Still (3), Hodge
Sat Mar 21	Atherton Collieries	A	Lge	D 1-1	Still
Tue Mar 24	Maghull	H	Lge	W 6-1	O.G., Steve Salt, Hodge, Togher, Jimmy Clark, Steven Perkins
Sat Mar 28	Blackpool Mechanics	A	Lge	W 2-0	Rigby, Togher
Wed Apr 1	Chadderton	A	Lge	D 1-1	Gary Winn
Sat Apr 4	Eastwood Hanley	H	League Cup	W 2-0	Togher (2)
Tue Apr 7	Ashton Town	A	Lge	W 4-3	Rigby (2), Owers (2)
Sat Apr 11	Eastwood Hanley	A	League Cup	L 1-3	Rigby
Sat Apr 18	Glossop	A	Lge	W 3-1	Togher (2), Quinn
Mon Apr 20	Holker Old Boys	H	Lge	W 6-1	Brenden Doyle, Quinn, Togher, Boland, Rigby (2)
Sat Apr 25	Cheadle Town	A	Lge	W 3-2	Knox, Still, Quinn
Thu Apr 30	Ashton United at Gigg Lane, Bury		League Cup Final	L 0-1	
Sat May 2	Westhoughton Town	A	Lge	L 2-4	Quinn, Perkins

1991-92 Season. Back left to right: Rod Cottam (Physio), Ian Hodge, Tommy Knox, Steve Salt, Brendan Doyle, Alan Robinson, Sean Togher, Norman Owers, Gary Winn, Alan Thompson, Kevin Sephton, John Thompson. Front left to right: Steven Perkins, Tony Rigby, Jimmy Clark, Paul Mahon (Asst. Manager), Frank Parr (Chairman), Russ Perkins (Manager), Tony Quinn, Kevin Still, Ian Owen. Kevin Still was voted the Club's Player of the Year.

1992-93 Season. Liverpool Senior Cup Finalists, pictured at Goodison Park.
Back left to right: Sean Togher, Ian Owen, Gary Martindale, Alan Robinson, Tommy Knox, Andy Doyle, Kevin Still, Brian Fairclough, Rod Cottam (physio). Front left to right: Gary Trewhitt, Brendan Doyle, Tony Quinn, Bobby Howard (Asst. Manager), Martin Lowe, Steven Perkins. Player of the Year was Ian Owen.

1992/93 Season
North West Counties Football League (Division One)

Date	Opponent	H/A	Competition	Result	Scorers
Sat Aug 15	Kidsgrove Athletic	H	Lge	L 0-2	
Tue Aug 18	St. Helens Town	H	Lge	W 3-2	Lee Nolan (2), Togher
Wed Aug 26	Darwen	A	Lge	W 3-2	Mike McDonald, Togher, Gary Harrison
Sat Aug 29	Bradford Park Avenue	A	F.A.Cup Prelim. Rd	D 1-1	Still
	played at Burscough				
Tue Sep 1	Bradford Park Avenue	H	F.A.Cup replay	L 1-2	Togher
Sat Sep 5	Chadderton	H	Lge	L 1-3	Togher
Tue Sep 8	Prescot	H	Lge	D 0-0	
Sat Sep 12	Salford City	A	Lge	D 2-2	Quinn (2)
Tue Sep 15	Darwen	H	Lge	W 1-0	Steve Nickson
Sat Sep 19	Flixton	A	Lge	L 1-2	Stephen Brough
Tue Sep 22	Skelmersdale United	A	Lge	L 0-3	
Sat Sep 26	Bacup Borough	H	Lge	W 4-1	Knox, Still, Brough, Togher
Sat Oct 3	Wythenshawe Amateurs	A	F.A.Vase Prelim. Rd	W 3-1	Brough, Still, Harrison
Sat Oct 10	Bamber Bridge	H	Lge	L 0-2	
Sat Oct 17	Newcastle Town	A	Lge	L 1-3	Brough
Tue Oct 20	St.Helens Town	H	Floodlit Trophy	W 3-1	Lee Barrett, Colin Stafford, Still
Sat Oct 24	Blackpool Mechanics	H	Lge	D 3-3	Still, Brough, Harrison
Sat Oct 31	Netherfield	H	F.A.Vase 1st Rd	W 2-1	Stafford, Still
Tue Nov 3	Blackpool Rovers	A	Lge	L 2-6	Stafford, Quinn
Sat Nov 7	Clitheroe	H	Lge	W 2-1	Togher, Still
Tue Nov 10	St. Helens Town	A	Floodlit Trophy	W 2-1	Andy Doyle, Stafford
Sat Nov 14	Bamber Bridge	A	Lge	L 0-1	
Tue Nov 17	Prescot	H	Floodlit Trophy	L 0-4	
Sat Nov 21	Lincoln United	H	F.A.Vase 2nd Rd	W 3-1	Togher (2), Still
Tue Nov 24	Bacup Borough	H	Lancs ATS Trophy	W 2-0	Quinn, Harrison
Sat Nov 28	Formby	A	League Cup	W 4-0	Still (2), Togher (2)
Tue Dec 1	Formby	H	Liverpool Senior Cup	W 5-1	Still (2), Quinn (2), Knox
Sat Dec 12	Ponteland United	H	F.A.Vase 3rd Rd.	W 1-0	Harrison
Sat Dec 19	Blackpool Mechanics	A	Lge	W 4-0	Quinn (2), Still, O.G.
Sat Dec 26	Skelmersdale United	H	Lge	W 1-0	Togher
Sat Jan 2	Bradford Park Avenue	H	Lge	D 2-2	Harrison, Still
Tue Jan 5	Bootle	A	Floodlit Trophy	D 1-1	Quinn
Sat Jan 9	Eastwood Hanley	H	Lge	D 0-0	
Tue Jan 12	Prescot	A	Floodlit Trophy	D 0-0	
Sat Jan 16	Cammell Laird	H	F.A.Vase 4th Rd	L 0-1	
	Attend: 500				
Tue Jan 19	Bootle	H	Floodlit Trophy	D 2-2	Bobby Howard, Quinn
Sat Jan 23	Penrith	H	Lge	D 0-0	
Tue Jan 26	Radcliffe Borough	H	Lancs ATS Trophy	L 1-2	Howard
Sat Jan 30	Glossop North End	A	Lge	W 2-1	B.Doyle, Still
Tue Feb 2	Clitheroe	H	League Cup	W 6-2	Martindale (2), Martin Lowe, Harrison, Still (2)
Sat Feb 6	Bamber Bridge	H	League Cup	W 4-1	Gary Martindale (2), Quinn, Togher
Sat Feb 13	Kidsgrove Athletic	A	League Cup	W 4-1	Martindale (2), Togher (2)
Tue Feb 16	St. Helens Town	H	Liverpool Senior Cup	W 1-0	Martindale
Sat Feb 20	Maine Road	H	Lge	L 0-1	
Tue Feb 23	Prescot	A	Lge	D 0-0	
Sat Feb 27	Nantwich Town	A	Lge	L 0-6	
Tue Mar 2	St. Helens Town	A	Lge	L 0-4	
Sat Mar 6	Prescot	H	League Cup S/F 1st leg	W 1-0	Quinn
Sat Mar 13	Prescot	A	League Cup S/F 2nd leg	D 2-2	Quinn, Togher
Tue Mar 9	Maine Road	A	Lge	W 2-1	B.Doyle, Martindale
Tue Mar 16	Atherton L.R.	H	Lge	D 0-0	
Sat Mar 20	Clitheroe	A	Lge	L 0-1	
Tue Mar 23	Flixton	H	Lge	W 4-1	Brian Fairclough, Martindale (2), B.Doyle
Sat Mar 27	Glossop North End	H	Lge	W 3-2	Martindale (2), Quinn
Mon Mar 29	Everton	A	Liverpool Senior Cup	W 2-0	A.Doyle, B.Doyle
	at Goodison Park - Attend: 693		Semi-final		
Sat Apr 3	Eastwood Hanley	A	Lge	W 1-0	Martindale
Wed Apr 7	Chadderton	A	Lge	D 2-2	Martindale, Togher
Sat Apr 10	Bradford Park Avenue	A	Lge	W 2-1	Martindale, Still
Mon Apr 12	Blackpool Rovers	H	Lge	D 2-2	Quinn (2)
Sat Apr 17	Newcastle Town	H	Lge	W 1-0	Knox
Tue Apr 20	Salford City	H	Lge	L 1-3	Fairclough
Thu Apr 22	Nantwich Town		League Cup Final	W 2-1	B.Doyle, Togher
	at Gigg Lane, Bury - Attend: 500				
Sat Apr 24	Bacup Borough	A	Lge	L 0-1	
Tue Apr 27	Atherton L.R.	A	Lge	L 0-1	
Sat May 1	Penrith	A	Lge	L 2-4	Lowe, Still
Thu May 6	Atherton L.R.	A	League Champions v. Lge Cup Winners	L 0-1	
Sat May 8	Nantwich Town	H	Lge	W 2-1	Still (2)
Tue May 11	Southport		Liverpool Senior Cup Final	L 1-2	Still
	at Goodison Park - Attend: 1,813				

1993/94 Season
North West Counties Football League (Division One)

Date	Opponent	H/A	Competition	Result	Scorers
Sat Aug 14	Maine Road	H	Lge	W 3-0	Mick McDonough, Quinn, McIlwaine
Wed Aug 18	Nantwich Town	A	Lge	D 3-3	Andy Doyle, Martindale, Quinn
Sat Aug 21	Maine Road	A	Lge	W 6-1	Martindale (3), Russell, M.McDonough, Togher
Tue Aug 24	Eastwood Hanley	H	Lge	D 1-1	Ged Nolan
Sat Aug 28	Caernarfon Town at Curzon Ashton F.C.	A	F.A.Cup Prelim. Rd	D 0-0	
Tue Aug 31	Caernarfon Town	H	F.A.Cup replay	W 2-0	McIlwaine, Alex Russell
Sat Sep 4	Bacup Borough	A	Lge	D 2-2	Quinn, M.McDonough
Tue Sep 7	Newcastle Town	H	Lge	L 1-2	Quinn
Sat Sep 11	Bootle	A	F.A.Cup 1st Qual. Rd	L 1-5	Russell
Sat Sep 18	Atherton L.R.	A	Lge	W 1-0	Russell
Tue Sep 21	Penrith	H	Lge	D 2-2	Martindale (2)
Sat Sep 25	Darwen	H	Lge	W 4-0	Russell (2), Martindale, M.McDonough
Mon Sep 27	Rossendale United	A	Lge	W 3-0	Martindale (2), McIlwaine
Sat Oct 2	Flixton	H	Lge	W 4-0	Quinn, Russell, M.McDonough (2)
Tue Oct 5	Skelmersdale United	A	Lge	D 2-2	Martindale, Howard
Sat Oct 9	Kidsgrove Athletic	A	Lge	W 2-1	Russell, McIlwaine
Tue Oct 12	Prescot	A	Floodlit Trophy	D 0-0	
Sat Oct 16	Clitheroe	H	Lge	D 1-1	M.McDonough
Sat Oct 23	Salford City	A	Lge	W 2-1	Martindale, M.McDonough
Tue Oct 26	Prescot	H	Floodlit Trophy	W 2-0	Martindale, M.McDonough
Tue Nov 2	Prescot	H	Lge	L 1-2	Quinn
Sat Nov 6	Eastwood Hanley	A	Lge	L 0-1	
Tue Nov 9	Marine	A	Liverpool Senior Cup	L 0-4	
Sat Nov 13	Atherton Collieries	H	League Cup	D 2-2	Martindale (2)
Sat Nov 20	Penrith	H	F.A.Vase 2nd Rd	L 2-3	Ian Owen, M.McDonough
Sat Nov 27	Atherton Collieries	A	League Cup replay	W 4-2	Martindale, Matt Helme, Russell, M.McDonough
Tue Nov 30	Darwen	H	Lancs ATS Trophy	W 1-0	M.McDonough
Sat Dec 4	Penrith	A	Lge	W 3-0	Martindale, Knox, Quinn
Tue Dec 7	Rossendale United	H	Lge	W 5-1	Martindale, M.McDonough (2), Quinn, Knox
Sat Dec 11	St. Helens Town	H	Lge	W 3-2	Quinn, Steve King, Martindale
Sat Dec 18	Newcastle Town	A	Lge	D 1-1	Quinn
Thu Dec 30	Prescot	A	Lge	D 2-2	Martindale (2)
Mon Jan 3	Blackpool Rovers	H	Lge	W 4-1	Nolan, M.McDonough, Formby, Martindale
Sat Jan 8	Maine Road	H	League Cup	D 1-1	Terry McDonough
Tue Jan 11	Maine Road	A	League Cup replay	L 1-3	Martindale
Sat Jan 15	Bamber Bridge	A	Lancs ATS Trophy	L 4-5	M.McDonough (2), Martindale, Perkins
Tue Jan 18	Newcastle Town	H	Floodlit Trophy	W 2-1	T.McDonough, Howard
Sat Jan 22	Bootle	H	Lge	L 0-2	
Tue Jan 25	Flixton	H	Floodlit Trophy	W 3-0	M.McDonough (2), Martindale
Sat Feb 5	Bradford Park Avenue	A	Lge	D 2-2	Martindale (2)
Tue Feb 8	Glossop North End	H	Lge	W 8-0	Kevin Formby (3), Martindale (2), T.McDonough, Knox, Still
Sat Feb 12	Chadderton	H	Lge	D 1-1	Martindale
Sat Feb 19	Clitheroe	A	Lge	W 5-0	Martindale (4), Knox
Sat Feb 26	Flixton	A	Lge	W 5-0	Howard, O.G., Formby, Martindale, Russell
Tue Mar 1	Glossop North End	A	Lge	L 0-3	
Sat Mar 5	Skelmersdale United	H	Lge	W 4-0	Still, Formby (2), Russell
Sat Mar 12	Salford City	H	Lge	W 4-2	Russell (2), Martindale (2)
Tue Mar 15	Bootle	H	Floodlit Trophy Semi-final	D 1-1	Gary Trewhitt
Sat Mar 19	Kidsgrove Athletic	H	Lge	D 2-2	Still, Russell
Tue Mar 22	Bacup Borough	H	Lge	W 4-3	Formby, Still, Howard, Knox
Sat Mar 26	St. Helens Town	A	Lge	W 1-0	Steve Fletcher
Tue Mar 29	Bootle	A	Floodlit Trophy Semi-final	L 1-3	Owen
Sat Apr 2	Chadderton	A	Lge	W 2-0	Helme, Still
Mon Apr 4	Bradford Park Avenue	H	Lge	D 1-1	Dave Billows
Thu Apr 7	Nantwich Town	H	Lge	W 9-3	Knox, Russell (4), Doyle, Howard, Billows (2)
Sat Apr 9	Blackpool Rovers	A	Lge	W 1-0	O.G.
Sat Apr 16	Atherton L.R.	H	Lge	L 0-1	
Sat Apr 23	Darwen	A	Lge	D 0-0	
Sat Apr 30	Bootle	A	Lge	L 2-4	Still, Togher

1994/95 Season
North West Counties Football League (Division One)

Date	Opponent	H/A	Comp	Result	Scorers
Sat Aug 13	Kidsgrove Athletic	A	Lge	W 3-0	Keith Vincent, John Brady (2)
Tue Aug 16	Bradford Park Avenue	H	Lge	L 1-2	Mick McDonough
Sat Aug 20	Prescot	H	Lge	D 2-2	Brady, Stevie Horrocks
Tue Aug 23	Maine Road	A	Lge	D 1-1	McDonough
Sat Aug 27	Bradford Park Avenue	A	F.A.Cup Prelim. Rd	W 3-0	Brady, Still, McDonough
Mon Aug 29	Skelmersdale United	H	Lge	W 6-3	Brady, Still, Helme (2), Stephen Baines, Robbie Cowley
Sat Sep 3	Eastwood Hanley	A	Lge	D 1-1	Brady
Tue Sep 6	Salford City	H	Lge	W 5-2	McDonough, Brady (2), Cowley (2)
Sat Sep 10	Horwich RMI	H	F.A.Cup 1st Qual. Rd	W 1-0	McDonough
Tue Sep 13	Bradford Park Avenue	A	Lge	D 2-2	Quinn, Darren Donnelly
Sat Sep 17	Eastwood Hanley	H	Lge	W 3-2	Brady, McDonough, Cowley
Tue Sep 20	Bacup Borough	H	Lge	W 5-1	Cowley, O.G.(2), McDonough, Horrocks
Sat Sep 24	Congleton Town	H	F.A.Cup 2nd Qual. Rd	D 0-0	
Wed Sep 28	Congleton Town	A	F.A.Cup replay	D 3-3	Brady (2), Horrocks
Sat Oct 1	Nantwich Town	A	Lge	L 1-2	Donnelly
Mon Oct 3	Congleton Town	H	F.A.Cup 2nd replay	D 2-2	Helme, Cowley
Thu Oct 6	Congleton Town	A	F.A.Cup 3rd replay	L 2-5	Vincent (2)
Tue Oct 11	Oldham Town	A	Floodlit Trophy 1st leg	L 2-5	Lee Bedson, Lee Steele
Sat Oct 15	Darwen	H	Lge	D 3-3	Vincent, Brady, Mark Sharrock
Sat Oct 22	Bacup Borough	A	Lge	W 2-1	Billows, Vincent
Tue Oct 25	Oldham Town	H	Floodlit Trophy 2nd leg	W 3-2	Brady, Billy Loughlin, Vincent
Sat Oct 29	Prescot	A	Lge	D 1-1	Bedson
Tue Nov 8	Newcastle Town	A	Lge	L 0-4	
Sat Nov 12	Stantondale	H	Lge Cup 2nd Rd	W 4-1	Cowley, Vincent, Bedson, Still
Tue Nov 15	Southport	H	Liverpool Senior Cup	L 2-3	Vincent, Brady
Sat Nov 19	Brigg Town	H	F.A.Vase 2nd Rd	W 2-0	Vincent, Cowley
Sat Nov 26	Nantwich Town	H	Lge	D 3-3	Bedson, Brady, Cowley
Mon Nov 28	Atherton L.R.	H	Lancs ATS Trophy	L 1-4	Helme
Sat Dec 3	Glossop North End	A	Lge	L 1-2	Vincent
Tue Dec 6	Penrith	H	Lge	W 4-0	Cowley (2), Helme, Bedson
Sat Dec 10	Arnold Town	A	F.A.Vase 3rd Rd	W 3-2	Cowley, Bedson, Mike Fagan
Sat Dec 17	Newcastle Town	H	Lge	L 1-2	Bedson
Tue Dec 20	Chadderton	H	Lge	W 3-1	Bedson, Vincent, Helme
Mon Dec 26	Skelmersdale United	A	Lge	W 4-1	Cowley (3), Bedson
Sat Dec 31	Trafford	H	Lge	W 4-0	Cowley (2), Bedson, Vincent
Sat Jan 7	Kidsgrove Athletic	H	Lge	L 2-3	Brady, Bedson
Sat Jan 14	Brandon United	H	F.A.Vase 4th Rd	W 3-0	Brady, Still, Cowley
Sat Jan 21	St. Helens Town	H	Lge	D 1-1	Cowley
Tue Jan 24	Atherton Collieries	H	Lge Cup 3rd Rd	L 2-5	Bedson (2)
Sat Feb 4	Cammell Laird	A	F.A.Vase 5th Rd	L 2-4	Brady, Vincent
Sat Feb 18	Bootle	H	Lge	D 1-1	Cowley
Mon Feb 20	Clitheroe	A	Lge	L 1-4	Cowley
Sat Feb 25	Penrith	A	Lge	W 2-1	Helme, Cowley
Sat Mar 4	Clitheroe	H	Lge	D 2-2	Cowley, Helme
Tue Mar 7	Glossop North End	H	Lge	D 2-2	Helme, Cowley
Tue Mar 14	Chadderton	A	Lge	W 5-0	Vincent (2), Chris Stanton, Jackson, Cowley
Sat Mar 25	Blackpool Rovers	H	Lge	D 3-3	Vincent, Bedson, Still
Tue Mar 28	Holker Old Boys	H	Lge	W 2-0	Still, Vincent
Sat Apr 1	Rossendale United	H	Lge	W 3-0	Still, Ray Birch (2)
Wed Apr 5	Holker Old Boys	A	Lge	D 1-1	Vincent
Sat Apr 8	Maine Road	H	Lge	W 3-1	Cowley, Horrocks, Birch
Tue Apr 11	Bootle	A	Lge	D 4-4	Birch, Helme, Andy Farley, Bedson
Sat Apr 15	Salford City	A	Lge	W 2-1	Steve Jackson, Cowley
Mon Apr 17	St. Helens Town	A	Lge	W 5-0	Stanton, Birch (2), Cowley, Bedson
Wed Apr 19	Trafford	A	Lge	D 0-0	
Sat Apr 22	Darwen	A	Lge	W 2-1	Cowley (2)
Tue Apr 25	Blackpool Rovers	A	Lge	L 1-4	Birch
Fri Apr 28	Rossendale United	A	Lge	W 4-0	Helme, Bedson, Vincent (2)

NORTH WEST COUNTIES LEAGUE - DIVISION ONE
1993-94 SEASON

	P	W	D	L	F	A	Pts
Atherton L.R.	42	25	13	4	83	34	88
Rossendale United	42	25	9	8	76	46	84
Burscough	**42**	**22**	**13**	**7**	**107**	**50**	**79**
Nantwich Town	42	22	11	9	80	54	77
Eastwood Hanley	42	22	11	9	75	52	77
Bootle	42	21	10	11	77	61	73
Penrith	42	20	11	11	62	44	71
Blackpool Rovers	42	19	10	13	64	57	67
Clitheroe	42	19	9	14	75	58	66
Kidsgrove Athletic	42	16	10	16	70	61	58
St. Helens Town	42	14	13	15	60	55	55
Prescot	42	14	13	15	46	47	55
Maine Road	42	14	13	15	58	64	55
Newcastle Town	42	14	10	18	66	67	52
Bradford Park Avenue	42	12	12	18	54	79	48
Darwen	42	12	8	22	38	61	44
Glossop North End	42	12	8	22	58	86	44
Salford City	42	11	10	21	50	67	43
Chadderton	42	10	8	24	49	85	38
Bacup Borough	42	9	9	24	57	85	36
Skelmersdale United	42	8	8	26	55	92	32
Flixton	42	9	5	28	35	90	32

NORTH WEST COUNTIES LEAGUE - DIVISION ONE
1995-96 SEASON

	P	W	D	L	F	A	Pts
Flixton	42	28	8	6	85	30	92
Newcastle Town	42	26	7	9	88	42	85
Trafford	42	26	5	11	89	45	83
Mossley	42	24	8	10	87	59	80
Burscough	**42**	**23**	**8**	**11**	**77**	**40**	**77**
Bootle	42	23	5	14	74	55	74
Clitheroe	42	20	12	10	63	44	72
St. Helens Town	42	19	13	10	71	53	70
Nantwich Town	42	20	7	15	64	59	67
Prescot Cables	42	17	11	14	70	66	62
Holker Old Boys	42	19	4	19	77	72	61
Glossop North End	42	14	15	13	52	48	57
Kidsgrove Athletic	42	15	9	18	61	64	54
Eastwood Hanley	42	12	15	15	60	57	51
Maine Road	42	12	14	16	60	71	50
Chadderton	42	14	8	20	52	69	50
Blackpool Rovers	42	11	9	22	49	74	42
Penrith	42	9	12	21	57	69	39
Darwen	42	9	10	23	57	77	37
Salford City	42	10	5	27	49	93	35
Rossendale United	42	6	10	26	32	114	28
Skelmersdale United	42	5	3	34	45	121	18

NORTH WEST COUNTIES LEAGUE - DIVISION ONE
1994-95 SEASON

	P	W	D	L	F	A	Pts
Bradford Park Avenue	42	30	4	8	96	43	94
Clitheroe	42	27	9	6	104	49	90
St. Helens Town	42	28	8	7	86	42	89
Trafford	42	27	5	10	98	50	86
Newcastle Town	42	24	7	11	75	57	79
Glossop North End	42	23	8	11	88	59	77
Blackpool Rovers	42	22	7	13	81	64	73
Burscough	**42**	**19**	**15**	**8**	**102**	**65**	**72**
Prescot	42	16	8	18	47	47	56
Penrith	42	16	7	19	72	72	55
Chadderton	42	15	7	20	56	70	52
Maine Road	42	14	9	19	69	83	51
Holker Old Boys	42	13	11	18	61	69	50
Kidsgrove Athletic	42	14	8	20	66	78	50
Eastwood Hanley	42	14	8	20	75	81	50
Nantwich Town	42	14	7	21	85	83	49
Darwen	42	14	5	23	65	82	47
Rossendale United	42	12	11	19	60	82	47
Bootle	42	11	10	21	46	68	43
Skelmersdale United	42	10	7	25	67	118	37
Salford City	42	9	9	24	45	85	36
Bacup Borough	42	3	6	33	35	132	15

1995/96 Season
North West Counties Football League (Division One)

Date	Opponent	H/A	Competition	Result	Scorers
Sat Aug 19	Glossop North End	A	Lge	D 1-1	McDonough
Tue Aug 22	Holker Old Boys	H	Lge	W 5-1	Andy Howard (2), Birch, Terry McPhillips (2)
Sat Aug 26	Northallerton	H	F.A.Cup Prelim. Rd	D 2-2	McDonough
Wed Aug 30	Northallerton	A	F.A.Cup replay	W 2-1	Bedson, Birch
Sat Sep 2	Holker Old Boys	A	Lge	W 3-1	Bedson (2), Jackson
Tue Sep 5	Chadderton	A	Lge	W 4-0	McDonough (2), Bedson, Birch
Sat Sep 9	Northwich Victoria	A	F.A.Cup 1st Qual. Rd	L 0-5	
Tue Sep 12	Eastwood Hanley	H	Lge	D 2-2	McDonough, Knox
Sat Sep 16	Kidsgrove Athletic	A	Lge	W 1-0	McDonough
Wed Sep 20	St. Helens Town	A	Lge	L 0-1	
Sat Sep 23	Chadderton	H	Lge	W 2-0	McDonough, Jackson
Tue Sep 26	Blackpool Rovers	H	Lge	W 4-2	Lee Trundle (4)
Tue Oct 3	St. Helens Town	H	Floodlit Trophy 1st leg	W 3-0	Bedson (2), Trundle
Sat Oct 7	Penrith	A	Lge	W 2-1	Bedson, Peter King
Tue Oct 10	St. Helens Town	H	Lge	L 0-2	
Sat Oct 14	Nantwich Town	H	Lge	W 2-1	Horrocks, Still
Wed Oct 18	St. Helens Town	A	Floodlit Trophy 2nd leg	L 0-5	
Sat Oct 21	Flixton	H	Lge	L 0-1	
Sat Oct 28	Newcastle Town	A	F.A.Vase	L 1-3	Howard
Tue Oct 31	Skelmersdale United	H	Lge	W 3-0	Jackson, Horrocks, Brady
Sat Nov 4	Maine Road	H	Lge	W 2-0	McDonough (2)
Mon Nov 6	Clitheroe	A	Lge	W 3-1	McPhillips (2), McDonough
Sat Nov 11	Stantondale	H	Lge Cup	W 6-0	McDonough, Howard (4), Darren Saint
Sat Nov 18	Salford City	A	Lge	W 7-0	Neil Hanson, McPhillips (3), McDonough, Jackson, Howard
Sat Nov 25	Mossley	A	Lge	L 0-1	
Mon Nov 27	Marine	H	Lancs ATS Trophy	D 3-3	McDonough (2), McPhillips
Sat Dec 2	Darwen	H	Lge	D 2-2	Nolan, O.G.
Tue Dec 5	Marine	A	Lancs ATS Trophy replay	L 0-2	
Sat Dec 9	Rossendale United	A	Lge	D 1-1	Brady
Sat Dec 16	Glossop North End	H	Lge	L 2-3	McPhillips (2)
Tue Dec 19	St. Helens Town	H	Liverpool Senior Cup	L 1-2	Brady
Sat Dec 23	Bootle	H	Lge	W 3-1	McPhillips, Jackson, Helme
Sat Jan 6	Prescot Cables	H	Lge	D 2-2	Howard, McPhillips
Sat Jan 13	Penrith	H	Lge	W 3-1	McPhillips, O.G., Howard
Sat Jan 20	Prescot Cables	H	Lge Cup	W 1-0	McPhillips
Sat Feb 3	Maine Road	A	Lge	D 2-2	Howard, McDonough
Sat Feb 17	Bootle	H	Lge	W 3-1	McDonough, Howard
Tue Feb 20	Trafford	A	Lge	W 1-0	Howard
Sat Feb 24	Mossley	H	Lge	W 1-0	McPhillips
Sat Mar 2	Eastwood Hanley	A	Lge	L 0-1	
Tue Mar 5	Clitheroe	H	Lge	W 2-0	McPhillips, McDonough
Sat Mar 9	Darwen	A	Lge Cup Q/Final	W 3-1	McPhillips (2), Billy Knowles
Sat Mar 16	Rossendale United	H	Lge	W 6-0	McPhillips (2), Howard, McDonough, Brendan Grant, Paul Dawson
Tue Mar 19	Newcastle Town	H	Lge	L 1-2	Howard
Sat Mar 23	Blackpool Rovers	A	Lge	L 0-1	
Sat Mar 30	Prescot Cables	A	Lge	L 0-2	
Sat Apr 6	Holker Old Boys	H	Lge Cup S/F 1st leg	W 3-0	Howard, Still, McDonough
Mon Apr 8	Skelmersdale United	A	Lge	W 1-0	Still
Wed Apr 10	Trafford	H	Lge	D 1-1	King
Sat Apr 13	Holker Old Boys	A	Lge Cup S/F 2nd leg	L 1-3	Howard
Thu Apr 18	Kidsgrove Athletic	H	Lge	W 2-1	O.G., Howard
Sat Apr 20	Nantwich Town	A	Lge	W 2-0	Hanson (2)
Tue Apr 23	Flixton	A	Lge	L 0-2	
Thu Apr 25	Flixton		League Cup Final	W 1-0	Phil Farrelly
	at Gigg Lane, Bury - Attend: 458				
Sat Apr 27	Salford City	H	Lge	W 1-0	Paul Gwyther
Tue Apr 30	Darwen	A	Lge	L 1-3	Hanson
Mon May 6	Newcastle Town	A	Lge	D 0-0	
Fri May 17	Flixton	A	Champions v Cup winners	W 1-0	Hanson

BURSCOUGH A.F.C.

Season	P	W	D	L	F	A	Pos.	Highlights	Goalscorers
Liverpool County Combination Div. 1									
1946-47	32	18	6	8	81	47	3		
1947-48	49	32	7	10	154	91	5	Lancs Junior Cup, Geo. Mahon Cup & Liverpool Challenge Cup winners	Wesley Bridge 57 goals
1948-49	43	23	5	15	120	82	8		Wesley Bridge 51 goals
1949-50	47	33	6	8	137	54	1	Lancs Junior Cup winners & League Champions	Wesley Bridge 51 goals
1950-51	51	28	9	14	134	68	6	Liverpool Challenge Cup winners	
1951-52	42	17	7	18	93	86	9		
1952-53	42	20	6	16	106	87	6	Louis Bimpson scored 7 goals on first team debut - transferred to Liverpool	Louis Bimpson 24 goals
Lancashire Combination Div. 2									
1953-54	55	41	5	9	180	49	1	League Champions & Reserves Champions County Comb. Div. 2	Johnny Vincent 60 goals
Lancashire Combination Div. 1									
1954-55	53	27	10	16	97	63	4	Reserves won Liverpool Challenge Cup	
1955-56	51	33	10	8	121	50	1	League Champions & Liverpool Senior Non-lge Cup winners	Joe Hart 32 goals
1956-57	44	21	7	16	100	75	5		Joe Hart 31 goals
1957-58	58	24	10	24	111	104	14	Lancs Comb Cup finalists	
1958-59	49	16	11	22	71	86	12		Ted Green 22 goals
1959-60	54	27	9	18	121	92	6	1st Rd F.A. Cup - lost 1-3 to Crewe Alexandra	Arthur Rowley 42 goals
1960-61	51	26	12	13	88	66	4		Harry Lyon 33 goals
1961-62	50	29	9	12	135	89	4		Harry Lyon 56 goals
1962-63	52	17	8	27	88	124	16		
1963-64	50	13	13	24	91	97	15		
1964-65	49	13	4	32	86	106	20		
1965-66	49	16	6	27	89	102	16		
1966-67	58	23	11	24	87	104	14	Lancs Junior Cup winners	
1967-68	53	17	13	23	74	86	14	Reserves County Comb Div. 2 & Lord Wavertree Cup winners	
1968-69	53	28	13	12	137	76	4	Lancs Comb Cup finalists	Brian Robinson 51 goals
1969-70	47	33	5	9	131	48	1	League Champions	Brian Robinson 42 goals

302

Cheshire County League

Season									
1970-71	49	26	12	11	116	79	2	Liverpool Senior Non-lge Cup winners	Leo Skeete 38 goals
1971-72	55	26	11	18	102	75	7		Brian Robinson 25 goals
1972-73	60	25	16	19	95	83	7		
1973-74	65	31	14	20	113	81	6	Runners-up Liverpool Senior Non-lge Cup & Cheshire League Cup	Joe Flaherty 28 goals
1974-75	66	32	16	18	111	73	7	Cheshire League Cup winners	Joe Flaherty 31 goals
1975-76	49	18	11	20	75	84	12		
1976-77	50	13	17	20	72	84	14		
1977-78	54	19	14	21	69	71	14	1st Rd F.A. Cup - lost 0-1 at Blyth Spartans	

Cheshire County League Div. 1

Season									
1978-79	47	20	15	12	65	42	5		Billy Jaycock 29 goals
1979-80	53	25	12	16	97	69	5	1st Rd F.A. Cup - lost 0-3 at Sheffield United	
1980-81	50	16	8	26	73	79	16		Billy Jaycock 25 goals
1981-82	56	31	13	12	100	57	3	1st Rd F.A. Cup - lost 1-2 to Altrincham	

North West Counties Football League Div. 1

Season									
1982-83	52	32	10	10	116	62	1	League Champions & winners Champions v Cup-winners Trophy	John Brady 27 goals
1983-84	48	25	10	13	104	68	4		John Coleman 30 goals
1984-85	53	31	9	13	108	71	3		John Coleman 39 goals
1985-86	48	17	13	18	55	53	9		
1986-87	50	16	13	21	75	70	12		
1987-88	42	17	7	18	52	61	10		
1988-89	40	13	10	17	48	67	10		
1989-90	41	10	12	19	47	53	17		

North West Counties Football League Div. 2

Season									
1990-91	49	17	11	21	56	75	9		
1991-92	51	28	8	15	114	73	4	League Cup finalists & promotion	

North West Counties Football League Div. 1

Season									
1992-93	68	31	15	22	108	96	10	League Cup winners & Liverpool Senior Cup finalists	Kevin Still 22 goals
1993-94	59	28	18	13	134	80	3	Three players transferred to Football League	Gary Martindale 36 goals
1994-95	58	26	18	14	137	101	8	Last 16 of the F.A. Vase	Robbie Cowley 30 goals
1995-96	58	31	10	17	105	67	5	League Cup winners & winners Champions v Cup-winners Trophy	

| TOTAL | 2553 | 1179 | 525 | 849 | 4979 | 3812 | | | |

THE GOALSCORERS

Most goals in a Game

PLAYER	GOALS	SEASON*
Louis Bimpson	7	1952-1953
Wesley Bridge	6	1947-1948
Wesley Bridge	5	1949-1950
Brian Robinson	5	1968-1969
Brian Robinson	5	1970-1971
Jackie Allen	4	1972-1973
Harry Bergin	4	1950-1951
John Coleman	4	1984-1985
John Disley	4	1956-1957
Alan Donnelly	4	1985-1986
Brendan Grant	4	1986-1987
Joe Hart	4	1953-1954
Andy Howard	4	1995-1996
Billy Jaycock	4	1978-1979
Stan Jones	4	1952-1953
Harry Lyon	4	1961-1962
Frank Makeating	4	1946-1947
Gary Martindale	4	1993-1994
A Murphy	4	1956-1957
Brian Murphy	4	1964-1965
Harry Penkeyman	4	1951-1952
Steve Robinson	4	1986-1987
Alex Russell	4	1993-1994
Tommy Saunders	4	1948-1949
Leo Skeete	4	1970-1971
Kevin Still	4	1991-1992
Lee Trundle	4	1995-1996
Johnny Vincent	4	1953-1954
Charlie Whiteside	4	1957-1958
Barry Brookfield	3	1960-1961
Owen Brown	3	1980-1981
Wally Burnett	3	1954-1955
Steve Cannon	3	1990-1991
Dave Carberry	3	1981-1982
Jimmy Cookson	3	1953-1954
Robbie Cowley	3	1994-1995
David Craig	3	1952-1953
Tommy Cronin	3	1954-1955
Bill Draper	3	1946-1947
Tony Duffy	3	1983-1984
Kenny Dumican	3	1969-1970
Joey Dunn	3	1989-1990
Albert Finley	3	1962-1963
Tony Fitzgerald	3	1965-1966
Joe Flaherty	3	1973-1974
Kevin Formby	3	1993-1994
Ted Green	3	1958-1959
Jimmy Hammell	3	1965-1966
John Hendry	3	1957-1958
Ian Hodge	3	1991-1992
Joe Kelly	3	1949-1950
Lol Lister	3	1964-1965
Dom McGrail	3	1950-1951
Ged McKenna	3	1981-1982
Terry McPhillips	3	1995-1996
Syl Nolan	3	1982-1983
Bill Parker	3	1952-1953
Bobby Pascoe	3	1981-1982
Barry Ravenscroft	3	1969-1970
Keith Reeder	3	1967-1968
Roy Rees	3	1963-1964
Lou Rigby	3	1962-1963
Robinson	3	1958-1959
John Rogers	3	1971-1972
Arthur Rowley	3	1959-1960
Steve Skeete	3	1983-1984
Phil Spencer	3	1973-1974
Des Steele	3	1957-1958
Brian Stokes	3	1976-1977
Ivor Swarbrick	3	1970-1971
Alan Swift	3	1968-1969
Tommy Tallon	3	1952-1953
Billy Thompson	3	1952-1953
Sean Togher	3	1991-1992
Turner	3	1950-1951
Dennis Walmsley	3	1960-1961
David Wassall	3	1972-1973
Len Wilkinson	3	1956-1957
Tony Williams	3	1974-1975
Ronnie Williams	3	1988-1989
Bernie Woods	3	1950-1951
Micky Worswick	3	1965-1966

* 1st season if more than once (4 goals or less)

Most goals in Total

PLAYER	GOALS*	PERIOD
Wesley Bridge	188	1947-1955
Brian Robinson	150	1968-1972
Kenny Dumican	121	1969-1977
Joe Hart	119	1954-1960
Billy Jaycock	90	1977-1981
Harry Lyon	89	1960-1962
Dennis Walmsley	88	1955-1966
John Disley	79	1953-1958
Arthur Rowley	79	1959-1962
John Brady	75	1981-1995
John Coleman	69	1983-1985
Phil Spencer	69	1973-1976
Johnny Vincent	67	1953-1960
Harry Bergin	66	1946-1951
Joey Flaherty	60	1973-1979
Joe Kelly	59	1947-1952
Leo Skeete	59	1970-1972
Jimmy Hammell	56	1964-1968
Kevin Still	54	1991-1996
Gary Martindale	51	1993-1994

* Some figures are best estimates based on information available.

Most goals in a Season

PLAYER	GOALS	SEASON
Johnny Vincent	60	1953-1954
Wesley Bridge	57	1947-1948
Harry Lyon	56	1961-1962
Wesley Bridge	51	1948-1949
Wesley Bridge	51	1949-1950
Brian Robinson	51	1968-1969
Brian Robinson	42	1969-1970
Arthur Rowley	42	1959-1960
John Coleman	39	1984-1985
Leo Skeete	38	1970-1971
Gary Martindale	36	1993-1994
Harry Lyon	33	1960-1961
Joe Hart	32	1955-1956
Joey Flaherty	31	1974-1975
Joe Hart	31	1956-1957
John Coleman	30	1983-1984
Robbie Cowley	30	1994-1995

BURSCOUGH v. SKELMERSDALE UNITED

Date	Competition	H/A	Result
Nov 9 1946	Liverpool County Comb	H	D 0-0
Dec 7 1946	Liverpool County Comb	A	W 3-1
Oct 11 1947	Liverpool County Comb	A	L 2-3
Feb 7 1948	Liverpool County Comb	H	D 1-1
May 8 1948	L'pool Challenge Cup Final at Southport		W 4-1
Sep 25 1948	Liverpool County Comb	H	W 3-1
Jan 29 1949	Liverpool County Comb	A	L 0-4
Jan 2 1950	Liverpool County Comb	A	W 6-2
Apr 15 1950	Liverpool County Comb	H	L 2-3
Oct 7 1950	Liverpool County Comb	H	L 0-1
Oct 14 1950	F..A. Cup	H	W 3-2
Nov 11 1950	Liverpool County Comb	A	D 3-3
Jan 1 1951	Liverpool Senior N/L Cup	H	W 2-0
Aug 25 1951	Liverpool County Comb	A	L 2-3
Apr 21 1952	Liverpool County Comb	H	D 2-2
Oct 4 1952	Liverpool County Comb	H	D 0-0
Mar 14 1953	Liverpool County Comb	A	L 1-3
Jan 1 1954	L'pool Senior N/L Cup S/F	A	W 3-0
Feb 11 1956	Lancs Junior Cup	A	D 1-1
Feb 18 1956	Replay	H	W 3-0
Sep 3 1956	L'pool Senior N/L Cup	A	L 1-4
Oct 20 1956	Lancs Comb	H	W 3-1
Mar 2 1957	Lancs Comb	A	W 3-2
Dec 25 1957	Lancs Comb	A	W 3-2
Dec 26 1957	Lancs Comb	H	W 6-2
Sep 13 1958	Lancs Comb Cup	H	L 1-3
Oct 11 1958	Lancs Comb	A	L 0-1
Apr 29 1959	Lancs Comb	H	D 2-2
Aug 24 1959	Lancs Comb Cup	A	D 1-1
Sep 7 1959	Replay	H	W 1-0
Sep 14 1959	Liverpool Senior N/L Cup	H	W 2-1
Apr 15 1960	Lancs Comb	A	L 1-2
Apr 18 1960	Lancs Comb	H	W 2-1
Aug 25 1960	Lancs Comb	A	L 2-3
Aug 31 1960	Lancs Comb	H	D 0-0
Aug 26 1961	Lancs Comb	A	W 5-2
Dec 23 1961	Lancs Comb	H	W 4-0
Aug 18 1962	Lancs Comb	A	L 0-1
Dec 15 1962	Lancs Comb	H	W 1-0
Aug 31 1963	Lancs Comb Cup	H	D 1-1
Sep 2 1963	Lancs Comb	H	W 5-1
Sep 17 1963	Lancs Comb Cup replay	A	L 1-3
Jan 11 1964	Lancs Comb	A	D 2-2
Aug 27 1964	Lancs Comb Cup	A	L 2-3
Dec 5 1964	Lancs Comb	H	W 3-2
Apr 17 1965	Lancs Comb	A	L 0-2
Sep 14 1965	Liverpool Senior N/L Cup	A	W 4-1
Sep 25 1965	Lancs Comb	A	L 1-3
Feb 5 1966	Lancs Junior Cup	A	W 3-2
Mar 19 1966	Lancs Comb	H	L 1-6
Sep 8 1966	Lancs Comb	A	L 0-6
Sep 27 1966	Lancs Comb Cup	A	D 1-1
Oct 4 1966	Replay	H	L 0-2
Apr 3 1967	Lancs Comb	H	W 2-1
Aug 31 1967	Lancs Comb	A	L 1-2
Apr 13 1968	Lancs Comb	H	D 2-2
Feb 24 1969	Liverpool Senior N/L Cup	A	L 2-6
Sep 24 1970	Cheshire League	H	L 0-4
Apr 6 1971	Cheshire League	A	W 5-1
Mar 16 1972	L'pool Senior N/L Cup S/F	H	W 3-0
Sep 4 1972	Liverpool Senior N/L Cup	H	L 0-2
Nov 23 1972	North West Floodlit Trophy	H	W 4-2
Apr 25 1974	L'pool Senior N/L Cup Final	H	L 1-2
Feb 12 1975	L'pool Senior N/L Cup S/F	H	L 1-2
Mar 19 1975	Lancs Floodlit Trophy S/F	H	W 1-0
Aug 6 1983	Cambrian Cup	H	L 0-1
Jul 31 1984	Cambrian Cup	H	W 2-1
Sep 15 1984	F.A. Cup	H	W 3-0
Oct 9 1984	Liverpool Senior Cup	H	L 1-2
Oct 27 1987	Liverpool Senior Cup	H	L 0-1
Nov 21 1987	North West Counties Lge	H	W 2-0
Mar 12 1988	North West Counties Lge	A	W 1-0
Oct 15 1988	North West Counties Lge	A	D 0-0
Feb 25 1989	North West Counties Lge	H	W 2-0
Oct 19 1991	N.W.C.League Cup	A	W 2-0
Sep 22 1992	North West Counties Lge	A	L 0-3
Dec 26 1992	North West Counties Lge	H	W 1-0
Oct 5 1993	North West Counties Lge	A	D 2-2
Mar 5 1994	North West Counties Lge	H	W 4-0
Aug 29 1994	North West Counties Lge	H	W 6-3
Dec 26 1994	North West Counties Lge	A	W 4-1
Oct 31 1995	North West Counties Lge	H	W 3-0
Apr 8 1996	North West Counties Lge	A	W 1-0

BURSCOUGH'S RECORD:

P.83 W.39 D.15 L.29 F.159 A.132

A CHRONOLOGICAL HISTORY OF VICTORIA PARK

1845	Area of Victoria Park and Mart Lane referred to on Ordnance Survey maps as 'Days Green.'
1887	Land owned by the Earl of Derby, farmed and occupied by Mr. William Spencer. Mart Lane was only developed in 1887 when James Martland Ltd. built their new premises there and obtained the area of land now known as Victoria Park.
1908	Burscough Wesleyans Cricket Club built a pavilion where the Community Centre now stands and played cricket on site of present football ground. Ground laid by Cricket Club President, Walter Martland.
1908-1914	Burscough Rangers played at 'Mart Lane Enclosure.' Played 30 yards nearer to railway and shared with Burscough Wesleyans football team. Teams changed in cricket pavilion.
1914-1919	Mart Lane ground cultivated during First World War.
1921	Burscough Rangers moved back to Mart Lane after a period on Travis' Field in Higgins Lane. Ground rented from James Martland Ltd. Now playing where present football ground is sited. Teams changed in 'Pavilion Cottage.'
1926	Grandstand erected by voluntary labour (400 seats). Built using materials from Everton's Bullens Road stand.
1931	Ground and Stand sold to Lathom & Burscough Urban District Council.
1934-1935	Burscough Rangers folded. Ground rented to Lancashire Electric Power Company for remainder of season.
1935-1937	Victoria Park home to Northern Nomads (1935-36 Reserves in Liverpool County Combination, 1936-37 Lancashire Combination side).
1937-1941	Burscough Vics and Lathom Juniors moved to Victoria Park. Vics continued playing there until 1941.
Dec 1943	British Restaurant opened, serving drinks and meals to service personnel - now the Community Centre.
1944-45	A 'Burscough F.C.' playing in Southport & District Amateur League, registered ground Victoria Park.

1945-46	Used by Burscough senior and junior teams, playing in Southport & District League.
1946	Present Burscough A.F.C. formed, agreed Security of Tenure on ground with local council.
1950	Covered accommodation at Crabtree End erected.
1951	Ground and Stand bought from Ormskirk Council for £400. Public Subscription Fund set up. Liverpool F.C. sent team for fund-raising game.
Sept 1957	Social Club opened beneath grandstand.
1959	Wall at Mart Lane end built.
1960	New canteen erected. Old canteen used as offices.
June 1963	Social Club (now The Barons) opened by Councillor S.C.Jones. Cost £6,000.
1970	Wall built between ground and rest of Victoria Park. Grant for half of cost obtained from Ormskirk Council. Cost £600.
1972	Floodlights installed. Switch on Thursday March 9th v. Oswestry Town in Cheshire League.
1983	Social Club sold.
1986-87	Old grandstand, which had been built in 1926, dismantled. Old canteen, situated between stand and new canteen, demolished. Floodlight pylons damaged in gales. New grandstand built using voluntary labour. New Floodlighting system installed at cost of £11,000.
Aug 1988	New 250 seater Grandstand officially opened by Mr. Syd Rudd, Life Vice-President of the Football Association. Celebration Match v. Liverpool followed opening.
1994	Covered standing accommodation for 500 spectators erected opposite main grandstand. Crabtree Lane End Stand refurbished. Floodlights upgraded.
1995	Flagpole erected at Mart Lane end. Donated by Vice-President, Mr. Ken Ainslie.
1996	Work commenced on extending dressing rooms under stand to meet latest ground grading requirements. Covered standing area terraced.

A fine picture of the old grandstand, taken in 1974.

The old stand comes down in 1987 after over 60 years service. New ground safety requirements meant the largely wooden structure was now deemed unsafe.

The new stand in the early stages of construction.

The impressive new stand, opened in 1988 with a visit by Liverpool Football Club. Seating 250, it also incorporates changing rooms, office accommodation, Boardroom, and a toilet block.

THE PRESENT

As we arrive at 1996, Burscough Football Club's Golden Jubilee, it is an opportune time to reflect on where the club stands today.

During the 116 years that Burscough has been represented in the game of Association Football, the village team has never attained a status higher than North West regional football. However, never in that 116 years has the village team been more prepared to take that further step into the wider world of what is now known as the Northern Premier League, which encompasses the whole of Northern England.

It is a credit to everyone, past and present, that the club is now, in its fiftieth year, in such a position of strength and continues to win major trophies. The pyramid structure of football now allows clubs such as Burscough to progress to the Unibond Northern Premier League, the GM Vauxhall Conference, and even, theoretically, to the Football League itself.

In recent years, Mark Parr has taken over the commercial side of the club which is so important in the modern game, and scaled new heights in terms of developing sponsorship, advertising and fund-raising activities. Gordon and Sylvia Cottle have spent many unglamorous hours foot-slogging around Burscough building up the weekly 'Cashline Lottery' to today's staggering total of almost 2,000 members, this remember, in a 'village' of little over 8,000 inhabitants. These activities are the lifeblood of this club, generating much needed weekly income throughout the year, income that is so essential to ensure that the club's ambitions can, firstly, be realised, and then, even more importantly, sustained. Mark Parr, for many years, and more recently, Stuart Heaps, have given many unpaid hours to administering a lottery which has now become virtually a full-time occupation.

Since refusing promotion in 1983 after winning the North West Counties League, the club has concentrated its efforts on improving the ground and building the kind of solid financial base so essential to ensure that any future opportunity to progress can be accepted. The present position has only been achieved through a tremendous amount of hard work and dedication, and the club has been well served over that period by its Management Committee. Chairman Frank Parr has been the driving force behind this progress, and the club has been wonderfully served over this period by vice-chairman, Stuart Heaps, who has taken on responsibility for so many of the thankless day to day tasks that endlessly require attention.

Frank Parr, Stuart Heaps, groundsman Bill Fairclough and committee members Stan Harvey, Roy Baldwin and, until recently, Dave Whittle, have worked tirelessly to make Victoria Park one of the finest football arenas in the North West of England. Bill Fairclough is responsible for maintaining the playing pitch and the compliments regularly voiced about the playing surface at Mart Lane bear true testament to his efforts. Roy Baldwin, with a lifetime devoted to serving local football, and the knowledge to prove it, is a popular, unassuming committeeman, who was awarded Lancashire Football Association's Order of Merit in 1993. Stan Harvey, with abundant energy, infectious enthusiasm, and a willingness to 'get stuck in', has proved a truly outstanding addition to the club's backroom staff. Treasurer Peter Nelson has brought financial expertise to the club, his knowledge of accounting procedures has proved invaluable in negotiating the complex demands now placed on clubs at this level. Gordon Cottle has concentrated on developing the club's community activities during recent seasons with spectacular results, the club now has a reputation second to none in providing facilities for young boy and girl footballers in West Lancashire. Committeeman Rod Cottam has been the club physio for many years now, totally reliable, respected, and armed with the confidence and expertise required to deal with any emergency. Barbara Cottam, Audrey Fairclough and Sylvia Cottle have taken over the running of the canteen, which provides a friendly matchday service for the club's supporters, as well as providing another source of valuable income for the club. Peter Nelson's son, Roger, mans the turnstile on matchdays and has brought some welcome publicity to the club while pursuing some of his more interesting pastimes, such as appearing on Granada TV's 'The Krypton Factor' programme.

The club has remained true to the ideals on which it was founded in 1946. We have a fine family atmosphere at Victoria Park, a ground to be proud of, the club continues to be administered in a sound and professional manner, and Burscough continue to compete successfully at the very highest level of North West non-league football.

Photographed in the Boardroom at Victoria Park and surrounded by cup winning teams of the past fifty years, the 1995-96 Management Committee pose with the North West Counties League Challenge Cup. Left to right: Bill Fairclough, P.G.Nelson (Treasurer), Roy Baldwin, Stan Harvey, Stuart Heaps (Vice-Chairman), Frank Parr (Chairman), Stan Strickland (Secretary), Gordon Cottle. Absent were Mark Parr and Rod Cottam.

Victoria Park today, one of the finest non-league football arenas in the North West. This excellent photograph, taken from the main stand in 1995 by Gordon Cottle, shows the ground's semi-rural setting. Opposite the main stand can be seen the new covered standing accommodation erected in 1994 and terraced in 1996.

CLUB OFFICIALS
1946 - 1996

PRESIDENT

1946-1953	John Parr-Sturgess
1953-1956	R.W.Charnock
1956-1961	Fred Price
1961-1964	Sam Curtis
1964-1965	Jim Turner
1965-1967	Dick Ashcroft ?
1967-1968	Harry Hague
1969-1970	John Hooper
1971-1975	Joe Gaskell
1975-1982	Frank Dobson
1982-1983	Roger Guy
1983-1984	Dan Hunter
1984-1985	J.Hargreaves
1985-1996	John Mawdsley

CHAIRMAN

1946-1950	Johnny Baldwin
	Tom Riley ?
1950-1956	Jimmy Johnson
1956-1957	Johnny Baldwin
1958-1960	Alf Marsden
1960-1970	Joe Hull
1970-1974	Bill Martland
1974-1996	Frank Parr

VICE-CHAIRMAN

1946-1947	Tom Riley
1949-1950	Jimmy Johnson
1953-1954	Andy Campbell
1955-1956	Johnny Baldwin
	Frank Parr
1971-1975	Jim Bridge
1975-1980	Gordon Hoskin
1981-1982	Gordon Gaskell
1982-1983	Bob Jones
1983-1986	Roy Baldwin
1986-1996	Stuart Heaps

SECRETARY

1946-1949	R.H. Holcroft
1949-1956	Ronnie Barker
1956-1960	Dick Ashcroft
1960-1962	Jim Turner
1962-1963	Chris Mahood
1963-1965	Bill Ward
1965-1966	Jim Meadows
1966-1967	Terry Kelly
1967-1975	Chris Mahood
1975-1977	Dave Raybould
1977-1980	Geoff Clarke
1980-1981	Les Foster
1981-1983	Gordon Hoskin
1983-1987	Ken Hilton
1987-1988	Bernie Charnock
1988-1991	Ken Hilton
1991-1993	Mike Woods
1993-1996	Stan Strickland

TREASURER

1946-1948	Teddy Dutton
1949-1950	Bill Parker
1950-1954	George Crabb
1954-1956	Dick Ashcroft
1956-1962	Jim Turner
1963-1964	E.Lawrence
1964-1975	Terry Kelly
1975-1979	Brian Lowe
1979-1980	Ken Hilton
1982-1983	Stan Petherbridge
1983-1987	Robert Crompton
1987-1993	Mike Woods
1993-1996	P.G. Nelson

MANAGER

1953-1958	Charlie Jones
1958-1959	P.J.Geran
1959-1960	Charlie Jones
1960-1963	Pat Murphy
1963-1965	Charlie Jones
1965-1971	Bob Langton
1971-1976	Kenny Spencer
1976-1977	Bob Jones
1977-1980	George Rooney
1980-1980	Cliff Roberts
1980-1981	David May
1981-1983	Bryan Griffiths
1983-1986	Mike McKenzie
1986-1987	Ray Coleman
1986-1987	Dennis Smith
1987-1988	Mike Ryman
1988-1989	Albie Donnerly
1989-1990	Mike Scott
1990-1991	Larry Carberry
1991-1995	Russ Perkins
1995-1996	John Davison

Even as this book was going to press, Burscough continued to win trophies. Following their League Challenge Cup victory, they travelled to Flixton on Friday 17th May 1996, to play for the annual Champions v Cup-winners challenge trophy. With one of their best performances of the season they beat the League Champions 1-0. Pictured left is the scorer of the final goal of the Club's first fifty years, defender-turned-forward Neil 'Jocky' Hanson (with a Flixton player in close attendance).

The following night at the Club's Presentation Evening in the Barons' Club, Andy Howard received the Supporter's Player of the Year award, with Hanson gaining the player's vote.

Pictured below with the two trophies, formerly the Lancashire Combination Cup and the Cheshire League Cup, are two of the hard-working canteen staff at Victoria Park, Audrey Fairclough (left) and Sylvia Cottle. Absent was Barbara Cottam.

LIST OF SUBSCRIBERS

1. Frank Parr
2. R. H. Holcroft
3.
4. Albert Gore
5. Ellen Baybutt
6. Charlie Jones
7. Jim Bridge
8. Chris Mahood
9. Eric Berry
10. Stuart Heaps
11. P. G. Nelson
12. Audrey & Bill Fairclough
13. Kenny Spencer
14. Dave Whittle
15. Philip Carver
16. Gordon & Sylvia Cottle
17. Colin Williams
18. Tom Walmsley
19. Roy W. Baldwin
20. Stan Harvey
21. Fred Milner
22. John H. Spencer
23. Brian Spencer
24. Tony Dutton
25. John & Barbara Moorcroft
26. Paul Hodgkinson
27. Paul Cowburn
28. Roy Thompson
29. John Thompson
30. Chris Thompson
31. Paul Thompson
32. Ian Rawstorne
33. Junior Linnets Supporters' Club
34. Julie & Gary Wright
35. W. Bleasdale
36. John Draper
37. Alan Wilson
38. Richard G. Spencer
39. Ray Walton
40. Neil Leatherbarrow ('Puskas')
41. Joe Pledger
42. Debbie Daniels
43. Joe Fisher
44. Tom Davies
45. Jack & Marion Crompton
46. John M. Morrison
47. Andrew S. Moffat
48. Raymond Lawson
49. Shelagh Greenwood
50. Kerrie Strickland
51. Joe McCall
52. Michael Braham
53. Jennie Strickland
54. Patrick White
55. K. J. Gane
56. Graham Orritt
57. Lorna Green (wife of the late Arthur Green)
58. Mrs. B. Crocker
59. Roy Walsh
60. Gilbert Ritchie
61. Robert John Ritchie
62. Daphne & John Dutton
63. John Porter
64. Robert Andrews
65. Bob Derbyshire
66. Derek Watkinson
67. Martland Brothers
68. Danny Hunter
69. J. L. Bimpson
70. Bob Warren
71. Christine Huyton (daughter of Bobby Langton)
72. John Parr
73. Bunty & Maurice Wright
74. Jim Aspinall
75. Bob Gibbons
76. T. P. Kelly
77. Sally Strickland
78. Mrs. Jean Draper

79.	Dennis Peters	122.	Rod & Barbara Cottam
80.	Mr. & Mrs. I. Craven	123.	Harry & Gladys Newton
81.	Tom Galvin	124.	Brian Sewell
82.	Adrian Galvin	125.	John Vincent
83.	Harold McKearney	126.	Ashley Berrington
84.	Kevin Naughton	127.	Frank Walmsley
85.	Stan Hurst	128.	Roderick Grubb (Nuneaton Borough F.C.)
86.	Hugh Caunce		
87.	Andrew M. H. Caunce	129.	John Melling
88.	Michael E. Milne	130.	John Disley
89.	Duncan Milne	131.	Sadie Jones (sister of the late Jimmy Jones)
90.	Ken Hilton		
91.	Desmond McLean	132.	John Francis Orritt
92.	E. Dutton Snr. & family	133.	Billy Flanagan (Liverpool County F.A.)
93.	E. Dutton Jnr. & family		
94.	F. Dutton & family	134.	Frank Postlethwaite
95.	Mrs. Lilly Dalton	135.	Tommy McGhee
96.	Roy Cheetham	136.	David A. Howgate
97.	Arthur Holden (Colwyn Bay F.C.)	137.	Geoff Wilde
		138.	Roly Howard
98.	Ken Smith	139.	John Mawdsley MBII
99.	Jim Fearnley	140.	Ron Lawson
100.	Elsie Halsall (wife of the late Bill Halsall)	141.	Geoff Swinnerton (Liverpool County F.A.)
101.	Gilly Houghton	142.	D. J. Walker
102.	Sheila & Jeff Styler	143.	Graham Stewart
103.	Colin Pickthall M.P.	144.	T. W. Saunders
104.	S. J. Pepper	145.	Joe Hart
105.	Jim Culshaw	146.	Paul Snowdon
106.	Graham Glover	147.	Norman Edmonson
107.	Ken J. Ainslie	148.	Brian Bannister
108.	Roy Hussey	149.	John Ortt
109.	Bill Ashcroft	150.	Tom McDonald
110.	Jim Moran	151.	R. Harper
111.	R. G. Nelson	152.	Donald Scott
112.	Anonymous	153.	Alison M. Smith
113.	Ian Bagshaw (Chorley F.C.)	154.	Paul Strickland
114.	Mark Taylor	155.	Graham Robinson
115.	Roger Musson	156.	Norman Porter
116.	Tom Park	157.	Tom Spencer
117.	Norman Lea	158.	Jim Disley
118.	Tom Bowen	159.	Kevin Suffell
119.	Dennis Walmsley	160.	Ronald S. Hyland
120.	Mrs. Pat Freeman	161.	Mrs. N. L. & Brian Strickland
121.	Eric Bridge	162.	Maurice Wilce

163.	Jim Spencer	205.	A. A. Booth
164.	Trevor Bridge	206.	John & Joan McKinlay
165.	Prescot Cables F.C.	207.	Jack Rothwell
166.	Walter Brogden (Penrith F.C.)	208.	Burscough Priory High School
167.	K. H. Dean (former Secretary to Lancashire Combination)	209.	David Alty
		210.	Jim Tyrer BEM
168.	Pauline, Sheila & Gordon Cottle Senior	211.	Bernard Alan Derbyshire
		212.	Ian Johnson
169.	Jimmy Gwyther	213.	Stephen Jacquest
170.	Derek W. Chislett	214.	Marion Knowles
171.	Brian Stokes	215.	Mrs. P. A. Hyland (daughter of Harry Waugh)
172.	John Spencer		
173.	Ted Green	216.	B. M. Gray
174.	Jim Harrison	217.	Gordon Mattocks
175.	Anne & Walter Carter	218.	Frank Lea
176.	Tom Martland	219.	Miss Beryl Parker
177.	Barry Brookfield	220.	Josie & George Ashton
178.	Alec McGregor	221.	Mickey Bridge
179.	Eric Hitchen	222.	Thomas Laird
180.	Myra Cartwright	223.	Joyce & Bill Hill
181.	Matt Brennan	224.	J. E. Watkinson
182.	William Weeks	225.	Peter Beament
183.	Anthony Bridge	226.	Edie Harrison
184.	Mary Benjamin	227.	Nell Disley
185.	Phil Cooper	228.	Diz Woodward
186.	Jean & David Bain	229.	Frank Clayton
187.	Blackburn Rovers F.C.	230.	Mrs. M. D. Williams
188.	Colin Urquhart	231.	Robert M. Smith
189.	P. Whittle	232.	J. G. Brine
190.	Trevor Harrison	233.	Ken Robinson
191.	W. Sloan	234.	Bob Bolton
192.	Dick Abram	235.	Mrs. Jane Gibbons (wife of the late Harry Gibbons)
193.	William Ollerton		
194.	Alan Alty	236.	In memory of Harry Gibbons
195.	In memory of George & Annie Fletcher	237.	In memory of Harry Gibbons
		238.	Kevin Downey
196.	Florrie Wilkes	239.	Keith Reeder
197.	John & Sheila Smith	240.	Albert Jackson
198.	Alex Russell	241.	Derrick Bradley
199.	Alex Russell Jnr.	242.	L. D. Bradley
200.	John Hooper	243.	In memory of J. E. Meadows
201.	Bill Parker	244.	In memory of William Parr
202.	George Ryley	245.	Mrs. Irene Prescott
203.	Mel Robson (Penrith F.C.)	246.	Russ Perkins
204.	David Johnson (Penrith F.C.)	247.	Paul Birch

248.	Andrew Brewer		293.	John S. Davies
249.	H. Lamb		294.	Gareth Owen
250.	Jimmy Vickers		295.	Nigel Hanks
251.	John Gibbons		296.	K. M. Rogers
252.	E. Mullis		297.	M. W. Stanley
253.	Ray Wall		298.	Phil Brough
254.	Steve Gallagher		299.	D. S. Corfield
255.	Alan Charles Birch		300.	Keith Stanton
256.	Geoffrey Prytherch		301.	Will & James Rankin
257.	Bob Baron		302.	Rodney Taylor & family
258.	Ann & Roy Harrison		303.	Dave Robertson
259.	Jimmy Howard		304.	Neil & Rachel Marsdin
260.	Tommy Knox		305.	Bryan Spittlehouse
261.	Barry Beesley		306.	Association of Sports Historians
262.	Bob Lamb		307.	Tim & Lorraine Marshall
263.	Trevor Ryding		308.	Roy & Pauline Baldwin
264.	Stan Petherbridge		309.	Ivor Swarbrick
265.	Gerry Brewer		310.	Ernest Swarbrick
266.	Terry Brewer		311.	James Brian Robinson
267.	William Baybutt		312.	Graham Henry Woods
268.	Richard H. Gilbody		313.	Gordon Gaskell
269.	Andy Howard		314.	Michael Gaskell
270.	James McLoughlin		315.	Ged Nolan
271.	Joel Duncan		316.	Paul Blasbery
272.	Ormskirk Plasterers		317.	Gordon Johnson
273.	Michael Parker		318.	Alex Blakeman
274.	Mr. & Mrs. Salter		319.	L. Ashton
275.	Flo Aspinall		320.	John R. Culshaw
276.	Bill Bolton		321.	Tony Fitzgerald
277.	Alan Tillotson		322.	Alison Vera Culshaw
278.	Dennis Monk		323.	Alf Pemberton
279.	Neil 'Jocky' Hanson		324.	Geoff Clarke
280.	Tom Derbyshire		325.	George & Wendy Moorcroft
281.	Stephen Foxcroft		326.	Michael Hodgson
282.	Len Wilkinson		327.	Tina Hodgson
283.	Jimmy Ashcroft		328.	Carl Ashcroft
284.	Bryan Miller		329.	Westbrook Packaging
285.	Mrs. Brenda Edington		330.	Eric Craven
286.	Ken Taylor		331.	Alan Bullen
287.	Brian Saint		332.	Mark Parr
288.	William Melling Forshaw		333.	Joanna Lisa Norris
289.	Mel Partridge		334.	Kevin & Joanne Parr
290.	L. A. Zammit		335.	Elizabeth Rose Parr
291.	George Rowles			
292.	Keith Forshaw			

BURSCOUGH FOOTBALL CLUB
ROLL *of* HONOUR

Lancashire Junior Cup Winners
1947/48, 1949/50, 1966/67

Liverpool Challenge Cup Winners
1947/48, 1950/51, 1954/55

George Mahon Cup Winners
1947/48

Liverpool County Combination Division One Champions
1949/50

Liverpool County Combination Division Two Champions
1953/54, 1967/68

*Lancashire Combination Champions
Division Two*
1953/54

*Lancashire Combination Champions
Division One*
1955/56, 1969/70

Liverpool Senior Non-League Cup Winners
1955/56, 1971/72

F.A. Cup 1st Round Proper
1959/60, 1977/78, 1979/80, 1980/81

Lord Wavertree Cup Winners
1967/68

Cheshire County League Runners-up
1970/71

Cheshire League Challenge Cup Winners
1974/75
Runners-up
1973/74

North West Counties League Division One Champions
1982/83

North West Counties Champions v Cup winners Challenge Trophy
1982/83, 1995/96

Bill Tyrer Memorial Trophy
1990

*League Cup Finalists
Promotion to Division One*
1991/92

North West Counties League Challenge Cup Winners
1992/93, 1995/96

Liverpool Senior Cup Finalists
1992/93